FOREWORD

Memorandum from the Prime Minister to Sir Edward Bridges
[Secretary to the War Cabinet] 8/11/40.

"Many of the executive departments naturally have set up and developed their own statistical branches.....I have my own statistical branch under Professor Lindemann ...... It is essential to consolidate and make sure that agreed figures only are used. The utmost confusion is caused when people argue on different statistical data: I wish all statistics to be concentrated in my own branch as Prime Minister and Minister of Defence, from which alone the final authoritative working statistics will issue.

Pray look into this and advise me how my wish can be most speedily and effectively achieved.

W.S.C."

Correct figures are the elusive raw material of effective government, and none was more aware of this than Winston Churchill in both his Administrations. To me, Churchill's memoranda, sometimes but not over-frequently adorned with a red "Action this day" label are the most interesting and significant part of his monumental six volumes "The Second World War". These fiery and imaginative missives analyse, criticise, encourage and direct- and rest for their effectiveness on correct data.

Churchill was well aware of the significant role that those responsible for collating, sifting and verifying the raw material were playing and he relied on them with justified confidence.

Even after his resignation from Office in April 1955, from time to time he would ask for the assistance of the Central Statistical Office, as will be seen from my letter, published here, and the meticulously careful reply: The question of our casualties in both World Wars had, as I remember it, arisen from a discussion that Churchill had with Robert Menzies, the Prime Minister of Australia, over a dinner at which I was present, Churchill was agreeably surprised that the global total for World War II was not higher, but then fastened on the unknown figure for China, which would have increased the melancholy sum very substantially.

It is most fitting that the story of the Central Statistical Office should now be made public. It is an important and far from dull addition to the knowledge of our affairs.

Anthony Montague Browne

Private Secretary to Winston Churchill
1952 - 1965

Knightsbridge 7972

28 Hyde Park Gate,
London, S.W.7.

14 December, 1960

Dear Robertson,

Some time ago when I was at Chartwell I telephoned your Office and through the Statistical Branch you gave me, for Sir Winston's information, the rough estimate of the total dead in the two World Wars. (These included all those who might be said to have lost their lives through the War, whether civilian or military). The figures were something like 63 million for the Second World War, and 20 million for the First.

These figures were given to me orally over the telephone, and Sir Winston has recently reverted to the subject and asked me if I will find out for him a little more detailed breakdown.

If the Statistical Branch can readily supply these figures I would be grateful for them, but as this is purely a matter of interest I know that Sir Winston would not wish anybody to be diverted from more important things to supply the figures.

Incidentally if you are able to give me the figures, could you let me know if they are confidential or not?

I shall not expect an answer to this letter for a long time!

Yours sincerely,

(Sgd.) ANTHONY MONTAGUE BROWNE

J.H. Robertson, Esq.

Central Statistical Office

FIGHTING with FIGURES

ISTICAL OFFICE

ague Brown
ett

INTRODUCTION AND GENERAL NOTES

The Statistical Digest of the War was first printed in 1951 as part of the United Kingdom Civil Series of war histories. Prepared by the Central Statistical Office, its purpose was to bring together the facts of the British war effort, which previously had been scattered amongst many historical volumes and Command papers.

Following a call by Sir Winston Churchill for regular and comprehensive statistics, the Economic Information Service was split into two sections, the Economics Section and the Central Statistical Office.

Under the direction of Harry Campion, the function of the CSO was to collect from Government departments regular series of ordered figures covering the development of the war effort in Britain.

This year marks the 50th anniversary of the end of the Second World War. In conjunction with this important occasion, the Central Statistical Office has published a revised edition of the original Statistical Digest of the Second World War. Retitled 'Fighting with Figures', the foreword has been written by Anthony Montague Brown, who was Winston Churchill's private secretary from 1952 to 1965. Text for each chapter has been written by Dr. Peter Howlett, the economics lecturer from the London School of Economics.

1. Area covered. Except where otherwise stated all statistics relate to the United Kingdom of Great Britain and Northern Ireland.

2. Period covered. In general the figures given in the Digest cover the period from September 1939 to August 1945. In some tables, however, figures for a pre-war year or years have been given where the comparison seems particularly valuable.

3. Time series. The Digest has no standard time series. Where possible annual totals are given throughout, but in many cases these are supplemented by quarterly totals, monthly averages and weekly averages according to the type of series dealt with. Except where it is stated to the contrary all statistics are for calendar years ended 31 December.

4. Change of basis. A line drawn across a column between two consecutive figures normally indicates that the figures above and below the line have been compiled on different bases and are not strictly comparable. In each case a footnote is added indicating the nature of the difference.

5. Consumption and stocks. Statistics of consumption and stocks should be used with particular caution. Figures given under the heading of "consumption" or "total disposals" are usually derived from statistics of releases from stocks by controls or manufacturers.
Figures of stocks may be affected to some degree by seasonal influences. Moreover, these figures often relate to only part of the total stocks in the country.

6. Definitions. In order to make this Digest as self-contained as possible a Definition Section is included at pages 242 to 277. The purpose of the notes and definitions given in this Section is to supplement the various footnotes given in the tables and to make it possible to interpret the figures fully without reference back to the basic sources of the statistics. It is important that each table should read in conjunction not only with footnotes appended to it but also with the appropriate paragraphs in the Definitions Section.

7. Rounding of figures. Where necessary, each figure has been rounded off to the nearest final digit. For this reason there may be in some tables an apparent slight discrepancy between the sum of the constituent items and the total as shown.

8. Symbols employed. The following symbols have been used throughout the Digest.

.. = not available
- = nil or negligible (less than half the final digit shown)
* = five week period

C.S.O. 34/1/6

MR. WOODS
Departmental Records

War casualties

You gave me Montague Browne's letter to Robertson asking for a breakdown of the numbers killed in the two World Wars; the letter quoted estimates of something like 63 millions, civilian and military, for the Second World War and 20 millions for the First.

I have assumed that the kind of analysis Sir Winston has in mind is the division between civilian and military and the distribution of casualties by country. Enclosures 1 and 2 provide estimates in this form. I cannot vouch for their accuracy but I have given the sources in each case. Clearly the figures for the U.K. will be more reliable than for the rest of the world and those for "military" probably more reliable than those for "civilian".

Enclosure 3 shows a further breakdown, for Europe only, distinguishing between "normal" deaths and war losses. The figures are taken from yet another source ("Population Changes in Europe since 1939" by Gregory Frumkin) but square up quite well with those in the other tables. This analysis and Enock's (Enclosure 1, reference 5) are of course the results of private researches, but I understand that they were carried out very carefully; Frumkin was in fact the editor of the "Statistical Year Book of the League of Nations" throughout its existence.

I am also enclosing Montague Browne's letter.

(H.E. BISHOP)

Central Statistical Office

26th January, 1961

ENCLOSURE 1

Casualties in the 1914-18 and 1939-45 Wars

United Kingdom	Military	Civilian	Total
1914 - 18	743,702[1]	8,389[2]	752,091
1939 - 45	270,687[3]	63,635[3]	369,405
World			
1914 - 18	8,500,000[4]	13,000,000[4]	21,500,000
1939 - 45	15,916,580[5]	13,252,197[5]	29,168,777

1. Hansard, March 9th 1923.

2. Greenwood. British Loss of Life in the wars of 1794-1815 and in 1914-18. Journal of the Royal Statistical Society, Vol.CV, 1942. Includes 6,330 sea passengers drowned.

3. Statistical Digest of the War. H.M.S.O. 1951. Figure for Armed Forces includes 6,244 still missing at 28 February, 1946.

4. Encyclopaedia Britannica, Vol. 23. 1947 ed. Figure for civilians is a global estimate of which no details are shown.

5. A.G. Enock. This War Business. 1951.

ENCLOSURE 2

Whitehall 9400 Ext 15.

The Library,
The War Office,
LONDON, S.W.1.

10 December, 1958.

Dear Sir,

Your letter of 19th November, 1958, enquiring about casualties in World Wars I and II, has been passed to me for reply.

I am enclosing with this letter details of the numbers killed and missing, as they are at present known, in a form in which I think you will find the answers to your questions; I was not certain if you meant to include British figures in your "allied" numbers, and I have, therefore, set these out separately so that you can select the items you require. I have also taken "servicemen" to include both Officers and Other Ranks of all the three Services. Unfortunately, I can find no figures for civilians for World War I.

You may like to know the sources from which we have compiled these figures, and which we find the most useful for answering enquiries of this kind. There are many varieties and discrepancies in most of them, and it is usually only possible to find approximate figures in most cases. They are as follows:-

1. WAR OFFICE. Statistics of the Military Effort of the British Empire during the Great War, 1914-1920. 1922 (H.M.S.O.)

2. WAR OFFICE. General Annual Reports on the British Army ... 1913-1919. 1921. (Cmd.1193). (H.M.S.O.)

3 MINISTRY OF DEFENCE. Strengths and Casualties of the Armed Forces and Auxiliary Services of the United Kingdom, 1939 to 1945. 1946. (Cmd. 6832). (H.M.S.O.)

4. COMMITTEE OF IMPERIAL DEFENCE. History of the Great War. Military Operations, France and Belgium, 1918. Vol. V (page 597) 1947 H.M.S.O.)

5. ENOCK, Arthur Guy. This War Business. 1951. (The Bodley Head).

I hope that this information will help you with your research.

Yours faithfully,

(D.W. KING)
Librarian.

Theodore H. MacDonald, Esq.,
Department of Zoology,
The University,
GLASGOW, 2.

KILLED IN ACTION, DIED OF WOUNDS AND OTHER CAUSES

WORLD WAR I

1. **British** (including India, Dominions and Colonies) 779,468

2. **Allied**

France	1,385,300	
Belgium	38,172	
Italy	460,000	
Portugal..	7,222	
Roumania..	335,706	
Serbia	127,535	
Greece	5,000	
Russia	1,700,000	
U.S.A.	115,660	
		4,174,595

3. **Enemy**

Germany	2,050,466	
Austria-Hungary	1,200,000	
Bulgaria..	201,000	
Turkey	300,000	
		3,751,466
	TOTAL	8,705,529

WORLD WAR II

1. **British**

(i) U.K. Armed Forces (i.e., excluding Women's Auxiliary Services) Home Guard, Merchant Navy, etc.) 264,443

(ii) Dominions, India and Colonies 108,929

373,372

2. **Allied**

Belgium	22,651	
China	1,500,000	
Denmark	6,400	
France	245,000	
Greece	253	
Netherlands	230,177	
Norway	1,598	
Sweden	3,318	
U.S.A.	520,433	
U.S.S.R...	4,500,000	
		7,029,830

3. **Enemy**

Germany	3,000,000	
Austria	220,000	
Bulgaria	18,500	
Italy	380,000	
Japan	2,565,878	
Poland	550,000	
Roumania	73,000	
Yugoslavia	1,706,000	
		8,513,378
	TOTAL	15,916,580

/CIVILIANS

CIVILIANS

(a) World War I — Not known

(b) World War II

Allied

United Kingdom	60,595
Belgium	90,000
China	An enormous number
Denmark	Unknown
France	152,000
Netherlands	242,000
Norway	3,638
U.S.S.R.	6,000,000
	6,548,233

Enemy

Germany	800,000
Austria	125,000
Italy	180,000
Japan	600,000
Poland	5,000,000
Yugoslavia	Large number
	6,705,000

ENCLOSURE 3

"Normal" Deaths in Belligerent Countries and War Losses during 1939-1945 (Europe only and excluding U.S.S.)

Thousands

Groups	Total deaths among belligerents	"Normal" deaths	War losses: Total	War losses: Military	Civilian losses: Non-Jewish	Civilian losses: Jewish
I. Western	16,345	14,642	1,703	935	537	231
II. Austria, Germany . .	11,524	6,990	4,534	3,730	524	280
III. Eastern	19,270	10,485	8,785	1,070	3,855	3,860
IV. Northern	925	829	96	89	6	1
All belligerents . .	48,064	32,946	15,118	5,824	4,922	4,372

Source: "Population Changes in Europe since 1939" Gregory Frumkin 1951. George Allen and Unwin. Table 7, page 181.

UNITS OF MEASUREMENT

I. British units of measurement and their metric equivalents

British unit			Metric equivalent
Length			
I inch (in.)			2.54 centimetres
I foot (ft.)	=	12 inches	30.48 centimetres
I yard (yd.)	=	3 feet	91.44 centimetres
I mile	=	1,760 yards	1.60934 kilometres
Surface			
I square foot (sq.ft)			0.09290 square metres
I square yard (sq.ft)	=	9 square feet	0.83613 square metres
I acre	=	4,480 square yards	40.47 ares
I square mile (sq.miles)	=	640 acres	258.99 hectares
Capacity			
I imperial gallon (gall.)	=	4 quarts	4.546 litres
I bulk barrel	=	36 gallons	1.63655
I cubic foot (cu.ft.)			0.02832 cubic metres
I cubic yard (cu.yd.)	=	27 cubic feet	0.76456 cubic metres
Weight			
I ounce avoirdupois (oz.)			28.35 grammes
I pound avoirdupois (lb.)	=	16 ounces	453.59 grammes
I hundredweight (cwt.)	=	112 pounds	50.80 kilogrammes
I long ton	=	2,240 pounds	1.01605 kilogrammes
I short ton	=	2,000 pounds	0.90718 metric tons

II. Miscellaneous units

Food and drink:	Butter	5,600 gallons milk = I ton butter (average)
	Cheese	2,240 gallons milk = I ton cheese
	Condensed milk	600 gallons milk = I ton full cream condensed milk 600 gallons skimmed milk = I ton skimmed condensed milk
	Dried egg	81,000 eggs = I ton dried egg
	Eggs	17,400 eggs = I ton
	Milk	I million gallons = 4,600 tons
	Milk powder	1,800 gallons milk = Iton full cream milk powder 2,400 gallons skimmed milk = I ton skimmed milk powder
	Sugar	100 tons raw sugar = 93 tons refined sugar
Fuel and power:	British thermal unit (B.Th.U.)	The amount of heat required to raise I lb. of water through I degree Fahrenheit at or near 39.1 degree Fahrenheit.
	Therm	100,000 British thermal units
	Unit of electricity	An output of I kilowatt over I hour
Shipping:	Deadweight tonnage Gross tonnage Net tonnage Standard displacement War load displacement	These terms are defined in the Definitions Section (pages 263 and 267)
Timber:	Softwood	I standard = 165 cubic feet
	Pitwood	I standard = 180 piled cubic feet

CONTENTS

6. RAW MATERIALS

7. PRODUCTION

ABBREVIATIONS

A.A.	Anti-aircraft
A.C.	Alternating current
A.F.V.	Armoured fighting vehicle
A.P.	Armour piercing
A.S.	Anti-submarine
A.S.R.	Air sea rescue
C.A.	Coastal artillery
D.C.	Direct current
Derv (fuel)	Diesel-engined road vehicle
G.O.	Gas operated
H.E.	High explosive
L.S.T.	Landing ship tank
P.I.A.T.	Projector infantry anti-tank
S.D.	Standard displacement
S.H.A.E.F.	Supreme Headquarters Allied Expeditionary Force
U.P.	Unrotated projectile
W.L.D.	War load displacement

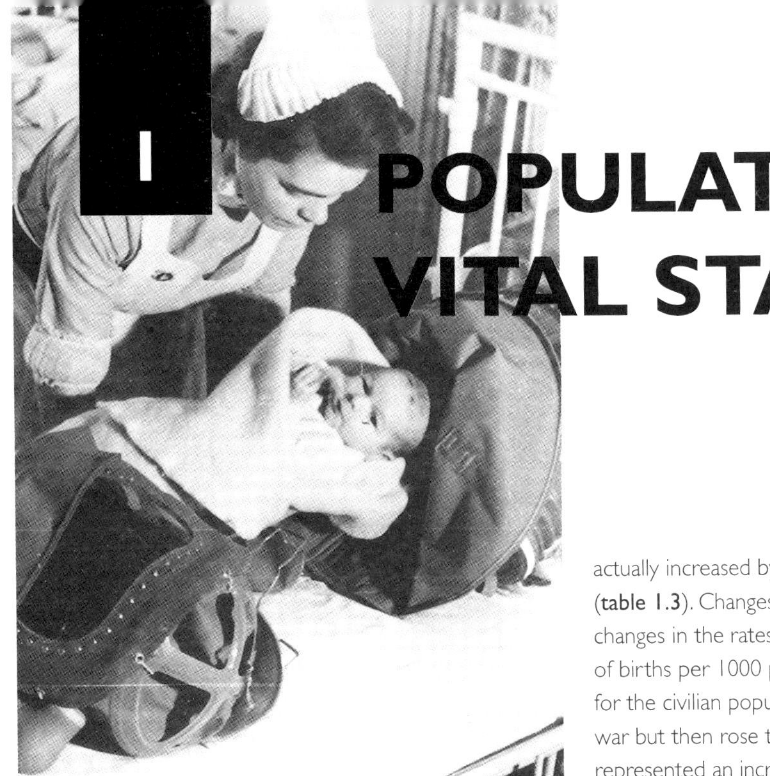

1 POPULATION & VITAL STATISTICS

War is most commonly associated with death and, in this respect, the Second World War was no different. The loss of human life was on an immense scale with more than 40 million people killed worldwide, including 25.6 million deaths suffered by the USSR, 6.5 million by Germany, 6 million by Poland and 2.4 million by Japan (Harrison and Gatrell 1993: 434; Milward 1977: 210-1). In absolute and proportionate terms the loss of life in Britain cannot compare with these figures, with an estimated 360,000 war related deaths (Hancock and Gowing 1949: 549). Indeed, the population of the UK actually increased by about three per cent during the war (**table 1.3**). Changes in the size of the population reflect changes in the rates of birth and death (that is the number of births per 1000 population). The birth rate of the UK for the civilian population fell in the first two years of the war but then rose to reach a peak of 17.9 in 1944, which represented an increase of almost a fifth on the 1939 rate. The death rate increased sharply in 1940 but then fell back again and was stable between 1942 and 1945 at 11.4 (with the exception of 1943 when it rose slightly to 11.8). The rate of natural increase (the difference between the birth rate and the death rate) fell from 3 per 1000 population in 1939 to a mere 0.8 in 1940 but thereafter increased to reach a peak of 6.5 in 1944; initially the dominant factor in changes in the rate of natural increase were changes in the death rate but after 1941 changes in the birth rate came to dominate population growth (**tables 1.3, 1.6 and 1.9**).

The bulk of the excess deaths due to the war were accounted for by the Armed Forces: 264,443 members of the Armed Forces were killed during the war (over half of these were in the Army, about a quarter in the Royal Air

1.1 Changes in the United Kingdom civilian population

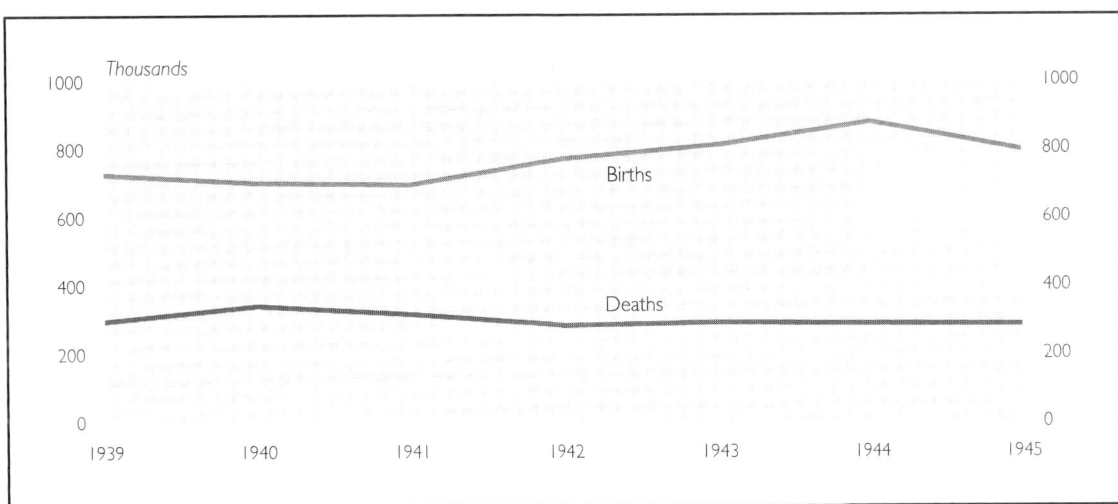

Force, and about a fifth in the Royal Navy) which, compared to the wartime peak size of the Armed Forces of 4.65 million in 1945, gives a rate of attrition of 5.7 per cent (**tables 3.8 and 3.3**). The Merchant Navy also experienced a heavy loss of life with more than 30,000 members killed during the war (Behrens 1955: 181-3; **table 3.3**). Civilian casualties due to the war were virtually all incurred due to the German bombing campaign: almost 70,000 tons of bombs were dropped on the UK during the war, the bulk of them between mid-1940 and mid-1941 (Titmuss 1950: 322-4). The total number of civilian deaths due to the operations of war were 67,635 (giving a war related rate of attrition among the civilian population of about 0.15 per cent), two-thirds of whom were killed in 1940 and 1941 (**tables 2.3-2.4**; Titmuss 1950: 325).

Turning to other causes of death among civilians we find that most initially experienced rising rates of incidence between 1939 and 1940 but thereafter, declined. For the most vulnerable group in society, those under 15 years of age, the reduction in the death rates per million population for many of these diseases was remarkable: scarlet fever fell from over 40 in the 1930s to 7 by 1945, diphtheria fell from almost 300 to 70, whooping cough from almost 200 to 85, and measles from over 200 to 21 (Stevenson 1984: 204; **tables 1.4-1.5 and 2.3-2.4**). This experience was in contrast to that of many other European countries: in the case of diphtheria, for example, whilst the number of child deaths from this disease in the UK fell from 3,000 in 1938 to 721 in 1945, countries such as Germany and Sweden were experiencing their worst epidemics for fifty years (Ferguson and Fitzgerald 1954: 163-4). An important exception to the large reductions in deaths from diseases during the war was tuberculosis (whose treatment was hampered by increased waiting lists for hospital beds and by a shortage of nursing staff) which experienced only a small decline between 1939 and 1945 (and in Scotland actually increased by 11 per cent between 1938 and 1945) (Ferguson and Fitzgerald 1954: 251-88; Titmuss 1950: 524-5; **tables 2.3-2.4**).

The chief reason for the decline in the number of deaths from many diseases in Britain was successful immunisation campaigns but other factors related to health and nutrition (such as the creation of the Emergency Medical Services, the introduction of school meals, the subsidised milk scheme for young children and expectant mothers, and the distribution of vitamins, orange juice and cod liver oil) all contributed to the wartime improvement in the health of the nation (Ferguson and Fitzgerald 1954: 155-71; Titmuss 1950: 509-10, 521). These changes also helped to reduce the rate of infant mortality (the number of deaths of infants under one year of age per 1000 live births), in contrast to the situation in the First World War when it had increased steadily (Ferguson and Fitzgerald 1954: 172). Infant mortality increased in 1940 and 1941 but thereafter declined and the level of infant mortality in 1945 in England and Wales was almost a fifth less than the average for 1935-8 (with a sharper reduction in Scotland of 27 per cent and a less sharp reduction in Northern Ireland of 14 per cent) (**table 1.8**).

The pressures and changes wrought by the war (including evacuation and military and industrial mobilisation) placed great pressure on the family, with declining rates of marriage and increases in the number of divorces and illegitimate births (Ferguson and Fitzgerald 1954: 103-9; Harris 1992: 26). An increase in the marriage rate (the

1.2 Divorce proceedings in England and Wales

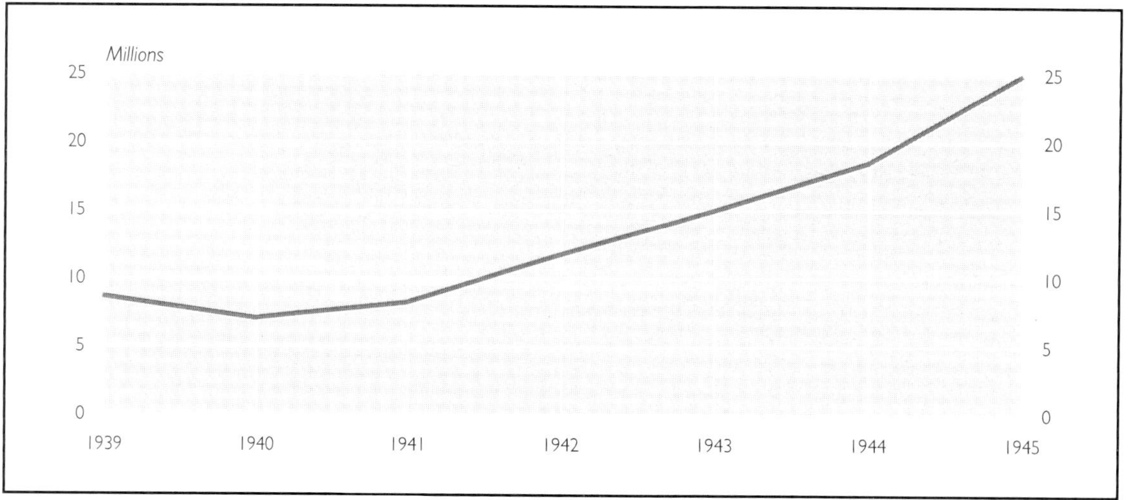

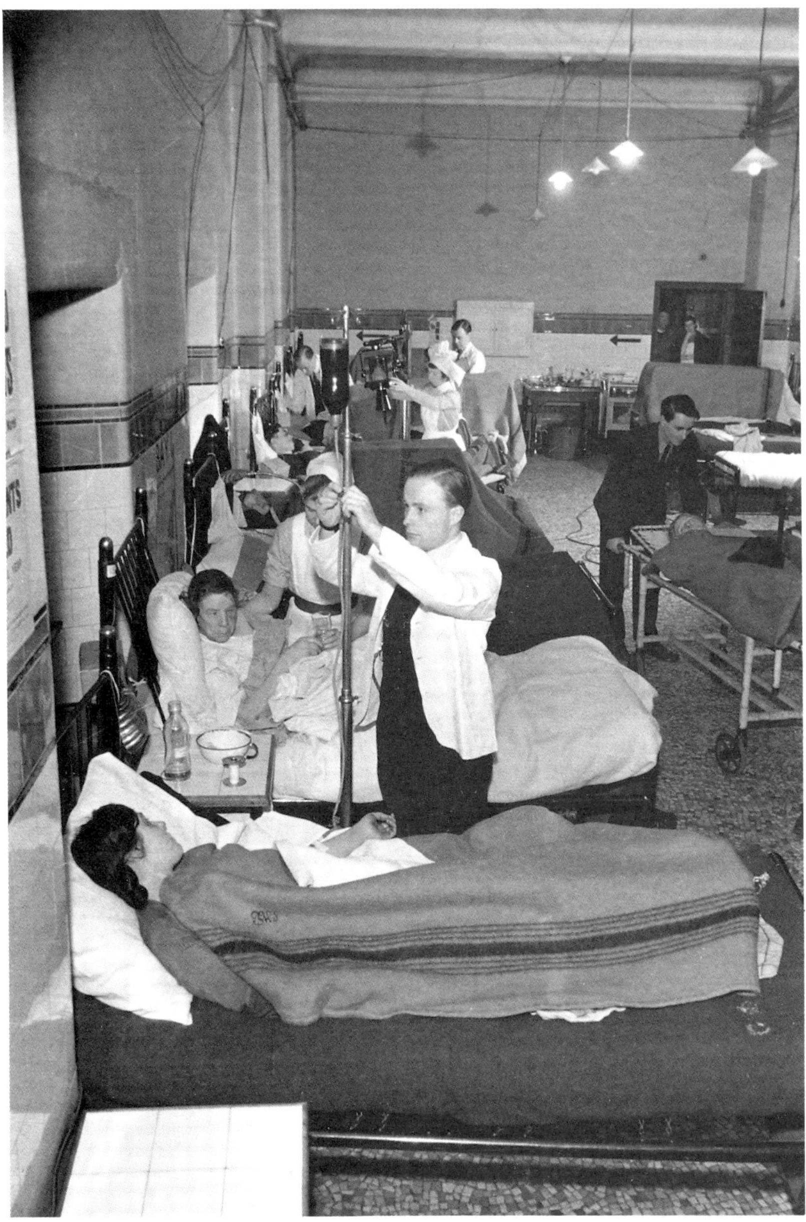

proportion filed by husbands rose from 45 per cent to 57 per cent (**table 2.18**). Finally, the ratio of illegitimate births to total live births rose from 4.2 per cent to 9.3 per cent in England and Wales, from 6.0 per cent to 8.7 per cent in Scotland and from 4.7 per cent to 5.4 per cent in Northern Ireland (**table 1.6**). One reason for this increase in illegitimate births was that wartime pressures prevented the marriage before the birth of their child of those women who conceived out of wedlock (in peacetime the 'regularisation' of such situations was fairly common) (Ferguson and Fitzgerald 1954: 90-2).

number of persons married per 1000 population) in England and Wales from 17.6 in 1938 to 22.5 in 1940 was followed by a decline to a low of 14.0 in 1943; Scotland experienced a similar trend although in Northern Ireland wartime marriage rates were generally higher than the 1938 figure of 13.4 (**table 1.10**). At the same time the number of divorces in England and Wales rose from 7,197 in 1939 to 19,482 in 1945 (a rise of 171 per cent -in Scotland they rose by 154 per cent), amongst the reasons divorces were filed, adultery increased its share from 56 per cent to 69 per cent of the total petitions and the

1.3 Population of the United Kingdom

United Kingdom Mid-year estimates *Thousands*

	United Kingdom			England and Wales			Scotland			Northern Ireland		
	Total	Males	Females	Total	Males	Females	Total	Males	Females	Total	Males	Females
Total population[1]												
1939[2]	47,762	22,962	24,799	41,460	19,920	21,540	5,007	2,412	2,594	1,295	630	665
1940	48,226	23,304	24,922	41,862	20,216	21,646	5,065	2,454	2,611	1,299	634	665
1941	48,216	23,266	24,950	41,748	20,141	21,607	5,160	2,492	2,668	1,308	633	675
1942	48,400	23,336	25,064	41,897	20,180	21,717	5,174	2,508	2,666	1,329	648	681
1943	48,789	23,574	25,215	42,259	20,397	21,862	5,189	2,521	2,668	1,341	656	685
1944	49,016	23,672	25,344	42,449	20,473	21,976	5,210	2,534	2,676	1,357	665	692
1945	49,182	23,723	25,459	42,636	20,549	22,087	5,187	2,508	2,679	1,359	666	693
Civilian population[3]												
1940	45,996	21,076	24,920	39,889	18,243	21,646	4,826	2,215	2,611	1,281	618	663
1941	44,849	20,003	24,846	38,743	17,228	21,515	4,818	2,160	2,658	1,288	615	673
1942	44,297	19,542	24,755	38,243	16,802	21,441	4,758	2,121	2,637	1,296	619	677
1943[4]	43,771	19,006	24,765	37,818	16,334	21,484	4,651	2,050	2,601	1,302	622	680
1944	43,743	18,852	24,891	37,785	16,188	21,597	4,641	2,035	2,607	1,316	629	687
1945	43,873	18,858	25,015	37,916	16,200	21,716	4,640	2,029	2,611	1,317	629	688

1. The total population includes all members of the armed forces and Merchant Navy whether at home or overseas.
2. Estimated population actually in the country (resident population). The figures exclude members of the armed forces serving overseas and merchant seamen at sea estimated at about a quarter of a million at June 1939.
3. The civilian population excludes members of the armed forces serving at home and abroad - it includes all members of the Merchant Navy.
4. From 1943, excluding certain classes of seamen previously included. The numbers so excluded at that date were: England and Wales, 122,000; Scotland, 26,000; Northern Ireland, 3,000.

Source: Registrars General

1.4 Age distribution of the resident population of the United Kingdom[1]

At 30 June 1939

Thousands

	United Kingdom			England and Wales			Scotland			Northern Ireland		
	Total	Males	Females	Total	Males	Females	Total	Males	Females	Total	Males	Females
Total all ages	47,762	22,962	24,799	41,460	19,920	21,540	5,007	2,412	2,594	1,295	630	665
Age groups:												
0- 4	3,376	1,719	1,657	2,861	1,458	1,403	402	204	198	114	58	56
5- 9	3,340	1,689	1,651	2,830	1,431	1,399	398	201	198	113	57	55
10-14	3,576	1,799	1,777	3,037	1,527	1,510	422	212	210	117	60	57
15-19	4,198	2,105	2,093	3,603	1,806	1,797	472	237	235	123	62	61
20-24	3,488	1,737	1,751	2,998	1,493	1,505	388	194	194	102	50	52
25-29	3,985	1,959	2,026	3,467	1,704	1,763	414	206	209	103	49	54
30-34	3,949	1,932	2,017	3,461	1,698	1,763	393	189	204	95	45	50
35-39	3,683	1,793	1,890	3,233	1,578	1,655	363	174	189	87	41	46
40-44	3,236	1,481	1,755	2,839	1,300	1,539	314	143	172	82	38	44
45-49	3,019	1,386	1,633	2,665	1,224	1,441	288	131	157	66	31	35
50-54	2,822	1,299	1,523	2,490	1,147	1,343	269	122	146	64	30	34
55-59	2,586	1,190	1,396	2,281	1,049	1,232	248	114	134	56	27	29
60 64	2,250	1,042	1,208	1,974	912	1,062	222	104	118	54	26	28
65-69	1,786	819	967	1,566	714	852	173	82	91	47	23	24
70 and over	2,463	1,010	1,453	2,155	279	1,276	239	99	140	71	32	39

1. See footnote 2 to Table 1.3.

Source: Registrars General

1.5 Age distribution of the resident population of the United Kingdom[1]

At 30 June 1945

Thousands

	United Kingdom			England and Wales			Scotland			Northern Ireland		
	Total	Males	Females	Total	Males	Females	Total	Males	Females	Total	Males	Females
Total all ages	49,182	23,723	25,459	42,636	20,549	22,087	5,187	2,508	2,679	1,359	666	693
Age groups:												
0- 4	3,678	1,881	1,797	3,126	1,600	1,526	418	212	206	134	69	65
5- 9	3,364	1,711	1,654	2,843	1,446	1,397	409	208	202	113	57	55
10-14	3,301	1,671	1,630	2,786	1,410	1,376	405	205	200	111	57	54
15-19	3,518	1,767	1,751	2,978	1,496	1,482	419	209	210	121	62	59
20-24	3,875	1,907	1,968	3,332	1,633	1,699	425	214	211	118	60	58
25-29	3,567	1,788	1,779	3,085	1,536	1,549	362	191	171	120	61	59
30-34	3,950	1,951	1,998	3,449	1,703	1,746	399	199	200	101	49	52
35-39	3,947	1,944	2,003	3,465	1,714	1,751	391	187	205	90	43	47
40-44	3,729	1,835	1,894	3,274	1,619	1,655	372	177	195	83	39	44
45-49	3,248	1,511	1,737	2,856	1,333	1,523	321	146	175	71	32	39
50-54	2,957	1,352	1,605	2,599	1,190	1,409	292	131	160	67	31	36
55-59	2,696	1,226	1,469	2,383	1,085	1,298	256	114	141	57	27	30
60-64	2,384	1,066	1,318	2,100	937	1,163	229	103	126	55	126	29
65-69	1,983	882	1,101	1,744	772	972	191	87	104	47	23	25
70 and over	2,986	1,232	1,753	2,616	1,075	1,541	298	126	171	72	32	40

1. See footnote 1 to Table 1.3.

Source: Registrars General

1.6 Births in the United Kingdom

	Live births										Still-births	
	Total	Males	Females	Legitimate	Illegitimate	Percentage of illegitimate	Total births per 1,000 population	Total births per 1,000 women aged 15-44	Legitimate births per 1,000 married women aged 16-44	Males born per 1,000 females	Thousands	Rate per 1,000 births (including still-births)
	Thousands											
United Kingdom												
1939	727	373	353	695	32	4.4	15.2	62.9	..	1,056	..	..
1940	702	360	342	670	32	4.6	14.6	60.6	..	1,053		
1941	696	357	338	657	38	5.5	14.4	60.3	..	1,056	..	..
1942	772	397	374	727	44	5.8	15.9	67.0	..	1,061		
1943	811	418	393	758	53	6.5	16.6	70.6	..	1,063	..	..
1944	878	453	425	814	65	7.3	17.9	76.7	..	1,065	..	..
1945	796	410	386	723	73	9.1	16.2	69.9	..	1,061	..	..
England and Wales												
1939	614	316	299	589	26	4.2	14.8	61.3	107.5	1,056	24	38
1940	590	303	288	564	26	4.3	14.1	58.7	98.5	1,053	23	37
1941	579	297	282	548	31	5.4	13.9	57.9	94.1	1,053	21	35
1942	652	336	316	615	36	5.6	15.6	65.2	103.8	1,063	22	33
1943	684	353	332	641	44	6.4	16.2	68.6	107.6	1,064	21	30
1944	751	388	364	696	55	7.3	17.7	75.7	117.4	1,065	21	28
1945	680	350	330	617	63	9.3	15.9	68.8	103.9	1,061	19	28
Scotland												
1939	87	45	42	82	5	6.0	17.4	72.1	141.1	1,060	4	42
1940	86	44	42	81	5	6.0	17.1	71.4	137.0	1,050	4	42
1941	90	46	44	84	6	6.6	17.4	73.5	138.1	1,059	4	40
1942	91	46	44	84	7	7.2	17.5	74.2	135.9	1,048	4	38
1943	95	49	46	88	7	7.6	18.2	78.7	140.6	1,051	3	36
1944	96	50	46	88	8	7.9	18.4	79.9	141.5	1,069	3	32
1945	87	45	42	79	8	8.7	16.8	73.1	126.1	1,063	3	33
Northern Ireland												
1939	25	13	12	24	1	4.7	19.5	82.5	..	1,044	..	..
1940	25	13	12	24	1	4.6	19.5	83.2	..	1,082	..	..
1941	27	14	13	26	1	4.8	20.6	85.4	..	1,096	..	..
1942	30	15	14	28	1	4.9	22.3	93.5	..	1,060	..	..
1943	32	16	15	30	2	5.5	23.5	99.5	..	1,076	..	..
1944	31	16	15	29	2	5.6	22.8	96.7	..	1,052	..	..
1945	29	15	14	27	2	5.4	21.3	91.0	..	1,063	..	..

Source: Registrars General

1.7 Reproduction rates

	England and Wales		Scotland	
	Gross	Effective	Gross	Net
1935	0.854	0.764	1.057	0.909
1936	0.862	0.774	1.069	0.914
1937	0.872	0.785	1.051	0.901
1938	0.897	0.810	1.077	0.933
1939	0.892	0.808	1.058	0.932
1940	0.850	0.772	1.042	0.896
1941	0.836	0.761	1.058	0.893
1942	0.934	0.853	1.087	0.948
1943	0.985	0.900	1.162	1.012
1944	1.089	0.996	1.183	1.041
1945	0.992	0.909	1.088	0.978

Source: Registrars General

1.8 Infantile mortality

Deaths of infants under 1 year of age per thousand live births

	United Kingdom			England and Wales			Scotland			Northern Ireland		
	Total	Males	Females	Total	Males	Females	Total	Males	Females	Total	Males	Females
1935	60	68	53	57	64	50	77	87	66	86	96	76
1936	62	70	54	59	66	51	82	92	72	77	86	67
1937	61	68	53	58	65	50	80	90	71	77	83	71
1938	55	62	48	53	60	46	70	77	62	75	79	71
1939	53	60	47	51	56	44	69	77	59	70	81	60
1940	60	69	52	57	64	49	78	90	66	86	95	76
1941	63	71	55	60	67	52	83	93	72	77	85	67
1942	53	59	46	51	57	44	69	78	60	76	87	65
1943	52	58	46	49	55	43	65	73	57	78	87	69
1944	48	53	42	45	50	40	65	73	56	67	74	61
1945	49	55	43	46	51	40	56	65	47	68	73	63

Source: Registrars General

1.9 Deaths analysed by age and sex[1]

Males

Thousands

	All ages	Under 1 year	1 and under 2	2-4	5-14	15-24	25-34	35-44	45-54	55-64	65-74	75 and over
United Kingdom												
1939	296.5	22.4	2.4	2.9	4.9	8.2	10.6	14.7	28.2	54.4	76.7	70.9
1940	340.6	25.0	3.3	4.1	6.2	9.4	13.1	18.8	33.4	63.3	85.6	78.3
1941	316.3	25.4	3.4	4.5	6.6	9.0	11.5	18.2	30.3	56.8	78.8	71.9
1942	283.2	23.5	2.2	3.0	4.9	6.6	8.6	14.5	26.4	51.0	74.7	67.8
1943	291.2	24.1	2.3	2.8	4.8	6.2	7.8	14.3	27.2	51.8	76.7	73.5
1944	287.2	24.0	2.0	2.6	4.8	5.8	7.2	14.0	26.4	51.5	76.5	72.9
1945	284.6	22.4	2.0	2.4	4.1	5.3	6.6	12.7	25.7	51.1	77.0	75.4
England and Wales												
1939	254.9	17.9	1.9	2.4	4.0	7.0	9.1	12.6	24.5	47.6	66.2	61.7
1940	294.2	19.7	2.7	3.3	5.2	8.1	11.4	16.3	29.3	55.9	74.2	68.2
1941	270.3	19.9	2.8	3.7	5.4	7.5	9.8	15.6	26.1	49.6	67.8	62.2
1942	242.1	18.6	1.8	2.5	4.1	5.4	7.3	12.4	22.6	44.6	64.4	58.5
1943	249.6	19.2	1.8	2.3	3.9	5.0	6.5	12.2	23.5	45.5	66.3	63.6
1944	246.9	19.2	1.6	2.1	4.0	4.7	6.1	12.0	22.8	45.2	66.3	63.1
1945	245.4	18.4	1.6	2.0	3.4	4.3	5.6	10.9	22.1	44.8	66.9	65.5
Scotland												
1939	32.9	3.5	0.4	0.4	0.7	1.0	1.2	1.7	3.0	5.5	8.1	7.3
1940	36.8	4.0	0.5	0.6	0.8	1.0	1.3	2.0	3.3	6.1	9.0	8.0
1941	36.2	4.3	0.5	0.6	0.9	1.1	1.3	2.1	3.4	5.8	8.6	7.6
1942	32.3	3.6	0.3	0.4	0.6	0.9	1.0	1.7	3.1	5.2	8.1	7.3
1943	32.8	3.5	0.4	0.4	0.7	0.9	1.0	1.7	3.0	5.2	8.2	7.9
1944	31.9	3.6	0.3	0.4	0.7	0.8	0.8	1.6	2.9	5.2	8.1	7.7
1945	31.1	2.9	0.3	0.3	0.6	0.8	0.8	1.5	2.9	5.2	8.1	7.8
Northern Ireland												
1939	8.7	1.0	0.1	0.1	0.2	0.2	0.3	0.4	0.7	1.3	2.4	1.9
1940	9.6	1.3	0.2	0.2	0.2	0.3	0.4	0.5	0.8	1.3	2.4	2.1
1941	9.8	1.2	0.1	0.2	0.3	0.4	0.4	0.5	0.8	1.4	2.4	2.1
1942	8.8	1.3	0.1	0.1	0.2	0.3	0.3	0.4	0.7	1.2	2.2	2.0
1943	8.8	1.4	0.1	0.1	0.2	0.3	0.3	0.4	0.7	1.1	2.2	2.0
1944	8.4	1.2	0.1	0.1	0.1	0.3	0.3	0.4	0.7	1.1	2.1	2.1
1945	8.1	1.1	0.1	0.1	0.1	0.2	0.2	0.3	0.7	1.1	2.0	2.1

1. Civilians only for England and Wales and Scotland from 3 September 1939 and for Northern Ireland from 1941.

Source: Registrars General

1.9 Deaths analysed by age and sex[1]

continued

Females

Thousands

	All ages	Under 1 year	1 and under 2	2-4	5-14	15-24	25-34	35-44	45-54	55-64	65-74	75 and over
United Kingdom												
1939	284.2	16.5	2.1	2.4	4.1	7.7	10.3	13.3	22.9	41.8	69.4	93.8
1940	322.9	17.9	2.9	3.6	5.3	10.0	12.2	15.6	25.9	47.4	77.9	104.5
1941	298.9	18.6	3.1	4.0	5.3	9.9	11.8	14.6	23.9	42.1	70.4	95.3
1942	268.1	17.3	1.8	2.6	3.8	7.8	9.8	12.6	21.0	38.5	64.4	88.5
1943	282.9	17.8	2.0	2.3	3.7	7.6	9.6	13.1	21.5	39.3	68.0	97.7
1944	273.8	17.8	1.7	2.0	3.6	7.3	9.2	12.4	20.9	38.0	66.2	94.7
1945	274.6	16.5	1.6	2.0	3.0	6.4	8.2	11.7	20.3	37.7	68.0	99.2
England and Wales												
1939	244.0	13.3	1.7	2.0	3.3	6.4	8.7	11.2	19.6	36.1	59.8	81.8
1940	278.4	14.2	2.2	2.8	4.4	8.5	10.4	13.4	22.6	41.1	67.5	91.3
1941	254.1	14.6	2.5	3.2	4.3	8.1	9.9	12.3	20.5	36.2	60.1	82.4
1942	228.6	13.7	1.4	2.1	3.1	6.3	8.1	10.6	18.1	33.1	55.3	76.7
1943	241.9	14.2	1.6	1.9	3.0	6.1	8.0	11.1	18.5	33.7	58.7	85.1
1944	234.2	14.3	1.4	1.6	2.9	5.9	7.7	10.5	18.0	32.7	57.0	82.1
1945	235.8	13.6	1.3	1.6	2.5	5.1	6.8	9.9	17.3	32.6	58.6	86.4
Scotland												
1939	31.4	2.5	0.3	0.3	0.6	1.0	1.2	1.6	2.6	4.5	7.3	9.6
1940	35.1	2.8	0.5	0.6	0.7	1.2	1.4	1.7	2.6	5.0	8.1	10.7
1941	34.9	3.1	0.5	0.6	0.7	1.4	1.5	1.8	2.7	4.6	7.8	10.3
1942	31.1	2.7	0.3	0.4	0.5	1.2	1.3	1.5	2.3	4.3	7.1	9.5
1943	32.4	2.6	0.3	0.3	0.6	1.2	1.3	1.6	2.4	4.5	7.3	10.2
1944	31.2	2.6	0.2	0.3	0.5	1.1	1.1	1.5	2.3	4.2	7.2	10.2
1945	30.6	2.0	0.2	0.3	0.4	1.0	1.1	1.4	2.4	4.1	7.4	10.3
Northern Ireland												
1939	8.8	0.7	0.1	0.1	0.2	0.3	0.4	0.5	0.7	1.2	2.3	2.4
1940	9.4	0.9	0.2	0.2	0.2	0.3	0.4	0.5	0.7	1.3	2.3	2.5
1941	9.9	0.9	0.1	0.2	0.3	0.4	0.4	0.5	0.7	1.3	2.5	2.6
1942	8.4	0.9	0.1	0.1	0.2	0.3	0.4	0.5	0.6	1.1	2.0	2.3
1943	8.6	1.0	0.1	0.1	0.1	0.3	0.3	0.4	0.6	1.1	2.0	2.4
1944	8.4	0.9	0.1	0.1	0.2	0.3	0.4	0.4	0.6	1.1	2.0	2.4
1945	8.2	0.9	0.1	0.1	0.1	0.3	0.3	0.4	0.6	1.0	2.0	2.5

1. Civilians only for England and Wales and Scotland from 1 June 1941 and for Northern Ireland from January 1941.

Source: Registrars General

1.10 Marriages

Thousands

	1938	1939	1940	1941	1942	1943	1944	1945
United Kingdom								
Number of marriages	409.1	495.1	533.9	448.5	428.8	344.8	349.2	456.7
Persons married per 1,000 population	17.2	20.6	22.1	18.6	17.7	14.1	14.3	18.6
Civil condition:								
Bachelors	375.9	459.9	498.0	413.1	393.0	309.9	312.7	414.2
Divorced men	4.8	6.2	6.0	5.6	5.9	7.0	8.8	12.0
Widowers	28.4	29.1	29.9	29.8	29.9	28.0	27.8	30.7
Spinsters	387.0	471.2	508.6	422.4	402.0	317.7	320.2	419.3
Divorced women	4.2	5.5	5.4	4.8	4.8	5.5	6.5	9.0
Widows	18.0	18.5	20.0	21.4	21.9	21.4	22.6	28.5
Age of males:								
Under 21 years	14.1	22.4	34.0	37.1	38.9	32.2	30.1	32.9
21 years and upwards	395.0	472.6	499.9	411.3	389.9	312.4	319.1	423.7
Age of females:								
Under 21 years	67.6	97.3	129.3	116.0	117.1	93.9	90.5	108.3
21 years and upwards	341.6	397.8	404.7	332.4	311.8	250.9	258.8	348.3
England and Wales								
Number of marriages	361.8	439.7	470.5	388.9	369.7	296.4	302.7	397.6
Persons married per 1,000 population	17.6	21.2	22.5	18.6	17.7	14.0	14.3	18.7
Civil condition:								
Bachelors	331.8	407.9	438.2	357.1	337.5	265.2	269.9	359.3
Divorced men	4.4	5.7	5.5	5.1	5.4	6.2	7.9	10.9
Widowers	25.6	26.1	26.9	26.7	26.8	25.1	24.9	27.5
Spinsters	341.4	417.8	447.3	365.1	345.5	272.0	276.4	363.6
Divorced women	3.8	5.0	4.9	4.3	4.3	4.9	5.8	8.0
Widows	16.6	16.9	18.4	19.5	19.9	19.5	20.6	26.1
Age of males:								
Under 21 years	12.2	19.5	30.2	32.7	34.3	28.2	26.4	28.8
21 years and upwards	349.7	420.1	440.4	356.2	335.4	268.1	276.3	369.0
Age of females:								
Under 21 years	59.3	86.6	115.8	102.6	103.1	82.2	79.5	95.2
21 years and upwards	302.5	353.1	354.8	286.3	266.7	214.2	223.3	302.4
Scotland								
Number of marriages	38.7	46.2	53.5	47.6	47.4	38.2	37.0	48.6
Persons married per 1,000 population	15.5	18.5	21.1	18.5	18.3	14.7	14.2	18.8
Civil condition:								
Bachelors	36.1	43.3	50.5	44.6	44.4	35.1	33.9	45.0
Divorced men	0.4	0.5	0.5	0.5	0.5	0.7	0.8	1.0
Widowers	2.2	2.5	2.5	2.5	2.5	2.4	2.4	2.7
Spinsters	37.2	44.5	51.7	45.6	45.2	35.9	34.6	45.6
Divorced women	0.4	0.5	0.5	0.5	0.5	0.6	0.7	1.0
Widows	1.2	1.3	1.4	1.5	1.7	1.6	1.7	2.1
Age of males:								
Under 21 years	1.6	2.6	3.4	3.8	4.1	3.5	3.3	3.6
21 years and upwards	37.1	43.6	50.1	43.8	43.3	34.6	33.7	45.1
Age of females:								
Under 21 years	7.1	9.3	11.9	11.1	11.8	9.8	9.3	11.2
21 years and upwards	31.6	36.9	41.7	36.5	35.6	28.4	27.7	37.5
Northern Ireland								
Number of marriages	8.6	9.2	9.8	12.0	11.7	10.2	9.5	10.5
Persons married per 1,000 population	13.4	14.2	15.1	18.3	17.6	15.1	14.0	15.4
Civil condition								
Bachelors	8.0	8.7	9.3	11.4	11.1	9.6	8.9	9.9
Divorced men	-	-	-	-	-	0.1	0.1	0.1
Widowers	0.6	0.5	0.5	0.6	0.6	0.5	0.5	0.5
Spinsters	8.4	8.9	9.6	11.7	11.3	9.8	9.2	10.1
Divorced women	-	-	-	-	-	-	-	-
Widows	0.2	0.3	0.2	0.3	0.3	0.3	0.3	0.3
Age of males:								
Under 21 years	0.3	0.3	0.4	0.6	0.5	0.5	0.4	0.5
21 years and upwards	8.3	8.9	9.4	11.4	11.2	9.7	9.1	10.0
Age of females:								
Under 21 years	1.2	1.4	1.7	2.3	2.2	1.9	1.7	1.9
21 years and upwards	7.4	7.8	8.1	9.7	9.5	8.3	7.8	8.6

Source: Registrars General

2 SOCIAL CONDITIONS

The impact of the war on social conditions cannot be underestimated: the evacuation of more than four million mothers and children from urban to rural areas over the course of the war brought about important changes in the scope and scale of welfare provision by the state at both central and local levels and in social attitudes; the medical services were placed under enormous strain as the wartime demands on them increased; crime rose; and the housing stock deteriorated in the face of German bombing and declining investment (Harris 1992). The war saw an expansion in the benefits system as pension coverage and payments improved and as many benefits moved from a means-tested basis to a non-means-tested basis (Titmuss 1950: 516; Johnson 1994: 286; **tables 2.7, 2.9 and 2.10**). The effect of the war itself created many new claimants for war pensions, grants and allowances: by 1945 their number had reached 717,000 and they were claiming a total of £24.2 million (**table 2.10**). This extension of benefits and of other welfare provisions during the war (such as the Emergency Medical Service) built on the rapid growth and innovation experienced in the 1930s (often at the level of local, rather than central, government) and they were to provide a solid foundation for the creation of the postwar Welfare State (Harris 1992: 22, 30; Titmuss 1950). The focal point for these developments was the Beveridge Report, published in 1942, which proposed overhauling the existing *ad hoc* social insurance schemes and replacing them with one scheme that would provide a welfare safety net 'from the cradle to the grave'.

The destruction and disruption that was caused by German bombing during the war (especially in the period from the late summer of 1940 to mid-1941) had a major impact on the social and physical fabric of the nation: in all two out of every seven houses were affected by enemy

2.1 Beneficiaries of war pensions, grants and allowances within the services in Great Britain

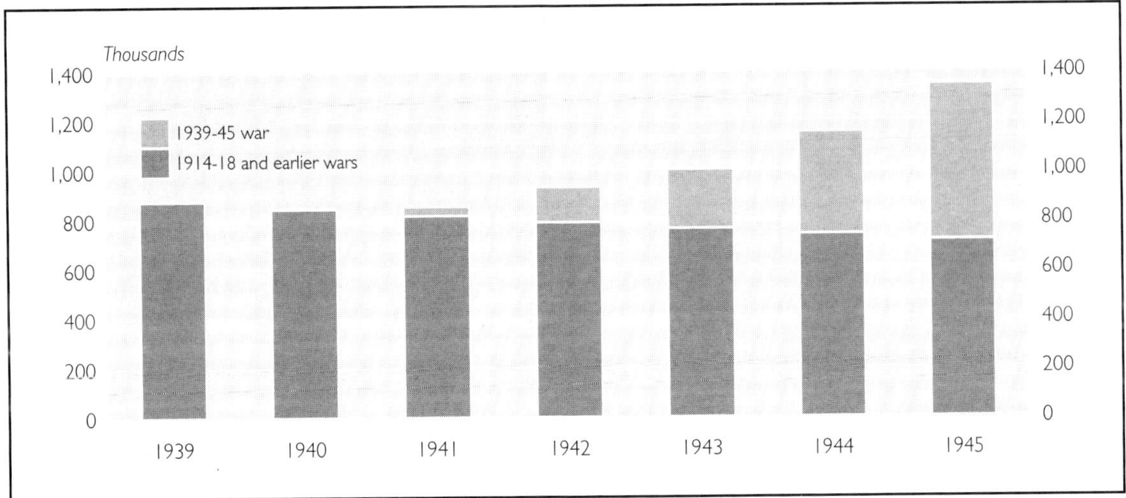

2.2 Persons found guilty of offences in England and Wales

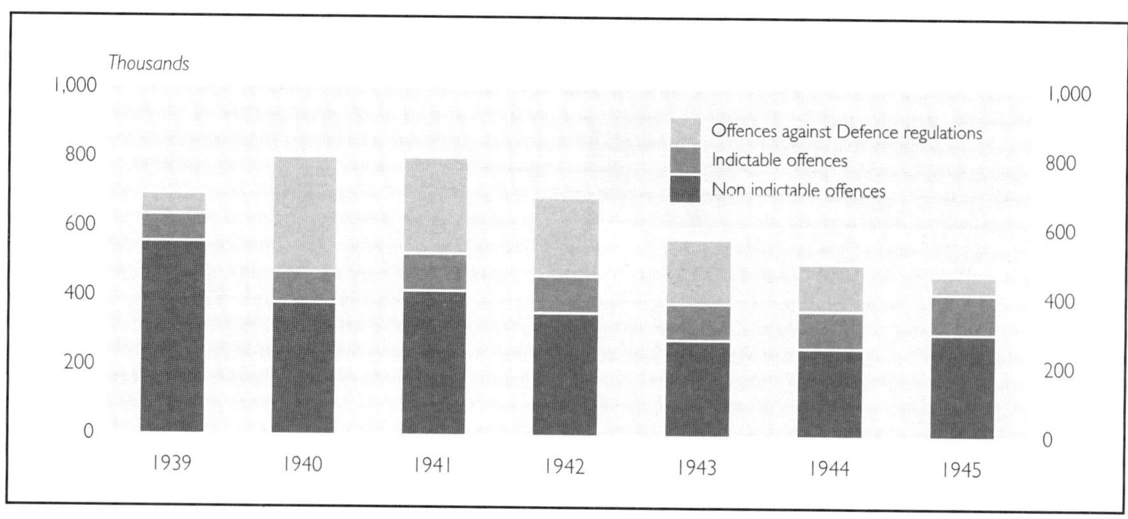

action (222,000 were destroyed and a further 3.5 million were damaged) and in some areas the proportion was much higher (in Bermondsey in London, for example, 90 per cent of the housing stock was affected in some way); furthermore, about 20 per cent of schools and hospitals were also put out of action (Titmuss 1950: 328-30, 462-3; Harris 1992: 22). House building did not have a high priority in the war and, as in Germany, it was deliberately squeezed to provide resources for war production (Overy 1988: 622). Thus, not only did overall investment fall sharply during the war (from 12 per cent of GDP in 1938 to 4 per cent in 1943) but the share of building in total gross domestic fixed capital formation also shrank (it fell from over a half of the total in 1939 to a third in 1940) (Feinstein 1972:T16, 86). In physical terms this meant that the total number of houses built in England and Wales between 1941-42 and 1944-45 was only 30,723 compared to 332,360 built in 1938-39 (**table 2.19**). This very low rate of house completion, plus the wartime damage to the existing housing stock, meant that by 1945 the nation faced an acute housing shortage.

The war also ushered in a new batch of laws (and rejuvenated some old ones) concerned with protecting morale, preventing black marketeering, regulating industry and the labour market, and enforcing the blackout. Not surprisingly convictions of people found guilty of breaking these laws rose dramatically at the beginning of the war: in England and Wales 61,000 people were convicted of such offences in 1939 and 340,000 in 1940, although thereafter the number of such convictions declined; in 1939 and 1940 more than 90 per cent of these convictions were for lighting offences but by 1945 this proportion had fallen to about a third of the total with convictions for offences against the Control of industry and employment rising in importance to account for 46 per cent of the total (Smithies 1982: 7-24, 58-91; **table 2.11**). Other crime also increased during the war: in England and Wales between 1939 and 1945 the number of indictable offences known to the police rose by 57 per cent (and the proportion of people per 100,000 found guilty rose from 149 to 223), juvenile convictions by 39 per cent, and female convictions almost doubled (Smithies 1982; Harris 1992: 28; **tables 2.11 and 2.14**). The result of this increased rate of conviction was that the average daily prison population increased by 42 per cent (**table 2.17**).

2.3 Civilian deaths registered: Analysis by cause and age[1]

Males

United Kingdom | *Number*

	All ages[2]	Age group									
		Under 1 year	1-4	5-9	10-14	15-24	25-34	35-44	45-44	55-64	65 and over
Deaths from all causes other than violence (1-162, 199 and 200):											
1939	277,627	21,880	4,588	2,141	1,584	6,146	8,285	12,646	25,738	51,287	143,331
1940	309,506	24,301	6,355	2,506	1,672	6,265	8,978	14,384	28,900	58,320	157,820
1941	285,352	24,697	6,610	2,448	1,535	5,788	7,895	13,571	25,794	52,080	144,929
1942	265,626	22,944	4,408	1,885	1,450	5,197	6,912	12,277	23,911	48,226	138,415
1943	275,509	23,542	4,235	1,853	1,364	4,922	6,431	12,442	24,945	49,418	146,357
1944	269,091	23,265	3,542	1,647	1,289	4,391	5,790	11,662	23,736	48,656	145,111
1945	270,291	21,740	3,477	1,422	1,151	4,115	5,636	11,174	23,783	48,956	148,833
Scarlet fever(8):											
1939	146	7	54	29	15	17	6	10	5	2	1
1940	106	7	36	31	8	9	7	1	3	1	3
1941	85	4	42	23	3	3	2	3	3	1	1
1942	61	3	18	20	6	2	3	4	-	2	3
1943	80	2	29	23	7	3	2	6	3	4	1
1944	61	4	25	17	3	2	2	3	1	3	1
1945	42	3	17	9	6	1	1	3	1	1	-
Whooping cough (9):											
1939	773	469	281	19	-	2	-	-	2	-	-
1940	485	282	189	14	-	-	-	-	-	-	-
1941	1,353	759	548	41	2	1	-	-	1	-	1
1942	423	277	142	3	-	-	-	-	-	1	-
1943	681	419	237	22	1	1	-	-	-	-	1
1944	597	412	168	14	1	-	-	-	1	-	1
1945	384	251	124	7	1	1	-	-	-	-	-
Diphtheria (10):											
1939	1,343	31	534	564	146	37	14	7	3	3	4
1940	1,624	50	671	659	160	47	15	8	6	5	3
1941	1,625	57	775	561	127	54	23	8	11	5	4
1942	1,073	34	457	404	103	43	13	9	5	3	2
1943	822	50	313	294	82	46	15	10	7	3	2
1944	560	29	220	201	63	24	7	2	6	2	6
1945	410	14	166	141	42	21	8	4	6	6	2
Tuberculosis of respiratory system (13):											
1939	15,039	37	67	33	73	2,055	2,944	2,923	3,148	2,670	1,089
1940	15,865	36	74	40	75	2,098	3,183	3,238	3,243	2,773	1,105
1941	15,821	48	133	56	88	2,020	3,020	3,284	3,301	2,741	1,130
1942	14,227	49	105	43	74	1,852	2,566	2,912	2,968	2,531	1,127
1943	14,767	77	98	49	56	1,701	2,461	3,038	3,234	2,820	1,233
1944	13,870	60	103	44	62	1,615	2,301	2,749	3,005	2,654	1,277
1945	13,641	43	97	43	68	1,550	2,288	2,708	2,917	2,602	1,325

See footnotes on page 15.

Source: Registrars General

2.3 Civilian deaths registered: Analysis by cause and age[1]
continued

Males

United Kingdom *Number*

	All ages[2]	Under 1 year	1-4	5-9	10-14	15-24	25-34	35-44	45-54	55-64	65 and over
		Age group									
Other forms of tuberculosis (14-22):											
1939	2,703	196	551	253	178	495	306	242	191	172	119
1940	2,934	251	637	254	191	521	355	241	204	163	117
1941	3,192	236	831	324	221	559	314	251	186	164	106
1942	2,925	220	647	291	215	503	313	256	210	148	122
1943	2,730	201	628	279	185	469	266	240	193	142	127
1944	2,539	186	568	260	191	416	244	215	190	161	108
1945	2,461	157	596	272	192	386	214	246	164	134	100
Influenza (33):											
1939	4,882	177	105	36	21	146	193	366	674	973	2 191
1940	7,387	311	217	33	31	170	283	622	1,079	1,761	2,880
1941	3,950	195	102	29	17	102	146	313	467	850	1,729
1942	2,053	124	58	14	13	57	62	137	295	473	820
1943	6,556	227	101	30	31	103	113	339	789	1,308	3,515
1944	2,294	148	58	17	13	43	35	129	281	489	1,081
1945	1,550	126	64	8	9	34	45	90	162	345	667
Measles (35):											
1939	174	55	94	23	1	-	1	-	-	-	-
1940	645	196	371	56	10	3	3	3	1	-	2
1941	691	214	366	82	12	5	3	2	-	2	5
1942	337	112	189	26	3	2	1	-	1	2	1
1943	428	146	228	32	6	4	4	3	-	2	3
1944	149	62	77	9	1	-	-	-	-	-	-
1945	434	170	215	31	7	2	1	3	1	1	3
Bronchitis (106):											
1939	10,266	615	142	20	24	100	130	311	991	1,890	6,043
1940	28,359	1,146	310	47	30	149	292	876	3,100	6,680	15,729
1941	21,030	1,240	285	51	20	100	195	619	2,027	4,678	11,815
1942	17,708	804	170	40	24	96	192	537	1,739	4,026	10,080
1943	19,485	859	159	38	22	93	177	541	1,939	4,246	11,411
1944	17,966	733	119	32	16	89	160	490	1,731	4,227	10,369
1945	19,329	718	114	30	20	81	146	518	1,833	4,573	11,295
Pneumonia (107-109):											
1939	14,573	3,212	1,066	149	77	309	457	855	1,645	2,492	4,311
1940	19,112	4,463	1,788	176	98	339	568	1,043	1,967	3,221	5,449
1941	16,915	4,322	1,428	176	84	293	380	896	1,672	2,837	4,827
1942	13,714	3,480	887	128	75	222	303	762	1,263	2,296	4,298
1943	15,650	4,083	886	134	76	212	247	789	1,462	2,474	5,287
1944	13,183	3,593	696	107	73	145	239	634	1,176	2,056	4,464
1945	12,576	3,649	651	97	53	148	202	479	1,025	1,946	4,326

See footnotes on page 15.

Source: Registrars General

2.3 Civilian deaths registered: Analysis by cause and age[1]

continued

Males

United Kingdom — *Number*

	All ages[2]	Age group: Under 1 year	1-4	5-9	10-14	15-24	25-34	35-44	45-54	55-64	65 and over
Deaths by violence (163-198):											
1939	18,918	495	726	672	450	2,116	2,379	2,157	2,478	3,119	4,325
1940	31,084	638	1,233	1,090	951	3,163	4,081	4,371	4,487	5,004	6,039
1941	30,941	722	1,342	1,351	1,182	3,132	3,706	4,601	4,412	4,822	5,650
1942	17,565	568	899	918	632	1,502	1,635	2,199	2,494	2,714	3,997
1943	15,710	612	787	918	595	1,263	1,282	1,955	2,218	2,396	3,679
1944	18,160	685	963	1,068	742	1,391	1,287	2,314	2,615	2,905	4,188
1945	14,283	630	842	915	616	1,156	980	1,572	1,905	2,108	3,553
Suicides (163-64):											
1939	3,667	-	-	-	2	198	417	520	715	1,000	815
1940	3,167	-	-	-	4	127	289	471	625	846	805
1941	2,568	-	-	-	5	109	237	406	475	647	689
1942	2,309	-	-	-	5	123	204	347	450	556	624
1943	2,421	-	-	-	5	109	198	404	487	575	643
1944	2,405	-	-	-	4	110	170	356	500	592	673
1945	2,429	-	-	-	6	84	179	342	511	572	735
Deaths of civilians due to operations of war (197) :											
1939	73	-	-	-	-	3	8	20	28	13	1
1940	11,851	102	412	388	463	1,463	1,992	2,079	1,894	1,731	1,320
1941	12,279	136	456	470	555	1,555	1,811	2,237	1,923	1,805	1,324
1942	2,098	16	66	102	140	211	246	338	396	326	257
1943	1,651	12	59	83	124	179	139	240	317	273	225
1944	4,541	53	184	198	256	376	382	698	844	802	747
1945	1,222	16	68	62	92	101	105	161	249	207	161

1. The figures in brackets following each cause of death are the reference numbers to that particular cause in the Fifth Revision of the International List.
2. Including a small number of unstated age.

Source: Registrars General

2.4 Civilian deaths registered: Analysis by cause and age[1]

Females

United Kingdom *Number*

	All ages	Age group									
		Under 1 year	1-4	5-9	10-14	15-24	25-34	35-44	45-54	55-64	65 and over
Deaths from all causes other than violence (1-162,199 and 200):											
1939	274,745	16,165	4,034	1,960	1,637	7,182	9,702	12,580	21,936	40,615	158,934
1940	302,418	17,395	5,586	2,278	1,696	7,923	10,073	13,463	23,501	44,680	175,823
1941	279,261	18,002	6,014	2,186	1,605	7,904	9,763	12,517	21,624	39,698	159,948
1942	257,771	16,824	3,815	1,691	1,390	7,168	9,105	11,758	20,060	37,272	148,687
1943	273,463	17,484	3,864	1,640	1,433	7,015	8,986	12,253	20,704	38,184	161,900
1944	260,910	17,226	3,095	1,447	1,240	6,416	8,152	11,155	19,479	36,319	156,381
1945	265,299	15,933	3,042	1,301	1,124	5,905	7,660	10,933	19,363	36,694	163,344
Scarlet fever (8):											
1939	156	4	59	40	12	21	4	6	7	3	-
1940	108	3	30	32	11	9	9	7	3	2	-
1941	83	4	35	13	7	8	9	3	3	-	1
1942	65	5	16	22	7	2	3	4	3	1	2
1943	82	3	25	23	7	5	11	4	2	1	1
1944	67	1	21	24	7	4	4	3	1	1	1
1945	61	1	17	16	7	7	8	2	1	1	1
Whooping cough (9):											
1939	965	523	413	23	3	-	1	-	-	2	-
1940	531	255	253	21	-	1	-	-	-	-	-
1941	1,848	900	885	54	5	-	-	1	-	-	3
1942	532	309	209	12	-	-	-	-	1	-	1
1943	851	469	360	20	1	1	-	-	-	-	-
1944	731	447	259	21	1	1	-	1	-	-	1
1945	501	273	208	17	2	1	-	-	-	-	-
Diphtheria (10):											
1939	1,293	29	466	541	141	57	24	9	12	9	5
1940	1,641	34	637	650	187	57	26	24	10	11	5
1941	1,643	41	646	611	158	98	31	22	15	13	8
1942	1,111	29	415	414	106	67	27	21	14	11	7
1943	821	39	281	265	79	65	26	21	23	17	5
1944	592	21	227	197	52	33	21	15	7	10	9
1945	443	6	155	157	40	21	20	18	9	10	7
Tuberculosis of respiratory system (13)											
1939	10,705	18	57	40	163	3,138	2,969	1,791	1,165	828	536
1940	11,585	34	70	40	183	3,503	3,225	1,962	1,145	853	570
1941	11,583	49	107	46	198	3,594	3,223	1,877	1,125	844	520
1942	10,407	45	87	33	144	3,275	2,852	1,661	1,011	779	520
1943	10,077	46	96	46	150	3,041	2,754	1,645	1,019	767	513
1944	9,677	43	96	47	138	2,951	2,676	1,607	918	705	496
1945	9,653	44	106	52	127	2,813	2,701	1,643	970	656	541

See footnotes on page 18.

Source: Registrars General

2.4 Civilian deaths registered: Analysis by cause and age[1]

continued

Females

United Kingdom

Number

	All ages	Age group									
		Under 1 year	1-4	5-9	10-14	15-24	25-34	35-44	45-54	55-64	65 and over
Other forms of tuberculosis (14-22):											
1939	2,415	160	454	216	191	488	300	183	142	132	149
1940	2,174	172	551	233	212	616	316	200	168	127	119
1941	3,098	174	749	311	226	700	290	221	154	133	140
1942	2,735	160	544	236	214	582	346	213	171	129	140
1943	2,734	155	564	260	206	623	292	201	149	118	166
1944	2,594	149	493	268	218	557	290	201	141	134	143
1945	2,242	157	506	251	213	500	230	182	137	119	147
Influenza (33):											
1939	5,467	112	85	22	44	133	241	333	483	812	3,202
1940	6,489	185	153	41	30	156	198	340	577	1,099	3,710
1941	4,060	155	75	34	20	87	116	178	343	574	2,478
1942	1,830	85	62	15	13	52	68	111	155	259	1,010
1943	7,510	190	118	38	52	126	208	366	546	908	4,958
1944	2,157	107	47	16	13	54	63	75	139	244	1,399
1945	1,461	71	44	8	5	24	34	59	114	214	888
Measles (35):											
1939	166	49	83	28	1	1	2	-	-	2	-
1940	663	200	365	62	5	9	7	4	1	5	5
1941	572	152	315	52	9	16	6	11	4	-	7
1942.	332	94	186	37	5	5	3	-	1	1	-
1943	463	162	225	45	9	6	6	5	1	1	3
1944	148	55	75	14	1	1	-	1	-	-	1
1945	405	131	214	32	2	7	7	2	1	2	7
Bronchitis (106):											
1939	8,568	505	140	22	21	58	80	153	329	853	6,407
1940	23,115	782	247	41	34	120	187	437	1,068	3,099	17,100
1941	16,984	869	218	27	20	108	123	259	731	1,904	12,725
1942	12,287	554	134	25	15	93	116	214	546	1,409	9,181
1943	15,123	626	141	20	18	81	130	306	631	1,625	11,545
1944	12,023	522	107	28	10	74	127	227	566	1,314	9,048
1945	13,281	496	109	24	11	71	107	249	577	1,628	10,009
Pneumonia (107-109):											
1939	11,376	2,329	910	145	103	262	385	503	758	1,336	4,645
1940	14,988	3,166	1,465	162	90	257	444	631	1,026	1,725	6,022
1941	13,828	3,289	1,266	159	83	264	385	554	829	1,451	5,548
1942	10,588	2,520	810	108	64	230	337	485	667	1,158	4,209
1943	13,089	3,022	849	114	85	275	405	573	816	1,402	5,548
1944	10,121	2,737	623	80	71	178	257	390	577	976	4,232
1945	10,218	2,808	586	69	54	165	233	361	541	986	4,415

See footnotes on page 18.

Source: Registrars General

2.4 Civilian deaths registered: Analysis by cause and age[1]

continued

Females

United Kingdom — *Number*

	All ages[2]	Age group										
		Under 1 year	1-4	5-9	10-14	15-24	25-34	35-44	45-54	55-64	65 and over
Deaths by violence (163-198):											
1939	9,485	384	432	288	132	478	605	677	935	1,219	4,335
1940	20,532	503	868	729	601	1,976	2,102	2,145	2,452	2,700	6,456
1941	19,561	614	986	881	664	2,008	1,995	2,015	2,255	2,414	5,725
1942	10,343	470	588	464	248	621	733	854	993	1,188	4,184
1943	9,443	431	531	397	264	522	635	828	890	1,054	3,891
1944	12,850	599	580	555	332	898	1,068	1,191	1,412	1,642	4,573
1945	9,360	520	538	406	196	464	606	747	914	1,054	3,915
Suicides (163-164):											
1939	1,911	-	-	-	1	94	283	353	470	413	297
1940	1,783	-	-	-	1	81	204	315	422	450	310
1941	1,484	-	-	-	-	59	219	249	350	365	242
1942	1,461	-	-	-	2	54	182	282	348	330	263
1943	1,472	-	-	-	1	56	193	319	325	321	257
1944	1,387	-	-	-	1	50	169	276	306	313	272
1945	1,556	-	-	-	1	63	191	288	367	354	292
Deaths of civilians due to operations of war (197):											
1939	-	-	-	-	-	-	-	-	-	-	--
1940	10,571	101	357	367	441	1,526	1,587	1,495	1,538	1,455	1,704
1941	10,058	135	419	467	480	1,551	1,443	1,423	1,427	1,288	1,422
1942	1,779	22	78	72	81	211	225	234	246	245	365
1943	1,486	16	56	69	106	176	165	219	205	202	272
1944	4,821	56	134	166	175	583	628	650	747	743	939
1945	1,205	14	43	58	47	149	156	189	199	160	190

1. The figures in brackets following each cause of death are the reference numbers to that particular cause in the Fifth Revision of the International List.
2. Including a small number of unstated age.

Source: Registrars General

2.5 Notifications of infectious diseases

Number

	1939	1940	1941	1942	1943	1944	1945
United Kingdom							
Diphtheria	58,052	63,018	64,794	52,074	44,176	31,428	25,134
Typhoid and paratyphoid fevers	1,909	3,761	5,945	1,170	1,004	848	730
Erysipelas	17,626	16,062	14,907	14,305	14,500	13,548	12,093
Scarlet fever	94,194	76,531	69,598	100,549	134,033	108,253	87,370
Smallpox	1	1	-	109	-	16	4
Dysentery	3,082	4,756	9,101	9,820	10,909	17,420	21,110
Ophthalmia neonatorum	5,947	5,563	5,117	5,556	5,543	4,603	4,044
Pneumonia (acute primary and acute influenzal)	52,482	61,977	64,549	54,901	67,141	50,740	44,637
Puerperal fever and pyrexia	11,034	9,161	8,957	10,244	9,976	9,336	8,276
Tuberculosis: Total	53,893	54,893	59,834	62,289	65,129	65,042	62,513
England and Wales							
Diphtheria	47,343	46,280	50,797	41,404	34,662	23,199	18,596
Typhoid and paratyphoid fevers	1,479	2,833	4,763	858	713	542	535
Erysipelas	14,141	13,123	12,232	11,598	11,833	11,148	9,853
Scarlet fever	78,101	65,302	59,433	85,084	116,034	92,671	73,687
Smallpox	1	1	-	7	-	16	6
Dysentery	1,941	2,860	6,670	7,296	7,905	13,025	16,278
Ophthalmia neonatorum	4,594	4,390	4,195	4,517	4,502	3,660	3,314
Pneumomia (acute primary and acute influenzal)	42,312	47,875	50,942	42,698	52,407	38,631	34,371
Puerperal fever and pyrexia	9,252	7,627	7,356	8,542	8,354	7,944	7,013
Tuberculosis:[1]: Total	46,206	46,572	50,964	52,619	54,342	54,313	52,110
Respiratory	34,930	36,151	39,499	40,629	42,410	43,794	42,166
Other	11,276	10,421	11,465	11,990	11,932	10,519	9,944
Scotland							
Diphtheria	9,476	15,069	12,395	9,474	7,944	6,835	5,679
Typhoid and paratyphoid fevers	345	859	1,070	225	200	183	137
Erysipelas	3,235	2,715	2,514	2,570	2,557	2,261	2,103
Scarlet fever	12,023	8,353	8,760	13,792	14,722	12,057	11,654
Smallpox	-	-	-	101	-	-	-
Dysentery	1,132	1,888	2,429	2,515	2,984	4,373	4,811
Ophthalmia neonatorum	1,328	1,152	902	1,023	1,019	930	722
Pneumonia (acute primary and acute influenzal)	9,455	13,658	13,316	11,855	14,428	11,852	10,049
Puerperal fever	784	735	709	775	814	680	617
Puerperal pyrexia	903	731	775	797	716	624	606
Tuberculosis:[1]: Total	7,097	7,722	8,294	9,048	10,088	9,933	9,658
Respiratory	4,657	5,212	5,739	6,224	7,215	7,282	7,316
Other	2,440	2,510	2,555	2,824	2,873	2,651	2,342
Northern Ireland							
Diphtheria	1,233	1,669	1,602	1,196	1,570	1,394	859
Typhoid and paratyphoid fevers	85	69	112	87	91	123	58
Erysipelas	250	274	161	137	110	139	137
Scarlet fever	4,070	2,876	1,405	1,673	3,277	3,525	2,029
Smallpox	-	-	-	1	-	-	-
Dysentery	9	8	2	9	20	22	21
Ophthalmia neonatorum	25	21	20	16	22	13	8
Pneumonia (acute primary and acute influenzal)	715	444	291	348	306	257	217
Puerperal fever	22	22	16	22	5	9	6
Puerperal pyrexia	73	46	101	108	87	79	34
Tuberculosis:[2]: Total	531	599	576	622	699	796	745

1. Formal notifications of new cases only.
2. Cases of acute infectious tuberculosis only.

Sources: Registrars General for England, Wales and Northern Ireland and Department of Health for Scotland

2.6 Venereal disease

Cases dealt with at civilian treatment centres in Great Britain[1]

Number

	1938	1939	1940	1941	1942	1943	1944	1945
Total all cases	149,218	137,746	121,754	130,054	137,330	142,377	139,034	145,387
Males	100,228	91,449	81,238	89,692	92,562	89,795	81,082	82,907
Females	48,990	46,297	40,516	40,362	44,768	52,582	57,952	62,480
Syphilis	64,377	63,138	59,832	62,963	72,654	80,656	81,155	81,024
Gonorrhoea	83,335	73,247	60,514	65,348	62,914	60,313	56,707	63,320
Soft chancre	1,506	1,361	1,408	1,743	1,762	1,408	1,172	1,043
New infection[2]	57,726	51,086	46,361	52,492	53,960	56,252	51,780	57,444
Males	42,272	37,789	34,470	37,705	36,082	34,848	30,121	34,531
Females	15,454	13,297	11,891	14,787	17,878	21,404	21,659	22,913
Syphilis	15,808	14,528	14,046	16,841	20,411	21,591	19,460	19,271
Gonorrhoea	40,826	35,579	31,230	34,337	32,326	33,695	31,545	37,458
Soft chancre	1,092	979	1.085	1,314	1,223	966	775	715

1. Cases from the services are included.
2. Cases in which treatment or observation was begun during the year. Included in the total of all cases.

Source: Health Departments

2.7 National Health Insurance

(i) Estimated numbers entitled to benefits

End of year — Thousands

	1939	1940	1941	1942	1943	1944	1945
Total	22,049	22,848	23,632	24,626	25,133	25,249	25,135
Males:							
Total	14,595	15,122	15,371	15,705	15,806	15,819	15,797
Approved societies	13,063	13,236	13,323	13,562	13,592	13,559	13,518
Navy and Army Fund	136	425	514	554	587	605	621
Deposit contributors	144	170	198	209	206	195	172
Exempt persons	7	5	3	2	2	2	2
Over age 65	1,245	1,286	1,333	1,378	1,419	1,458	1,484
Females:							
Total	7,454	7,726	8,261	8,921	9,327	9,430	9,338
Approved societies	6,944	6,968	7,401	7,980	8,320	8,390	8,288
Navy and Army Fund	-	14	43	64	72	73	74
Deposit contributors	157	179	208	244	273	277	258
Exempt persons	6	5	3	2	2	2	1
Over age 60	347[1]	560	606	631	660	688	717

Source: *Ministry of National Insurance*

(ii) Receipts, expenditure and accumulated funds

£ thousand

	1939	1940	1941	1942	1943	1944	1945
Receipts:							
Total	45,157	43,383	47,029	59,189	58,134	58,060	57,221
Contributions from employers and workers	31,007	31,499	31,577	40,574	41,070	40,204	39,176
Interest, etc., on funds	6,382	3,530	6,952	9,155	6,389	6,765	6,882
Parliamentary votes and grants	7,768	8,354	8,500	9,460	10,675	11,091	11,163
Expenditure:							
Total	41,350	41,012	39,026	47,288	51,916	54,013	54,247
Benefits:							
Total	35,180	34,978	32,657	40,602	45,468	47,381	47,401
Sickness	11,251	12,353	11,053	15,808	19,285	19,406	18,725
Disablement	6,502	5,984	5,329	7,200	7,636	8,272	8,804
Maternity	1,762	1,701	1,705	1,877	2,104	2,256	2,042
Medical	12,689	12,475	12,452	13,453	14,138	15,074	15,449
Other	2,976	2,465	2,118	2,264	2,305	2,373	2,381
Administration:							
Total	6,170	6,034	6,369	6,686	6,448	6,632	6,846
Approved societies and insurance committees	5,034	5,047	5,149	5,530	5,308	5,509	5,547
Central departments	1,136	987	1,220	1,156	1,140	1,123	1,299
Accumulated funds (at end of year)	147,046	148,510	155,606	166,073	171,084	174,289	176,303

1. Over 65 years of age

Source: *Ministry of National Insurance*

2.8 Unemployment Insurance

(i) Persons insured

Great Britain — July of each year — *Thousands*

	1939	1940	1941	1942	1943	1944	1945
Total	15,548	14.803	14,922	15,061	14,630	14,150	13,640
General scheme	14,838	14,158	14,292	14,406	13,945	13,465	12,965
Agricultural scheme	710	645	630	655	685	685	675

Source: Ministry of Labour and National Service

(ii) Receipts, expenditure and fund

Years ended 31 March — *£ thousand*

	1939	1940	1941	1942	1943	1944	1945
Receipts							
Total	68,543	71,480	78,941	80,306	80,159	77,797	89,834
General scheme	66,992	70,047	77,485	78,729	78,546	76,165	88,140
Agricultural scheme	1,551	1,433	1,456	1,577	1,613	1,632	1,694
Contributions from:							
Employers and employees:							
General scheme	43,969	46,479	50,803	50,501	49,068	46,604	45,208
Agricultural scheme	996	930	907	960	956	959	972
Defence departments	138	-	-	-	-	-	8,060
Exchequer:							
General scheme	22,032	23,233	25,396	25,250	24,534	23,301	26,633
Agricultural scheme	494	465	453	480	478	480	486
Income from investments:							
General scheme	839	325	1,282	2,975	4,942	6,258	8,234
Agricultural scheme	61	38	96	137	179	193	236
Other receipts:							
General scheme	14	10	4	3	2	2	5
Agricultural scheme	-	-	-	-	-	-	-
Expenditure							
Total	84,414	65,621	9,079	6,301	5,490	6,753	17,105
General scheme	83,346	64,992	8,710	6,021	5,242	6,491	16,765
Agricultural scheme	1,068	629	369	280	248	262	340
Benefit, transitional payments and unemployment allowances:							
General scheme: Direct	34,854	18,938	5,592	3,185	2,600	3,472	12,374
Association	1,791	864	213	79	38	49	271
Agricultural scheme: Direct	871	451	196	97	66	79	155
Administrative expenses:							
General scheme	5,335	4,256	2,589	2,477	2,327	2,704	3,855
Agricultural scheme	185	174	170	180	179	180	182
Interest on advances and reduction of debt	40,864	40,578	-	-	-	-	-
Other payments and refunds:							
General scheme	502	356	316	280	277	266	265
Agricultural scheme	12	4	3	3	3	3	3
Fund							
Balance of fund at end of period:							
General scheme	24,156	29,211	97,986	170,694	243,998	313,672	385,047
Agricultural scheme	3,254	4,058	5,145	6,442	7,807	9,177	10,531
Investments (at cost) at end of period	27,511	33,230	103,150	177,187	251,872	322,892	396,271
Treasury advances outstanding	39,354	-	-	-	-	-	-

1. This figure relates to the war years when such contributions were in abeyance.

Source: Ministry of National Insurance

2.9 Pensions

(i) Old age pensions payable from age 70

Number

	1939	1940	1941	1942	1943	1944	1945
Number of pensions payable[1] (Thousands)							
Total	1,906	1,944	1,986	2,043	2,128	2,186	2,255
Under Contributory Pensions Act	1,299	1,372	1,439	1,519	1,622	1,707	1,797
Other	607	572	547	524	506	479	458
Men:							
Under Contributory Pensions Act	608	633	656	684	724	756	789
Other	182	174	169	163	161	152	145
Women:							
Under Contributory Pensions Act	691	739	783	835	898	951	1,008
Other	425	398	378	362	345	327	313
Full rate:							
Under Contributory Pensions Act	1,296	1,369	1,434	1,514	1,616	1,700	1,789
Other	580	546	522	499	480	454	434
Reduced rate:							
Under Contributory Pensions Act	30	3	5	5	6	7	8
Other		26	25	25	26	25	24
Total amount of pensions paid in year ended 31 March (£ thousand)	49,348	49,816	50,694	51,844	53,709	56,538	57,398

Source: Ministry of National Insurance and H.M. Customs and Excise

(ii) Pensions insured and beneficiaries under the Widows', and Old Age Pensions Act, 1936

End of year — Thousands

	1939	1940	1941	1942	1943	1944	1945
Estimated numbers insured:							
Total	21,835	22,640	23,361	24,242	24,736	24,863	24,767
Men	14,635	15,188	15,380	15,622	15,683	15,714	15,693
Women	7,200	7,452	7,981	8,620	9,053	9,149	9,074
Number of beneficiaries:							
Total	2,016	2,349	2,423	2,467	2,507	2,544	2,585
Widows: Contributory	664	699	743	765	789	811	829
Non-contributory	179	161	144	130	117	104	93
Children: Contributory	282	274	261	249	241	234	225
Non-contributory	3	1	-	-	-	-	
Pensioners under 70[2]: Men	551	566	586	601	613	622	634
Women	337	648	689	722	747	773	804

1. At the last Friday in March in each year.
2. Men aged 65 and over; women aged 65 and over up to 30 June 1940 and 60 and over thereafter.

Source: Ministry of National Insurance

(iii) Contributory pension: Receipts, expenditure and accumulated funds

Years ended 31 March — £ thousand

	1939	1940	1941	1942	1943	1944	1945
Receipts							
Total	52,004	55,443	67,761	72,949	75,855	77,804	77,189
Contributions	33,771	34,481	45,679	49,564	5,154	52,859	52,096
Parliamentary vote	17,415	19,989	20,989	21,999	22,999	22,999	22,999
Interest, etc	818	973	1,093	1,386	1,702	1,946	2,094
Expenditure							
Total	49,133	50,292	57,466	61,502	62,575	64,575	65,055
Widows' and orphans' pensions:							
Contributory	19,698	20,505	21,580	22,543	22,759	23,212	23,748
Non-contributory	5,357	4,785	4,286	3,888	3,447	3,105	2,767
Pensioners under 70[1]	22,108	22,926	29,326	32,607	33,694	35,90	35,655
Administration	1,669	1,747	1,943	1,974	1,750	1,923	1,894
Payments to National Health Insurance:							
Central Fund	329	331	316	-	-	-	-
Unemployment Arrears Fund	301	-	-	174	925	945	991
Accumulated funds	24,869	30,020	40,315	51,762	65,042	78,271	90,405

1. See footnote 2 on page 23.

Source: Ministry of National Insurance

2.10 War pensions, grants and allowances

(i) Expenditure

Years ended 31 March — £ thousand

	1939	1940	1941	1942	1943	1944	1945
Total	39,175	38,238	39,458	42,596	46,075	50,946	62,081
Pensions, gratuities and allowances: Total	37,450	36,481	36,922	39,558	42,507	46,808	57,087
Services:							
1914-18 war and earlier wars:							
Officers, nurses and dependants	4,063	3,941	3,804	3,688	3,600	3,511	3,499
Other ranks and dependants	33,387	32,475	31,602	30,548	29,803	29,007	29,387
1939-45 war:							
Officers, nurses and dependants	-	17	233	554	9,73	1,672	2,946
Other ranks and dependants	-	15	524	2,530	5,500	9,310	16,659
Mercantile marine:							
Officers and dependants	-	6	79	252	498	740	897
Seamen and dependants	-	12	116	336	610	777	947
Civilians:							
Men, women and dependants	-	14	565	1,651	1,524	1,790	2,752
Medical treatment to pensioners	1,007	983	1,295	1,405	1,658	1,957	2,415
Miscellaneous	32	27	30	72	83	163	305
Administration: Local and central	686	748	1,212	1,561	1,827	2,017	2,274

Source: Ministry of Pensions

(ii) Estimated number of beneficiaries

At 31 March in each year — *Number*

	1939	1940	1941	1942	1943	1944	1945
Total	877,400	850,570	869,915	980,050	1,061,05 5	1,224,070	1,431,385
Services							
1914-18 war and earlier wars:							
Total	877,400	846,150	817 815	789,865	763,970	740,445	714,745
Officers and dependants:							
Disabled officers	21,520	21,140	20,690	20,265	19,850	19,475	19,095
Widows	7,700	7,590	7,465	7,335	7,190	7,060	6,945
Adult dependants	3,700	3,500	3,270	3,005	2,770	2,560	2,345
Other[1]	600	250	105	40	25	380	535
Nurses and dependants:							
Disabled nurses	885	870	865	845	830	810	800
Dependants	20	20	20	20	20	15	15
Other ranks and dependants:							
Disabled other ranks	404,685	395,675	387,100	378,395	370,360	361,605	352,725
Widows	116,520	114,380	112,590	110,640	108,785	106,855	104,895
Adult dependants	196,730	183,000	171,040	159,110	148,425	136,865	125,790
Other[1]	125,040	119,725	114,670	110,210	105,715	104,820	101,600
1939-45 war:							
Total	-	3,470	37,095	193,725	238,690	412,780	652,405
Officers and dependants:							
Disabled officers	-	-	100	755	1,455	3,030	5,630
Widows	-	100	1,225	2,810	4,625	7,515	10,950
Adult dependants	-	10	120	325	580	1,045	1,630
Other[1]	-	95	1,100	2,625	4,155	8,430	15,765
Other ranks and dependants:							
Disabled other ranks	-	20	5,840	35,905	64,440	116,110	177,920
Widows	-	1,285	8,050	18,670	30,030	46,210	69,260
Adult dependants	-	190	2,195	5,610	9,490	15,710	25,390
Other[1]	-	1,770	18,465	77,025	123,915	214,730	325,860
Mercantile marine							
Officers:							
Disabled officers	-	-	10	75	245	910	1,550
Widows	-	115	675	1,860	2,890	3,365	3,555
Adult dependants	-	15	125	370	605	835	900
Other[1]	-	135	665	1,770	2,580	3,700	4,570
Seamen:							
Disabled seamen	-	-	145	485	810	1,840	3,195
Widows	-	230	1,250	2,895	4,720	5,165	5,115
Adult dependants	-	30	315	900	1,545	2,045	2,190
Other[1]	-	385	1,775	4,580	7,170	9,155	9,725
Civilians							
Disabled civilians	-	-	185	8,675	11,200	13,695	18,465
Widows	-	20	4,610	8,485	9,015	9,285	10,845
Dependants	-	-	330	880	900	960	1,105
Other[1]	-	20	4,920	15,485	16,715	19,890	23,020

1. Wives of disabled officers or men, children living with parents, and orphans.

Source: Ministry of Pensions

2.11 Offences known to the police and persons proceeded against and found guilty

England and Wales *Number*

	1939	1940	1941	1942	1943	1944	1945
All offences[1]							
Persons proceeded against	745,148	863,749	879,692	759,763	623,972	554,035	517,543
Persons found guilty	695,814	803,721	802,999	689,238	569,825	500,488	467,700
Indictable offences							
Offences known to police	303,771	305,114	358,655	364,889	372,760	415,010	478,394
Persons proceeded against	86,645	99,017	118,746	118,295	115,508	118,849	128,733
Persons found guilty:							
Total	78,058	89,814	107,571	107,150	104,868	106,550	115,974
Breaking and entering	11,714	13,353	14,762	14,625	14,548	16,554	21,260
Frauds and false pretences[2]	2,401	1,860	3,312	2,953	2,907	2,684	2,350
Larceny	55,341	65,117	77,206	75,189	72,620	72,829	75,975
Receiving	2,591	4,060	6,238	6,597	6,051	6,331	7,014
Sexual offences	2,214	1,987	2,510	2,971	3,392	3,078	3,228
Violence against the person: Total	1,708	1,445	1,589	1,622	1,846	1,898	2,459
Murder	28	22	24	31	29	20	21
Manslaughter	61	63	64	85	62	80	101
Wounding	1,413	1,177	1,259	1,250	1,370	1,404	1,869
Other offences against the person	206	183	242	256	385	394	468
Other offences	2,089	1,992	1,954	3,193	3,504	3,176	3,688
Non-indictable offences[3]							
Persons proceeded against	597,117	424,392	474,590	406,934	313,673	291,096	330,692
Persons found guilty:							
Total	557,825	381,462	417,066	354,369	278,132	255,865	297,438
Assaults	9,959	9,847	10,079	9,605	10,571	10,785	11,390
Betting and gaming[4]	13,035	7,550	8,936	10,359	9,811	8,950	10,626
Bye-laws and Police Regulations	28,688	23,998	23,070	21,478	19,832	16,150	13,755
Drunkenness and other offences under Intoxicating Liquor Laws	54,812	48,863	43,778	29,778	29,314	24,910	22,188
Education Acts	3,375	5,690	13,357	17,800	18,778	16,378	10,102
Game Laws	1,774	1,449	1,481	1,354	1,398	1,161	1,508
Labour Laws	5,883	2,754	1,792	1,878	2,220	1,943	1,774
Malicious damage	8,384	9,778	12,059	12,343	12,082	11,361	12,632
Offences by prostitutes	1,977	1,761	1,621	2,122	2,371	1,630	2,096
Railway offences	7,373	6,145	9,192	11,001	11,929	12,275	14,382
Revenue Laws	28,375	24,899	27,286	28,813	24,134	21,304	18,248
Stealing	1,898	2,333	4,651	4,568	5,187	3,780	3,394
Traffic offences	359,669	208,152	232,938	170,680	101,337	91,798	148,419
Vagrancy Acts(5)	4,986	3,294	2,587	2,977	3,028	3,060	3,482
Wireless Telegraphy Acts	3,683	648	579	1,433	815	440	356
Other offences	23,954	24,301	23,660	28,180	25,325	29,940	23,086
Offences against Defence Regulations							
Persons proceeded against	61,386	340,340	286,356	234,534	194,791	144,090	58,118
Persons found guilty:							
Total	59,931	332,445	278,362	227,719	186,825	138,073	54,288
Lighting offences	59,758	299,260	210,934	154,080	109,757	73,831	17,594
Looting	-	426	2,508	415	255	561	93
Control of industry	20	5,624	13,543	22,832	30,071	24,237	17,472
Control of employment	-	-	275	4,114	12,583	10,124	7,597
Strikes and lockouts	-	-	50	582	1,284	-	125
Traffic offences	34	18,498	37,716	30,371	11,297	5,978	4,495
Other offences	119	8,637	13,336	15,325	21,578	23,342	6,912

1. Including offences against Defence Regulations.
2. Including offences in connection with bankruptcy.
3. Excluding offences against Defence Regulations.
4. Including gaming offences under the Vagrancy Acts.
5. Excluding gaming offences under the Vagrancy Acts.

Source: Home Office

2.12 Crimes and offences made known to the police and persons proceeded against, convicted or found guilty

Scotland — *Number*

	1939	1940	1941	1942	1943	1944	1945
All crimes and offences[1]							
Crimes and offences made known to police	197,089	221,752	211,701	191,526	174,739	166,163	161,671
Persons proceeded against	133,459	149,061	149,095	129,369	115,726	106,436	92,440
Charge proved without finding of guilt	5,815	6,061	5,237	5,006	4,621	4,799	4,872
Persons convicted or found guilty	110,719	118,277	114,559	99,492	90,291	85,144	74,487
Crimes							
Crimes made known to police	60,104	62,266	67,494	69,127	70,944	71,583	86,075
Persons proceeded against	22,086	25,140	27,119	27,440	26,917	25,741	28,109
Charge proved without finding of guilt	4,657	5,209	4,585	4,404	4,027	3,878	4,024
Persons convicted or found guilty:							
Total	15,227	17,705	20,150	20,492	21,141	19,828	21,816
Frauds and false pretences[2]	1,403	787	1,039	1,070	1,003	915	975
Housebreaking	2,228	2,613	2,890	3,306	3,737	3,567	4,933
Malicious mischief	2,372	3,089	3,244	3,328	3,188	3,181	3,735
Reset (Receiving)	220	447	574	609	576	692	735
Sexual offences	361	336	378	453	433	391	479
Theft[3]	6,685	8,636	9,872	9,676	9,477	8,785	9,024
Violence against the person: Total	1,541	1,256	1,385	1,273	1,426	1,483	994
Murder	-	-	-	-	-	3	4
Culpable homicide	21	13	6	13	13	9	15
Assaults	1,220	1,008	1,123	999	1,105	1,180	707
Other crimes against the person	300	235	256	261	308	291	268
Other crimes	417	541	768	777	1,301	814	941
Miscellaneous offences[4]							
Offences made known to police	136,985	100,866	99,423	86,602	72,970	64,716	65,801
Persons proceeded against	111,373	88,297	87,934	74,958	64,262	58,136	56,597
Charge proved without finding of guilt	1,158	770	602	555	504	835	776
Persons convicted or found guilty:							
Total	95,492	65,930	61,549	53,003	46,061	43,864	45,701
Betting and gaming	3,348	1,749	1,972	2,183	1,861	1,838	1,644
Breach of the peace	16,019	13,275	12,662	12,265	12,393	11,617	11,802
Drunkenness and other offences against the Intoxicating Liquor Laws	13,929	12,345	9,646	6,150	5,179	3,569	2,777
Education Acts	132	146	825	1,495	2,065	2,082	1,779
Game Laws	250	147	160	180	167	166	182
Labour Laws	596	353	251	304	263	216	177
Police Regulations	8,342	8,420	7,198	6,569	6,017	5,217	5,168
Prostitution	125	33	40	125	246	298	235
Railway offences	373	306	310	292	375	720	551
Revenue Laws	555	326	319	208	246	231	264
Road Acts[5]	39,766	23,124	22,576	17,548	12,155	12,299	16,577
Streets and buildings	616	497	594	488	414	341	454
Vagrancy Acts	1,090	743	561	673	733	828	861
Other offences	10,351	4,466	4,435	4,523	3,947	4,442	3,230
Offences against war legislation							
Offences made known to police	-	58,620	44,784	35,797	30,825	29,864	9,795
Persons proceeded against	-	35,624	34,042	26,971	24,547	22,559	7,734
Charge proved without finding of guilt	-	82	50	47	90	86	72
Persons convicted or found guilty:							
Total	-	34,642	32,860	25,997	23,089	21,452	6,970
National Registration Act, 1939.	-	96	271	473	322	1,214	274
Defence Regulations:							
Lights in buildings	-	25,142	20,403	13,683	8,228	3,408	. .
Lights on vehicles	-	6,148	5,234	3,602	3,288	2,982	. .
Other offences		3,256	6,952	8,239	11,251	13,848	. .

1. Including offences against war legislation.
2. Including offences in connection with bankruptcy.
3. Including embezzlement.
4. Excluding offences against war legislation.
5. Including cases of "furious and reckless driving".

Source: Scottish Home Department

2.13 Offences known to the police and persons proceeded against and found guilty

Northern Ireland

Number

	1939	1940	1941	1942	1943	1944	1945
All offences[1]							
Persons proceeded against	44,109	49,076	55,746	52,955	54,047	54,522	44,815
Persons found guilty	40,498	46,017	52,634	49,307	50,178	50,813	41,908
Indictable offences							
Offences known to police	2,579	2,990	3,586	4,307	4,566	5,123	5,709
Persons proceeded against	2,249	2,810	2,861	3,412	3,518	3,266	3,157
Persons found guilty:							
Total	2,009	2,469	2,546	2,933	2,980	2,752	2,697
Breaking and entering	382	449	443	433	499	448	505
Frauds and false pretences[2]	58	43	73	82	70	65	65
Larceny	1,286	1,627	1,644	1,879	1,873	1,764	1,643
Receiving	95	179	202	260	256	244	199
Sexual offences	26	20	24	31	28	31	43
Violence against the person:							
Total	63	34	52	76	81	77	62
Murder	1	-	-	7	1	4	1
Manslaughter	4	4	5	4	1	4	1
Wounding	12	7	7	3	6	15	5
Other offences against the person	46	23	40	62	73	54	55
Other offences	99	117	108	172	173	123	180
Non-indictable offences[3]							
Persons proceeded against	36,593	28,892	30,476	32,059	30,365	35,383	35,244
Persons found guilty:							
Total	33,398	26,525	28,172	29,676	28,248	32,790	33,020
Assaults	491	469	441	481	661	505	621
Betting and gaming[4]	3,382	2,180	1,938	2,043	2,193	2,434	2,754
Byelaws and Police Regulations	1,755	1,415	1,398	1,641	1,796	2,306	2,522
Drunkenness and other offences under Intoxicating Liquor Laws	4,023	3,149	2,689	1,874	1,696	1,476	1,456
Education Acts	1,265	1,527	1,705	1,856	2,585	2,654	2,040
Game Laws	68	66	56	64	24	51	77
Labour Laws	496	257	178	121	87	63	77
Malicious damage	289	267	333	391	485	476	496
Offences by prostitutes	27	2	15	171	185	129	156
Railway offences	49	55	26	146	208	182	94
Revenue Laws	1,287	1,084	874	1,121	1,589	1,811	1,135
Stealing	60	127	217	1,121	241	184	159
Traffic offences	17,637	13,917	15,020	15,733	13,957	16,634	18,816
Vagrancy Acts[5]	429	323	235	378	386	467	353
Wireless Telegraphy Acts	6	17	3	2	1	2	8
Other offences	2,134	1,674	3,134	3,437	2,154	3,416	2,256
Offences against Defence Regulations							
Offences known to police	5,267	17,374	22,411	17,485	20,164	15,873	6,414
Persons proceeded against	5,267	17,374	22,409	17,484	20,164	15,873	6,414
Persons found guilty:							
Total	5,091	17,023	21,916	16,698	18,950	15,271	6,191
Lighting offences	5,060	15,589	18,420	12,584	11,254	9,405	3,606
Looting	-	-	153	-	-	-	-
Other offences	31	1,434	3,343	4,114	7,696	5,866	2,585

1. Including offences against Defence Regulations.
2. Including offences in connection with bankruptcy.
3. Excluding offences against Defence Regulations.
4. Including gaming offences under the Vagrancy Acts.
5. Excluding gaming offences under the Vagrancy Acts.

Source: Ministry of Home Affairs

2.14 Juvenile delinquency[1]

England and Wales *Number*

	1939	1940	1941	1942	1943	1944	1945
Juveniles found guilty							
All offences	53,106	66,080	72,483	66,522	68,049	68,069	73,620
Indictable offences:							
Total	30,835	42,187	43,594	38,549	38,763	40,554	43,503
Larceny	21,476	29,545	29,698	25,291	25,378	25,931	26,443
Breaking and entering	7,715	10,275	10,982	10,512	10,281	11,544	13,664
Receiving	558	971	1,202	937	969	939	979
Sexual offences	495	465	540	503	621	594	636
Frauds, etc.	100	138	163	167	135	130	94
Violence against the person	136	141	176	124	180	176	244
Other offences	355	652	833	1,015	1,199	1,240	1,443
Non-indictable offences:							
Total	21,291	20,341	24,160	24,347	24,816	23,391	27,575
Highway Acts	8,376	5,766	5,826	5,184	4,421	4,532	8,109
Police Regulations	2,048	1,508	1,250	1,564	1,700	1,651	1,903
Malicious damage	5,091	6,776	8,530	9,068	8,497	8,113	8,717
Railway offences	2,110	1,793	1,949	2,274	3,252	3,249	3,361
Stealing	1,040	1,530	3,319	3,198	3,697	2,719	2,241
Betting and gaming	602	866	1,131	878	777	499	439
Other offences	2,024	2,102	2,155	2,181	2,472	2,628	2,805
Offences against Defence Regulations:							
Total	980	3,552	4,729	3,626	4,470	4,124	2,542
Lighting offences	974	3,183	3,315	2,772	2,594	2,307	1,481
Looting	-	220	946	137	118	150	25
Control of industry	-	9	36	105	136	148	115
Preservation of agricultural land	-	29	163	165	724	530	176
Other offences	6	111	269	447	898	989	745

1. Young persons under 17 years of age.

Source: Home Office

2.15 Juvenile delinquency[1]

Scotland — *Number*

	1939	1940	1941	1942	1943	1944	1945
Alll crimes and offences[2]	..	..	..	..	..	..	4,292
Charges proved without finding of guilt							
Juveniles found guilty	10,957	13,885	14,290	1 5,138	15,170	15,264	15,952
Crimes							
Charges proved without finding of guilt	..	..	..	..	..	..	3,679
Juveniles found guilty	5,404	8,250	8,757	8,663	8,526	7,702	8,539
Miscellaneous offences[3]							550
Charges proved without finding of guilt	..	..	..	..	..	..	
Juveniles found guilty	5,553	5,238	4,967	5,921	6,647	6,977	7,141
Offences against war legislation							
Charges proved without finding of guilt	..	..	..	..	..	..	63
Juveniles found guilty	-	397	566	554	597	585	272

1. Young persons under 17 years of age.
2. Including offences against war legislation.
3. Excluding offences against war legislation.

Source: Scottish Home Department

2.16 Juvenile delinquency[1]

Northern Ireland — *Number*

	1939	1940	1941	1942	1943	1944	1945
Juveniles found guilty							
All offences	1,706	1,971	1,826	1,888	2,032	2,234	2,069
Indictable offences							
Total	717	1,126	906	929	898	811	701
Larceny	455	781	598	608	554	516	417
Breaking and entering	206	281	252	243	222	209	186
Receiving	15	35	22	20	35	33	16
Sexual offences	6	1	1	4	3	1	2
Frauds, etc.	-	7	4	3	-	3	2
Violence against the person..	5	-	-	-	-	3	2
Other offences	30	21	29	51	84	46	76
Non-indictable offences							
Total	960	814	817	882	1,001	1,275	1,329
Highways Acts	389	292	194	190	240	353	348
Police Regulations	351	282	241	230	237	432	497
Malicious damage	145	128	213	197	248	227	270
Railway offences	12	13	8	49	58	76	45
Stealing	20	52	89	144	136	110	86
Betting and gaming	-	1	4	3	9	11	18
Other offences	43	46	68	69	73	66	65
Offences against Defence Regulations							
Total	29	31	103	77	133	148	39
Lighting offences	29	26	33	58	53	54	18
Looting	-	-	43	-	-	-	-
Other offences	-	5	27	19	80	94	21

1. Young persons under 16 years of age.

Source: Ministry of Home Affairs

2.17 Prison population: Receptions and daily average population

Number

	1939	1940	1941	1942	1943	1944	1945
England and Wales							
Receptions:							
Total	44,513	40,455	48,089	51,217	45,084	47,135	48,094
Males	39,766	34,202	42,101	43,938	37,343	38,530	40,713
Females	4,747	6,253	5,988	7,279	7,741	8,605	7,381
Committals on remand or for trial	7,628	6,347	4,023	11,259	9,084	9,896	10,699
Committals by civil process (non-payment of monies, etc.)[1]	7,116	6,347	4,023	3,900	3,136	2,956	3,276
Committals in default of payment of fines	7,139	4,474	3,510	3,702	4,031	3,737	3,302
Sentences of imprisonment without the option of a fine[2]	20,690	502	27,641	29,870	26,438	27,788	26,815
Sentences of penal servitude[2]	522	502	523	813	831	1,098	1,560
Sentences of Borstal detention	1,418	1,289	1,739	1,673	1,564	1,660	2,442
Daily average population:							
Total	10,326	9,377	10,634	12,400	12,790	12,915	14,708
Unconvicted[3]	1,034	1,781	1,450	1,440	1,281	1,333	1,433
Convicted	9,292	7,596	1,450	1,440	1,281	11,582	13,275
Scotland							
Receptions:	13,953	13,251	12,143	11,397	11,085	10,884	12,360
Total	11,882	11,432	10,629	9,967	9,363	9,266	10,849
Males	2,071	1,819	1,514	1,430	1,722	1,618	1,511
Females							
Ordinary prisoners[4]	13,739	13,112	11,943	29	28	34	11,993
Convicts[5]	33	17	20	29	28	34	58
Offenders sentenced to Borstal detention	152	107	163	243	270	218	291
Others	29	14	17	25	15	15	18
Daily average population	1,350	1,320	1,337	1,559	1,560	1,606	1,958
Northern Ireland							
Receptions:							
Total	2,183	2,115	1,991	2,243	1,836	1,977	1,866
Males	1,743	1,699	1,676	1,828	1,378	1,517	1,502
Females	440	1,699	1,676	415	1,378	460	1,502
Committals on remand or for trial	272	263	508	683	507	513	605
Committals by civil process (non-payment of monies, etc.)[1]	34	263	508	22	507	27	29
Committals in default of payment of fines	985	920	354	282	273	257	259
Sentences of imprisonment without the option of a fine[2]	850	51	1,040	39	955	1,114	886
Sentences of penal servitude[2]	10	51	27	39	34	13	7
Sentences of Borstal detention	32	47	44	39	48	53	80
Daily average population:							
Total	373	363	445	550	499	516	490
Unconvicted[3]	21	31	28	29	36	21	26
Convicted	352	332	417	521	463	495	464

1. Including committals in default of sureties.
2. Including sentences imposed by Courts Marital.
3. Prisoners on remand or awaiting trial and prisoners committed by civil process.
4. Convicted and untried and forfeited and revoked licence-holders under the Penal Servitude Acts.
5. New sentences of penal servitude and death.

Source: Prison Commission for England and Wales, Scottish Home Department and Ministry of Home Affairs, Northern Ireland

2.18 Divorce proceedings[1]

Number

	1939	1940	1941	1942	1943	1944	1945
England and Wales[2]							
Dissolution of marriage:							
Petitions filed	8,517	6,915	8,079	11,613	14,887	18,390	24,857
On grounds of: Adultery	4,731	3,931	4,781	7,116	9,513	12,006	17,091
Desertion	2,813	2,326	2,667	3,630	4,342	5,100	6,227
Cruelty	705	467	437	605	736	963	1,223
Lunacy	208	159	173	223	265	278	283
Presumed decease	60	32	21	39	31	43	33
By husbands	3,822	3,485	4,279	6,303	8,100	10,154	14,271
By wives	4,695	3,430	3,800	5,310	6,787	8,236	10,586
Decrees nisi granted	7,019	7,111	6,318	8,608	10,724	14,356	18,982
Nullity of marriage:							
Petitions filed	186	171	226	390	498	579	854
By husbands	96	100	127	247	288	328	503
By wives	90	71	99	143	210	251	351
Decrees nisi granted	178	139	143	230	330	406	500
Scotland[2]							
Divorce:							
Actions in which final judgment given	884	805	772	1,027	1,317	1,745	2,237
On grounds of: Adultery	439	380	370	490	732	1,067	1,517
Desertion	392	370	349	467	509	583	619
Cruelty	32	33	40	53	48	77	73
Insanity	21	22	13	17	28	18	28
At instance of: Husbands	426	421	402	552	775	1,088	1,546
Wives	458	384	370	475	542	657	691
Divorce granted	869	794	760	1,011	1,301	1,711	2,205
Northern Ireland							
Divorce:							
Petitions filed	31	107	67	117	119	131	174
Nullity of marriage:							
Petitions filed	3	3	3	6	3	4	9

1. Excluding proceedings for judicial separation and for the restitution of conjugal rights.
2. The increase in the number of proceedings during the years 1939 to 1945 is to some extent due to the introduction of new legislation which gave additional grounds for divorce.

Source: Lord Chancellor's Department (England and Wales), Scottish Home Department and High Court of Justice (Northern Ireland)

2.19 Number of houses built[1]

Number

	Total	Permanent houses built by local authorities[2]: Assisted	Permanent houses built by local authorities[2]: Un-assisted	Permanent houses built by private builders[2]: Assisted	Permanent houses built by private builders[2]: Un-assisted	War destroyed houses re-built: By local authorities	War destroyed houses re-built: By private builders under licence	Houses built by Government departments[2]: Permanent	Houses built by Government departments[2]: Temporary	Temporary houses erected by local authorities
England and Wales[5]										
1935-38 (average)	334,405	48,579	12,336	1,177	272,313	-	-			-
1938-39	332,360	88,776	12,968	4,207	226,409	-	-	-		-
1939-40	195,962	40,231	10,221	2,849	142,661	-	-	-		-
1940-41	42,498	11,802	3,606	648	26,442	-	-	-		-
1941-42	9,841	1,676	1,237	118	5,483	-	-	1,327		-
1942-43	9,577	586	792	40	2,454	-	-	5,705		-
1943-44	5,768	1,437	1,102	12	1,067	-	-	2,150		-
1944-45	5,537	1,691	741	108	1,744	-	-	1,253		-
1945 (April to December)	10,384	366	-	901		142	36	-	-	8,939
Scotland										
1935-38 average	24,426	15,850	990	5	7,581	-	-	..	..	-
1939	25,529	18,902	216	58	6,353	-	-	..	..	-
1940	14,206	10,357	117	228	3,504	-	-	..	..	-
1941	5,406	4,676	38	68	624	-	-	..	..	-
1942	3,296	3,034	38	21	203	-	-	..	..	-
1943	2,809	2,717	-	28	64	-	-	..	..	-
1944	2,553	2,383	-	36	134	-	-	..	..	-
1945	2,006	1,428	-	27	111	-	3	..	..	437
Northern Ireland[5]										
1935-38 (average)	2,951	158	-	2,395	385	-	-	13	-	-
1938-39	1,324	1,100	16	-	207	-	-	1	-	-
1939 (April to December)	267	169	-	-	96	-	-	2	-	-
1940	400	400	-	-	-	-	-	-	-	-
1941	206	206	-	-	-	-	-	-	-	-
1942	-	-	-	-	-	-	-	-	-	-
1943	-	-	-	-	-	-	-	-	-	-
1944	27	-	-	-	10	-	-	17	-	-
1945	81	-	-	-	21	-	-	60	-	-

1. Including flats, each flat being counted as one unit.
2. The Scottish National Housing Companies, Scottish Housing association and the Northern Ireland Housing Trust are included in the figures for local authorities, but other housing associations are included in the figures for private builders.
3. Accommodation for the families of police, prison staffs, defence services and other Government employees and, in Northern Ireland, houses built on behalf of the Irish Sailors' and Soldiers' Land Trust.
4. Excluding houses in England and Wales having a rateable value exceeding £78 (or 105 in the Metropolitan Police District).
5. Years ended 31 March, from 1934-35 to 1944-45 for England and Wales, and from 1934-35 to 1938-39 for Northern Ireland. Thereafter calendar years.

Source: Health Departments

2.20 Construction activity[1]: Estimated value of work done

Great Britain — *£ million*

Type of work	Description	1940	1941	1942	1943	1944	1945
Total		425	470	425	350	290	290
Military construction	Airfields, camps and training establishments, defence works, storage depots, etc.	140	120	125	122	49	12
Industrial facilities	Factories, warehouses and storage premises	80	76	65	46	29	25
Civil defence	Air raid precautions, public shelters, static water supplies etc.	..	42	23	12	9	-
Residential building	Construction of hostels and houses	..	22	16	6	13	30
Roads and streets	Strengthening, widening and major maintenance	..	2	3	3	3	2
Public and institutional buildings	Hospitals, schools, etc.	..	6	6	9	6	5
Public utilities	Electricity, gas, water, sewerage, railways, ports, canals, tramways, etc.	..	19	16	12	8	12
Mining	Mines and opencast coal production	..	-	2	7	13	14
Air raid damage	Repairs, demolition and debris clearance	6	63	61	50	58	113
All other work	Including conversion, adaptation, maintenance and repair (other than war damage repair) of houses	..	120	108	83	102	77

1. Output of firms in the twelve main trades of the building and civil engineering industries, excluding the output of firms consisting solely of working principals.

Source: Ministry of Works

3 MANPOWER

In September 1939, in marked contrast with the situation in August 1914, the British state began the war with Germany in the belief that the conflict would be a long one and that it could only be won by adopting a policy of 'armament in depth' (Handcock and Gowing 1949: 68,71). This meant mobilising the resources available to the economy as fully and effectively as possible in order to supply troops for the Armed Forces and to arm those troop. Furthermore, when Churchill became Prime Minister in May 1940 his government abandoned financial controls and planning and adopted physical planning as its main means of managing the economy; the former relied on the monetary resources available to the economy and to the state, on determining government programmes on the basis of pounds and pence, whereas the latter relied on the physical resources available to the state, on determining government programmes on the basis of, for example, the amount and type of labour or steel available.

The supply and distribution of labour was one of the chief constraints facing the economy and by late 1942 the Manpower Budget (which allocated the available labour supply to government departments, and particularly to those representing the armed forces and the munitions industries) had emerged as probably the key economic tool used by the War Cabinet to plan the economy (Hancock and Gowing 1949: 438-52). Thus, manpower planning and manpower statistics were at the very heart of the wartime economy. The Manpower Budget was the focal point of many of the disputes between various Ministers as it dictated the manpower balance between the Armed Forces and civil employment and, within civil employment, the balance between the munitions industries and the non-munitions industries, and so reflected the strategic and economic priorities of the state.

The control and allocation of manpower by the state could not be achieved without a range of compulsory powers to

3.1 Expansion of the Armed Forces in the United Kingdom

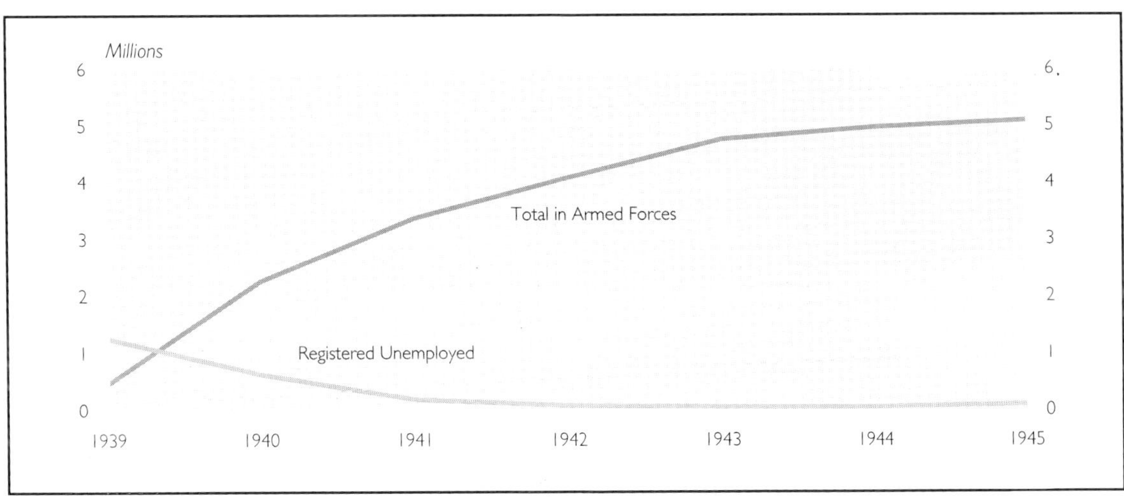

3.2 The relative importance of industries in the United Kingdom

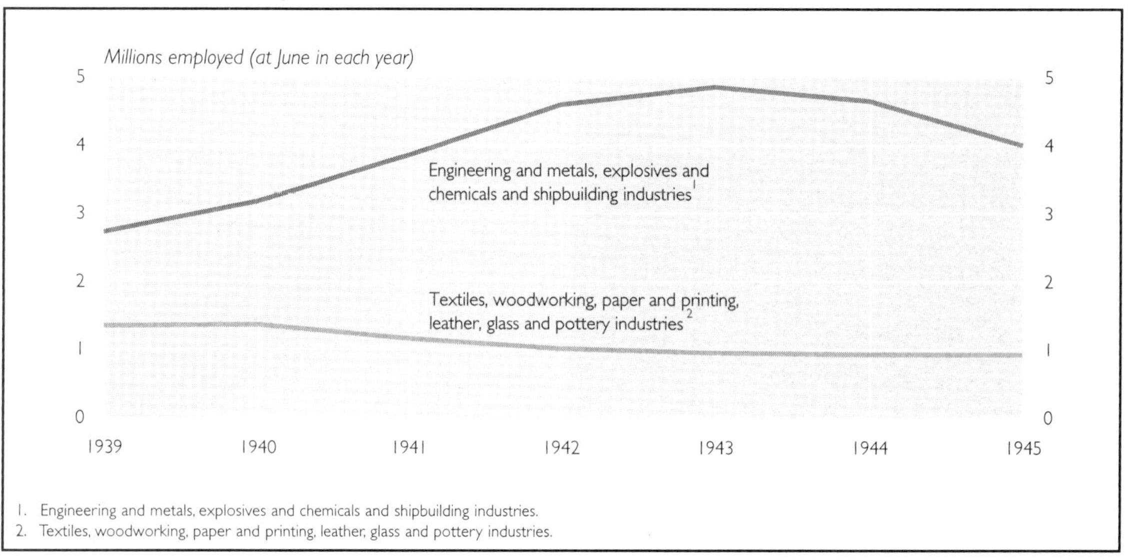

1. Engineering and metals, explosives and chemicals and shipbuilding industries.
2. Textiles, woodworking, paper and printing, leather, glass and pottery industries.

allow it to intervene directly in the labour market. These powers were mainly exercised by the Ministry of Labour and National Service. They included: the wartime National Service Acts of 1939-42 which made males aged 18-50 liable for military service and made women liable to be called up for service in the Women's Auxiliary Services (the female branches of the army, navy and air force and the nursing services) or the Civil Defence services; the Schedule of Reserved Occupations, which ensured that industries vital to the war effort did not lose workers unnecessarily to the Armed Forces; and the Essential Works Orders, which were used to control the supply and movement of labour (Ince 1946: 18-27). Compulsion on its own might have alienated the labour movement and thus to balance this the state also used wage incentives and supported improvements in working conditions and welfare; furthermore, the responsibility of wielding the tools of compulsion were placed in the hands of one of the leading trade unionists of the interwar period, Ernest Bevin, who was appointed by Churchill as the Minister of Labour in 1940. Although these measures did not prevent worker discontent, the labour movement was more co-operative with the state than it had been in the First World War: for example, the average numbers of days lost per year due to strike action between 1939 and 1945 was roughly a third of the average for 1914-1918 (**table 3.30**; Department of Employment and Productivity 1971: 396).

The main strategic priority was to raise a large military force to combat the menace from the Axis powers (Germany, Italy and Japan). The expansion of the military services was rapid: they increased by almost three million between 1939 and 1941 and had reached five million by 1945, accounting for almost a quarter of the working population (**table 3.3**). Of these, more than 90 per cent were men serving in the Armed Forces; and of the Armed Forces the Army was the largest, followed by the Royal Air Force and then the Royal Navy (in June 1945 they accounted for, respectively, 63 per cent, 20 per cent and 17 per cent of the total Armed Forces) (**table 3.4**). The remainder were women serving in the Women's Auxiliary Services (which was created in 1940) who provided many essential support services during the war. As with most wars the fighting was done primarily by young men: in June 1943, for example, a quarter of the Armed Forces were aged 22 or younger and another quarter were aged between 23 and 27; by the end of the war 63 per cent of all UK men aged between 20 and 29 were serving in the Armed Forces (**tables 3.5 and 1.5**).

The expansion of the Armed Forces was fed by two main sources: reduced unemployment (in the 1930s Britain had experienced very high levels of unemployment and at the beginning of 1940 there were still more than one million people unemployed) and the recruitment of workers from civil employment. This recruitment was fuelled mainly by conscription - less than a third of the wartime intake of the Armed Forces were volunteers (**table 3.6**). Despite the large outflow of labour from industry civil employment remained fairly stable during the war because the overall size of the working population actually increased (from 19.5 million in 1938 to a wartime peak of 22.3 million in 1943). This mainly reflected an increase in the female participation rate (new female workers accounted for four out of every five of the new labour market entrants) which meant that the sharp fall in male civil employment was countered by a sharp rise in female civil employment (**table 3.3**).

Within civil employment there was also a marked transformation in the importance of different industries: the strategic priorities of the war called for the expansion of the munitions and related industries (metals, engineering, vehicles, shipbuilding, chemicals, explosives, paints, oils, etc.) at the expense of the non-munitions industries. Thus, the munitions and related industries saw their share of civil employment increase from 16 per cent in 1939 to a wartime peak of 23 per cent in 1943 whilst those industries considered 'less essential' to the war effort (such as textiles, commercial services, leather, wood and paper) saw their share decline from 49 per cent in 1939 to 28 per cent in 1944 (Howlett, 1944: 22-24; **tables 3.12-3.25**) Furthermore, many workers in these 'less essential' industries were engaged in the manufacture of supplies for the Armed Forces: in December 1943, for example, such work occupied 43 per cent of workers in the textile industries, 41 per cent in the hats and caps industries, 53 per cent in the furniture and upholstery industry and 42 per cent in the paper industry (**tables 3.19-3.22**). Finally, the establishment of the war economy also went hand-in-hand with an expansion in the size of the state. New Ministries were established (such as the Ministries of Aircraft Production, Economic Warfare, Food, Shipping, Supply and Works and Buildings) and the number of civil servants more than doubled from 0.6 million in April 1939 to the wartime peak of 1.4 million four years later (**tables 3.26 and 3.27**).

3.3 Distribution of total manpower[1]

Great Britain — At June in each year — *Thousands*

	1938	1939	1940	1941	1942	1943	1944	1945
Total working population	19,473	19,750	20,676	21,332	22,056	22,285	22,008	21,649
Males	14,476	14,656	15,104	15,222	15,141	15,032	14,901	14,881
Females	4,997	5,094	5,572	6,110	6,915	7,253	7,107	6,768
Total in Armed Forces and Auxiliary Services	385	480	2,273	3,383	4,091	4,761	4,967	5,090
Males	385	480	2,218	3,278	3,784	4,300	4,500	4,653
Females	-	-	55	105	307	461	467	437
Registered insured unemployed	1,710	1,270	645	198	87	60	54	103
Males	1,325	1,013	434	100	61	44	40	68
Females	385	257	211	98	26	16	14	35
Ex.members of H.M. Forces not yet in employment	–	–	–	–	–	20	20	40
Males	–	–	–	–	–	13	14	27
Females	–	–	–	–	–	7	6	13
Total in civil employment	17,378	18,000	17,758	17,751	17,878	17,444	16,967	16,416
Males	12,766	13,163	12,452	11,844	11,296	10,675	10,347	10,133
Females	4,612	4,837	5,306	5,907	6,582	6,769	6,620	6,283
Agriculture and fishing	949	950	925	981	1,002	1,047	1,048	1,041
Mining and quarrying	849	873	886	820	823	818	813	799
Metals, engineering, vehicles and ship-building	2,590	2,812	3,198	3,753	4,372	4,659	4,496	3,899
Chemicals, explosives, paints, oils, etc.	276	294	361	487	618	574	515	447
Textiles	861	1,002	1,074	871	723	669	635	634
Clothing, boots and shoes	717	752	748	674	550	493	455	481
Food, drink and tobacco	640	654	621	597	567	519	508	518
Cement, bricks, pottery, glass, etc.	271	265	220	211	188	170	159	159
Leather, wood, paper, etc.	844	859	725	614	573	539	536	555
Other manufactures	164	177	181	190	163	123	129	127
Building and civil engineering	1,264	1,310	1,064	1,043	893	726	623	722
Gas, water and electricity supply	240	242	213	214	214	200	193	196
Transport and shipping	1,225	1,233	1,146	1,194	1,217	1,176	1,237	1,252
Distributive trades	2,882	2,887	2,639	2,332	2,173	2,009	1,927	1,958
Commerce, banking, insurance and finance	414	413	370	358	317	282	268	264
National and Local Government	1,386 (bracketed: both rows)	1,385	1,448	1,636	1,728	1,786	1,809	1,903
Civil Defence, Fire Service and Police		80	345	383	384	323	282	127
Miscellaneous services	1,806	1,812	1,594	1,393	1,373	1,331	1,334	1,334

1. Men aged 14-64, women aged 14-59. Including employers and self-employed as well as employees, but excluding indoor private domestic service. Women in part-time paid employment are included, two being counted as one unit. Figures exclude prisoners-of-war, but include such other foreign workers as entered civilian employment.

Source: Ministry of Labour and National Service

3.4 Strength of the Armed Forces and Women's Auxiliary Services

United Kingdom End of month *Thousands*

		Armed Forces[1]				Women's Auxiliary Services[2]				
		Total	Royal Navy[3]	Army[4]	Royal Air Force	Total	Women's Royal Naval Service	Auxiliary Territorial Service[5]	Women's Auxiliary Air Force	Nursing Services[6]
1939	September	1,270	180	897	193	. .	1.6	. .	. .	2.4
	December	1,557	214	1,128	215	43.1	3.4	23.9	8.8	7.0
1940	March	1,842	241	1,361	240	. .	4.4	. .	8.9	8.2
	June	2,212	271	1,650	291	56.6	5.6	31.5	11.9	7.6
	September	2,615	307	1,888	420	69.3	7.9	36.1	17.4	7.9
	December	2,899	333	2,075	491	75.1	10.0	36.4	20.5	8.2
1941	March	3,090	365	2,166	559	85.8	12.3	37.5	27.0	9.0
	June	3,278	395	2,221	662	105.3	15.1	42.8	37.4	10.0
	September	3,483	424	2,292	767	157.5	18.0	65.0	64.1	10.4
	December	3,602	449	2,340	813	216.0	21.6	85.1	98.4	10.9
1942	March	3,690	477	2,397	816	258.6	24.8	111.1	110.8	11.9
	June	3,784	496	2,453	835	307.5	28.6	140.2	125.7	13.0
	September	3,918	529	2,494	895	351.1	33.5	162.2	141.5	13.9
	December	4,068	566	2,566	936	400.6	39.3	180.7	166.0	14.6
1943	March	4,186	610	2,628	948	435.9	45.0	195.3	180.1	15.5
	June	4,300	660	2,673	967	461.6	53.3	210.3	181.6	16.4
	September	4,371	710	2,679	982	470.7	60.4	212.5	180.3	17.5
	December	4,435	756	2,680	999	467.5	64.8	207.5	176.8	18.4
1944	March	4,448	768	2,680	1,000	468.8	68.6	206.2	175.7	18.3
	June	4,500	778	2,720	1,002	466.4	73.5	199.0	174.4	19.5
	September	4,509	776	2,741	992	463.7	74.0	198.2	171.2	20.3
	December	4,525	780	2,760	985	457.1	73.4	196.4	166.2	21.1
1945	March	4,553	781	2,802	970	449.7	73.2	195.3	159.7	21.5
	June	4,653	783	2,920	950	437.2	72.0	190.8	153.0	21.4

Source: Service Departments

1. Excluding men locally enlisted abroad.
2. Including women locally enlisted abroad.
3. Including men serving with the Royal Navy on T.124 agreements, Royal Marine Police and, up to June 1941, prisoners-of-war and missing.
4. Including men serving with the India Unattached List, but excluding the British Indian Service. Men locally enlisted abroad are included up to September 1941.
5. Excluding those locally enlisted abroad on modified forms of Auxiliary Territorial Service engagements whose documents were maintained outside the United Kingdom. From June 1944 all women locally enlisted abroad whose documents were maintained outside the United Kingdom are excluded.
6. Including Queen's Army Schoolmistresses.

3.5 Age distribution of the Armed Forces and Women's Auxiliary Services

Thousands

<table>
<tr><th></th><th colspan="5">Armed Forces[1]</th><th colspan="5">Women's Auxiliary Services[1]</th></tr>
<tr><th></th><th>1941 December</th><th>1942 June</th><th>1943 June</th><th>1944 June</th><th>1945 June</th><th>1941 December</th><th>1942 June</th><th>1943 June</th><th>1944 June</th><th>1945 June</th></tr>
<tr><td>Age:</td><td></td><td></td><td></td><td></td><td></td><td></td><td></td><td></td><td></td><td></td></tr>
<tr><td>18 and under</td><td>63.3</td><td>66.0</td><td>149.1</td><td>78.5</td><td>76.2</td><td>29.4</td><td>18.1</td><td>17.3</td><td>9.5</td><td>7.4</td></tr>
<tr><td>19</td><td>155.0</td><td>143.5</td><td>184.7</td><td>195.3</td><td>186.3</td><td>23.4</td><td>34.4</td><td>40.2</td><td>25.6</td><td>22.7</td></tr>
<tr><td>20</td><td>253.5</td><td>213.2</td><td>222.1</td><td>226.3</td><td>215.4</td><td>25.7</td><td>36.4</td><td>60.3</td><td>39.6</td><td>30.3</td></tr>
<tr><td>21</td><td>311.1</td><td>272.6</td><td>241.0</td><td>239.5</td><td>228.5</td><td>31.6</td><td>46.4</td><td>62.5</td><td>64.2</td><td>36.8</td></tr>
<tr><td>22</td><td>252.8</td><td>300.8</td><td>281.1</td><td>254.6</td><td>236.6</td><td>18.2</td><td>41.2</td><td>66.5</td><td>61.8</td><td>57.5</td></tr>
<tr><td>23</td><td>210.9</td><td>236.3</td><td>297.9</td><td>277.9</td><td>248.2</td><td>11.5</td><td>21.8</td><td>56.3</td><td>61.0</td><td>54.1</td></tr>
<tr><td>24</td><td>190.7</td><td>208.0</td><td>231.3</td><td>306.3</td><td>272.8</td><td>8.7</td><td>14.5</td><td>29.3</td><td>51.6</td><td>52.4</td></tr>
<tr><td>25</td><td>211.9</td><td>183.9</td><td>203.2</td><td>235.2</td><td>304.5</td><td>8.5</td><td>11.6</td><td>20.6</td><td>27.9</td><td>43.7</td></tr>
<tr><td>26</td><td>201.3</td><td>203.9</td><td>183.1</td><td>197.6</td><td>237.5</td><td>6.8</td><td>10.9</td><td>13.8</td><td>19.7</td><td>23.6</td></tr>
<tr><td>27</td><td>191.3</td><td>196.1</td><td>212.9</td><td>184.2</td><td>201.3</td><td>6.1</td><td>8.6</td><td>12.6</td><td>12.7</td><td>15.9</td></tr>
<tr><td>28</td><td>179.5</td><td>189.4</td><td>205.2</td><td>212.4</td><td>180.3</td><td>4.6</td><td>7.7</td><td>10.4</td><td>11.9</td><td>10.3</td></tr>
<tr><td>29</td><td>176.0</td><td>177.8</td><td>196.6</td><td>205.5</td><td>209.7</td><td>3.9</td><td>6.2</td><td>8.8</td><td>9.3</td><td>10.0</td></tr>
<tr><td>30</td><td>161.7</td><td>176.6</td><td>185.5</td><td>197.7</td><td>202.5</td><td>3.3</td><td>5.6</td><td>7.0</td><td>8.2</td><td>7.9</td></tr>
<tr><td>31</td><td>145.8</td><td>158.8</td><td>184.5</td><td>187.5</td><td>194.5</td><td>2.9</td><td>4.4</td><td>6.0</td><td>6.9</td><td>7.0</td></tr>
<tr><td>32</td><td>119.8</td><td>146.6</td><td>168.3</td><td>184.1</td><td>184.5</td><td>2.5</td><td>3.9</td><td>4.9</td><td>5.9</td><td>5.8</td></tr>
<tr><td>33</td><td>113.9</td><td>121.6</td><td>159.9</td><td>171.4</td><td>182.1</td><td>2.2</td><td>3.2</td><td>4.2</td><td>4.7</td><td>5.3</td></tr>
<tr><td>34</td><td>104.6</td><td>114.9</td><td>136.9</td><td>161.6</td><td>170.1</td><td>1.9</td><td>2.6</td><td>3.5</td><td>3.9</td><td>4.0</td></tr>
<tr><td>35</td><td>99.3</td><td>108.9</td><td>127 8</td><td>138.6</td><td>160.8</td><td>1.9</td><td>2.4</td><td>3.1</td><td>3.1</td><td>3.2</td></tr>
<tr><td>36</td><td>74.7</td><td>102.7</td><td>120.0</td><td>130.0</td><td>136.4</td><td>1.6</td><td>2.2</td><td>2.6</td><td>2.8</td><td>2.6</td></tr>
<tr><td>37</td><td>62.1</td><td>78.7</td><td>112.2</td><td>122.7</td><td>127.1</td><td>1.5</td><td>1.9</td><td>2.3</td><td>2.4</td><td>2.3</td></tr>
<tr><td>38</td><td>49.4</td><td>65.3</td><td>88.7</td><td>114.5</td><td>119.4</td><td>1.3</td><td>1.8</td><td>2.1</td><td>2.1</td><td>2.0</td></tr>
<tr><td>39</td><td>44.0</td><td>54.3</td><td>74.4</td><td>90.6</td><td>112.5</td><td>1.1</td><td>1.5</td><td>1.9</td><td>1.7</td><td>1.7</td></tr>
<tr><td>40</td><td>40.6</td><td>50.2</td><td>62.2</td><td>76.1</td><td>87.9</td><td>1.0</td><td>1.3</td><td>1.6</td><td>1.6</td><td>1.4</td></tr>
<tr><td>41</td><td>29.5</td><td>44.2</td><td>57.5</td><td>61.6</td><td>72.8</td><td>1.1</td><td>1.2</td><td>1.3</td><td>1.4</td><td>1.3</td></tr>
<tr><td>42</td><td>20.1</td><td rowspan="5">159.2</td><td>50.2</td><td>57.8</td><td>58.5</td><td>1.1</td><td rowspan="5">4.7</td><td>1.1</td><td>1.2</td><td>1.1</td></tr>
<tr><td>43</td><td>16.4</td><td rowspan="4">157.0</td><td>50.3</td><td>74.8</td><td>0.8</td><td rowspan="4">5.0</td><td>1.0</td><td>1.0</td></tr>
<tr><td>44</td><td>14.1</td><td>33.5</td><td>48.0</td><td>0.6</td><td>1.1</td><td>0.8</td></tr>
<tr><td>45</td><td>13.6</td><td rowspan="2">123.7</td><td>33.5</td><td>0.4</td><td rowspan="2">3.4</td><td>0.8</td></tr>
<tr><td>46 and over</td><td>82.0</td><td>91.6</td><td>1.0</td><td>2.3</td></tr>
<tr><td>All ages</td><td>3,589.0</td><td>3,773.7</td><td>4,293.3</td><td>4,515.1</td><td>4,654.4</td><td>204.7</td><td>294.4</td><td>445.2</td><td>446.2</td><td>415.2</td></tr>
</table>

1. The differences between the total figures given in this table and in Table 3.3 are explained as follows. The figures for the Royal Navy in this table exclude Royal Marine Police, merchant seamen on T.124 agreements, and prisoners-of-war; those for the Army include personnel locally enlisted abroad; and those for the Women's Auxiliary Services exclude the Nursing Services.

Source: Service Departments

3.6 Intake and outflow of the Armed Forces and Women's Auxiliary Services[1]

Thousands

	Armed Forces[2]							Women's Auxiliary Services				
	Intake			Outflow				Intake		Outflow		
	Called up under National Service Acts	Volunteers[3]	Direct officer intake	Casualties and other deaths	Medical discharges	Transfers to and from reserve, releases, etc. (net)[4]	Net change in strength	Volunteers	Called up under National Service Acts	Medical discharges	Transfers to and from reserve, releases, etc. (net)[4]	Net change in strength
1939 Sept. 3 to Dec. 31	122.2	193.5	17.3	3.2	6.8	+60.8	+869.1[5]	..	-	..	..	..
1940	1,044.6	461.0	38.6	68.9	69.1	+67.7	+1,338.4	..	-	..	..	..
1941	632.7	272.3	28.0	55.4	104.8	-68.8	+704.3	155.49	-	1.67	-15.56	+138.27
1942	547.2	194.9	14.2	126.7	96.8	-64.1	+468.6	146.61	67.15	6.09	-26.81	+180.90
1943	347.4	186.9	10.3	68.3	77.4	-34.9	+364.4	58.65	50.35	8.28	-37.58	+63.14
1944	254.5	83.5	7.4	98.5	93.3	-62.3	+91.6	40.38	7.48	8.58	-52.43	-13.16
1945	231.3	66.6	4.1	+121.2[6]	141.5	-1,253.2	-971.9	29.27	0.01	8.75	-176.30	-155.76
1939 Sept. 3 to Dec. 31	122.2	193.5	17.3	3.2	6.8	+60.8	+869.1[5]	..	-	..	..	..
1940 1st Qtr.	304.3		9.0	2.2	14.2	-10.0	+286.9	..	-	..	..	..
2nd Qtr.	414.8		11.6	17.5	18.0	-21.5	+369.4	..	-	..	..	..
3rd Qtr.	452.0		9.7	37.8	15.9	-8.3	+399.7	..	-	..	..	..
4th Qtr.	334.3		8.3	11.4	20.9	-27.9	+282.4	..	-	..	..	..
1941 1st Qtr.	242.5		8.3	7.1	25.4	-27.3	+191.0	14.39	-	0.34	-4.04	+10.01
2nd Qtr.	236.5		6.1	18.5	30.8	-6.6	+186.7	23.21	-	0.28	-4.55	+18.37
3rd Qtr.	259.5		6.4	17.9	26.8	-14.7	+206.6	55.11	-	0.38	-2.90	+51.83
4th Qtr.	166.7		7.1	11.8	21.9	-20.1	+119.9	62.79	-	0.67	-4.06	+58.06
1942 1st Qtr.	182.8		3.3	56.2	20.9	-20.3	+88.7	45.12	3.51	0.95	-6.15	+41.56
2nd Qtr.	163.6		3.4	14.3	24.8	-28.4	+99.3	37.04	18.38	1.37	-6.32	+47.76
3rd Qtr.	207.1		3.7	40.4	27.4	-11.0	+132.2	33.17	18.91	1.90	-7.51	+42.67
4th Qtr.	188.4		3.8	15.7	23.7	-4.6	+148.3	31.28	26.35	1.89	-6.83	+48.91
1943 1st Qtr.	108.3	47.3	2.8	16.2	19.4	-5.0	+118.3	25.35	18.39	1.80	-7.60	+34.33
2nd Qtr.	101.0	48.5	2.7	19.6	17.1	-5.7	+110.3	15.42	19.99	1.92	-8.55	+24.94
3rd Qtr.	66.6	49.3	2.8	17.5	19.9	-7.3	+74.0	11.24	8.80	2.28	-9.83	+7.92
4th Qtr.	71.4	41.5	2.1	14.7	21.1	-17.1	+62.1	6.67	3.16	2.28	-11.60	-4.04
1944 1st Qtr.	50.5	25.0	1.9	20.6	24.1	-18.1	+14.4	9.84	6.90	2.21	-13.16	+1.36
2nd Qtr.	78.3	26.1	2.2	19.9	26.5	-6.6	+53.7	13.86	0.49	2.44	-15.46	-3.53
3rd Qtr.	72.8	19.4	1.9	33.9	24.7	-28.2	+7.7	9.75	0.08	2.30	-11.09	-3.58
4th Qtr.	52.9	13.6	1.2	24.1	18.5	-9.5	+15.7	6.95	0.03	1.64	-12.73	-7.42
1945 1st Qtr.	62.5	14.1	1.3	13.0	27.6	-10.8	+26.6	7.95	0.01	2.08	-13.73	-7.85
2nd Qtr.	57.6	14.1	0.7	+103.1[6]	33.8	-38.8	+ 103.0	9.71	-	2.69	-19.43	-12.40

Source: Service Departments

1. Excluding men and women locally enlisted abroad. Figures for the Army and A.T.S., however, include those whose documents are maintained in the United Kingdom.
2. Excluding men serving with the Royal Navy on T.124 agreements (and variants), but including Royal Marine Police.
3. From January 1945 including intake into the Royal Navy from Deferred List.
4. From June 1945 including Class A and B releases.
5. Including about 485,400 mobilized and embodied at the outbreak of war.
6. The number of prisoners repatriated exceeded casualties.

3.7 Releases from the Armed Forces, Women's Auxiliary Services and Nursing Services[1]

Number

	Armed Forces					Women's Auxiliary Services					Nursing Services		
	Total	Class A releases	Class B releases	Class C releases	Other releases and dis-charges	Total	Class A releases	Class B releases	Class C releases	Other releases and dis-charges	Total	Class A releases	Other releases and dis-charges
1945 June 18-30	32,120	22,108	-	21	9,991	11,694	9,110	-	36	2,548	457	403	54
July	76,884	59,919	2,051	174	14,740	32,330	28,771	5	239	3,315	1,079	931	148
August	111,437	88,629	6,492	489	15,827	30,232	25,292	9	424	4,507	824	737	87
September	131,543	102,856	9,815	3,307	15,565	22,293	19,000	39	918	2,336	992	881	111
October	266,595	200,700	20,598	4,706	40,591	24,006	19,023	182	1,032	3,769	952	796	156
November	377,371	317,764	29,046	6,762	23,799	24,535	20,824	716	1,150	1,845	1,020	911	109
December	346,157	294,883	24,653	5,805	20,816	21,144	17,916	920	733	1,575	925	794	131
1946 January	422,135	381,100	25,843	3,677	11,515	30,869	28,635	583	761	890	931	844	87
February	329,665	288,202	26,921	2,520	12,022	31,886	30,328	192	523	843	985	875	110
March	335,547	289,408	34,933	2,219	8,987	32,618	30,759	270	492	1,097	1,173	1,078	95
April	255,509	210,271	32,243	1,396	11,599	21,734	20,441	445	389	459	938	876	62
May	254,712	224,589	20,586	1,271	8,266	23,378	22,155	180	358	685	931	852	79
June	218,559	201,780	10,207	732	5,840	21,128	20,325	90	276	437	1,036	967	69
July	174,259	156,711	11,029	600	5,919	14,960	14,281	87	265	327	747	664	83
August	132,827	120,942	6,516	351	5,018	10,568	9,802	82	193	491	650	573	77
September	145,235	135,779	5,009	239	4,208	10,678	9,837	96	238	507	549	466	83
October	108,573	98,827	3,579	281	5,886	9,333	8,007	67	194	1,065	856	776	80
November	88,454	82,344	1,597	283	4,230	7,603	6,924	32	179	468	818	757	61
December	79,740	75,195	883	309	3,353	6,011	5,599	31	142	239	670	633	37
1947 January	41,951	36,250	764	545	4,392	4,039	3,336	14	142	547	423	345	78
February	33,545	29,372	386	662	3,125	3,246	2,731	12	159	344	257	211	46
March	47,483	43,495	361	626	3,001	3,649	3,226	10	166	247	389	311	78
April	51,938	46,473	1,400	300	3,765	3,786	3,192	12	152	430	374	339	35
May	63,657	56,721	2,146	251	4,539	3,793	3,228	10	123	432	299	267	32
June	57,779	51,787	1,730	302	3,960	3,472	3,009	16	73	374	231	197	34
July	55,316	48,808	1,545	358	4,605	4,259	3,637	10	105	507	272	219	53
August	37,870	32,828	1,144	211	3,687	4,465	4,005	7	122	331	183	153	30
September	39,415	33,404	1,593	225	4,193	3,884	3,347	14	114	409	142	112	30
October	52,295	46,930	848	265	4,252	3,750	3,258	11	99	382	224	207	17
November	53,163	48,622	647	163	3,731	2,824	2,485	7	74	258	161	140	21
December	57,236	53,261	425	120	3,430	2,476	2,272	2	25	177	163	140	28

1. Excluding releases for a temporary period, but including those released locally abroad or repatriated from the United Kingdom.

Source: Service Departments

3.8 Casualties suffered during the war by the Armed Forces, Auxiliary Services and Merchant Navy[1]

Number

	Total					War against Germany				War against Japan			
	Total	Killed	Missing[2]	Wounded	Prisoners-of-war	Killed	Missing	Wounded	Prisoners-of-war	Killed	Missing	Wounded	Prisoners-of-war
Armed Forces[3]													
Total	755,439	264,443	41,327	277,077	172,592	234,475	35,075	260,548	135,009	29,968	6,252	16,529	37,583
Royal Navy	73,642	50,758	820	14,663	7,401	46,911	416	14,360	5,518	3,847	404	303	1,883
Army	569,501	144,079	33,771	239,575	152,076	121,484	29,255	224,427	119,764	22,595	4,516	15,148	32,312
Royal Air Force	112,296	69,606	6,736	22,839	13,115	66,080	5,404	21,761	9,727	3,526	1,332	1,078	3,388
Women's Auxiliary Services													
Total	1,486	624	98	744	20	..	..	..	..	..	..	..	..
Women's Royal Naval Service	124	102	-	22	-	..	..	..	..	..	..	..	..
Auxiliary Territorial Service[4]	751	335	94	302	20	..	..	..	..	..	..	..	..
Women's Auxiliary Air Force	611	187	4	420	-	..	..	..	..	..	..	..	..
Merchant Navy	45,329	30,248	4,654	4,707	5,720	28,748	30	4,467	4,675	1,500	4,624	240	1,045

1. From 3 September 1939 to 14 August 1945 as reported to 28 February 1946.
2. Including 6,244 still missing at 28 February 1946 and 39,835 who rejoined their units.
3. Including men from overseas serving in the United Kingdom forces, in particular from Newfoundland and Southern Rhodesia.
4. Including Army Nursing Services.

Source: Service Departments

3.9 Strength of the Home Guard and Royal Observer Corps

Thousands

	Home Guard		Royal Observer Corps				
				Full-time[1]		Part-time[1]	
	Men	Women	Total	Men	Women	Men	Women
1940 June	1,456	-	27.9	2.3	-	25.6	-
1941 June	1,603	-	33.2	4.0	-	29.3	-
December	1,530	-	34.8	4.4	-	30.0	0.4
1942 June	1,565	-	34.0	5.1	0.2	28.0	0.8
December	1,741	-	32.4	5.5	0.4	25.6	0.9
1943 March	1,793	-	32.8	5.7	0.7	25.2	1.1
June	1,784	4	32.9	5.9	1.0	24.8	1.2
September	1,769	16	32.9	6.2	1.4	24.1	1.3
December	1,754	22	33.0	6.4	2.1	23.2	1.3
1944 March	1,739	28	32.8	6.5	2.5	22.4	1.4
June	1,727	31	32.7	6.4	2.6	22.1	1.5
September	1,698	32	32.5	6.4	2.8	21.9	1.5
December	1,685	-	32.2	6.4	2.9	21.4	1.4
1945 March	-	-	32.1	6.5	3.0	21.2	1.4
June	-	-	8.7	5.7	2.1	0.9	-

1. Figures before 1942 are estimated.

Source: War Office and Air Ministry

3.10 Numbers employed in the Civil Defence services

Great Britain *Thousands*

	Whole-time						Part-time					
	A.R.P. Services[1]		National Fire Services[2]		Casualty Services[3]		A.R.P. Services[1]		National Fire Service[2]		Casualty Services[3]	
	Males	Females	Males	Females	Males	Females	Males	Females	Male	Females	Males	Females
1940 March	117.5	15.9	72.9	5.4	17.0	31.6	..	..	153.9	7.6	41.9	125.0
June	108.7	14.9	72.2	4.7	14.9	33.0	719.4	136.9	161.6	8.9	46.7	134.2
September	112.0	14.9	82.1	4.2	15.2	35.0	774.0	153.0	168.0	9.0	51.2	137.0
December	112.3	15.2	88.0	5.4	15.1	35.4	774.7	149.9	163.4	8.9	49.8	129.1
1941 March	112.0	15.8	92.5	4.5	14.9	35.3	778.4	152.2	168.1	9.8	48.0	122.8
June	110.1	16.8	96.8	5.4	14.5	36.0	759.2	148.3	159.4	10.0	47.2	122.2
September	109.0	17.5	..	..	13.6	37.2	734.7	140.6	..	..	45.6	117.7
December	107.1	19.1	106.8	19.7	13.4	37.9	668.0[4]	127.2[4]	136.5	8.2	42.9	107.6
1942 March	99.7	19.4	108.6	26.0	11.8	36.1	710.8	127.2	122.1	9.6	39.8	97.1
June	88.7	17.6	107.7	28.5	9.3	30.7	739.6	137.3	129.9	11.1	39.7	95.2
September	78.9	14.9	101.8	30.4	8.2	26.2	746.2	148.1	141.1	18.6	41.2	101.9
December	74.4	13.5	98.0	31.9	7.5	24.8	777.4	165.5	176.6	33.1	44.5	114.2
1943 March	69.6	12.4	95.5	32.2	7.2	23.2	782.5	165.3	200.3	42.6	48.2	120.3
June	66.5	11.7	93.8	30.7	7.1	21.8	773.4	167.1	214.8	47.0	47.5	116.6
September	62.2	11.0	92.6	29.4	6.9	20.3	797.9	175.7	224.5	51.1	49.0	117.7
December	59.6	10.4	90.6	27.3	6.7	19.3	799.3	177.4	233.2	53.8	49.0	116.2
1944 March	57.7	10.2	88.6	25.7	6.6	18.7	802.5	178.4	234.9	53.6	49.4	115.0
June	56.9	10.0	86.6	24.1	7.1	17.8	799.4	179.8	231.9	54.6	49.8	114.2
September	54.3	9.5	84.4	22.2	6.5	17.8	791.7	177.4	228.5	53.0	48.9	112.6
December	28.5	5.0	71.7	20.0	4.1	9.6	651.8	150 8	160.4	46.3	37.8	81.9
1945 March	24.8	4.4	57.9	15.1	3.4	7.7	622.7	142.3	136.6	35.7	29.3	63.0
June	..	..	46.2	10.6	..	..	..	..	102.9	5.2	..	..
September	..	..	36.5	5.5	..	..	..	..	47.6	9.8	..	..

1. Civil Defence (General) Services: wardens, rescue and first-aid parties, report and control centres, messengers
2. Until September 1941 regular Fire Brigades and Auxiliary Fire Service. Including Works Brigades.
3. Emergency ambulance service and first-aid post service.
4. Excluding non-effectives previously included. They numbered 37.3 thousand males and 11.9 thousand females in December 1941.

Source: Home Office

3.11 Numbers employed in the Police services

Great Britain *Thousands*

	Whole-time				Part-time	
	Regular		Auxiliary[1]		Auxiliary[2]	
	Males	Females	Males	Females	Males	Females
1939 September	68.4	0.3	36.1[3]	0.1	180.2	. .
December	65.4	0.3	34.4	0.1	. .	. .
1940 March	64.6	0.3	33.8	0.1	. .	0.5
June	64.4	0.3	31.9	0.2	159.3	0.6
September	64.0	0.3	35.6	0.2	160.5	0.7
December	64.1	0.3	36.3	0.3	159.0	0.8
1941 March	64.5	0.3	37.5	0.3	158.1	0.7
June	64.4	0.4	38.2	0.3	156.2	0.7
September	62.8	0.4	39.5	0.8	160.4	0.9
December	62.0	0.4	39.1	2.2	145.5	1.2
1942 March	61.3	0.4	38.5	2.7	145.1	1.2
June	60.4	0.4	36.8	3.6	145.3	1.6
September	56.1	0.4	36.4	4.5	147.0	1.8
December	54.6	0.4	36.0	4.8	147.7	1.9
1943 March	53.8	0.4	35.1	5.0	146.0	1.9
June	51.6	0.4	34.1	5.0	145.0	1.9
September	50.0	0.4	33.1	4.9	143.3	1.9
December	48.8	0.4	28.1	4.8	142.3	1.9
1944 March	49.6	0.4	26.8	4.7	141.1	2.0
June	48.9	0.4	25.3	4.6	138.9	1.9
September	48.3	0.4	23.5	4.5	137.2	1.8
December	47.9	0.4	21.1	4.3	132.1	1.8
1945 March	47.4	0.4	19.8	4.2	122.3	1.7
June	46.8	0.4	18.6	4.0	103.6	1.3
September	49.6	0.5	16.8	3.7	52.7	0.6

1. Police War Reserve, First Police Reserve, special constables, and Women's Auxiliary Police Corps, but excluding civilian employees. From September 1941 the Police Auxiliary Messenger Service is included.
2. Special constables and Women's Auxiliary Police Corps, but excluding civilian employees. From September 1941 the Police Auxiliary Messenger Service is included. From September 1939 to September 1941 the figures relate to persons enrolled for employment.
3. This figure does not include whole-time special constables.

Source: Home Office and Scottish Home Department

3.12 Numbers employed in agriculture

Great Britain | *Thousands*

	All workers[1]			Regular workers[2]		Casual workers		Women's Land Army[3]
	Total	Males	Females	Males	Females	Males	Females	
1939 June	711	618	93	546	55	72	39	. .
1940 June	712	602	110	530	58	72	52	8.8
December	669	591	79	514	46	76	32	8.8
1941 June	759	619	141	531	71	88	69	15.9
December	729	598	131	504	72	94	59	23.5
1942 June	824	627	197	530	110	97	87	44.4
December	789	614	175	516	104	98	71	59.0
1943 June	843	621	223	517	128	104	95	77.7
December	805	619	186	514	121	105	66	80.3
1944 June	863	647	216	522	95	100	73	78.0
December	835	652	182	514	83	91	54	71.6
1945 June	887	683	204	521	90	104	71	65.3

1. Workers on holdings of more than one acre. Excluding the occupier, his wife and domestic servants, but including relatives of the occupier (or of his wife) who work on the holding, members of the Women's Land Army, members of H.M. Forces, prisoners of war, etc., but not school children.
2. Including before June 1944, in the case of England and Wales, and December 1945 in the case of Scotland, prisoners of war and members of the Women's Land Army employed as regular workers but not then returned separately. For subsequent dates they are included only in the figures for all workers.
3. The figures include all those in full-time employment in agricultural, horticultural and timber work.

Source: Agricultural Departments

3.13 Numbers employed in engineering and metals[1], explosives and chemicals and shipbuilding industries[2]

Great Britain

Thousands

		Total numbers employed			Numbers employed on					
					Manufacture of equipment and supplies for the Forces					
		Total	Males	Females	Total	Orders for Admiralty	Orders for Ministry of Supply	Orders for Ministry of Aircraft Production	Orders for export	Orders for home market
1939	June	2,742.0	2,254.0	488.0	..	..	..	..	..	..
1940	June	3,170.1	2,523.6	646.5	2,099.8	..	..	..	259.2	811.1
	September	3,339.8	2,616.2	723.6	2,371.5	..	..	..	225.9	742.4
	December	3,461.4	2,699.1	762.3	2,554.8	619.7	937.3	997.8	199.0	707.6
1941	March	3,651.6	2,744.7	906.9	2,734.2	619.9	1,021.7	1,092.6	191.8	725.6
	June	3,852.7	2,789.4	1,063.3	2,979.2	642.4	1,168.9	1,167.9	166.9	706.6
	September	4,003.3	2,832.7	1,170.6	3,154.1	656.8	1,284.5	1,212.8	156.6	692.6
	December	4,260.7	2,900.8	1,359.9	3,397.0	676.4	1,133.9	1,286.7	136.7	727.0
1942	March	4,438.5	2,930.4	1,508.1	3,590.0	685.8	1,540.0	1,364.2	125.2	723.3
	June	4,589.5	2,949.2	1,640.3	3,772.1	704.7	1,629.2	1,438.2	110.3	707.1
	September	4,712.5	2,991.9	1,720.6	3,893.1	728.9	1,658.7	1,505.5	98.6	720.8
	December	4,809.9	3,006.4	1,803.5	3,982.9	741.9	1,686.0	1,555.0	92.1	734.9
1943	March	4,839.8	3,004.6	1,835.2	4,020.0	766.0	1,670.3	1,583.7	84.6	735.2
	June	4,847.8	2,992.2	1,855.6	4,019.6	786.8	1,627.7	1,605.1	85.5	742.7
	September	4,820.4	2,975.9	1,844.5	3,997.5	805.3	1,536.9	1,655.3	86.5	736.4
	December	4,799.1	2,959.9	1,839.2	3,977.6	806.5	1,459.5	1,711.6	86.8	734.7
1944	March	4,736.0	2,928.5	1,807.5	3,915.4	806.1	1,422.2	1,687.1	88.4	732.2
	June	4,642.6	2,877.7	1,764.9	3,810.4	793.2	1,377.6	1,639.6	87.6	744.6
	September	4,536.1	2,832.3	1,703.8	3,709.6	780.3	1,338.7	1,590.6	91.6	734.9
	December	4,362.4	2,761.2	1,601.2	3,503.6	756.1	1,277.0	1,470.5	104.8	754.0
1945	March	4,208.0	2,694.2	1,513.8	3,301.4	720.1	1,250.5	1,330.8	122.0	784.6
	June	3,998.6	2,601.4	1,397.2	2,953.8	667.7	1,156.1	1,130.0	154.9	889.9

1. Excluding iron and steel manufacture and the tinplate, tube and wire industries.
2. Males under 65 and females under 60, but excluding non-manual workers earning over £420 per annum. Part-time female workers are included, two being counted as one unit.

Source: Ministry of Labour and National Service

3.14 Numbers employed in the explosives, chemicals, paints, oils, etc., industries[1]

Great Britain

Thousands

	Total numbers employed			Numbers employed on					
				Manufacture of equipment and supplies for the Forces					
	Total	Males	Females	Total	Orders for Admiralty	Orders for Ministry of Supply	Orders for Ministry of Aircraft Production	Orders for export	Orders for home market
1939 June	284.4	210.5	73.9	. .	. .	. .	. .	. .	. .
1940 June	339.9	236.9	103.0	156.6	. .	. .	. .	43.5	139.8
September	362.4	240.7	121.7	175.7	. .	. .	. .	37.8	148.9
December	394.9	257.2	137.7	224.8	26.8	173.2	24.8	34.7	135.4
1941 March	432.4	268.4	164.0	254.2	31.6	196.9	25.7	40.2	138.0
June	477.7	269.8	207.9	312.9	25.0	256.2	31.7	30.6	134.2
September	516.9	275.7	241.2	365.0	28.2	315.6	21.2	29.7	122.2
December	559.5	282.6	276.9	401.0	31.3	342.4	27.3	27.3	131.2
1942 March	598.3	287.5	310.8	436.5	35.1	372.9	28.5	25.7	136.1
June	610.2	288.8	321.4	453.7	33.2	394.9	25.6	23.5	133.0
September	605.4	286.1	319.3	449.2	37.1	381.6	30.5	21.5	134.7
December	600.5	283.8	316.7	436.5	37.0	371.1	28.4	20.4	143.6
1943 March	586.1	281.6	304.5	420.9	38.2	351.6	31.1	17.5	147.7
June	565.3	272.9	292.4	398.8	38.8	328.7	31.3	19.2	147.3
September	548.1	267.5	280.6	383.1	39.6	312.6	30.9	19.2	145.8
December	529.7	260.6	269.1	366.4	40.2	292.8	33.4	19.3	144.0
1944 March	515.2	256.6	258.6	351.8	39.0	278.4	34.4	19.0	144.4
June	506.3	256.3	250.0	344.4	39.5	269.0	35.9	19.7	142.2
September	493.0	253.7	239.3	333.5	39.3	260.2	34.0	19.0	140.5
December	465.6	246.0	219.6	307.1	38.2	238.7	30.2	20.1	138.4
1945 March	457.2	248.1	209.1	298.0	36.7	233.5	27.8	21.9	137.3
June	438.1	240.4	197.7	264.0	34.1	207.1	22.8	26.0	148.1

1. See footnote 2 to Table 3.13.

Source: Ministry of Labour and National Service

3.15 Numbers employed in shipbuilding and ship repairing[1]

Great Britain *Thousands*

	Total	Naval vessels				Merchant vessels		
				Private yards				
	Total	Total	H.M. dockyards	New work	Repairs and conversions	Total	New work	Repairs and conversions
1939 June	144.7	. .	. .	. .	. .	. .	. .	. .
1940 June	203.1	130.3	26.4	62.4	41.5	72.8	28.8	44.0
September	208.6	131.3	28.6	65.8	36.9	77.3	28.1	49.2
December	215.5	135.2	29.5	68.5	37.2	80.3	30.6	49.7
1941 March	221.7	139.8	30.0	67.1	42.7	81.9	31.6	50.3
June	232.4	141.9	30.1	73.0	38.8	90.5	36.0	54.5
September	234.9	141.9	30.1	74.3	37.5	93.0	36.6	56.4
December	239.5	146.3	33.5	75.1	37.7	93.2	35.9	57.3
1942 March	244.3	148.6	34.9	75.3	38.4	95.7	37.2	58.5
June	249.3	153.6	35.4	78.2	40.0	95.7	38.2	57.5
September	257.7	158.7	36.2	89.3	41.1	99.0	42.9	58.5
December	272.3	168.5	36.1	88.0	40.6	102.2	42.2	59.1
1943 March	244.3	148.6	36.3	83.0	44.0	101.8	37.2	59.0
June	249.3	153.6	36.7	87.5	43.3	104.8	38.2	62.8
September	272.5	170.1	36.7	89.3	44.1	102.4	42.9	59.5
December	272.3	168.5	37.8	88.0	42.7	103.8	42.2	61.6
1944 March	244.3	148.6	37.5	87.7	44.5	102.0	40.7	61.3
June	249.3	153.6	37.4	88.3	38.9	106.5	41.3	65.2
September	272.5	170.1	37.4	86.2	45.2	96.7	41.0	55.7
December	272.3	168.5	37.1	82.7	47.7	93.1	40.0	53.1
1945 March	258.7	161.4	36.7	77.0	47.7	97.3	41.6	55.7
June	252.3	148.4	35.7	73.9	38.8	103.9	42.5	61.4

1. See footnote 2 to Table 3.13.

Source: Admiralty and Ministry of Labour and National Service

3.16 Numbers employed in engineering and allied industries[1]

Great Britain | *Thousands*

		Total numbers employed			Numbers employed on					
					Manufacture of equipment and supplies for the Forces					
		Total	Males	Females	Total	Orders for Admiralty	Orders for Ministry of Supply	Orders for Ministry of Aircraft Production	Orders for export	Orders for home market
1939	June	2,312.9	1,901.7	411.2	..	..	..	..	..	..
1940	June	2,627.1	2,087.4	539.7	1,812.9	..	..	..	215.7	598.5
	September	2,768.8	2,171.6	597.2	2,064.5	..	..	..	188.1	516.2
	December	2,851.0	2,232.4	618.6	2,194.8	457.7	764.1	973.0	164.3	491.9
1941	March	2,997.5	2,260.8	736.7	2,340.2	448.5	824.8	1,066.9	151.6	505.7
	June	3,142.6	2,294.0	848.6	2,524.4	475.5	912.7	1,136.2	136.3	481.9
	September	3,251.5	2,330.0	921.5	2,647.2	486.7	968.9	1,191.6	126.9	477.4
	December	3,461.7	2,388.6	1,073.1	2,849.7	498.8	1,091.5	1,259.4	109.4	502.6
1942	March	3,595.9	2,410.8	1,185.1	3,004.9	502.1	1,167.1	1,335.7	99.5	491.5
	June	3,730.0	2,425.5	1,304.5	3,164.8	517.9	1,234.3	1,412.6	86.8	478.4
	September	3,849.4	2,464.8	1,385.6	3,285.2	533.1	1,277.1	1,475.0	77.1	487.1
	December	3,948.9	2,482.5	1,466.4	3,388.1	546.6	1,314.9	1,526.6	71.7	489.1
1943	March	3,988.6	2,480.4	1,508.2	3,435.8	564.5	1,318.7	1,552.6	67.1	485.7
	June	4,010.2	2,472.6	1,537.6	3,453.3	580.5	1,299.0	1,573.8	66.3	490.6
	September	3,999.8	2,461.6	1,538.2	3,444.3	595.6	1,224.3	1,624.4	67.3	488.2
	December	3,997.1	2,453.2	1,543.9	3,442.7	597.8	1,166.7	1,678.2	67.5	486.9
1944	March	3,949.1	2,427.1	1,522.0	3,393.9	597.4	1,143.8	1,652.7	69.4	485.8
	June	3,865.2	2,377.8	1,487.4	3,301.4	589.1	1,108.6	1,603.7	67.9	495.9
	September	3,777.6	2,339.0	1,438.6	3,207.3	572.2	1,078.5	1,556.6	72.6	497.7
	December	3,636.2	2,278.3	1,357.9	3,029.0	550.4	1,038.3	1,440.3	84.7	522.5
1945	March	3,492.1	2,209.7	1,282.4	2,842.0	522.0	1,017.0	1,303.0	100.1	550.0
	June	3,308.2	2,130.6	1,177.6	2,541.4	485.2	949.0	1,107.2	128.9	637.9

1. See footnote 2 to Table 3.13. The industries included are those shown in detail in Table 3.17.

Source: Ministry of Labour and National Service

3.17 Numbers employed in engineering and metals industries[1]

Great Britain | *Thousands*

	Engineering, boilermaking, etc. (including marine engineering)			Motor vehicles cycles and aircraft manufacture and repair			Construction and repair of railway and other carriages, etc.			Bolts, nuts, screws, hand tools, cutlery, brass and allied metal ware and miscellaneous metal goods		
	Total	Males	Females	Total	Males	Females	Total	Males	Females	Total	Males	Females
1939 June	939.8	841.5	98.3	473.3	428.1	45.2	65.6	62.3	3.3	378.1	241.3	136.8
1940 June	1,114.5	967.4	147.1	561.9	489.0	72.9	61.8	58.2	3.6	406.5	246.7	159.8
September	1,193.1	1,016.0	177.1	626.4	531.5	94.9	57.6	53.9	3.7	408.7	250.0	158.7
December	1,237.9	1,045.8	192.1	676.9	563.7	113.2	56.1	52.5	3.6	396.7	249.1	147.6
1941 March	1,277.8	1,035.6	242.2	756 4	603.0	153.4	56.7	52.2	4.5	412.6	251.0	161.6
June	1,381.3	1,083.0	298.3	780.1	600.8	179.3	59.6	53.8	5.8	419.2	243.9	175.3
September	1,441.3	1,099.9	341.4	814.3	603.9	204.4	60.1	53.6	6.5	425.0	248.2	176.8
December	1,540.6	1,122.1	418.5	899.8	647.1	252.7	58.5	50.9	7.6	435.5	248.1	187.4
1942 March	1,615.7	1,134.5	481.2	946.4	657.9	288.5	59.4	50.9	8.5	440.0	250.5	189.5
June	1,685.0	1,147.3	537.7	995.2	677.9	317.3	59.5	50.7	8.8	448.0	242.2	205.8
September	1,735.3	1,165.4	569.9	1,044.3	696.5	347.8	59.9	50.4	9.5	448.6	240.0	208.6
December	1,787.0	1,178.4	608.6	1,080.2	703.3	376.9	59.8	50.3	9.5	449.9	237.7	212.2
1943 March	1,799.9	1,174.5	625.4	1,101.7	708.2	393.5	59.1	49.5	9.6	448.4	235.5	212.9
June	1,790.9	1,159.7	631.2	1,121.8	711.7	410.1	59.1	49.5	9.6	447.8	233.7	214.1
September	1,776.7	1,150.7	626.0	1,128.2	713.9	414.3	60.7	50.7	10.0	446.4	233.4	213.0
December	1,760.3	1,136.3	624.0	1,140.2	722.5	417.7	61.0	50.7	10.3	445.9	232.9	213.0
1944 March	1,730.3	1,124.3	606.0	1,129.1	714.6	414.5	61.2	51.0	10.2	445.0	232.1	212.9
June	1,673.3	1,091.6	581.7	1,116.9	709.2	407.7	61.2	51.2	10.0	440.4	229.5	210.9
September	1,630.4	1,070.1	560.3	1,093.8	700.4	393.4	61.1	51.3	9.8	430.8	226.0	204.8
December	1,568.0	1,045.6	522.4	1,031.6	673.1	358.5	60.7	51.4	9.3	422.9	223.2	199.7
1945 March	1,508.4	1,017.2	491.2	964.3	640.7	323.6	60.8	51.6	9.2	415.3	219.5	195.8
June	1,438.0	989.8	448.2	876.2	597.2	279.0	61.2	52.0	9.2	405.7	215.9	189.8

1. See footnote 2 to table 3.13.

Source: Ministry of Labour and National Service

3.17 Numbers employed in engineering and metals industries[1]

continued

Great Britain | *Thousands*

	General iron founding, heating and ventilating apparatus			Electric cables, apparatus, etc.			Scientific instruments watches, clocks, plate, jewellery, etc.			Non-ferrous metal manufacture		
	Total	Males	Females	Total	Males	Females	Total	Males	Females	Total	Males	Females
1939 June	117.3	106.1	11.2	195.9	116.4	79.5	87.0	54.8	32.2	55.9	51.2	4.7
1940 June	98.6	86.6	12.0	222.7	122.9	99.8	92.6	55 0	37.6	68.5	61.6	6.9
September	91.3	78.7	12.6	227 2	123.1	104.1	93.3	55.1	38.2	71.2	63.3	7.9
December	89.5	77.0	12.5	227 4	123.1	104.3	92.5	56.2	36.3	74.0	65.0	9.0
1941 March	88.6	75.6	13.0	233.7	120.4	113.3	95.2	56.3	38.9	76.5	66.7	9.8
June	89.4	75.2	14.2	237.3	117.1	120.2	98.0	56.1	41.9	81.7	68.1	13.6
September	89.0	77.0	12.0	242.1	114.8	127.3	98.2	61.4	36.8	85.5	69.2	16.3
December	88.5	74.2	14.3	254.5	115.4	139.1	98.4	61.3	37.1	85.9	69.5	16.4
1942 March	88.2	73.1	15.1	257.1	113.7	143.4	98.6	60.3	38.3	90.5	69.9	20.6
June	87.8	68.3	19.5	261.4	114.7	146.7	98.7	53.2	45.5	94.4	71.2	23.2
September	93.0	68.4	24.6	270.2	117.4	152.8	98.5	52.4	46.1	99.6	74.3	25.3
December	89.7	66.8	22.9	280.5	118.8	161.7	97.8	51.1	46.7	104.0	76.1	27.9
1943 March	89.4	65.6	23.8	285.4	118.8	166.6	98.0	50.5	47.5	106.7	77.8	28.9
June	85.8	64.6	21.2	291.0	118.8	172.2	99.4	51.3	48.1	114.4	83.3	31.1
September	82.1	61.8	20.3	293.1	117.8	175.3	99.3	51.0	48.3	113.3	82.3	31.0
December	81.4	61.4	20.0	296.5	116.9	179.6	98.8	50.4	48.4	113.0	82.1	30.9
1944 March	80.3	60.6	19.7	295.6	115.7	179.9	97.2	48.9	48.3	110.4	79.9	30.5
June	74.8	56.3	18.5	295.0	114.7	180.3	96.9	48.6	48.3	106.7	76.7	30.0
September	74.7	56.3	18.4	290.4	114.0	176.4	95.6	48.0	47.6	100.8	72.9	27.9
December	74.6	56.2	18.4	292.0	114.0	178.0	94.4	47.2	47.2	92.0	67.6	24.4
1945 March	74.6	56.2	18.4	289.3	113.5	175.8	93.1	46.6	46.5	86.3	64.4	21.9
June	72.2	55.1	17.1	279.9	112.2	167.7	91.0	45.4	45.6	84.0	63.0	21.0

1. See footnote 2 to Table 3.13.

Source: Ministry of Labour and National Service

3.18 Numbers employed in the iron and steel industry[1]

Great Britain | *Thousands*

	Total numbers employed			Numbers employed in				
	Total	Males	Females	Pig iron production	Steel melting, iron and steel rolling, etc.	Tin plate production	Iron and steel tube manufacture	Wire, wire netting and ropes manufacture
1939 June	259.1	246.1	13.0	15.5	160.0	25.1	31.7	26.8
1940 June	273.3	255.0	18.3	16.7	167.3	24.3	33.8	31.2
1941 June	299.9	267.1	32.8	17.6	193.9	16.7	37.2	34.5
1942 June	318.8	258.4	60.4	17.3	207.4	16.3	39.9	37.9
1943 June	303.9	239.7	64.2	17.4	195.4	13.8	41.3	36.0
1944 June	292.3	230.6	61.7	17.9	189.1	12.3	39.1	33.9
1945 June	267.7	216.8	50.9	15.9	174.8	12.4	34.7	29.9

1. See footnote 2 to Table 3.13

Source: Ministry of Labour and National Service

3.19 Numbers employed in the textile industries[1]

Great Britain — *Thousands*

	All textile industries						Cotton spinning and weaving					
				Numbers employed on						Numbers employed on		
	Total	Males	Females	Manufacture of equipment and supplies for the Forces	Orders for export	Orders for home market	Total	Males	Females	Manufacture of equipment and supplies for the Forces	Orders for export	Orders for home market
1939 June	987.9	388.3	599.6	..	..	..	339.9	119.2	220.7	..	..	..
1940 June	1,040.9	378.3	662.6	..	..	..	363.8	115.7	248.1	..	..	..
December	970.0	346.8	623 2	..	..	..	339.2	107.4	231.8	..	..	..
1941 June	855.0	298.3	556.7	..	..	..	276.1	84.4	191.7	..	..	..
December	752.4	258.8	493.6	254.6	166.2	331.6	237.3	71.6	165.7	83.2	57.6	96.5
1942 June	708.2	243.0	465.2	276.2	112.0	320.0	233.8	70.5	163.3	89.2	44.0	100.6
December	677.4	230.2	447.2	276.3	90.0	311.1	231.0	68.8	162.2	90.3	37.7	103.0
1943 June	654.1	219.8	434.3	270.7	87.1	296.3	227.3	65.8	161.5	83.9	40.9	102.5
December	636.1	216.0	420.1	270.9	86.5	278.7	223.5	65.4	158.1	76.2	46.4	100.9
1944 June	622.4	210.3	412.1	273.5	92.1	256.8	220.1	63.6	156.5	81.7	45.5	92.9
December	615.4	209.9	405.5	273.9	93.4	248.1	214.9	63.4	151.5	78.9	45.5	90.5
1945 June	619.2	210.3	408.9	224.6	111.0	283.6	212.9	62.7	150.2	56.4	52.6	103.9

Thousands

	Woollen and Worsted						Silk and Rayon					
				Numbers employed on						Numbers employed on		
	Total	Males	Females	Manufacture of equipment and supplies for the Forces	Orders for export	Orders for home market	Total	Males	Females	Manufacture of equipment and supplies for the Forces	Orders for export	Orders for home market
1939 June	207.6	90.3	117.3	..	..	..	72.2	34.6	37.6	..	..	..
1940 June	222.3	89.6	132.7	..	..	..	75.7	35.7	40.0	..	..	..
December	212.1	84.5	127.6	10.0	140.7	64.4	65.7	29.8	35.9	13.0	21.2	31.5
1941 June	195.3	76.5	118.8	80.2	45.3	69.8	58.6	24.8	33.8	10.2	23.5	24.9
December	176.1	67.6	108.5	66.7	40.2	69.2	52.7	22.2	30.5	8.1	20.5	24.1
1942 June	162.1	63.4	98.7	70.4	23.0	68.7	50.0	21.0	29.0	14.2	13.2	22.6
December	152.3	60.0	92.3	62.6	20.9	68.8	47.5	20.0	27.5	19.6	8.7	19.2
1943 June	143.5	56.4	87.1	62.1	17.7	63.7	45.9	19.2	26.7	19.4	7.7	18.8
December	136.0	54.1	81.9	61.6	14.3	60.1	45.4	19.3	26.1	20.1	7.9	17.4
1944 June	129.1	51.1	78.0	55.0	16.5	57.6	44.1	19.0	25.1	22.2	8.7	13.2
December	127.5	50.6	76.9	56.8	16.2	54.5	44.7	19.4	25.3	23.0	8.9	12.8
1945 June.	129.8	50.1	79.7	50.3	20.3	59.2	45.9	19.9	26.0	21.2	10.1	14.6

1. See footnote 2 to Table 3.13.

Source: Ministry of Labour and National Service

3.19 Numbers employed in the textile industries[1]

continued

Great Britain *Thousands*

	Hosiery and lace						Linen, jute, hemp, etc.					
				Numbers employed on						Numbers employed on		
	Total	Males	Females	Manufacture of equipment and supplies for the Forces	Orders for export	Orders for home market	Total	Males	Females	Manufacture of equipment and supplies for the Forces	Orders for export	Orders for home market
1939 June	139.3	34.2	105.1	..	..	..	55.4	20.7	34.7	..	..	..
1940 June	136.9	31.8	105.1	..	..	..	61.1	20.4	40.7	..	..	..
December	123.4	27.5	95.9	23.5	14.5	85.4	55.6	18.2	37.4	19.9	7.7	28.0
1941 June	110.9	24.9	86.0	18.0	11.3	81.6	49.9	15.7	34.2	18.7	6.6	24.6
December	92.6	21.2	71.4	14.9	11.6	66.1	47.9	14.1	33.8	19.8	5.1	23.0
1942 June	81.4	18.1	63.3	17.7	7.6	56.1	48.3	13.8	34.5	22.9	3.9	21.5
December	77.6	16.1	61.5	19.6	3.9	54.1	46.3	13.4	32.9	23.9	3.1	19.3
1943 June	74.3	15.4	58.9	17.0	3.2	54.1	42.9	12.6	30.3	25.3	2.8	14.8
December	69.1	14.5	54.6	15.2	3.1	50.8	42.0	12.5	29.5	27.3	2.7	12.0
1944 June	67.9	14.3	53.6	17.8	5.1	45.0	41.5	12.3	29.2	26.4	2.8	12.3
December	68.2	14.4	53.8	18.7	5.4	44.1	39.9	11.8	28.1	25.2	2.5	12.2
1945 June	69.6	14.7	54.9	14.9	5.5	49.2	39.7	11.8	27.9	20.1	4.3	15.3

Thousands

	Textile bleaching, printing, dyeing and finishing						Other textile industries					
				Numbers employed on						Numbers employed on		
	Total	Males	Females	Manufacture of equipment and supplies for the Forces	Orders for export	Orders for home market	Total	Males	Females	Manufacture of equipment and supplies for the Forces	Orders for export	Orders for home market
1939 June	79.6	56.7	22.9	..	..	..	93.9	32.6	61.3	..	..	..
1940 June	80.0	55.0	25.0	..	..	..	101.1	30.1	71.0	..	..	..
December	75.2	50.4	24.8	23.6	25.3	26.3	98.8	29.0	69.8	44.6	12.5	41.7
1941 June	71.1	46.8	24.3	22.5	25.8	22.8	93.1	25.2	67.9	44.5	11.2	37.4
December	63.2	40.5	22.7	21.8	21.7	19.7	82.6	21.6	61.0	40.1	9.5	33.0
1942 June	57.2	36.8	20.4	22.0	13.9	21.3	75.4	19.4	56.0	39.8	6.4	29.2
December	53.5	33.9	19.6	19.6	11.6	22.3	69.2	18.0	51.2	40.7	4.1	24.4
1943 June	51.7	32.6	19.1	21.1	10.7	19.9	68.5	17.8	50.7	41.9	4.1	22.5
December	51.8	32.5	19.3	23.9	9.5	18.4	68.3	17.7	50.6	46.6	2.6	19.1
1944 June	51.8	32.4	19.4	24.2	10.6	17.0	67.9	17.6	50.3	46.2	2.9	18.8
December	52.0	32.3	19.7	24.6	11.7	15.7	68.2	18.0	50.2	46.7	3.2	18.3
1945 June	52.2	32.0	20.2	21.1	12.6	18.5	69.1	19.1	50.0	40.6	5.6	22.9

1. See footnote 2 to Table 3.13.

Source: Ministry of Labour and National Service

3.20 Numbers employed in certain clothing industries[1]

Great Britain *Thousands*

		Tailoring						Hats and caps					
					Numbers employed on						Numbers employed on		
		Total	Males	Females	Manufacture of equipment and supplies for the Forces	Orders for export	Orders for home market	Total	Males	Females	Manufacture of equipment and supplies for the Forces	Orders for export	Orders for home market
1939	June	234.6	66.6	168.0	..	..	..	29.6	11.1	18.5	..	..	..
1940	June	243.3	54.8	188.5	..	..	..	23.7	8.2	15.5	..	..	..
	December	238.7	50.7	188.0	..	..	..	22.3	7.1	15.2	4.9	3.0	14.4
1941	June	242.0	49.3	192.7	128.2	2.8	111.0	23.2	7.0	16.2	4.4	1.9	16.9
	December	208.0	43.8	164.2	..	..	..	20.4	5.9	14.5	3.1	3.0	14.3
1942	June	194.6	41.4	153.2	..	..	..	19.1	5.6	13.5	5.1	2.9	11.1
	December	190.7	40.3	150.4	..	..	..	15.0	4.5	10.5	4.1	1.4	9.5
1943	June	178.1	38.0	140.1	49.5	1.5	127.1	12.7	3.8	8.9	3.3	0.7	8.7
	December	165.0	36.3	128.7	..	..	..	11.6	3.3	8.3	4.7	1.1	5.8
1944	June	158.5	34.9	123.6	60.3	2.7	95.5	11.4	3.3	8.1	4.3	1.5	5.6
	December	158.2	31.2	127.0	65.0	2.1	91.1	11.5	3.3	8.2	4.9	1.3	5.3
1945	June	172.2	37.4	134.8	45.0	2.1	125.1	12.7	3.7	9.0	5.1	2.1	5.5

Thousands

		Shirts, collars, etc.						Boots and shoes, etc.					
					Numbers employed on						Numbers employed on		
		Total	Males	Females	Manufacture of equipment and supplies for the Forces	Orders for export	Orders for home market	Total	Males	Females	Manufacture of equipment and supplies for the Forces	Orders for export	Orders for home market
1939	June	93.5	10.1	83.4	..	..	..	135.0	78.4	56.6	..	..	..
1940	June	91.5	8.9	82.6	..	..	..	132.9	73.6	59.3	..	..	..
	December	83.1	8.9	74.2	28.2	4.0	50.9	129.8	69.6	60.2	23.6	6.9	99.3
1941	June	77.7	6.8	70.9	26.8	2.3	48.6	127.8	65.0	62.8	27.0	3.2	97.6
	December	66.4	5.3	61.1	19.5	3.0	43.9	118.9	58.2	60.7	22.1	4.1	92.7
1942	June	58.4	5.1	53.3	16.6	3.7	38.1	107.0	54.3	52.7	22.5	3.1	81.4
	December	56.8	4.9	51.9	15.2	1.4	40.2	99.9	52.2	47.7	22.1	1.8	76.0
1943	June	55.1	4.7	50.4	10.6	0.9	43.6	96.3	51.1	45.2	19.1	0.9	76.3
	December	52.1	4.5	47.6	12.0	0.9	39.2	93.7	50.2	43.5	15.8	1.0	76.9
1944	June	49.6	4.4	45.2	12.7	1.0	35.9	92.2	49.5	42.7	16.8	1.0	74.4
	December	47.7	4.2	43.5	12.3	1.0	34.4	91.9	49.1	42.8	17.8	0.9	73.2
1945	June	52.5	4.2	48.3	11.1	1.4	40.0	95.3	51.1	44.2	14.0	1.0	80.3

1. See footnote 2 to Table 3.13.

Source: Ministry of Labour and National Service

3.21 Numbers employed in woodworking and furniture industries[1]

Great Britain *Thousands*

	Sawmilling and machined woodwork, wooden box and packing-case making and other woodworking						Furniture, upholstery, etc.					
				Numbers employed on						Numbers employed on		
	Total	Males	Females	Manufacture of equipment and supplies for the Forces	Orders for export	Orders for home market	Total	Males	Females	Manufacture of equipment and supplies for the Forces	Orders for export	Orders for home market
1939 June	101.6	90.0	11.6	..	..	..	138.4	111.5	26.9	..	..	..
1940 June	88.3	75.4	12.9	..	..	..	107.7	81.1	26.6	..	..	..
December	86.6	74.7	11.9	37.3	10.1	39.2	93.7	67.8	25.9	30.4	3.0	60.3
1941 June	91.4	74.0	17.4	47.9	9.7	33.8	78.2	52.8	25.4	30.8	1.5	45.9
December	97.1	73.5	23.6	52.4	8.2	36.5	72.9	46.8	26.1	30.6	0.7	41.6
1942 June	107.8	79.6	28.2	65.1	7.1	35.6	70.4	44.4	26.0	30.3	0.6	39.5
December	119.5	83.7	35.8	78.6	5.2	35.7	68.5	42.6	25.9	31.8	0.5	36.2
1943 June	118.9	82.5	36.4	79.9	3.2	35.8	61.5	37.5	24.0	32.4	0.3	28.8
December	121.1	82.5	38.6	82.9	3.3	34.9	59.6	36.4	23.2	31.6	0.2	27.8
1944 June	127.8	84.6	43.2	90.1	3.1	34.6	57.8	35.4	22.4	29.8	0.2	27.8
December	127.8	84.5	43.3	89.3	3.7	34.8	58.3	35.9	22.4	28.9	0.3	29.1
1945 June	124.9	83.6	41.3	75.1	5.2	44.6	62.4	39.8	22.6	21.1	0.6	40.7

1. See footnote 2 to Table 3.13.

Source: Ministry of Labour and National Service

3.22 Numbers employed in certain paper and printing industries[1]

Great Britain *Thousands*

	Paper, paper board, cardboard box, etc. making						Printing, publishing and bookbinding, etc.					
				Numbers employed on						Numbers employed on		
	Total	Males	Females	Manufacture of equipment and supplies for the Forces	Orders for export	Orders for home market	Total	Males	Females	Manufacture of equipment and supplies for the Forces	Orders for export	Orders for home market
1939 June	152.1	79.7	72.4	..	..	..	304.3	198.9	105.4	..	..	..
1940 June	134.2	66.6	67.6	..	..	..	233.5	143.0	90.5	..	..	..
December	123.9	61.9	62.0	16.4	23.8	83.7	205.1	123.3	81.8	5.0	26.2	173.9
1941 June	120.4	57.7	62.7	23.6	14.3	82.5	190.2	111.3	78.9	7.7	21.0	161.5
December	113.0	50.8	62.2	27.6	11.6	73.8	185.9	108.3	77.6	10.1	17.3	158.5
1942 June	108.7	49.9	58.8	31.1	8.3	69.3	175.8	99.4	76.4	23.9	13.2	138.7
December	104.3	48.6	55.7	30.0	6.1	68.2	169.3	95.4	73.9	18.2	12.5	138.6
1943 June	97.8	45.1	52.7	33.8	5.3	58.7	165.0	92.9	72.1	17.0	14.8	133.2
December	99.6	45.8	53.8	42.3	5.3	52.0	163.8	92.0	71.8	21.9	13.1	128.8
1944 June	97.8	44.1	53.7	42.6	5.4	49.8	162.5	90.6	71.9	23.1	13.5	125.9
December	95.9	43.8	52.1	39.2	5.8	50.9	164.8	91.5	73.3	23.3	14.2	127.3
1945 June	98.2	45.4	52.8	35.4	7.8	55.0	173.4	97.0	76.4	18.8	14.9	139.7

1. See footnote 2 to Table 3.13.

Source: Ministry of Labour and National Service

3.23 Numbers employed in leather and rubber manufacture[1]

Great Britain *Thousands*

	Leather, leather goods and fur						Rubber manufacture (excluding rubber garments)					
				Numbers employed on						Numbers employed on		
	Total	Males	Females	Manufacture of equipment and supplies for the Forces	Orders for export	Orders for home market	Total	Males	Females	Manufacture of equipment and supplies for the Forces	Orders for export	Orders for home market
1939 June	73.0	45.1	27.9	..	..	..	70.2	41.1	29.1	..	..	..
1940 June	73.7	42.7	31.0	..	..	..	80.8	45.2	35.6	..	..	..
December	69.0	38.8	30.2	28.9	7.8	32.3	82.7	43.7	39.0	50.5	8.9	23.3
1941 June	67.8	36.5	31.3	26.3	6.6	34.9	85.8	42.8	43.0	43.9	9.5	32.4
December	62.6	32.6	30.0	26.0	6.8	29.8	78.9	38.9	40.0	43.7	5.3	29.9
1942 June	60.3	31.5	28.8	27.8	5.5	27.0	67.5	34.6	32.9	40.4	1.5	25.6
December	55.6	29.2	26.4	27.8	3.4	24.4	61.0	31.2	29.8	37.7	2.5	20.8
1943 June	53.3	28.2	25.1	29.6	3.5	20.2	60.6	31.2	29.4	43.1	1.8	15.7
December	52.1	27.5	24.6	..	..	..	61.4	32.3	29.1	45.1	1.4	14.9
1944 June	49.5	27.0	22.5	30.4	4.0	15.1	62.1	33.2	28.9	46.5	1.6	14.0
December	50.2	27.3	22.9	30.0	4.1	16.1	62.8	34.0	28.8	46.3	1.7	14.8
1945 June	51.6	27.6	24.0	26.8	6.4	18.4	62.3	34.3	28.0	43.7	2.4	16.2

1. See footnote 2 to Table 3.13.

Source: Ministry of Labour and National Service

3.24 Numbers employed in glass and pottery manufacture[1]

Great Britain *Thousands*

	Glass manufacture (excluding bottles and scientific glass)						Pottery, earthenware, etc.					
				Numbers employed on						Numbers employed on		
	Total	Males	Females	Manufacture of equipment and supplies for the Forces	Orders for export	Orders for home market	Total	Males	Females	Manufacture of equipment and supplies for the Forces	Orders for export	Orders for home market
1939 June	30.6	22.5	8.1	..	..	..	67.0	30.0	37.0	..	..	..
1940 June	28.3	19.2	9.1	..	..	..	59.3	23.9	35.4	..	..	..
December	27.8	18.5	9.3	5.2	6.8	15.8	55.2	21.0	34.2	10.7	22.6	21.9
1941 June	25.9	16.3	9.6	6.6	6.9	12.4	52.1	19.1	33.0	5.3	21.6	25.2
December	25.2	15.2	10.0	5.3	4.0	15.9	44.5	16.3	28.2	4.7	18.6	21.2
1942 June	26.1	15.6	10.5	7.6	2.9	15.6	39.7	15.4	24.3	4.2	16.6	18.9
December	24.9	14.6	10.3	8.6	1.6	14.7	37.5	14.9	22.6	5.5	10.0	22.0
1943 June	24.4	14.0	10.4	8.8	1.1	14.5	36.7	14 6	22.1	4.9	9.8	22.0
December	24.4	14.0	10.4	9.5	2.4	12.5	36.6	14.6	22.0	4.6	10.3	21.7
1944 June	24.3	14.0	10.3	9.6	2.6	12.1	36.2	14.3	21.9	4.5	10.0	21.7
December	25.1	14.8	10.3	7.9	2.7	14.5	37.1	14.5	22.6	5.1	11.1	20.9
1945 June	25.7	15.5	10.2	7.0	3.8	14.9	39.0	14.7	24.3	7.5	12.9	18.6

1. See footnote 2 to Table 3.13.

Source: Ministry of Labour and National Service

3.25 Railway staff: Numbers employed

Great Britain — At March in each year — *Number*

	1939	1940	1941	1942	1943	1944	1945
Total staff	588,517	583,627	587,864	599,608	612,596	616,756	622,369
Men and boys:							
Total	563,264	557,711	547,030	525,648	524,132	523,439	531,062
Officers, supervisory, clerical, etc.	86,049	82,930	81,127	77,487	72,240	70,076	69,440
Conciliation	330,571	332,629	332,775	317,785	319,382	319,607	326,301
Shop and artisan	112,113	107,246	102,958	100,569	101,668	101,469	102,438
Police, electrical generating station and miscellaneous	6,605	6,981	7,611	7,816	7,814	7,742	8,126
Ancillary	27,926	27,925	22,559	21,991	23,028	24,545	24,757
Women and girls:							
Total	25,253	25,916	40,834	73,960	88,464	93,317	91,307
Officers, supervisory, clerical, etc.	12,229	13,372	17,595	26,665	29,291	29,641	30,294
Conciliation	–	–	9,260	24,255	32,280	36,093	35,612
Shop and artisan	990	884	2,348	10,474	13,933	13,976	11,355
Police, electrical generating station and miscellaneous	6,160	5,997	5,463	5,732	5,939	6,412	6,790
Ancillary	5,874	5,663	6,168	6,834	7,021	7,195	7,256

Source: Ministry of Transport

3.26 Industrial staff in the Civil Service[1]

Great Britain | *Thousands*

		Total	Admiralty	War Office	Air Ministry	Ministry of Supply[2]	Ministry of Aircraft Production	Post Office	Forestry Commission	Ministry of Transport	Ministry of Works	Other departments
1939	April 1	240.2	71.6	68.3	25.8	_	_	51.1	5.2	2.0	6.6	9.6
1940	January 1	294.4	80.4	38.3	38.3	65.7	_	43.5	7.2	3.5	7.4	10.1
	April 1	322.7	87.0	42.2	41.5	74.8	_	42.2	10.7	5.5	6.6	12.2
	July 1	366.1	94.0	46.5	45.5	97.8	2.5	43.8	13.8	4.7	6.6	10.9
	October 1	398.8	99.6	43.5	48.7	116.3	7.4	43.9	16.2	4.2	7.1	11.9
1941	January 1	427.1	103.2	44.9	53.2	131.1	6.0	44.5	16.9	4.3	10.6	12.4
	April 1	475.5	106.7	47.3	54.7	181.8	5.0	45.7	5.3[3]	3.9	12.6	12.5
	July 1	538.6	112.3	49.5	52.6	238.4	5.4	47.1	5.2	4.7	13.4	10.0
	October 1	596.6	119.0	49.5	50.6	287.5	9.1	47.7	5.0	4.8	13.4	10.0
1942	January 1	654.0	122.6	53.3	52.2	332.6	10.1	49.1	4.8	5.1	14.0	10.2
	April 1	690.0	125.9	54.7	54.1	357.4	12.1	50.5	5.1	5.0	14.6	10.6
	July 1	697.4	125.2	55.2	57.3	358.6	15.2	50.5	5.4	5.6	13.6	10.8
	October 1	700.3	128.8	55.7	61.9	351.4	16.6	49.9	5.4	6.2	13.4	11.0
1943	January 1	729.8	146.5	60.4	65.2	351.9	17.9	50.2	5.2	6.5	15.0	11.0
	April 1	737.8	151.2	66.5	66.9	346.0	18.2	50.3	5.3	6.6	15.8	11.0
	July 1	724.7	152.6	64.9	55.4	331.6	31.9	49.9	5.1	6.1	16.4	10.8
	October 1	727.0	156.5	72.0	56.7	319.1	33.1	49.9	5.1	5.6	17.4	11.6
1944	January 1	716.5	159.5	71.7	57.6	305.5	33.2	48.9	4.8	5.4	18.2	11.7
	April 1	710.3	160.3	75.3	59.0	294.1	32.7	48.1	4.7	5.4	18.8	11.9
	July 1	698.6	158.8	78.0	58.9	282.1	32.1	47.3	4.9	5.5	19.5	11.5
	October 1	692.8	160.8	78.9	58.0	274.8	32.6	46.8	4.8	4.6	20.3	11.2
1945	January 1	675.3	156.6	77.5	56.4	265.4	31.3	46.8	4.7	4 2	21.4	11.0
	April 1	665.3	154.8	76.5	56.2	260.3	30.5	46.5	4.7	3.7	20.4	11.7
	July 1	620.8	151.3	72.3	54.5	227.2	26.9	46.3	4.9	3.7	20.3	13.4
	October 1	514.8	148.1	64.0	52.8	138.6	22.1	47.2	5.1	3.3	20.1	13.5

1. Including part-time workers, two part-time workers being counted as one whole-time worker. Excluding staff in Northern Ireland other than reserved and agency services.
2. Including some staff which in 1939 were employed by the War Office or Air Ministry.
3. Between April 1940 and April 1941, home-grown timber production work was transferred from the Forestry Commission to the Ministry of Supply.

Source: Treasury

3.27 Non-industrial staff in the Civil Service: Departmental analysis

Great Britain *Thousands*

	Total[1]	Post Office	Ad-miralty	War Office	Air Ministry	Ministry of Supply	Ministry of Aircraft Produc-tion	Ministry of Labour and National Service	Ministry of Food	Ministry of Trans-port	Ministry of Works	Other depart-ments
1939 April 1	387.7	196.6	12.9	19.8	19.7	–	–	28.3	–	3.0	6.3	101.1
1940 January 1	433.9	186.9	17.6	28.2	26.9	16 0	–	27.9	13.7	3.2	7.1	106.4
April 1	454.8	188.4	20.1	32.6	28.7	18.7	–	26.0	19.3	6.5	7.4	107.1
July 1	482.1	188.0	21.6	33.3	19.8	23.0	12.4	28.9	23.7	3.1	7.8	120.5
October 1	492.2	188.0	23 5	34.1	21.2	27.0	7.9	29.7	24.9	3.1	8.2	124.5
1941 January 1	520.3	188.7	23.9	39.0	23.5	30.6	8.9	30.4	29.0	3.0	8.3	135.0
April 1	554.5	195.3	25.9	44.2	26.2	37.0	10.0	32.4	29.8	11.3	9.2	133.2
July 1	605.3	198.9	28.2	49.5	33.2	41.8	10.9	39.0	40.4	12.4	10.1	140.9
October 1	620.5	202.6	29.7	54.9	34.6	48.3	12.0	38.2	33.6	12.8	11.1	142.7
1942 January 1	640.7	204.1	32.0	55.1	35.4	54.2	12.9	39.3	35.4	13.2	12.0	147.1
April 1	657.4	204.8	33.7	58.6	36.2	58.7	13.8	40.3	36.8	13.7	12.8	148.0
July 1	674.4	206.1	34.7	62.6	36.6	61.4	14.9	42.0	38.9	14.4	13.5	149.3
October 1	688.4	207.2	36.4	64.0	37.9	64.5	15.6	42.5	38.3	15.0	14.2	152.8
1943 January 1	704.1	207.4	42.1	66.3	39.6	67.7	16.4	43.0	38.1	15.2	14.5	153.8
April 1	710.6	207.6	43.4	69.2	39.6	67.9	16.2	43.8	39.4	15.6	14.4	153.5
July 1	719.2	206.3	45.8	68.6	36.5	68.0	18.8	43.3	49.2	15.7	14.2	152.8
October 1	715.5	204.9	47.7	69.5	36.5	67.9	19.7	41.2	45.0	15.9	14.6	152.6
1944 January 1	708.1	203.4	49.0	69.2	36.7	66.4	20.3	39.8	42.3	16.0	14.3	150.7
April 1	704.4	202.7	50.2	68.7	37.3	64.0	20.6	39.4	40.0	16.1	14.5	150.9
July 1	712.7	203.5	51.9	68.3	37.1	63.1	21.1	40.3	44.7	16.6	14.8	151.3
October 1	705.9	205.2	52.7	67.9	36.6	62.1	21.6	38.4	39.3	16.3	14.8	151.0
1945 January 1	704.6	207.4	53.4	68.1	36.2	61.6	21.5	37.1	38.2	15.0	15.3	150.8
April 1	704.7	208.6	54.4	67.5	35.7	60.8	21.5	35.6	37.9	14.9	14.3	153.5
July 1	703.8	210.5	54.4	63.8	34.7	58.6	21.0	36.6	43.0	14.5	15.1	151.6
October 1	690.0	220.4	52.7	61.3	33.7	50.4	20.0	36.0	38.3	13.4	15.8	148.0

1. Established and unestablished, excluding staff in Northern Ireland other than reserved and agency services. In arriving at the totals two part-time workers are counted as one whole-time worker.

Source: Treasury

3.28 Male operatives employed on the Government building programme in Great Britain[1]

End of month

Thousands

	Total	For Services and Supply Departments: Total	Admiralty	War Office[2]	Air Ministry[2]	Ministry of Supply	Ministry of Aircraft Production[2]	Ministry of Transport[2]	For Civil Departments[2,3]	New house construction (including site preparation)
1941 July	541.8	342.6	34.2	55.1	109.3	100.5	32.8	10.7	199.2	
August	543.8	341.0	33.2	55.7	109.3	100.0	32.1	10.7	202.8	
September	557.8	347.2	32.2	55.5	109.9	108.1	30.6	10.9	210.6	
October	560.9	348.5	32.6	56.5	108.7	105.9	32.3	12.5	212.4	
November	537.7	346.0	31.0	56.5	106.7	106.4	34.3	11.1	191.7	
December	517.6	333.7	29.5	55.9	99.3	103.0	34.9	11.1	183.9	
1942 January	503.7	330.8	28.6	54.7	102.5	92.3	40.6	12.1	171.9	1.0
February	496.7	329.8	28.7	50.2	105.3	92.8	40.5	12.3	165.9	1.0
March	510.2	332.7	27.0	52.1	106.5	92.6	41.7	12.8	176.0	1.5
April	514.0	337.7	26.2	50.7	112.6	91.5	43.5	13.2	174.7	1.6
May	495.5	328.3	26.4	48.0	109.8	82.1	49.1	12.9	165.6	1.6
June	480.9	319.4	26.6	44.2	112.8	75.3	48.0	12.5	159.8	1.7
July	466.7	319.3	25.0	45.0	117.1	65.2	54.9	12.1	145.6	1.8
August	464.7	327.3	28.3	52.8	120.7	60.5	53.3	11.7	134.7	2.7
September	460.5	331.0	26.5	62.0	126.1	52.1	53.1	11.2	126.8	2.7
October	460.7	336.3	27.0	71.2	129.6	48.9	49.4	10.2	121.7	2.7
November	445.2	328.5	27.9	72.8	130.1	45.1	43.4	9.2	114.2	2.5
December	426.6	320.5	27.2	75.6	129.8	41.9	37.9	8.1	103.6	2.5
1943 January	425.3	323.5	27.7	78.3	130.2	38.9	39.7	8.7	99.7	2.1
February	419.9	319.9	30.0	76.9	127.8	37.7	39.0	8.5	97.9	2.1
March	405.7	312.4	32.2	72.5	124.5	37.5	37.7	8.0	91.2	2.1
April	388.7	296.4	31.6	61.3	123.8	36.2	35.3	8.2	89.9	2.4
May	372.3	280.3	31.4	51.4	119.1	35.6	33.7	9.1	89.7	2.3
June	356.1	263.1	32.2	44.9	109.8	34.7	32.6	8.9	90.7	2.3
July	347.1	247.1	31.9	38.2	103.9	34.1	29.6	9.4	96.1	3.9
August	351.4	244.4	31.8	37.8	102.2	33.0	29.6	10.0	101.0	6.0
September	344.8	235.8	31.4	36.9	99.0	31.5	26.6	10.4	101.7	7.3
October	335.4	224.9	31.8	34.4	94.5	29.4	25.2	9.6	101.6	8.9
November	330.5	221.4	31.9	33.2	87.6	35.0	24.7	9.0	100.3	8.8
December	316.7	215.6	30.8	34.1	78.3	40.1	23.9	8.4	91.5	9.6
1944 January	317.3	213.3	30.7	35.1	71.9	45.2	22.4	8.0	94.6	9.4
February	316.8	207.7	29.4	34.4	63.8	47.9	23.1	9.1	100.5	8.6
March	306.3	190.7	27.7	32.2	53.8	46.0	21.9	9.1	107.7	7.9
April	295.6	175.6	25.1	31.2	47.9	42.7	20.3	8.4	113.0	7.0
May	273.4	153.1	22.2	29.9	39.9	33.7	18.8	8.6	114.0	6.3
June	267.5	146.2	20.5	28.9	38.9	31.6	17.6	8.7	115.5	5.8
July	249.4	134.4	19.3	26.3	32.9	31.3	16.4	8.2	110.3	4.7
August	231.5	133.2	18.5	24.4	31.6	36.6	14.4	7.7	93.7	4.6
September	222.1	124.2	18.5	23.0	30.0	31.5	13.3	7.9	93.1	4.8
October	216.5	114.0	19.2	22.0	30.4	23.1	11.5	7.8	97.6	4.9
November	201.9	105.0	18.4	21.0	28.6	21.0	9.4	6.5	92.0	4.9
December	195.0	98.6	17.6	18.9	27.0	20.3	8.7	6.1	91.4	5.0
1945 January	189.7	93.8	16.3	17.6	26.9	20.3	7.2	5.5	90.5	5.4
February	198.2	94.5	16.4	17.6	26.5	21.2	7.1	5.7	95.3	8.4
March	200.1	92.3	15.1	17.0	25.9	22.1	6.4	5.8	94.7	13.1
April	207.1	91.0	15.3	16.7	25.6	21.5	5.7	6.2	99.6	16.5
May	218.1	91.9	15.0	15.9	25.4	23.0	5.6	7.0	105.7	20.5
June	219.9	87.0	14.4	15.0	23.3	23.6	4.3	6.4	106.3	26.6
July	242.5	87.4	14.6	14.0	22.8	24.2	4.5	7.3	122.8	32.3

1. Aged 16 and over
2. Labour employed on licensed work sponsored by War Office, Air Ministry, Ministry of Aircraft Production and Ministry of Transport is included under " Civil Departments " before January 1943.
3. Including repair of houses made uninhabitable by war damage; salvage operations and war debris clearance; and first aid repairs carried out by the Special Repair Service.

Source: Ministry of Works

3.29 Training of civilians in Government training centres and emergency training establishments[1]

		Number in training		Number admitted to training		Number completed training	
		Males	Females[2]	Males	Females[2]	Males	Females[2]
		End of period		Weekly averages			
1940	3rd Quarter	24,039	-	1,829	-	515	-
	4th Quarter	24,286	-	1,616	-	1,160	-
1941	1st Quarter	20,741	6,576	1,729	861	1,482	245
	2nd Quarter	28,256	10,231	2,200	1,147	1,099	644
	3rd Quarter	19,670	10,280	1,052	1,104	1,371	789
	4th Quarter	12,254	14,399	824	1,524	1,235	971
1942	1st Quarter	9,283	12,041	695	1,362	800	1,345
	2nd Quarter	8,436	12,132	706	1,336	644	1,164
	3rd Quarter	6,140	12,073	513	1,318	575	1,156
	4th Quarter	5,780	11,940	447	1,146	396	1,022
1943	1st Quarter	5,184	11,166	418	1,046	397	989
	2nd Quarter	4,521	9,512	395	937	394	943
	3rd Quarter	3,216	6,460	281	636	319	729
	4th Quarter	3,345	5,786	274	538	218	523
1944	1st Quarter	3,172	3,796	253	308	203	417
	2nd Quarter	3,236	3,191	225	276	191	287
	3rd Quarter	2,654	1,985	187	170	187	215
	4th Quarter	2,634	953	189	78	153	142
1945	1st Quarter	2,596	443	167	37	129	71
	2nd Quarter	2,851	291	162	23	116	28
	3rd Quarter	3,498	270	190	19	101	18

1. Excluding coal mining training centres.
2. Women were admitted to Government training centres in January 1941.

Source: Ministry of Labour and National Service

3.30 Industrial stoppages[1]

Working days lost as a result of disputes

Thousands of days

	1939	1940	1941	1942	1943	1944	1945
Working days lost through the stoppages which began in the year[2]	1,354	941	1,077	1,530	1,832	3,696	2,847
Analysis by number of workers involved:							
Under 100	90	66	82	66	82	105	151
100 and under 250	192	111	84	92	146	136	197
1,000 and under 2,500	280	309	229	459	338	392	391
2,500 and under 5,000	132	69	82	151	185	158	203
5,000 and upwards	95	156	218	449	606	2,398	1,413
Working days lost each year through all stoppages in progress[3]							
Analysis by industry:							
All industries and services	1,356	940	1,079	1,527	1,808	3,714	2,835
Building and contracting	131	73	36	29	25	7	5
Mining and quarrying	612	508	338	862	889	2,495	644
Metals, engineering and shipbuilding	332	163	556	526	635	1,048	528
Textiles	100	77	36	26	17	47	10
Clothing	13	40	16	19	7	5	68
Transport and communications	56	13	54	35	181	85	1,491
Other industries and services	112	66	43	30	54	27	89

1. Stoppages involving fewer than ten workers or lasting less than one day have been omitted except when the aggregate number of working days lost exceeded 100.
2. The figures relate to stoppages beginning in the years shown and the figures for working days lost include days lost in subsequent years where the stoppage extended into the following calendar year
3. This analysis shows the total working days lost within each year as a result of stoppages in progress in that year whcther beginning in that or an earlier year.

Source: Ministry of Labour and National Service

4 AGRICULTURE AND FOOD

Before the war more than 22 million tons of food and animal feeding-stuffs were imported into the UK but by 1942 less than 11 million tons were being imported (Hammond 1951: 392); thus, between 1939 and 1942 imports of butter and sugar fell by roughly two-thirds and wheat imports fell by a third (**table 8.8**). The loss of food imports was partly due to the loss of access to markets controlled by the Axis powers, and to enemy action, but the main factors were financial constraints (at least until the advent of Lend-lease in March 1941) and the need to economise on scarce shipping capacity (**tables 4.19-4.20**). State policy towards the agricultural sector was driven by two related concerns: the need to increase domestic production to replace the loss of imported foodstuffs and the desire to maintain a high nutritional level for the population. This in turn meant that the state was less concerned with the volume of agricultural output and more concerned about its calorific output (Murray 1955: 241).

The consequence of this for domestic production was that arable farming was encouraged at the expense of livestock farming. Thus, in Britain between 1939 and 1943 arable production increased (wheat production by 81 per cent, potatoes by 92 per cent, fodder crops by 27 per cent and vegetables by 30 per cent) whilst livestock numbers, with the exception of cattle (because of the importance of milk output), fell (the pig population by 58 per cent, sheep and lambs by 24 per cent and poultry by 45 per cent)' (**tables 4.1-4.9**). There were also significant gains in yields per acre in arable farming, particularly in grain production (**table 4.7**). Even more impressive than the increases in yield per acre was the performance of the agricultural sector in terms of food value: net calorie output increased by 91 per cent during the war and calorific reliance on imports was cut from 70 per cent to 60 per cent (Murray 1955: 242).

4.1 Estimated food supplies per head of civilian population

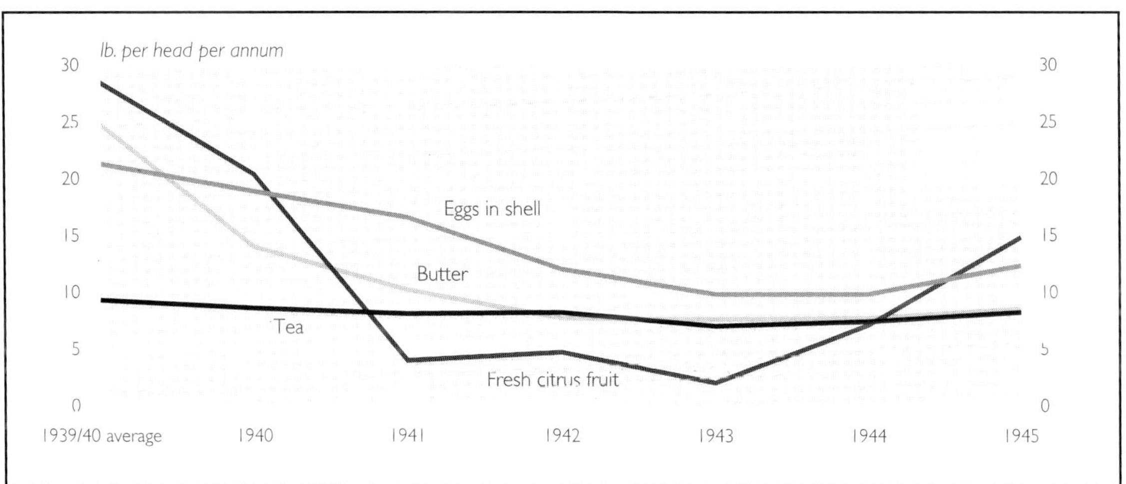

4.2 Estimated food supplies per head of civilian population

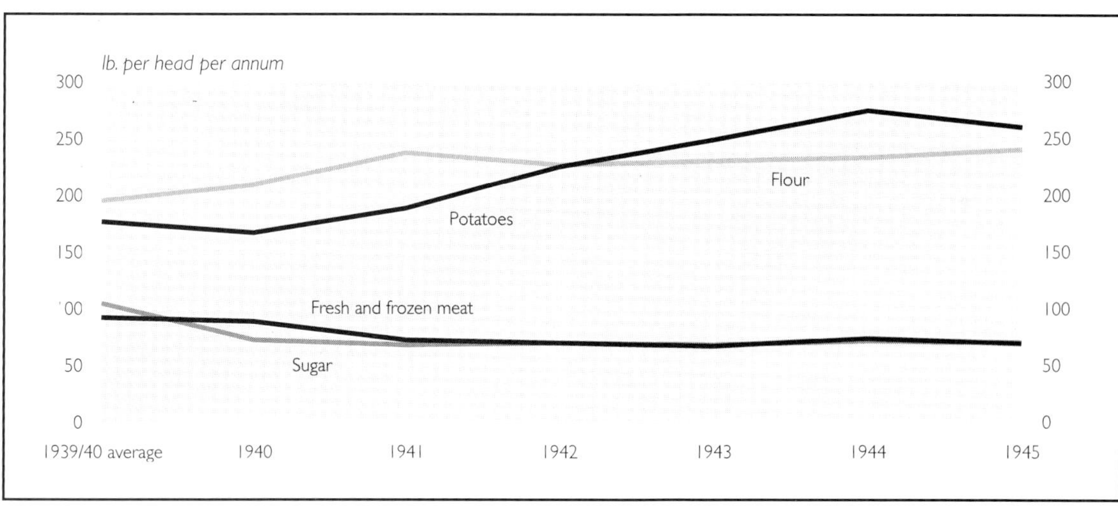

The increases in wartime agricultural output were probably a reflection of increased inputs of land and capital rather than an improved labour input. Although employment in agriculture did increase during the war many of these new workers were inexperienced in agriculture (such as the female recruits of the Women's Land Army and prisoners-of-war) or were working in new sectors within agriculture (i.e., the experienced livestock workers who were transferred to the arable sector) and thus it is likely that the quality of the labour input declined (Williams 1954: 333-5; **table 3.12**). Increases in the amount of arable land from 11.9 million acres in 1939 to 17.9 million acres in 1944 (the result of the 'ploughing-up' campaign promoted by the state) undoubtedly helped raise output, although this was mirrored by a decline in the area devoted to permanent grasslands (reflecting the declining importance of livestock) (**table 4.3**). The key to increased output and yields was, however, the greater use made by farmers of fertilisers and machinery, and their growing acceptance of scientific methods of production and modern methods of farm management (Pollard 1983: 206; **tables 4.12, 6.15 and 7.30**; Murray 1955: 243-4).

The state played a key role in agriculture during the war both in terms of the support and encouragement it offered to farmers and in terms of the food policy it pursued towards consumers. State support to farmers came in two main forms: first, through central direction and financial incentives (in the forms of subsidies and grants) the state encouraged farmers to make improvements to their land and to make greater and more effective use of fertilisers and machinery; second, price incentives were used to encourage production (Pollard 1983: 206). The increased prices paid to farmers were not passed on to consumers and this led to a massive rise in the food subsidy borne by the state: over the course of the war the net annual cost of food subsidies borne by the Ministry of Food rose from £13 million to £162 million (Hammond 1951: 398).

Another important prop of wartime food policy was rationing (Howlett 1994a: 291-2). This was primarily used as an anti-inflationary tool and, by being seen to promote equality, it also served as a method of social control. However, another important function of rationing was to make the best possible use of the limited food supplies, which included a successful attempt to ensure that the nutritional status of the population did not deteriorate (Milward 1977: 281). Rationing was first introduced in 1940 and by the end of the war had been extended so that it encompassed most basic foodstuffs, petrol, clothing, and other consumer goods. The inflationary pressures present in the economy following the end of the war meant that the state continued rationing into the postwar period and even extended it (bread, for example, was first rationed in 1946) and for many foodstuffs rationing did not end until the mid-1950s.

4.3 Area of crops and grassland

Great Britain — *Thousand acres*

	1936-38 average	1939	1940	1941	1942	1943	1944	1945
Crops and grass[1]								
Total	29,359	29,201	29,098	29,057	28,926	28,807	28,745	28,758
Arable land	11,991	11,870	13,203	14,991	16,175	17,387	17,936	17,866
Permanent grassland	17,368	17,331	15,089	14,066	12,752	11,420	10,809	10,892
Tillage								
Total	8,471	8,342	9,826	11,916	12,839	13,659	13,708	13,063
Wheat	1,851	1,763	1,797	2,247	2,504	3,451	3,215	2,272
Barley	926	1,010	1,321	1,457	1,513	1,771	1,957	2,201
Oats	2,130	2,135	3,002	3,501	3,658	3,210	3,215	3,305
Mixed corn	96	85	258	529	529	485	415	435
Rye (threshed)	15	14	17	40	58	128	119	79
Potatoes	597	589	695	966	1,116	1,193	1,219	1,207
Sugar beet	335	345	329	351	425	417	431	417
Fodder crops:								
Beans	119	135	90	193	222	248	286	206
Peas	40	37	38	64	69	64	57	46
Turnips and swedes	753	688	720	808	832	806	798	793
Mangolds	226	215	229	265	268	285	307	307
Other	297	284	332	482	514	502	523	506
Hops	18	19	19	18	18	19	20	20
Mustard (seed)	27	24	24	17	22	16	13	18
Flax for fibre (as straw)	1	2	18	38	45	52	60	44
Fruit	299	293	291	300	292	291	288	285
Vegetables	277	290	301	371	418	419	499	508
Flowers and nursery stock	24	25	18	14	12	9	9	11
Other crops	17	18	20	35	44	52	47	56
Bare fallow	423	374	306	219	280	240	231	347
Temporary grassland								
Total	3,520	3,528	3,376	3,075	3,336	3,728	4,228	4,803
For hay	1,730	1,689	1,698	1,547	1,858	2,095	2,266	2,589
For grazing	1,790	1,838	1,678	1,528	1,478	1,633	1,962	2,213
Permanent grassland								
Total	17,368	17,331	15,896	14,066	12,752	11,420	10,809	10,892
For hay	4,699	4,786	4,398	3,883	3,343	2,811	2,433	2,524
For grazing	12,669	12,545	11,497	10,184	9,409	8,609	8,379	8,369
Rough grazings	15,944	16,006	15,995	16,344	16,289	16,420	16,278	16,554

1. Excluding rough grazings.

Source: Agricultural Department

4.4 Area of crops and grassland

Northern Ireland | *Thousand acres*

	1936-38 average	1939	1940	1941	1942	1943	1944	1945
Crops land grass[1]								
Total	2,478	2,478	2,331	2,296	2,277	2,252	2,263	2,265
Arable land	1,097	1,036	1,143	1,249	1,323	1,341	1,337	1,318
Permanent grassland	1,382	1,442	1,188	1,047	955	910	926	947
Tillage								
Total	472	471	660	798	828	851	840	786
Wheat	6	3	12	18	12	14	5	2
Barley	3	3	18	18	15	14	16	14
Oats	273	291	397	449	475	470	441	448
Mixed corn	-	-	5	15	17	15	9	7
Rye (threshed)	-	-	-	-	-	1	1	1
Potatoes	127	115	137	157	187	197	198	190
Fodder crops:								
Beans	-	-	1	2	1	1	2	1
Turnips and swedes	29	23	26	29	26	24	22	21
Mangolds	1	1	2	2	2	1	1	1
Other	1	1	2	3	4	4	4	4
Flax for fibre (as straw)	22	21	46	90	73	93	125	80
Fruit	8	8	9	10	10	10	10	10
Vegetables	2	2	3	4	4	4	4	4
Other crops	1	1	1	1	1	2	2	2
Temporary grassland								
Total	625	565	483	451	495	491	497	532
For hay	209	212	211	202	245	238	225	240
For grazing	416	353	272	249	250	252	272	291
Permanent grassland								
Total	1,382	1,442	1,188	1,047	955	910	926	947
For hay	216	1,223	221	199	191	180	180	179
For grazing	1,165	1,218	968	848	764	730	746	769
Rough grazings	533	534	644	659	670	700	707	706

1. Excluding rough grazings.

Source: Ministry of Agriculture, Northern Ireland

4.5 Estimated quantity of crops and grass harvested

Great Britain — *Thousand tons*

	1936-38 average	1939	1940	1941	1942	1943	1944	1945
Wheat	1,646	1,642	1,628	2,000	2,556	3,435	3,134	2,174
Barley	762	889	1,089	1,127	1,432	1,632	1,737	2,096
Oats	1,676	1,733	2,514	2,815	3,125	2,670	2,574	2,862
Mixed corn	76	73	222	423	447	380	341	366
Rye (grain)	10	10	11	26	45	94	87	58
Potatoes	4,085	4,354	5,375	6,783	8,162	8,537	8,026	8,702
Sugar beet	2,741	3,529	3,176	3,226	3,923	3,760	3,267	3,886
Fodder crops:								
Beans	96	111	54	153	162	194	190	161
Peas	29	23	30	42	51	43	33	31
Turnips and swedes	10,557	9,699	10,366	11,570	12,844	11,677	11,811	11,946
Mangolds	4,065	4,050	4,229	5,090	5,404	5,785	5,543	6,508
Straw:								
Wheat	2,062	1,986	1,854	2,347	2,810	3,759	3,327	2,304
Barley	720	838	961	1,083	1,282	1,425	1,492	1,776
Oat	2,212	2,227	2,858	3,515	3,805	3,197	3,072	3,263
Hops	13	14	14	13	13	14	13	14
Mustard (seed)	11	11	9	6	9	5	4	6
Flax for fibre (as straw)	2	3	30	61	79	107	105	90
Fruit	428	797	558	293	714	644	612	450
Vegetables	2,355	2,389	2,596	2,851	3,659	3,113	3,387	1,213
Hay from temporary grassland	2,337	2,273	2,315	2,139	2,669	3,038	2,894	3,843
Hay from permanent grassland	4,539	4,783	3,898	3,786	3,233	2,844	2,093	2,659

Source: Agricultural Departments

4.6 Estimated quantity of crops and grass harvested

Northern Ireland — *Thousand tons*

	1936-38 average	1939	1940	1941	1942	1943	1944	1945
Wheat	6	3	13	18	11	12	4	2
Barley	3	3	15	17	14	13	15	12
Oats	264	270	378	432	428	394	379	383
Mixed corn	-	-	4	15	16	14	8	6
Rye (grain)	-	-	-	-	-	1	1	1
Potatoes	788	864	1,030	1,221	1,231	1,285	1,070	1,089
Fodder crops:								
Beans	-	-	-	1	1	1	1	1
Turnips and swedes	433	385	448	466	380	336	318	324
Mangolds	17	19	29	30	22	20	17	16
Straw:								
Wheat	8	4	15	23	14	16	6	2
Barley	3	4	18	19	16	15	19	15
Oat	382	383	528	579	585	557	553	537
Mixed corn	-	1	6	20	21	18	11	9
Flax for fibre (as straw)	43	42	93	180	146	187	249	161
Fruit	23	27	25	28	35	13	54	7
Vegetables	15	13	21	32	31	30	35	29
Hay from temporary grassland	339	315	338	314	387	400	344	352
Hay from permanent grassland	458	419	460	390	371	387	359	338

Source: Ministry of Agriculture, Northern Ireland

4.7 Estimated yield per acre

Great Britain

	Unit	1936-38 average	1939	1940	1941	1942	1943	1944	1945
Wheat	Cwts.	17.7	18.6	18.1	17.8	20.4	19.9	19.5	19.1
Barley	"	16.4	17.6	16.5	15.5	18.9	18.4	17.7	19.0
Oats	"	15.7	16.2	16.8	16.1	17.1	16.6	16.0	17.3
Mixed corn	"	15.8	17.2	17.2	16.1	17.0	15.7	16.5	16.8
Rye (grain)	"	12.5	13.7	12.6	13.2	15.4	14.7	14.7	14.6
Potatoes	Tons	6.9	7.4	7.7	7.0	7.3	7.2	6.6	7.2
Sugar beet	"	8.2	10.3	9.7	9.3	9.3	9.1	7.7	9.4
Fodder crops:									
Beans	Cwts.	16.3	16.4	12.0	16.0	14.7	15.8	13.4	15.7
Peas	"	14.6	12.7	16.0	13.3	15.2	13.7	12.3	13.6
Turnips and swedes	Tons	14.1	14.1	14.4	14.3	15.4	14.5	14.9	15.1
Mangolds	"	18.0	18.9	18.5	19.3	20.3	20.4	18.1	21.3
Straw:									
Wheat	Cwts.	22.3	22.5	20.6	20.9	22.4	21.8	20.7	20.3
Barley	"	15.5	16.6	14.5	14.9	17.0	16.1	15.2	16.1
Oat	"	20.8	20.9	19.0	20.1	20.8	19.9	19.1	19.8
Hops	"	13.5	15.3	14.5	14.5	14.2	14.9	13.0	14.1
Mustard (seed)	"	8.5	9.3	7.6	6.9	8.7	7.0	7.1	7.6
Flax for fibre (as straw)	Tons	1.8	1.8	1.6	1.6	1.7	2.0	1.9	2.0
Hay from temporary grassland	Cwts.	26.9	26.9	27.3	27.7	28.8	29.0	25.5	29.7
Hay from permanent grassland	"	19.2	20.0	17.7	19.5	19.4	20.2	17.2	21.1

Source: Agricultural Departments

4.8 Estimated yield per acre

Northern Ireland

	Unit	1936-38 average	1939	1940	1941	1942	1943	1944	1945
Wheat	Cwts.	20.7	20.4	21.5	20.6	18.5	17.6	17.9	17.5
Barley	"	19.0	17.8	17.0	19.6	18.1	17.9	18.4	17.4
Oats	"	19.3	18.5	19.0	19.2	18.0	16.8	17.2	17.1
Mixed corn	"	-	18.5	18.7	19.1	18.5	17.7	17.9	17.7
Rye (grain)	"	12.5	13.7	12.6	13.2	15.4	14.8	14.7	14.7
Potatoes	Tons	6.2	7.5	7.5	7.8	6.6	6.5	5.4	5.7
Fodder crops:									
Beans	Cwts.	16.3	16.4	12.2	15.9	14.6	15.7	13.2	15.6
Peas	"	-	-	-	13.5	15.3	13.7	12.6	13.6
Turnips and swedes	Tons	15.0	16.4	16.9	16.3	14.8	14.2	14.5	15.2
Mangolds	"	15.8	16.3	17.2	15.3	14.0	14.4	14.6	14.3
Straw:									
Wheat	Cwts.	27.8	24.8	25.6	26.7	23.0	23.3	25.4	24.7
Barley	"	23.5	20.5	20.5	22.1	20.7	21.2	24.0	21.4
Oat	"	27.9	26.3	26.6	25.8	24.6	23.7	25.1	24.0
Mixed corn	"	-	26.3	26.6	25.8	24.6	23.7	25.1	24.0
Flax for fibre (as straw)	Tons	2.0	2.0	2.0	2.0	2.0	2.0	2.0	2.0
Hay from temporary grassland	Cwts.	32.4	29.7	32.0	31.1	31.7	33.6	30.5	29.3
Hay from permanent grassland	"	42.3	37.5	41.7	39.2	38.9	42.9	39.9	37.8

Source: Ministry of Agriculture, Northern Ireland

4.9 Number of cattle, sheep, pigs and poultry on agricultural holdings

Great Britain — At June in each year — *Thousands*

	1936	1937	1938	1939	1940	1941	1942	1943	1944	1945
Cattle										
Total	7,853	7,909	8,030	8,119	8,361	8,153	8,248	8,428	8,616	8,697
Cows and heifers in milk	2,596	2,583	2,606	2,628	2,647	2,667	2,587	2,674	2,686	2,673
Cows in calf but not in milk	461	450	429	447	455	489	545	596	605	576
Heifers in calf with first calf	514	530	541	539	596	552	751	729	744	747
Bulls being used for service	101	104	106	109	110	111	120	126	127	129
Other cattle:										
Two years old and over	1,109	1,117	1,099	1,144	1,214	1,056	1,086	1,092	1,188	1,311
One year and under two	1,583	1,590	1,601	1,677	1,671	1,702	1,513	1,556	1,591	1,634
Under one year	1,490	1,535	1,649	1,575	1,667	1,577	1,646	1,654	1,674	1,628
Sheep and lambs										
Total	24,205	24,712	25,882	25,993	25,465	21,445	20,764	19,700	19,435	19,496
Ewes for breeding	10,548	10,606	10,406	10,572	10,309	8,865	8,520	7,899	7,820	7,916
Rams for service	327	338	296	305	298	249	246	237	235	234
Other sheep:										
One year old and over	2,315	2,120	3,825	3,451	3,734	3,407	2,982	3,109	3,167	3,218
Under one year	11,015	11,649	11,355	11,664	11,125	8,924	9,016	8,454	8,213	8,127
Pigs										
Total	4,040	3,883	3,822	3,767	3,631	2,207	1,872	1,571	1,631	1,903
Sows for breeding	512	487	463	479	426	216	221	162	226	218
Boars for service	37	35	33	33	30	18	18	15	19	19
Other pigs:										
Five months old and over				677	827	633	547	573	487	628
Two months and under five	3,491	3,361	3,326	1,616	1,567	933	679	515	522	651
Under two months				963	781	408	406	307	377	386
Poultry										
Total	70,005	63,704	64,053	64,137	62,121	49,126	43,212	35,299	38,481	44,665
Total fowls	65,698	59,830	59,920	60,234	58,545	46,233	40,160	32,241	34,986	40,615
Six months and over	29,142	27,997	26,475	26,610	29,554	28,418	20,446	16,247	15,976	17,533
Under six months	36,556	31,833	33,445	33,624	28,991	17,815	19,714	15,994	19,010	23,083
Ducks	2,843	2,499	2,564	2,467	2,263	1,796	1,981	1,939	2,234	2,542
Geese	661	577	634	611	608	620	648	707	779	866
Turkeys	804	797	934	825	705	477	423	411	483	542

Source: Agricultural Departments

4.10 Number of cattle, sheep, pigs and poultry on agricultural holding

Northern Ireland — At June in each year — *Thousands*

	1936	1937	1938	1939	1940	1941	1942	1943	1944	1945
Cattle										
Total	770	730	732	753	732	787	827	832	886	919
Cows and heifers in milk	250	237	229	213	202	211	222	236	242	245
Cows in calf but not in milk	..[1]	..[1]	..[1]	32	33	35	43	44	47	49
Heifers in calf with first calf	25	23	30	25	24	34	51	44	50	53
Bulls being used for service	5	4	5	5	5	4	5	5	5	5
Other cattle:										
Two years old and over	81	75	85	85	87	111	128	134	155	186
One year and under two	199	194	191	190	186	191	180	170	179	180
Under one year	210	198	192	204	196	200	197	198	208	201
Sheep and lambs										
Total	835	829	893	895	854	812	742	683	672	654
Ewes for breeding	382	377	402	403	854	364	332	301	300	295
Rams for service	11	10	13	12	12	11	10	9	10	9
Other sheep:										
One year old and over	39	36	46	43	51	71	60	61	65	71
Under one year	403	406	433	437	413	366	340	312	297	279
Pigs										
Total	522	570	561	627	475	351	271	257	237	249
Sows for breeding	57	54	58	63	42	29	28	24	26	27
Boars for service	2	2	2	2	1	0.6	0.5	0.3	0.4	0.4
Other pigs:										
Five months old and over			83	90	93	78	65	41	31	34
Two months and under five	463	514	230	255	212	181	133	153	142	149
Under two months			189	217	128	61	45	40	38	39
Poultry										
Total	10,570	10,182	10,193	10,220	9,122	12,933	14,601	15,430	16,646	17,471
Fowls	9,543	9,222	9,199	9,295	8,120	11,850	13,342	14,130	15.256	16,050
Ducks	499	428	425	415	396	530	664	701	759	794
Geese	139	112	113	104	103	115	118	114	123	124
Turkeys	389	420	456	406	413	438	478	485	508	504

1. Included with "other cattle".

Source: Ministry of Agriculture, Northern Ireland

4.11 Horses grazed on agricultural land

At June in each year — *Thousands*

	1936	1937	1938	1939	1940	1941	1942	1943	1944	1945
Great Britain										
Total	1,013	1,005	1,002	987	959	962	917	871	829	796
Used for agricultural purposes[1]	672	663	668	649	642	667	585	616	577	545
Unbroken horses:										
One year old and over	108	114	122	131	126	114	105	90	87	87
Under one year	57	61	60	57	50	42	39	37	87	34
Stallions being used for service	4	4	5	5	4	3	3	3	3	3
Other[2]	171	162	148	146	136	136	184	125	126	127
Northern Ireland										
Total	99	98	99	97	97	97	95	90	88	85
Used for agricultural purposes[1]	81	81	80	76	77	80	80	77	75	72
Unbroken horses:										
One year old and over[3]	5	6	7	9	8	7	6	5	4	4
Under one year	4	4	5	5	4	3	3	2	3	3
Other[2]	8	7	6	8	8	7	7	6	6	6

1. Including mares kept for breeding.
2. Including all other horses grazed on agricultural holdings exceeding one acre in Great Britain, or one quarter of an acre in Northern Ireland regardless of the use to which they are put.
3. Including stallions being used for service.

Source: Agricultural Departments

4.12 Agricultural tractors, machines and implements in use[1]

Great Britain — *Number*

	1942 May	1944 April	1946 January
Tractors:			
Total	116,830	173,370	203,420
Tracklayers	5,600	9,090	12,350
Three and four-wheeled	104,780	153,350	175,050
Two-wheeled market garden type	6,450	10,930	16,020
Mouldboard ploughs:			
Total	465,630	466,860	482,190
Horse drawn	353,180	312,710	303,240
Tractor drawn	112,450	154,150	178,950
Disc harrows	33,840	58,860	65,200
Cultivators or grubbers	161,690	191,410	247,790
Toolbars	14,340	23,100	33,710
Corn drills[2]	101,550	108,640	115,510
Mowing machines	220,420	210,590	228,320
Binders	131,600	144,040	149,500
Threshing machines	13,150[3]	14,960[3]	14,960
Combined harvester-threshers	1,000	2,500	3,800[3]
Potato spinners	37,030	53,460	59,470
Milking machines	29,510	37,790	48,290

1. Owned by farmers, contractors, the agricultural executive committees and the Department of Agriculture for Scotland.
2. Including combined seed and fertilizer drills.
3. Estimated numbers in use at harvest.

Source: Agricultural Departments

4.13 Movement off farms of cereals, potatoes and sugar beet

Weekly averages — *Thousand tons*

	Year	Jan*	Feb	Mar	Apr*	May	Jun	Jul*	Aug	Sep	Oct*	Nov	Dec
Cereals:													
Wheat [1]													
1940	18.3	22.8	24.0	19.8	13.4	12.5	5.5	2.4	21.8	31.3	25.6	23.0	20.5
1941	18.4	20.0	19.5	18.3	12.2	10.0	6.5	2.0	4.3	31.0	34.0	33.0	31.0
1942	31.1	33.2	48.8	49.8	32.8	29.3	10.5	1.8	8.8	36.8	41.4	43.5	40.3
1943	44.6	41.6	47.8	47.0	41.8	46.8	34.0	11.6	30.8	62.3	61.8	60.5	53.0*
1944	47.9	64.0	67.0	70.0	58.8	57.8	38.5	14.0	38.0	49.5	43.6	39.5	37.0
1945	39.6	44.4	52.5	50.5	50.8	45.8	44.5	18.6	30.3	50.5	32.2	30.5	28.3
Barley [2]													
1941	13.6	..	..	..	..	..	..	1.2	2.0	21.8	23.0	28.3	30.0
1942	17.2	22.8	23.0	18.0	7.0	3.8	2.3	1.0	9.5	37.5	23.0	29.0	33.3
1943	24.8	30.4	32.3	30.0	16.2	11.5	6.5	6.8	34.8	36.3	28.6	39.0	29.2*
1944	23.7	30.2	30.8	27.3	15.0	10.3	5.5	4.0	28.5	42.0	32.6	31.3	30.5
1945	32.1	28.6	35.3	35.0	22.8	14.8	9.3	6.8	45.8	55.8	44.0	47.5	46.3
Oats [2]													
1941	4.5	..	..	..	..	..	..	1.7	1.2	5.6	6.2	7.8	8.3
1942	8.1	7.2	8.8	9.5	7.0	6.8	6.8	4.6	5.3	5.5	10.2	13.3	13.0
1943	10.8	14.0	15.5	16.0	14.2	14.5	11.8	8.6	4.8	3.3	8.8	9.0	9.8*
1944	6.9	9.6	9.8	8.8	8.0	5.8	6.0	4.0	2.8	5.3	7.2	8.3	7.5
1945	6.7	5.6	6.5	5.8	5.4	4.3	4.5	2.8	3.5	9.8	10.2	11.5	11.0
Potatoes [2]													
1940	63.9	67.4	72.0	68.5	72.2	54.8	38.0	54.4	53.5	60.5	69.8	72.8	80.5
1941	80.4	83.6	98.0	100.5	95.6	96.5	59.3	54.8	71.5	68.5	75.4	78.0	85.8
1942	97.1	87.6	121.3	112.3	88.6	90.8	94.0	98.8	81.3	92.3	91.2	102.3	110.5
1943	113.9	116.0	118.0	115.5	123.6	128.5	114.0	117.0	92.5	98.3	102.4	113.0	124.6*
1944	122.8	139.8	141.0	140.5	142.2	110.0	113.3	107.0	103.0	116.0	114.2	123.3	120.8
1945	118.2	117.6	150.5	123.5	127.4	104.0	89.3	101.2	102.8	127.5	117.6	137.5	121.8
Sugar [3]													
1939	9.5	1.1	-	-	-	-	-	-	-	0.8	27.8	36.5	33.6
1940	9.6 [4]	12.8	-	-	-	-	-	-	-	-	31.5	34.3	33.8
1941	8.1	10.0	-	-	-	-	-	-	-	-	19.4	35.0	32.9
1942	9.1	18.2	0.7	-	-	-	-	-	-	-	22.8	35.9	31.7
1943	10.5	24.3	4.5	-	-	-	-	-	-	-	26.2	32.7	31.2*
1944	7.5	14.4	0.5	-	-	-	-	-	-	0.3	20.9	28.5	24.3
1945	8.6	13.9	0.4	-	-	-	-	-	-	-	27.0	33.9	26.9

1. Receipts by flour millers.
2. For human consumption, processing and stock feeding under Ministry schemes.
3. Production of refined sugar from home-grown sugar beet.
4. Year ended January 1940.

* Average of five weeks.

Source: Ministry of Food

4.14 Animals purchased for slaughter[1]

Weekly averages — *Thousand*

	Year	Jan*	Feb	Mar	Apr*	May	Jun	Jul*	Aug	Sept	Oct*	Nov	Dec
Cattle:													
Total													
1939	42.0	..	..	..	..	..	..	..	..	..	..	..	..
1940	38.7	42.8	34.6	37.7	36.7	28.6	30.0	31.0	42.0	57.6	57.1	37.2	25.9
1941	36.8	36.1	41.3	36.2	34.2	34.2	31.7	33.8	40.4	36.1	39.9	46.3	32.5
1942	30.9	25.7	22.3	25.2	28.2	31.1	27.8	30.6	37.7	37.8	44.7	35.2	22.9
1943	30.1	21.4	23.6	28.4	33.8	39.5	33.6	30.6	37.9	32.5	34.2	28.8	20.0*
1944	33.5	20.8	24.3	29.7	36.1	36.3	28.8	36.4	38.0	40.4	46.8	39.5	23.6
1945	35.9	22.9	27.8	28.5	32.1	29.8	24.8	45.4	47.5	51.6	49.3	44.9	24.8
Imported fat cattle													
1939	3.7	..	..	..	..	..	..	..	..	..	..	..	..
1940	2.9	5.0	3.5	2.3	1.2	0.3	1.3	2.9	2.8	4.9	4.1	3.8	2.1
1941	5.7	2.5	3.5	2.3	1.5	0.4	1.8	4.9	5.9	7.0	9.4	15.9	14.0
1942	3.8	9.3	3.0	1.1	0.7	0.3	1.7	6.7	5.9	5.0	4.6	3.4	2.1
1943	1.5	0.8	1.4	0.8	0.3	-	1.7	3.1	3.0	3.6	2.5	1.1	0.2 *
1944	2.2	-	-	-	-	-	0.6	4.9	4.0	5.5	5.4	3.5	2.1
1945	3.3	0.8	0.9	0.2	-	-	1.6	7.1	6.6	8.1	4.4	6.3	3.3
Home fed cattle:													
Steers and heifers[2]													
Home-bred													
1940	17.1	15.1	16.6	17.9	17.6	13.9	14.0	11.9	18.6	27.1	26.6	14.3	10.7
1941	16.0	16.1	19.5	17.0	16.7	18.0	16.0	13.5	18.1	16.3	16.1	15.9	9.4
1942	14.8	8.4	10.7	14.5	17.3	19.9	15.6	12.4	16.9	17.8	21.4	14.6	8.6
1943	13.0	8.1	9.6	12.9	16.5	20.9	16.1	13.0	17.3	14.1	13.6	9.3	5.9*
1944	13.3	7.0	9.2	12.7	16.8	17.9	12.4	13.9	15.7	15.9	17.6	13.5	6.4
1945	14.5	7.3	10.5	12.2	15.1	14.3	9.3	18.4	20.6	21.9	20 6	15.9	7.6
Imported from Eire as stores													
1940	8.4	10.0	7.8	8.2	8.3	6.6	6.1	6.1	10.0	13.4	12.3	6.7	4.7
1941	4.6	7.0	7.5	7.0	6.9	6.6	5.1	3.3	3.9	3.1	2.2	2.0	1.0
1942	3.3	1.0	1.2	2.0	3.0	3.9	3.5	3.4	5.1	5.7	5.4	3.3	2.0
1943	5.1	2.5	3.5	6.0	8.5	10.2	7.2	5.5	7.5	4.3	3.6	2.1	1.3 *
1944	5.6	2.6	4.6	6.7	9.8	9.5	5.7	6.5	7.3	5.5	4.4	2.6	1.3
1945	5.6	2.5	4.2	6.1	8.8	8.0	4.1	7.8	8.3	7.0	5.0	3.2	1.5
Cows, bulls and others													
1940	10.3	12.7	6.7	9.3	9.5	7.8	8.6	10.1	10.6	12.2	14.1	12.5	8.5
1941	10.5	10.5	10.8	9.9	9.1	9.2	8.8	12.1	12.5	9.7	12.2	12.5	8.1
1942	9.0	7.0	7.4	7.6	7.2	7.0	7.0	8.1	9.8	9.3	13.3	13.9	10.2
1943	10.5	10.0	9.1	8.7	8.5	8.4	8.6	9.0	10.1	10.5	14.4	16.3	12.6*
1944	12.4	11.2	10.5	10.3	9.5	8.9	10.1	11.1	11.0	13.5	19.4	19.9	13.8
1945	12.5	12.3	12.2	10.0	8.2	7.5	9.8	12.1	12.0	14.6	19.3	19.5	12.4

See footnotes on page 76.

Source: Ministry of Food

4.14 Animals purchased for slaughter[1]

continued

Weekly averages — *Thousands*

	Year	Jan*	Feb	Mar	Apr*	May	Jun	Jul*	Aug	Sep	Oct*	Nov	Dec
Calves													
1939	15.4	..	..	..	..	..	..	..	..	..	..	..	..
1940	16.5	10.4	19.0	21.4	19.1	12.5	11.6	15.6	16.1	20.9	21.6	15.9	14.4
1941	20.3	18.7	22.6	27.8	28.1	23.2	19.6	20.2	17.2	17.3	18.6	16.0	13.6
1942	21.5	16.3	20.8	28.0	25.4	20.5	16.9	19.6	19.7	22.5	26.7	22.0	19.0
1943	25.5	23.1	26.8	36.3	31.7	23.2	17.6	17.6	20.0	26.0	31.3	29.4	23.6*
1944	25.9	24.9	30.2	36.0	25.2	15.9	14.9	17.3	22.1	30.0	36.6	33.2	24.2
1945	26.9	28.7	34.4	36.1	25.8	16.7	14.0	17.6	21.3	31.0	38.3	32.8	25.0
Sheep and lambs													
1939	227.1	..	..	..	..	..	..	..	..	..	..	..	..
1940	212.5	154.4	168.6	158.7	94.3	100.3	152.3	242.6	288.1	328.8	376.1	294.5	186.5
1941	158.4	186.7	149.0	142.9	141.0	101.3	106.4	172.5	172.9	139.3	149.5	264.8	170.1
1942	152.5	169.9	145.8	142.4	126.8	86.7	70.4	113.8	142.6	145.2	223.5	266.4	190.6
1943	140.7	181.7	139.7	136.9	139.6	89.9	72.5	83.5	102.5	121.3	162.7	232.3	207.6*
1944	127.2	166.9	149.8	137.7	86.1	63.7	56.2	75.5	87.8	111.0	181.2	238.1	172.7
1945	121.4	163.5	131.3	131.7	97.2	64.2	48.6	65.0	83.2	120.3	160.7	221.0	169.3
Pigs[3]:													
Baconers													
1939	41.8	..	..	..	..	..	..	..	..	..	..	..	..
1940	49.4	17.8	21.9	42.4	46.0	57.6	63.0	53.6	60.7	64.3	56.1	59.4	56.8
1941	39.6	54.6	58.3	59.9	57.9	36.9	37.4	34.0	28.6	25.0	25.1	26.4	27.5
1942	24.4	25.8	24.8	26.5	25.6	25.8	26.9	25.8	22.7	21.6	20.9	22.6	23.8
1943	22.4	23.4	22.0	24.3	26.3	26.7	27.0	25.8	21.8	19.4	17.7	17.6	17.1*
1944	18.8	16.4	18.0	17.9	20.6	21.1	19.3	20.5	17.9	17.2	17.7	19.1	19.8
1945	25.9	20.4	25.0	27.0	29.6	29.2	29.4	33.3	25.2	24.0	22.3	22.7	21.9
Porkers[4]													
1940	30.6	12.0	47.2	48.9	48.4	40.0	31.1	26.9	18.1	29.7	28.6	19.3	18.8
1941	12.9	22.5	25.2	26.2	26.5	14.5	10.6	7.7	5.3	4.0	3.6	3.3	3.6
1942	3.2	3.7	4.0	4.2	3.7	2.5	2.2	2.4	2.5	2.9	2.8	3.8	4.0
1943	2.4	4.4	4.0	3.9	3.1	2.5	2.1	1.7	1.6	1.5	1.2	1.4	1.5*
1944	2.0	1.2	1.6	1.2	1.5	1.8	1.7	1.9	2.3	2.4	2.3	2.6	3.5
1945	3.5	4.4	4.8	4.2	4.3	3.1	2.1	7.7	2.8	2.0	1.9	2.2	2.1
Sows, boars and other[4]													
1940	9.5	5.4	10.2	14.2	13.2	9.9	8.7	8.8	9.2	11.0	7.4	8.3	7.9
1941	5.0	8.3	9.6	8.6	8.9	5.5	4.5	3.6	2.6	2.0	1.7	1.7	1.6
1942	1.9	1.6	1.7	2.0	2.0	2.0	1.7	1.7	1.7	1.8	1.8	2.1	2.3
1943	1.5	2.5	2.3	2.1	2.0	1.7	1.5	1.3	1.0	0.8	0.8	0.9	0.9*
1944	2.0	0.9	0.9	1.1	1.3	2.0	4.0	4.1	2.6	1.8	1.7	1.9	1.9
1945	2.2	2.1	2.7	3.0	2.9	2.5	2.4	2.3	1.9	1.7	1.6	1.8	1.5

1. Great Britain only. Fat cattle, sheep and lambs sent from Eire and Northern Ireland are included. Detailed records begin in January 1940; earlier figures are estimated.
2. Including cow-heifers.
3. Excluding pigs fattened by self suppliers.
4. The number of pigs other than baconers slaughtered in 1939 was 3,011 thousand (weekly average, 57.9).

* Average of five weeks.

Source: Ministry of Food

4.15 Milk: Sales through the Marketing Schemes

Monthly averages or calendar months — *Million gallons*

	Year	Jan	Feb	Mar	Apr	May	Jun	Jul	Aug	Sep	Oct	Nov	Dec
Total sales													
1939	108.3	90.1	85.8	100.0	107.2	130.3	131.2	128.8	124.6	114.3	108.0	91.8	87.6
1940	102.3	85.0	82.6	93.6	99.6	129.3	127.8	121.3	118.0	101.2	95.1	85.7	87.7
1941	101.9	88.3	83.2	97.7	100.3	121.4	127.7	119.5	110.9	103.8	100.5	86.5	83.5
1942	105.8	83.8	79.1	95.5	104.3	130.1	137.4	129.3	119.4	109.3	102.6	89.5	88.8
1943	112.0	90.9	86.6	105.1	117.5	147.0	145.6	132.6	118.0	106.4	104.4	94.2	95.8
1944	114.8	99.3	97.4	112.2	122.2	152.6	142.8	129.3	116.6	104.9	105.0	96.3	99.4
1945	118.7	101.9	96.9	115.8	130.0	155.3	145.6	133.9	121.2	106.7	109.3	102.0	105.6
Liquid sales													
1939	72.0	73.2	68.4	74.8	71.7	75.6	74.2	74.7	72.1	67.6	70.2	69.4	71.5
1940	78.1	73.2	70.0	74.6	74.4	77.6	77.4	77.9	80.9	80.1	83.9	82.9	84.2
1941	88.6	86.1	81.6	92.8	85.1	89.5	88.6	93.6	92.6	91.4	95.3	85.1	82.2
1942	92.9	82.7	76.1	87.7	90.0	97.4	101.7	105.0	100.9	98.2	99.1	88.5	87.0
1943	97.4	89.7	83.9	96.0	95.0	109.5	107.1	105.7	97.9	97.6	100.2	93.0	93.4
1944	100.4	95.7	91.1	98.0	95.9	113.2	110.7	105.0	101.4	100.4	103.1	95.2	95.4
1945	103.6	97.7	89.9	102.4	103.7	112.5	111.8	110.9	104.8	102.5	106.2	99.3	101.1
Used for manufacture[1]													
1939	36.3	16.9	17.4	25.2	35.5	54.7	57.0	54.1	52.5	46.7	37.8	22.4	16.1
1940	24.2	11.8	12.6	19.0	25.2	51.7	50.4	43.4	37.1	21.1	11.2	2.8	3.5
1941	13.3	2.2	1.6	4.9	15.2	31.9	39.1	25.9	18.3	12.4	5.2	1.4	1.3
1942	12.9	1.1	3.0	7.8	14.3	32.7	35.7	24.3	18.5	11.1	3.5	1.0	1.8
1943	14.6	1.2	2.7	9.1	22.5	37.5	38.5	26.9	20.1	8.8	4.2	1.2	2.4
1944	14.4	3.6	6.3	14.2	26.3	39.4	32.1	24.3	15.2	4.5	1.9	1.1	4.0
1945	15.1	4.2	7.0	13.4	26.3	42.8	33.8	23.3	16.4	4.2	3.1	2.7	4.5

1. Manufacture into m[illegible] products together with the quantity used on farms for cheese-making.

Source: Ministry of Food

4.16 Processed food: Production[1]

Thousand tons

	1939	1940	1941	1942	1943	1944	1945
Flour milling:							
Wheat milled	5,627[2]	5,973	6,067	5,326	5,026	5,348	5,716
Flour produced	3,939[2]	4,391	4,600	4,394	4,527[3]	4,470[3]	4,524
Offals produced	1,744[2]	1,676	1,535	905	866[3]	825[3]	1,106
Oat milling:							
Oats milled by oatmeal millers	..	..	219	314	449	396	321
Oatmeal produced	..	..	124	178	252	221	176
Seed crushing:							
Oilseeds and nuts processed	1,596	1,618	1,370	1,448	1,264	1,292	1,336
Crude oil produced	515	622	578	599	529	538	570
Oilcake and meal produced	1,082[4]	969	766	810	671	715	735
Vegetable oil consumption[5]							
Total disposals	..	787	819	768	696	745	782
For food	..	475	517	447	425	456	475
Whale, herring and seal oil consumption[5]:							
Total disposals	..	185	152	127	104	73	121
For food	..	157	128	108	86	55	93
Production of home-killed meat[6]:							
Total	1,180	1,072	902	772	754	783	812
Beef	602	557	523	453	445	487	517
Veal	23	25	28	28	33	32	34
Mutton and lamb	238	227	176	171	159	142	134
Pork[7]	201	155	74	29	27	30	34
Offal[7]	116	108	101	91	90	92	93
Production of bacon and ham[7]	199	207	174	121	123	139	149
Production of animal fats:							
Lard	..	8	4	3	2	2	3
Other edible fats	..	35	31	34	45	41	32
Production of milk products:							
Butter[8]	21	16	8	10	9	10	8
Cheese[9]	43	32	30	20	22	18	22
Condensed milk	..	178	72	96	97	111	94
Milk powder	..	15	9	14	23	23	29
Cream	33	15	-	-	-	-	-
Sugar: production from home-grown sugar-beet (as refined sugar)	487[10]	501	419	474	557	391	449
Production of compound edible fats:							
Margarine	226	359	419	406	392	399	406
Compound cooking fat	132	159	145	62	53	32	85
Production of other processed foods:							
Jam and marmalade	220[11]	72	86	195	324	192	273
Syrup and treacle	95[11]	72	86	82	96	108	106
Canned vegetables	160	190	209	195	177	192	204
Canned and bottled fruit	..	..	16	42	25	6	10
Canned meat	..	..	..	43	60	79	54
Canned fish	..	..	1	3	2	1	2
Biscuits	300	330	361	358	278	272	261
Breakfast cereals	..	..	45	47	45	47	47
Chocolate confectionery	..	173	187	162	145	148	127
Sugar confectionery	..	150	149	128	107	114	111
Cocoa and drinking chocolate	..	19	26	29	24	27	28
Starch	..	..	42	35	37	38	38
Pearl barley and barley products	4	13	16	12	13	19	27

1. Figures for 1939 relate to the calendar year except where otherwise: stated. From 1940 onwards figures are for periods of 52 weeks (53 weeks in 1943) except for condensed milk and milk powder.
2. Year ended 31 July.
3. Including small quantities produced from barley, rye and oats.
4. Including castor cake which is unfit for animal feed.
5. As crude oil.
6. Including production from fat cattle and fresh meat and offal imported from Eire.
7. Including meat and offal produced by pig clubs, etc.
8. Excluding farmhouse butter.
9. Including farmhouse cheese.
10. Year ended January 1940.
11. Year ended 30 June.

Source: Ministry of Food

4.17 Food and animal feeding stuffs: Consumption[1]

Thousand tons

	1940	1941	1942	1943	1944	1945
Cereal products and sugar:						
Flour:						
Total disposals	4,573	5,149	4,967	5,138	5,234	5,433
For food in the United Kingdom	4,497	5,086	4,856	4,982	5,095	5,161
Rice	188	156	92	84	86	36
Sugar:						
Total disposals	1,657	1,550	1,533	1,540	1,765	1,761
For food in thle United Kingdom	1,588	1,453	1,478	1,519	1,641	1,629
Syrup and treacle	72	78	86	95	110	108
Starch	..	153	134	106	119	114
Oatmeal and flakes	..	167	210	257	223	217
Other breakfast cereals	..	45	51	45	47	47
Meat and fish:						
Fresh and frozen meat and offal	2,151	1,728	1,681	1,672	1,826	1,706
Canned corned meat	31	40	81	105	89	117
Other canned meat	26	44	178	193	220	259
Bacon and ham	440	417	408	401	508	365
Fresh, frozen and cured fish (landed weight):						
Total disposals	495	425	493	504	560	735
For food in the United Kingdom	455	421	485	499	543	709
Canned fish	120	89	82	82	95	118
Dairy products:						
Butter	290	205	166	170	161	183
Cheese	186	187	297	261	232	232
Condensed milk	224	189	224	219	205	175
Milk powder	32	18	62	97	79	105
Eggs in shell	399	344	248	207	203	257
Dried egg	2	3	40	57	59	81
Frozen liquid egg	49	31	6	4	9	1
Fats:						
Margarine	343	399	395	394	410	424
Lard and compound cooking fat	193	208	248	253	256	234
Fruit and vegetables:						
Dried fruit	159	173	192	151	223	202
Canned and bottled fruit	..	39	59	75	25	18
Jam and marmalade	227	251	290	363	345	290
Potatoes[2]:						
Total disposals	3,404	4,194	5,058	6,043	6,421	6,111
For food in the United Kingdom	3,356	3,850	4,602	5,460	6,154	5,820
Canned vegetables	..	174	255	201	211	244
Dried peas, beans and lentils	111	150	132	132	156	157
Other foods:						
Chocolate and sugar confectionery	..	..	..	249	258	241
Biscuits	..	..	352	272	272	260
Tea	213	184	181	164	168	191
Raw coffee	26	25	27	31	40	47
Cocoa beans	141	121	132	115	155	127
Barley:						
For brewing	..	..	..	797	883	1,039
For food	..	..	..	424	50	44
For animal feed	..	..	..	4	307	280
Maize:						
Total disposals	2,037	809	180	124	116	406
Animal feed	1,889	702	61	6	6	294
Oilcake and meal	1,329	899	902	690	786	825
Milling offals	1,989	1,600	886	898	817	1,108
Fish and meat meal	118	67	51	55	69	69

1. Figures relate to periods of 52 weeks (53 weeks in 1943) except for fresh, frozen and cured fish, condensed and powdered milk and cocoa beans, the figures for which are for calendar years.
2. Excluding seed and chat potatoes.

Source: Ministry of Food

4.18 Estimated food supplies per head of civilian population

lb. per head per annum

	1934-38 average	1940	1941	1942	1943	1944	1945
Cereal products and sugar:							
Flour	194.5	208 .6	237.1	226.6	230.2	233.5	240.7
Rice	4.4	6.6	6.4	3.5	2.9	3.2	0.9
Sugar[1]	103.9	71.8	67.4	69.2	67.7	71.4	70.5
Starch	2.2	1.9	1.7	1.9	1.2	1.3	1.3
Oatmeal and flakes	5.4	5.0	8.0	9.8	10.8	10.1	9.9
Other breakfast cereals	1.8	1.8	2.2	2.3	2.0	2.1	2.2
Meat and fish:							
Fresh and frozen meat	91.4	87.9	71.7	69.2	66.5	73.7	69.6
Offal	7.4	7.1	6.1	5.5	5.6	6.8	5.6
Canned corned meat	2.1	-	0.4	2 4	3.3	0.1	3.5
Other canned meat	0.8	1.1	2.0	5.0	4.6	5.8	4.9
Bacon and ham	27.3	20.2	19.1	19.4	18.5	23.6	16.8
Fresh, frozen and cured fish	21.8	11.1	11.3	13.1	14.2	16.0	20.2
Canned fish	3.6	5.2	3.4	2.8	3.1	3.3	3.4
Dairy products:							
Butter	24.8	14.0	10.2	7.7	7.6	7.7	8.5
Cheese	8.8	8.2	8.3	14.0	11.5	10.3	9.7
Condensed milk	12.3	8.0	5.5	5.2	4.9	4.2	4.3
Milk powder	1.6	1.6	0.8	2.9	4.2	3.1	3.5
Eggs in shell	21.3	18.9	16.6	12.0	9.8	9.8	12.3
Dried egg	-	0.1	0.1	1.9	2.6	2.8	3.0
Frozen liquid egg	1.9	2.4	1.5	0.3	0.2	0.5	-
Fats:							
Margarine	8.7	15.4	17.5	17.4	17.0	17.8	17.1
Lard and compound cooking fat	9.3	9.1	10.0	11.9	11.8	12.1	10.1
Other edible oils and fats	8.2	7.5	6.7	6.6	5.5	5.5	5.3
Fruit and vegetables:							
Dried fruit	8.0	7.2	7.9	8.5	6.1	9.6	8.1
Fresh citrus fruit	28.5	20.4	4.0	4.7	2.0	7.1	14.8
Fresh tomatoes	10.4	8.2	6.9	8.6	8.9	8.2	9.1
Canned and bottled fruit	12.0	7.6	1.9	2.9	2.9	0.7	0.1
Jam and marmalade[2]	0.1	-	0.3	-	2.0	2.1	1.0
Potatoes	176.0	166.4	188.2	224.9	248.8	274.6	260.2
Canned vegetables	2.0	1.9	1.9	1.5	1.1	0.2	1.4
Dried peas, beans and lentils	7.4	4.6	6.3	5.0	4.2	4.6	4.7
Other foods:							
Tea	9.3	8.6	8.1	8.2	7.0	7.4	8.2
Raw coffee	0.7	1.2	1.2	1.2	1.0	1.2	1.2
Cocoa beans	4.7	5.8	5.3	4.6	3.5	4.2	4.3

1. Including sugar in all home-produced manufactured foods.
2. Imported only.

Source: Ministry of Food

4.19 Arrivals of Lend-Lease foodstuffs from the United States of America[1,2]

Thousand tons

		Total arrivals	Cereal products and sugar							Meat and fish			
			Maize	Pulses	Rice	Soya beans, flour and gifts	Other cereals and cereal products	Starch-maize	Sugar (as refined sugar)	Fresh and frozen meat and offal	Canned meat	Bacon and ham	Caned fish
1941	April to December	1,073	274	81	-	10	9	55	-	-	51	78	24
1942		1,427	98	27	-	20	12	90	-	33	170	114	64
1943		1,705	59	64	76	78	2	76	10	200	182	86	97
1944		1,280	21	57	6	20	2	51	-	289	22	92	12
1945[3]		709	199	27	5	9	10	38	-	100	-	31	4
1941	2nd Quarter	27	-	5	-	-	-	-	-	-	-	1	-
	3rd Quarter	382	61	46	-	5	1	24	-	-	20	34	7
	4th Quarter	664	213	30	-	5	8	31	-	-	31	43	17
1942	1st Quarter	405	23	3	-	5	12	12	-	-	27	16	31
	2nd Quarter	281	-	6	-	5	-	21	-	1	52	34	7
	3rd Quarter	403	40	6	-	7	-	37	-	23	54	46	6
	4th Quarter	338	35	12	-	3	-	20	31	9	37	18	20
1943	Ist Quarter	287	-	3	9	13	-	18	-	43	8	23	28
	2nd Quarter	475	19	18	22	23	2	25	10	43	47	24	20
	3rd Quarter	531	38	16	28	21	-	16	-	45	102	26	17
	4th Quarter	412	2	27	17	21	-	-	17	69	25	13	32
1944	Ist Quarter	276	-	8	2	9	17	-	-	102	11	21	6
	2nd Quarter	406	20	22	1	4	1	7	-	117	1	49	-
	3rd Quarter	286	1	13	1	2	-	10	-	34	9	16	1
	4th Quarter	312	-	14	2	5	1	-	36		11	6	5
1945	Ist Quarter	289	63	16	-	2	5	12	-	60	-	18	-
	2nd Quarter	319	129	1	5	7	4	15	-	40	-	12	3
	3rd Quarter	101	7	10	-	-	1	11	-	-	-	1	1

See footnotes on page 82.

Source: Ministry of Food

4.19 Arrivals of Lend-Lease foodstuffs from the United States of America[1,2]

continued

Thousand tons

		Dairy products				Fats		Fruit and vegetables						
		Cheese	Condensed and dried milk	Eggs in shell	Egg products	Lard and compound cooking fats	Other oils and fats	Dried fruit	Fruit pulp	Canned fruit	Canned vegetables	Fruit juices	Other fruit and vegetable products	Other foodstuffs
1941	April to Dec	38	150	15	25	95	-	70	14	16	59	1	4	4
1942		122	224	2	57	215	5	91	28	4	18	7	14	12
1943		56	199	-	75	239	18	124	10	6	5	19	7	17
1944		110	162	-	66	181	2	125	9	14	3	15	9	12
1945[3]		29	63	-	17	68	-	59	14	5	2	5	22	2
1941	2nd Quarter	3	3	6	-	1	-	7	-	-	1	-	-	-
	3rd Quarter	15	57	6	12	50	-	21	2	3	16	-	-	2
	4th Quarter	20	90	3	13	44	-	42	12	13	42	1	4	2
1942	1st Quarter	28	103	2	14	39	-	49	6	4	18	-	11	2
	2nd Quarter	26	25	-	18	66	1	8	4	-	-	2	1	4
	3rd Quarter	25	50	-	11	69	1	11	9	-	-	3	1	4
	4th Quarter	43	46		14	41	3	23	9	-	-	2	1	2
1943	1st Quarter	8	48	-	17	15	4	39	2	-	1	2	4	2
	2nd Quarter	10	75	-	22	70	6	23	5	-	-	7	3	1
	3rd Quarter	18	45	-	11	91	8	26	3	5	4	5	-	6
	4th Quarter	20	31	-	25	63	-	36	-	1	-	5	-	8
1944	1stQuarter	18	6	-	16	29	-	25	4	5	-	2	3	2
	2nd Quarter	28	19	-	18	47	-	53	3	3	-	8	3	2
	3rd Quarter	25	47	-	17	86	1	14	-	2	1	3	-	3
	4th Quarter	39	90	-	15	19	1	33	2	4	2	2	3	5
1945	1st Quarter	7	18	-	-	27	-	33	8	2	2	1	14	1
	2nd Quarter	8	16	-	10	27	-	25	5	3	-	2	6	1
	3rd Quarter	14	29	-	7	14	-	1	1	-	-	2	2	-

1. Figures refer to 52-week years except for 1943, when there were 53 weeks.
2. In addition there were the following arrivals from other countries:-(thousand tons)

Source: *Ministry of Food*

		Rice	Other oils and fats	Raw sugar			Granulated sugar		
		Brazil	Iceland	San Domingo	Haiti	Cuba	Porto Rico	Cuba	Java
1942	1st Quarter	-	-	5	-	-	-	-	-
	2nd Quarter	-	-	24	-	-	-	-	-
	3rd Quarter	-	8	31	3	-	-	8	1
	4th Quarter	1	14	58	-	-	-	-	1
1943	1st Quarter	8	1	86	15	-	-	-	-
	2nd Quarter	3	-	99	-	101	-	-	-
	3rd Quarter	-	10	131	-	88	105	-	-
	4th Quarter	-	8	41	8	345	82	-	-
1944	1stQuarter	-	4	35	-	16	24	-	-
	2nd Quarter	-	-	4	-	-	-	-	-

3 to 30 September 1945. There were no arrivals in the fourth quarter of 1945.

4.20 Losses of food and feeding-stuffs at sea

Monthly averages or calendar months — *Thousand tons*

	Total losses	Cereal products and sugar: Total grains and pulses	Wheat	Animal feeding-stuffs	Sugar	Meat	Dairy products	Oilseeds, oils and fats	Fruit and veget-ables	Beverages: Tea	Other	Other food
1939[1]	35.6	22.3	15.1	-	7.9	1.7	0.9	0.3	0.8	1.2	0.2	0.3
1940	60.7	38.8	26.0	1.9	5.7	5.7	2.2	3.0	2.2	0.3	0.2	0.7
1941	65.6	31.8	24.6	2.5	5.2	3.8	1.5	15.5	1.3	1.2	1.4	1.4
1942	43.4	13.3	10.9	0.1	4.4	7.2	2.4	10.3	2.0	1.9	0.5	1.3
1943	30.9	10.2	8.5	-	3.1	5.1	2.1	8.2	0.4	1.0	0.1	0.7
1944	3.3	0.2	0.1	-	0.3	0.6	-	1.4	0.1	0.2	0.5	-
1939 September	62.8	38.7	29.0	-	24.1	-	-	-	-	-	-	-
October	42.1	25.3	13.9	0.1	7.1	0.4	0.1	1.1	3.1	4.9	-	0.1
November	22.0	19.9	12.2	-	0.2	0.4	-	-	-	-	0.9	0.6
December	15.4	5.4	5.4	-	-	5.8	3.7	-	-	-	-	0.5
1940 January	60.7	59.9	49.8	-	-	0.2	-	-	-	-	-	0.6
February	19.6	9.8	9.0	-	-	6.5	0.7	-	2.7	-	-	0.1
March	13.8	5.4	4.8	-	-	0.3	0.1	6.4	0.9	-	-	0.7
April	-	-	-	-	-	-	-	-	-	-	-	-
May	14.5	9.8	-	-	-	4.2	0.4	-	-	-	-	-
June	72.0	56.2	32.7	-	7.6	1.7	0.6	1.4	3.9	-	-	0.3
July	129.8	94.0	63.4	3.8	7.3	14.3	1.5	1.0	5.6	-	-	2.2
August	90.7	55.2	22.9	2.1	8.2	7.9	2.6	10.1	3.2	0.3	1.0	0.2
September	71.6	38.4	36.4	3.5	17.6	3.5	1.0	6.6	-	-	0.6	0.5
October	84.9	54.2	46.2	4.1	8.7	7.2	3.2	0.1	5.7	-	0.1	1.7
November	97.4	45.9	12.8	3.0	15.5	12.8	9.8	3.0	3.9	1.9	0.6	0.9
December	73.5	36.6	34.6	5.9	3.3	9.5	7.0	7.3	0.1	1.9	-	1.9
1941 January	65.2	43.4	27.2	4.7	2.7	3.6	0.6	5.0	-	2.8	-	2.4
February	78.6	19.0	11.6	10.7	-	6.0	0.8	33.2	1.6	3.4	1.5	2.4
March	110.4	58.7	45.0	3.4	12.7	0.1	0.8	24.1	-	3.6	3·2	3.8
April	95.8	68·1	63.9	4.7	3·5	5·9	2.2	6.4	1.4	1.9	1.3	0.3
May	107.8	55.2	47.7	5.1	6.6	16.5	2.6	20.1	1.1	-	-	0.6
June	84.8	37.7	25.0	0.8	12.3	5.0	1.0	22.7	2.1	0.1	1.3	1.8
July	17.8	3.1	-	-	7.0	-	-	7.7	-	-	-	-
August	32.9	6.4	5.9	-	-	-	-	21.4	3.2	-	1.6	0.3
September	87.2	33.1	30.2	-	-	0.5	2.7	38.9	1.2	0.7	8.4	1.7
October	28.1	17.7	15.1	-	-	3.2	3.5	1.1	2.2	-	-	0.4
November	49.0	18.5	4.8	-	17.6	3.2	1.6	4.3	1.3	1.9	-	0.6
December	30.0	20.5	18.6	-	-	1.7	2.7	1.5	1.7	-	-	1.9
1942 January	30.9	16.2	8.1	-	5.1	0.1	1.1	7.2	0.3	-	0.1	0.8
February	48.3	26.5	26.5	0.2	2.7	9.4	1.9	3.7	1.1	0.8	-	2.0
March	47.8	12.7	10.4	0.9	3.5	4.0	1.6	14.2	7.9	1.0	-	2.0
April	14.9	0.6	-	-	7.1	1.2	1.7	0.8	2.8	0.3	0.1	0.3
May	25.6	21.0	21.0	-	-	2.8	0.1	-	-	-	-	1.7
June	31.0	0.6	0.6	-	4.0	6.2	10.5	7.9	1.6	-	0.2	-
July	28.8	13.5	6.0	-	3.3	6.0	-	4.3	-	-	1.6	0.1
August	73.6	19.1	15.6	-	13.0	11.7	3.4	16.7	4.9	2.4	0.6	1.8
September	33.8	5.6	3.4	-	0.3	16.5	2.9	4.9	0.5	1.8	0.1	1.2
October	75.1	19.1	19.1	-	6.7	16.9	0.8	19.2	3.1	5.9	2.8	0.6
November	84.2	24.0	19.7	-	7.1	9.7	4.5	24.5	2.1	7.5	0.3	4.5
December	26.4	-	-	-	-	1.6	0.9	20.3	-	2.9	0.5	0.2

1. Four months, September to December.

Source: Ministry of Food

4.20 Losses of food and feeding-stuffs at sea

continued

Monthly averages or calendar months — *Thousand tons*

		Total losses	Cereal products and sugar				Meat	Dairy products	Oilseeds, oils and fats	Fruit and veget-ables	Beverages		Other food
			Total grains and pulses	Wheat	Animal feeding-stuffs	Sugar					Tea	Other	
1943	January	15.4	10.3	9.7	-	-	-	-	4.6	0.5	-	-	-
	February	23.9	14.1	13.5	-	-	3.3	2.2	-	1.3	2.4	-	0.6
	March	169.8	45.4	38.7	-	31.6	32.3	15.6	34.0	2.5	2.4	0.9	5.1
	April	64.8	11.7	7.8	-	-	20.1	4.7	23.1	0.1	3.4	-	1.7
	May	48.1	23.7	21.2	-	2.3	1.4	0.1	18.3	0.1	1.9	0.1	0.2
	June	4.4	1.3	1.1	-	-	0.1	0.2	2.1	0.5	-	-	0.2
	July	13.6	5.7	5.7	-	-	-	0.5	7.4	-	-	-	-
	August	2.0	0.2	-	-	0.9	0.3	0.5	-	0.1	-	-	-
	September	10.1	4.2	-	-	-	3.6	0.2	0.9	-	1.2	-	-
	October	8.0	4.1	4.1	-	-	-	0.3	1.1	-	2.3	-	0.2
	November	-	-	-	-	-	-	-	-	-	-	-	-
	December	11.3	1.2	-	-	2.6	-	0.8	6.7	-	-	-	-
1944	January	3.4	-	-	-	-	2.4	0.3	0.3	0.4	-	-	-
	February	2.1	-	-	-	-	-	-	-	0.1	-	1.8	0.2
	March	5.4	-	-	-	-	-	-	5.4	-	-	-	-
	April	4.1	-	-	-	3.9	-	-	-	-	-	0.2	-
	May	-	-	-	-	-	-	-	-	-	-	-	-
	June	-	-	-	-	-	-	-	-	-	-	-	-
	July	1.0	-	-	-	-	-	-	-	0.4	-	0.5	-
	August	6.0	-	-	-	-	-	-	3.8	-	2.2	-	-
	September	-	-	-	-	-	-	-	-	-	-	-	-
	October	7.3	0.5	-	-	-	2.2	-	4.6	-	-	-	-
	November	-	-	-	-	-	-	-	-	-	-	-	-
	December	10.7	2.0	1.5	-	-	3.0	-	2.2	0.5	-	3.0	-
1945	January	11.2	11.2	10.6	-	-	-	-	-	-	-	-	-
	February	-	-	-	-	-	-	-	-	-	-	-	-
	March	0.9	-	-	0.6	-	-	-	0.3	-	-	-	-
	April	-	-	-	-	-	-	-	-	-	-	-	-
	May	-	-	-	-	-	-	-	-	-	-	-	-

Source: Ministry of Food

5 FUEL AND POWER

The performance of the coal industry during the war was poor: production declined from 231 million tons in 1939 to 183 million tons in 1945, absenteeism showed a marked increase, and the average output per manshift at the coal face fell by about 10 per cent (**tables 5.3 and 5.6**). The first coal crisis emerged in the winter of 1940-41 but this was mainly the result of disruption in the transportation system rather than a crisis in production (an important outcome of these difficulties was a successful drive to increase coal stocks to protect against such crises in the future) (Court 1951: 87-106; **table 5.3**). Production problems emerged in 1941 but part of their origins can be traced back to the loss of labour earlier in the war. The fall of France in 1940 and the loss of other overseas markets led to a marked decline in exports (from 37 million tons in 1939 to 20 million tons in 1940 and to a mere 5 million tons in 1941) and this had serious repercussions on the industry: unemployment in the export-orientated coal regions rose and miners left to find employment in other industries or in the Armed Forces (Supple 1987: 503-5; **table 9.12**). Thus, the labour force fell from a peak of 767,000 in June 1940 to 690,000 by May 1941 and although state intervention (including the 'Bevin Boys' scheme which recruited approximately 20,000 new workers for the industry in 1944 and 1945) did reverse this trend, it never managed to restore the former level of employment (Court 1951: 304-6; **table 5.6**).

Furthermore, the percentage of total manshifts worked at the coal face was also declining and these factors, combined with increasing absenteeism and poor industrial relations (the coal industry accounted for by far the largest share of total days lost through industrial disputes, peaking in 1944 when 2.5 million days were lost) resulted in the falling output and productivity that characterised the industry during the war (Supple 1987: 504-16, 525-7; **tables 5.6 and 3.30**).

5.1 War-time performance of the coal industry

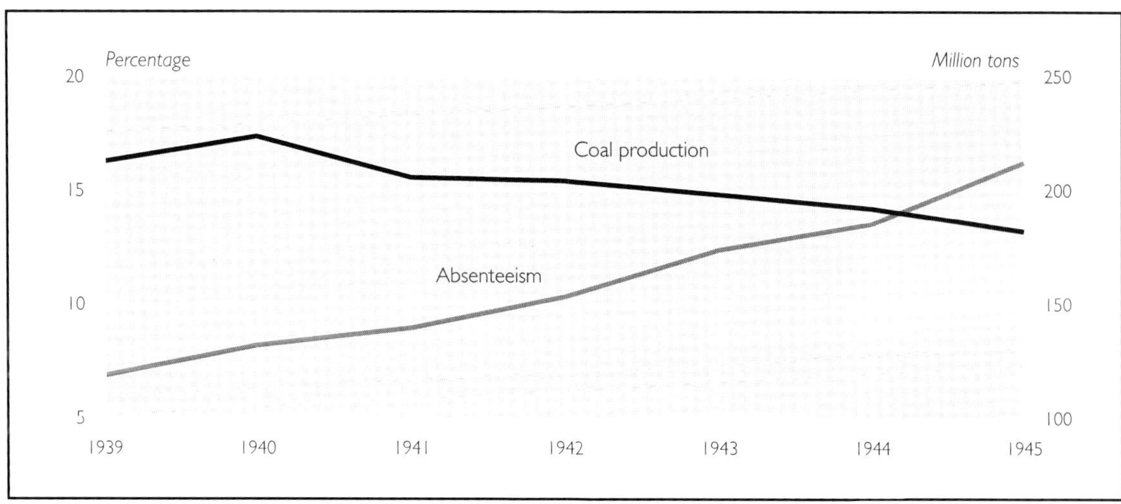

The shortfall in energy supplies created by problems in the coal industry was compensated by expansion in the gas industry and, particularly, the electricity industry: gas output increased by 18 per cent between 1939 and 1944 (**tables 5.9 and 5.11**). However, their expansion was not without its cost: about a fifth of the demand for coal came from the gas and electricity industries and their combined consumption rose from 39 million tons in 1939 to 45 million tons by 1944 (**table 5.4**). Whilst coal consumption by both industrial and domestic users declined continuously from 1940, electricity sales to industrial users increased by 71 per cent between 1939 and 1944 and by 32 per cent to domestic users (the latter helped by changes in the price structure which saw domestic electricity prices remain stable while domestic coal prices rose by two-thirds) (Hannah 1979: 305; court 1951: 147-62; **tables 5.4 and 5.12**).

In the early period of the war electricity sales had been adversely affected by the 'blackout' but the expansion of munitions production led to a rapid increase in consumption after 1940 (Hannah 1979: 291). To meet this increased demand the capacity of power stations was increased by 35 per cent; furthermore, the National Grid was extended to service factories that were relocated to Wales and the north to reduce the threat from bombing (Hannah 1979: 295,298). Although employment fell from 120,000 to 90,000 labour was used more intensively (longer hours were worked, there was more shift working and holidays were staggered) and productivity rose (Hannah 1979: 298-300).

The Second World War was a mechanised war and the aircraft, tanks and other motorised vehicles of the British forces needed oil and, given the disruption of wartime trade routes, that oil would, primarily come from the USA. Although the production of petroleum products from indigenous materials increased during the war in terms of the overall supply it remained unimportant (**table 5.15**). There was some domestic processing of imported oil but this declined and was of significance to the overall supply only in the cases of bitumen and lubricating oils (Paynton-Smith 1971: 187-93, 273-/; **table 5.14**). Thus, the supply of petroleum products was heavily reliant on imports, which increased from 11.4 million tons in 1940 to 20.2 million tons in 1944 (77 per cent), although most of this increase came in 1943 and 1944 (**table 5.13**). These imports were dominated by aviation, motor and industrial spirits (which increased by an impressive 162 per cent and whose share of total petroleum imports increased from approximately one-third to a half) and fuel oil (which increased in volume by 65 per cent and accounted for more than a quarter of total imports) (**table 5.13**).

Although the supply did increase, most of it was used to meet the rising demands from both the British and American forces (by mid-1944 the United States Army Air Force accounted for nearly half of the total aviation spirit consumption), and civilian consumption was squeezed (for example civilian consumption of motor spirit fell by approximately a third between 1941 and 1943)(Paynton-Smith 1971: 288-93, 389-97; **table 5.17**). The defining event of the war, from the perspective of petroleum, was the build-up to D-Day and the invasion of Europe which required increased supplies of motor fuel and aviation spirit; as this process began in mid-1943 monthly oil consumption dramatically rose by 25 per cent (Paynton-Smith 1971: 391).

5.2 Electricity production

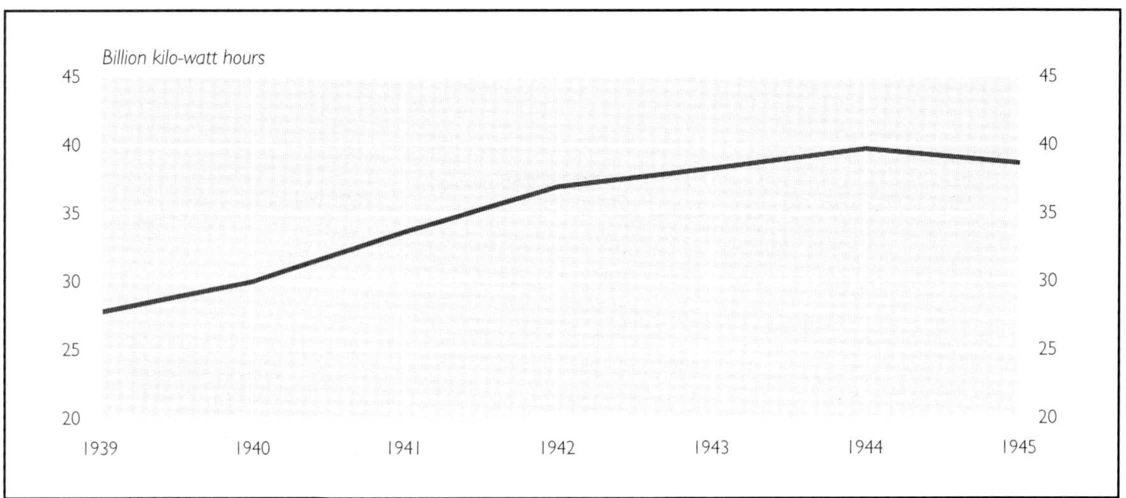

5.3 Coal: production, consumption and stocks

Thousand tons

	Production[1]			Consumption (including exports)			Stocks[1] (end of period)		
	Total	Saleable mined coal	Opencast coal[2]	Total	Inland consumption[3]	Overseas shipments and bunkers[4]	Distributed	Opencast on sites or central stocking grounds	Colliery stocks held on pitbanks and in trucks[5]
Annual totals									
1939	231,338	231,338	-	232,919	186,401	46,518	14,550	-	5,186
1940	224,299	224,299	-	222,301	195,666	26,635	17,259	-	4,475
1941	206,344	206,344	-	206,073	196,704	9,369	18,679	-	3,326
1942	204,944	203,633	1,311	205,124	197,404	7,720	18,625	254	2,950
1943	198,920	194,493	4,427	198,414	190,380	8,034	17,656	1,602	2,946
1944	192,746	184,098	8,648	193,403	187,296	6,107	16,031	2,324	2,552
1945	182,773	174,658	8,115	188,028	179,500	8,528	12,314	716	2,229
Weekly averages									
1939	4,437	4,437	-	4,467	3,575	892	14,550	-	5,186
1940	4,290	4,290	-	4,252	3,743	509	17,259	-	4,475
1941	3,957	3,957	-	3,952	3,772	180	18,679	-	3,326
1942	3,930	3,905	25	3,934	3,786	148	18,625	254	2,950
1943	3,815	3,730	85	3,805	3,651	154	17,656	1,602	2,946
1944	3,687	3,521	166	3,699	3,582	117	16,031	2,324	2,552
1945	3,506	3,350	156	3,606	3,442	164	12,314	716	2,229
1940 January	4,136*	4,136*	-	..	..	820	..	-	4,505
February	4,413	4,413	-	..	..	737	..	-	3,963
March	4,339	4,339	-	..	..	659	..	-	3,437
April	4,864	4,864	-	..	..	743	..	-	3,219
May	4,701*	4,701*	-	4,448	3,665	783	10,679	-	3,084
June	4,758	4,758	-	4,217	3,609	608	12,631	-	3,197
July	4,365*	4,365*	-	4,050	3,627	423	15,078	-	3,322
August	4,087	4,087	-	3,744	3,441	303	16,563	-	3,465
September	4,130	4,130	-	3,741	3,404	337	17,872	-	3,762
October	4,029*	4,029*	-	3,927	3,616	311	18,493	-	4,228
November	3,935	3,935	-	4,052	3,826	226	18,311	-	4,461
December	3,638	3,638	-	4,083	3,907	176	17,259	-	4,475
1941 January	3,813*	3,813*	-	4,212	4,021	191	15,022	-	4,416
February	3,890	3,890	-	4,272	4,071	201	13,740	-	4,318
March	4,047	4,047	-	4,263	4,041	222	12,975	-	4,135
April	3,839*	3,839*	-	4,098	3,880	218	12,345	-	3,779
May	4,051	4,051	-	3,987	3,790	197	13,856	-	3,536
June	3,913	3,913	-	3,721	3,523	198	12,952	-	3,395
July	3,980*	3,980*	-	3,582	3,384	198	15,612	-	3,287
August	3,624	3,624	-	3,513	3,357	156	16,620	-	3,161
September	4,129	4,129	-	3,701	3,561	140	18,041	-	3,141
October	4,135*	4,135*	-	3,907	3,748	159	19,124	-	3,289
November	4,194	4,194	-	4,097	3,957	140	19,318	-	3,393
December	3,851	3,851	-	4,179	4,040	139	18,679	-	3,326
1942 January	3,954	3,954	-	4,277	4,119	158	16,314	-	3,380
February	4,022	4,022	-	4,459	4,304	155	14,608	-	3,337
March	4,072	4,072	-	4,268	4.128	140	13,550	-	3,291
April	3,787*	3,782*	5*	3,942	3,808	134	12,850	..	3,166
May	3,770	3,766	4	3,758	3,606	152	13,146	..	3,031
June	3,986	3,973	13	3,673	3,510	163	13,918	..	3,008
July	3,914*	3,871*	43*	3,680	3,518	162	15,317	..	2,776
August	3,455	3,410	45	3,454	3,320	134	15,688	..	2,889
September	4,097*	4,046*	51*	3,728	3,575	153	17,515	..	2,839
October	4,158	4,104	54	3,888	3,741	147	18,620	..	3,050
November	4,141	4,105	36	4,088	3,945	143	18,959	..	2,987
December	3,765*	3,728*	37*	4,110	3,974	136	18,625	254	2,950

See footnotes on page 88

Source: Ministry of Fuel and Power

5.3 Coal: production, consumption and stocks

continued

Thousand tons

		Production[1]			Consumption (including exports)			Stocks[1] (end of period)		
		Total	Saleable mined coal	Opencast coal[2]	Total	Inland consumption[3]	Overseas shipments and bunkers[4]	Distributed	Opencast on sites or central stocking grounds	Colliery stocks held on pitbanks and in trucks[5]
1943	January	3,995	3,967	28	4,107	3,974	133	17,800	..	3,009
	February	4,010	3,976	34	4,119	3,986	133	17,517	..	3,103
	March	4,339	4,020	56	4,038	3,899	139	17,377	..	3,043
	April	3,726*	3,657*	69*	4,038	3,656*	165	17,284	..	2,932
	May	4,021	3,937	84	3,821	3,605	171	17,745	..	3,033
	June	3,684	3,606	78	3,556	3,378	178	18,264	..	3,197
	July	3,801*	3,682*	119*	3,500	3,324*	176	19,434	..	2,973
	August	3,278	3,166	121	3,276	3,156	120	19,510	..	2,957
	September	3,931*	3,808*	123*	3,669	3,491*	178	20,283	..	2,976
	October	4,015	3,888	127	3,852	3,685	167	20,328	..	2,980
	November	3,903	3,796	107	3,982	3,840	142	19,757	..	3,025
	December	3,532*	3,455*	77*	4,034	3,885*	149	17,656	1,602	2,946
1944	January	3,793	3,705	88	4,049	3,906	143	16,047	1,716	3,041
	February	3,847	3,738	109	4,103	3,959	144	14,727	1,854	2,997
	March	3,634*	3,508*	126*	4,023	3,893*	130	13,134	1,953	2,820
	April	3,460	3,338	122	3,533	3,425	108	12,699	1,956	2,714
	May	3,969	3,772	197	3,666	3,569	97	13,643	1,526	2,713
	June	3,749*	3,538*	211*	3,437	3,324*	113	15,017	1,721	2,701
	July	3,686	3,447	239	3,313	3,218	95	16,373	1,931	2,733
	August	3,185	2,944	241	3,097	3,005	92	16,886	2,155	2,620
	September	3,818*	3,622*	196*	3,495	3,381*	114	18,072	2,284	2,646
	October	3,876	3,680	196	3,753	3,648	105	18,457	2,327	2,648
	November	3,911	3,744	167	4,011	3,887	124	18,017	2,323	2,602
	December	3,538*	3,425*	113*	3,994	3,864*	130	16,031	2,324	2,552
1945	January	3,506	3,385	121	4,108	3,978	130	13,205	2,367	2,732
	February	3,693	3,578	115	4,147	3,993	154	11,372	2,360	2,612
	March	3,717*	3,529*	188*	3,918	3,745*	173	10,376	2,402	2,550
	April	3,591	3,414	177	3,590	3,436	154	10,142	2,353	2,516
	May	3,161	3,010	151	3,333	3,186	147	10,079	2,197	2,394
	June	3,778*	3,599*	179*	3,463	3,293*	170	11,562	1,917	2,374
	July	3,386	3,222	164	3,201	3,033	168	12,644	1,640	2,401
	August	2,501	2,363	138	2,877	2,716	161	12,058	1,358	2,286

Source: Ministry of Fuel and Power

1. Great Britain.
2. The opencast production figures have not been adjusted to allow for subsequent losses in stocking nor for some coal of inferior quality not included in the stock figures for the later periods.
3. Including shipments to Northern Ireland. Up to December 1942, computed from figures for calendar months.
4. Computed from figures for calendar months. The figures include bunkers for fishing vessels proceedingoutside territorial waters, but exclude coastwise bunkers.
5. A large proportion of the coal which was held by collieries in these years was of very inferior quality.

* Average of five weeks.

5.4 Coal: Inland consumption

Thousand ton

	Public utility undertakings[1]			Coke ovens	Industrial consumers[2,3]			Domestic[3]			Collieries[3]	Miscellaneous[3,6]
									Merchants' disposals[5]			
	Gas	Electricity[4]	Railways		Iron and steel	Engineering and other metal trades	Other industries	Miners' coal	House	Anthracite and boiler fuel		
Annual lotals												
1939	18,966	15,9255	12,930	20,423		..		4,627	..		12,089	..
1940	18,083	18,112	13,474	22,275		45,000		4,821	46,400		12,321	15,180
1941	19,419	20,435	14,010	21,129	11,600	3,900	30,600	4,671	45,800		12,125	13,015
1942	20,734	22,283	14,724	21,581	11,383	5,214	29,265	4,711	42,800		12,046	12,663
1943	20,840	22,599	14,970	20,891	11,305	4,864	27,758	4,461	36,256	2,103	11,600	12,733
1944	20,730	24,074	15,202	20,135	10,336	4,486	26,690	4,624	33,327	2,221	11.141	14,330
1945	20,967	23,493	14,935	20,102	9,572	4,083	25,838	4,595	30,055	2,278	10,540	13,042
Weekly averages												
1939	364	305	248	392		..		89	..		232	..
1940	346	346	258	426		861		92	887		236	291
1941	372	392	269	405	222	75	587	90	878		233	249
1942	398	427	282	414	218	100	561	90	821		231	244
1943	400	433	287	401	217	93	532	86	695	40	222	245
1944	397	460	291	385	198	86	510	88	637	42	213	275
1945	402	451	286	386	184	78	496	88	576	44	202	249
1940 January	447*	429*	260*	430*	..	..	..	103	960		247	..
February	428	403	268	428	..	..	..	112	960		246	..
March	382	346	261	433	..	..	..	96	920		235	..
April	366	340	266	441	..	..	..	102	946		252	..
May	320*	310*	248*	446*	215	69	565	90	875		243	284
June	307	308	253	442	215	69	564	74	869		228	280
July	308*	308*	256*	430*	203	65	534	87	918		237	281
August	310	300	254	417	197	63	517	81	806		229	267
September	289	311	248	409	201	65	529	83	777		228	264
October	315*	343*	253*	407*	220	71	578	94	819		235	281
November	352	374	262	411	234	75	613	94	884		230	297
December	383	390	266	404	232	75	609	94	924		227	303
1941 January	414*	444*	272*	404*	236	76	621	100	947		241	266
February	420	437	276	404	242	78	635	97	972		241	269
March	403	415	278	405	245	79	644	102	967		236	267
April	377*	390*	273*	402*	235	76	617	94	924		235	257
May	356	371	265	403	229	76	604	91	907		237	251
June	330	336	252	405	208	60	553	79	842		225	233
July	315*	329*	250*	403*	195	55	521	79	783		230	224
August	324	336	252	398	195	56	512	72	781		209	227
September	344	365	263	405	214	63	544	85	808		234	236
October	368*	398*	272*	408*	222	79	599	90	827		237	248
November	414	444	285	413	232	97	617	90	873		230	262
December	427	448	287	412	225	102	611	96	925		240	267
1942 January	466	514	290	412	231	113	624	99	863		243	264
February	471	524	301	416	244	123	642	115	944		248	276
March	447	487	297	417	240	112	626	104	893		240	265
April	399*	421*	286*	409*	224	107	584	94	806		234	244
May	371	397	278	413	212	93	554	84	752		221	231
June	357	383	268	408	212	79	536	84	722[7]		236	225
July	345*	370*	269*	410*	193	77	493	84	820		231	226
August	341	356	263	406	182	74	475	71	737		202	213
September	356*	389*	273*	417*	212	83	511	84	788		233	229
October	378	410	285	417	219	98	552	89	817		236	240
November	420	262	293	420	227	117	582	92	846		233	253
December	434*	448*	288*	414*	227	126	584	97	868		233	255

See footnotes on page 90.

Source: Ministry of Fuel and Power

5.4 Coal: Inland consumption

continued

Thousand ton

	Public utility undertakings[1]				Industrial consumers[2,3]			Domestic[3]				
									Merchants' disposals[5]			
	Gas	Electricity[4]	Railways	**Coke ovens**	Iron and steel	Engineering and other metal trades	Other industries	Miners' coal	House	Anthracite and boiler fuel	**Collieries** [3]	**Miscellaneous** [3,6]
1943 January	457	478	293	415	226	128	578	96	770	42	229	262
February	446	463	300	416	238	132	570	98	783	42	235	263
March	432	452	296	416	235	126	562	97	743	46	235	259
* April	396	408	285	408	223	101	531	85	713	41	222	243
May	381	405	282	401	221	83	526	85	711	42	226	242
June	356	379	272	402	206	68	490	75	647	39	217	227
* July	351	377	277	390	190	62	472	74	656	38	214	223
August	346	367	268	383	187	58	450	67	584	32	202	212
* September	370	418	286	392	213	65	497	80	673	39	224	234
October	396	453	292	395	219	81	556	84	699	40	223	247
November	431	498	300	395	228	104	581	92	686	41	227	257
* December	457	521	296	395	220	115	581	94	686	41	219	260
1944 January	451	525	302	395	218	115	577	100	654	45	226	298
February	452	530	312	396	229	117	571	101	674	48	227	302
* March	449	526	311	384	220	116	566	97	665	46	215	298
April	386	437	295	363	193	80	502	86	579	39	203	262
May	367	432	296	389	202	72	512	89	675	43	219	273
* June	348	392	281	385	187	61	471	83	610	39	213	254
July	339	381	274	381	172	55	448	75	604	39	204	246
August	333	366	264	375	164	52	412	68	520	40	211	258
* September	356	427	282	383	190	62	464	80	628	40	211	258
October	389	472	292	387	199	84	515	90	679	43	220	278
November	434	520	302	395	207	106	554	98	702	48	223	298
* December	462	528	297	396	198	111	547	95	674	46	214	296
1945 January	490	587	303	390	197	129	561	101	669	46	216	289
February	479	544	308	392	211	122	548	107	720	51	221	290
* March	434	479	308	390	199	100	527	99	677	48	213	271
April	393	424	290	389	185	76	495	89	601	45	200	249
May	368	401	275	379	167	65	461	80	530	39	189	232
* June	358	398	287	390	184	65	483	86	561	43	204	240
July	347	368	277	384	166	49	443	76	469	40	192	222
August	341	342	252	359	142	42	381	61	400	32	165	199

1. Excluding consumption of coal at waterworks, which amounts on an average to 8,000 tons per week.
2. Undertakings with an annual consumption of 100 tons or more of coal and/or coke.
3. Calculated from four-weekly or monthly figures until December 1942; from then onwards figures are on a four or five week-basis.
4. Authorized electricity undertakings and railway and transport authorities only.
5. Including disposals to shops, offices and other establishments, partly or entirely non-residential, with an annual consumption of less than 100 tons of coal and/or coke. Including landsale deliveries until December 1942.
6. Including shipments to Northern Ireland, and consumption by Service departments and at waterworks.
7. In June 1942, a revised form of return was instituted, designed to cover all controlled premises, including industrial consumers with an annual consumption of less than 100 tons. On the old basis the figure for June 1942 was about 701,000 tons.

* Average of five weeks.

Source: Ministry of Fuel and Power

5.5 Coal: Distributed stocks[1]

End of period — *Thousand tons*

	Public utility undertakings: Gas	Public utility undertakings: Water	Public utility undertakings: Electricity	Public utility undertakings: Railways	**Coke ovens**	Industrial consumers[2]: Iron and steel	Industrial consumers[2]: Engineering and other metal trades	Industrial consumers[2]: Other industries	Merchants' stocks: House coal	Merchants' stocks: Anthracite and boiler fuel	**Government dumps**	**Miscellaneous[3]**
1939	2,811	117	2,827	1,306	393	..	..	..	..		..	..
1940	3,467	147	3,477	1,634	476	587	761	3,312	1,500		768	1,130
1941	3,079	170	3,367	1,765	537	734	912	3,688	1,671	185	1,625	946
1942	2,887	154	3,712	1,021	596	737	1,067	3,475	1,808	248	1,772	1,148
1943	2,188	134	3,305	1,401	454	650	706	3,171	1,664	143	2,389	1,451
1944	2,391	136	3,247	898	484	701	736	3,184	1,073	114	2,217	850
1945	1,838	117	2,839	614	422	471	501	2,493	1,324	153	848	694
1939 September	3,235		2,900	1,293	434	..	..	..	..		..	..
October	3,186		2,945	1,295	423	..	..	..	..		..	..
November	3,123		2,966	1,317	445	..	..	..	..		..	..
December	2,928		2,827	1,306	393	..	..	..	..		..	..
1940 January	2,314		2,324	1,201	298	..	..	..	..		..	235
February	1,956		2,111	1,031	301	..	..	..	..		..	213
March	1,938		2,161	914	312	..	..	..	..		..	244
April	2,120		2,292	925	336	..	..	..	665		..	262
May	2,606		2,576	1,002	376	354	459	1,999	992		..	315
June	3,141		2,891	1,128	417	436	566	2,462	1,225		..	365
July	3,845		3,336	1,308	462	533	692	3,012	1,266		150	474
August	4,095		3,587	1,398	488	598	776	3,376	1,413		232	600
September	4,244		3,740	1,535	524	642	833	3,627	1,592		374	761
October	4,241		3,800	1,669	547	647	840	3,654	1,670		489	936
November	4,059		3,691	1,707	562	632	820	3,567	1,585		628	1,060
December	3,614		3,477	1,634	476	587	761	3,312	1,500		768	1,130
1941 January	2,965		2,992	1,469	486	531	689	2,999	1,008		916	967
February	2,556		2,740	1,367	465	500	647	2,814	840		1,003	808
March	2,226		2,570	1,277	487	490	635	2,765	744		1,047	734
April	1,939		2,463	1,166	477	491	637	2,771	591		1,084	726
May	1,977		2,572	1,193	520	515	569	3,004	679		1,095	828
June	2,070		2,773	1,255	520	565	661	3,196	743		1,108	965
July	2,442		3,149	1,404	556	639	743	3,456	1,092		1,135	996
August	2,698		3,269	1,484	491	657	907	3,725	1,226		1,157	1,006
September	3,104		3,422	1,620	531	708	1,003	3,960	1,479		1,194	1,020
October	3,457		3,565	1,730	571	722	998	3,962	1,778		1,299	1,042
November	3,469[4]		3,547[4]	1,772	583	744	955	3,822	1,982		1,437	1,007
December	3,249		3,367	1,765	537	734	912	3,688	1,856		1,625	946
1942 January	2,723		2,783	1,627	496	665	758	3,172	1,502		1,683	905
February	2,453		2,452	1,504	496	614	672	2,968	974		1,688	787
March	2,238		2,272	1,358	532	612	641	2,849	713		1,602	733
April	2,106		2,234	1,210	494	599	721	2,711	563		1,521	691
May	2,227		2,341	1,159	453	622	778	2,824	606		1,436	700
June	2,340		2,547	1,100	504	667	871	2,988	738		1,388	775
July	2,662		2,884	1,054	587	705	987	3,215	966		1,394	863
August	2,741		3,050	936	478	700	1,016	3,305	1,143		1,375	944
September	3,049		3,391	947	539	747	1,129	3,598	1,623		1,439	1,053
October	3,268		3,599	924	581	768	1,147	3,664	1,946		1,555	1,168
November	3,248		3,608	955	615	773	1,124	3,609	2,155		1,698	1,174
December	3,041		3,712	1,021	596	737	1,067	3,475	2,056		1,772	1,148

See footnotes on page 92.

Source: Ministry of Fuel and Power

5.5 Coal: Distributed stocks[1]

continued

End of period — *Thousand tons*

	Public utility undertakings					Industrial consumers[2]		Merchants' stocks			
	Gas	Water	Electricity	Railways	Coke ovens	Iron and steel	Engineering and other metal trades	Other industries	House coal	Anthracite and boiler fuel	Government dumps	Miscellaneous[3]
1943 January	2,634		3,558	1,038	555	698	986	3,265	1,701	240	1,843	1,282
February	2,480		3,581	1,098	564	651	940	3,155	1,646	223	1,888	1,291
March	2,394		3,632	1,106	537	636	883	3,119	1,681	193	1,948	1,248
April	2,335		3,691	1,105	511	641	862	3,138	1,608	174	2,010	1,209
May	2,343		3,813	1,176	556	654	897	3,248	1,617	162	2,065	1,214
June	2,405		3,924	1,231	520	678	933	3,374	1,676	151	2,130	1,242
July	2'544		4'071	1,343	540	734	982	3'656	1,808	148	2,241	1,367
August	2,461		4,042	1,314	434	727	998	3,721	1,834	138	2,313	1,528
September	2,627		4,105	1,380	477	740	980	3,962	1,940	134	2,392	1,546
October	2,714		4,062	1,412	495	748	956	3,883	2,000	140	2,408	1,510
November	2,680		3,839	1,449	503	724	860	3,672	2,022	153	2,405	1,450
December	2,322		3,305	1,401	454	650	706	3,171	1,664	143	2,389	1,451
1944 January	1,918	127	2,894	1,317	452	612	605	2,840	1,551	133	2,366	1,232
February	1,808	125	2,549	1,247	464	546	524	2,573	1,413	116	2,341	1,021
March	1,698	121	2,242	1,109	450	461	453	2,167	1,165	87	2,311	870
April	1,673	126	2,251	1,026	453	484	529	2,035	971	96	2,262	793
May	1,939	135	2,530	1,133	510	538	590	2,250	911	101	2,218	78
June	2,214	138	2,898	1,202	519	623	681	2,671	1,014	110	2,202	745
July	2,470	146	3,244	1,252	537	663	785	3,027	1,159	124	2,197	769
August	2,492	146	3,449	1,151	414	673	842	3,220	1,305	123	2,195	876
September	2,741	150	3,676	1,040	450	715	915	3,550	1,505	127	2,217	986
October	2,893	150	3,794	1,009	484	732	900	3,626	1,532	130	2,221	986
November	2,807	148	3,707	989	525	733	843	3,520	1,467	131	2,218	929
December	2,391	136	3,247	898	484	701	736	3,184	1,073	114	2,217	850
1945 January	1,815	125	2,574	734	401	619	570	2,688	734	105	2,114	726
February	1,406	114	2,212	580	423	558	481	2,383	562	98	1,914	641
March	1,199	110	2,191	461	467	545	479	2,229	439	102	1,574	580
April	1,090	107	2,247	513	442	533	529	2,197	399	110	1,391	584
May	1,038	106	2,322	510	363	524	550	2,215	417	111	1,289	634
June	1,278	113	2,789	543	445	567	629	2,533	717	121	1,097	730
July	1,406	123	3,099	532	443	590	694	2,791	1,028	134	1,023	781
August	1,183	125	3,041	410	273	552	718	2,823	1,059	132	966	776

1943 figures for Gas and Water are combined.

1. Great Britain.
2. Undertakings with an annual consumption of 100 tons or more of coal and or coke.
3. Including coal held by Service departments.
4. From November 1941 coal held in wagons at the sidings of the gas, water and electricity undertakings and in barges alongside power stations is included. At the end of November the stocks in these categories were estimated to be 50,000 tons for gas and 55,000 tons for electricity.

Source: Ministry of Fuel and Power

5.6 Mined coal: Productivity[1]

Weekly averages

	Number of wage-earners on colliery books	Average number of shifts worked per wage-earner on colliery books per week[2]	Average number of shifts possible per wage-earner on colliery books per week[2]	Absenteeism percentages overall[2]	Average output in tons per manshift worked[2]		Manshifts at the coal face as percentage of total[2]
	Thousands				Overall	At the coal face	
1939	766	5.15	5.53	6.94	1.14	3.00	37.85
1940	749	5.27	5.75	8.26	1.10	2.97	37.04
1941	698	5.37	5.91	9.03	1.07	2.99	35.96
1942	709	5.34	5.96	10.40	1.05	2.91	35.94
1943	708[3]	5.12[4]	5.85[4]	12.46[4]	1.03	2.75[4]	37.48[4]
1944	710	4.96	5.74	13.61	1.00	2.70	37.19
1945	709	4.73	5.65	16.31	1.00	2.70	36.96
1939 September	748.6	5.36	5.77	7.08	1.12	2.98	37.57
October	755.2	5.40	5.80	6.92	1.14	3.02	37.74
*November	759.1	5.60	6.00	6.74	1.15	3.05	37.84
December	759.8	4.88	5.24	6.95	1.13	3.01	37.54
1940 *January	759.0	5.17	5.71	9.44	1.12	2.98	37.43
February	760.4	5.22	5.87	11.16	1.13	3.04	37.33
March	762.3	5.01	5.51	9.15	1.13	3.03	37.13
April	763.1	5.70	6.15	7.35	1.15	3.07	37.58
*May	763.3	5.62	6.08	7.66	1.14	3.03	37.55
June	766.9	5.46	5.89	7.26	1.11	2.95	37.50
*July	761.1	5.41	5.84	7.48	1.11	2.99	36.97
August	757.1	5.14	5.61	8.34	1.07	2.90	36.88
September	746.0	5.13	5.58	8.02	1.07	2.90	36.76
*October	731.2	5.35	5.79	7.60	1.09	2.96	36.63
November	712.4	5.18	5.60	7.62	1.09	2.99	36.36
December	702.7	4.86	5.30	8.22	1.08	2.98	36.06
1941 *January	698.9	5.29	5.85	9.49	1.08	2.99	36.26
February	694.6	5.29	5.86	9.72	1.09	3.00	36.15
March	692.0	5.31	5.87	9.57	1.09	3.02	35.99
*April	690.4	5.32	5.83	8.70	1.08	3.00	35.89
May	690.2	5.58	6.11	8.73	1.08	3.02	35.78
June	690.6	5.29	5.74	7.78	1.06	2.97	35.67
*July	692.1	5.55	6.02	7.87	1.07	3.00	35.85
August	697.3	4.86	5.30	8.25	1.06	2.98	35.58
September	704.0	5.60	6.16	9.16	1.08	2.98	36.14
*October	706.7	5.67	6.27	9.53	1.08	2.99	36.13
November	707.5	5.37	5.94	9.66	1.08	2.99	36.17
December	707.9	5.32	5.90	9.76	1.06	2.96	35.93
1942 *January	707.5	5.36	6.09	11.94	1.05	2.92	36.12
February	706.8	5.49	6.18	11.13	1.07	2.94	36.26
March	705.6	5.41	6.05	10.63	1.07	2.96	36.18
*April	706.0	5.25	5.81	9.59	1.05	2.92	35.92
May	707.9	5.07	5.64	10.13	1.04	2.91	35.86
June	708.9	5.52	6.14	10.06	1.04	2.91	35.88
*July	709.6	5.46	6.04	9.62	1.05	2.92	35.82
August	701.7	4.64	5.20	10.80	1.02	2.87	35.45
*September	711.4	5.58	6.20	10.02	1.05	2.93	35.97
October	711.0	5.58	6.21	10.21	1.06	2.95	36.01
November	712.9[3]	5.39	6.02	10.41	1.06	2.94	35.95
*December	713.3	5.35	5.97	10.31	1.05	2.90	36.05

See footnotes on page 94.

Source: Ministry of Fuel and Power

5.6 Mined coal: Productivity[1]

continued

Weekly averages

		Number of wage-earners on colliery books	Average number of shifts worked per wage-earner on colliery books per week[2]	Average number of shifts possible per wage-earner on colliery books per week[2]	Absenteeism percentages overall[2]	Average output in tons per manshift worked[2]		Manshifts at the coal face as percentage of total[2]
		Thousands				Overall	At the coal face	
1943	January	714.1	5.33	6.07	12.32	1.04	2.78	37.48
	February	713.7	5.33	6.10	12.53	1.04	2.78	37.61
	March	712.3	5.31	6.08	12.62	1.05	2.79	37.51
	*April	711.0	5.01	5.71	12.23	1.03	2.75	37.29
	May	710.3	5.36	6.05	11.45	1.03	2.77	37.30
	June	708.9	4.99	5.62	11.27	1.02	2.72	37.40
	*July	707.1	5.06	5.72	11.48	1.03	2.73	37.60
	August	705.6	4.50	5.13	12.29	1.00	2.68	37.19
	*September	704.4	5.25	6.00	12.49	1.03	2.73	37.63
	October	703.0	5.33	6.07	12.25	1.04	2.76	37.65
	November	701.9	5.22	6.03	13.47	1.04	2.76	37.54
	* December	702.2	4.84	5.66	14.40	1.02	2.71	37.44
1944	January	703.0	5.22	5.96	12.44	1.01	2.70	37.37
	February	703.4	5.25	5.96	12.00	1.01	2.70	37.44
	* March	704.3	4.95	5.67	12.68	1.01	2.70	37.20
	April	706.5	4.76	5.44	12.44	0.99	2.67	37.23
	May	709.8	5.22	5.98	12.67	1.02	2.72	37.38
	* June	713.1	4.94	5.67	12.89	1.01	2.71	37.05
	July	713.6	4.85	5.58	13.14	1.00	2.70	36.90
	August	713.6	4.26	5.02	15.21	0.97	2.65	36.56
	*September	713.8	5.04	5.94	15.14	1.01	2.70	37.23
	October	713.4	5.08	5.97	14.86	1.01	2.73	37.16
	November	713.2	5.14	6.02	14.55	1.02	2.73	37.41
	*December	713.7	4.80	5.65	15.04	1.00	2.69	37.21
1945	January	715.6	4.81	5.77	16.60	0.98	2.65	37.11
	February	716.9	4.98	5.95	16.40	1.00	2.69	37.20
	* March	717.4	4.92	5.83	15.55	1.00	2.70	37.09
	April	717.1	4.80	5.68	15.46	0.99	2.68	37.03
	May	716.0	4.32	5.09	15.10	0.97	2.65	36.77
	* June	713.6	5.01	5.87	14.69	1.01	2.71	37.20
	July	709.3	4.63	5.49	15.78	0.98	2.67	36.77
	August	706.2	3.62	4.42	18.00	0.92	2.57	35.98

1. Great Britain.
2. Up to and including 1942, the figures are obtained from returns collected by the Joint Accountants to the industry for the purpose of wages ascertainment.
3. The introduction of a revised form of return in November 1942 resulted in a net increase of about 1,250 in the total wage-earners.
4. Owing to the introduction of a revised forrn of return the figures are not comparable with those for previous years. On the old basis the figures for 1943 are: shifts worked, 5.24; shifts possible, 5.96; absenteeism percentage, 12.06; average output, 2.86; percentage of shifts at the coal face, 35.94.

* Average of five weeks.

Source: Ministry of Fuel and Power

5.7 Coke: Production, consumption and stocks

Thousand tons

	Production[1]			Consumption			Stocks[1] (end of period)		
	Total	At coke ovens	At gas-works	Total	Inland con-sumption[2]	Overseas ship-ments[3]	Total	At coke ovens	At gas-works
Annual totals									
1939	24,226	14,026	10,200	24,226	21,758	2,468	..	487	706
1940	25,268	15,351	9,917	25,488	24,544	944	2,731	441	532
1941	25,099	14,547	10,552	25,140	24,697	443	2,690	160	572
1942	26,104	14,900	11,204	26,100	25,819	281	2,694	183	453
1943	25,861	14,453	11,408	25,485	25,192	293	3,070	332	680
1944	25,576	14,081	11,495	26,546	26,433	113	2,100	82	290
1945	25,622	13,986	11,636	25,545	25,362	183	2,177	77	279
Weekly averages									
1939	465	269	196	465	417	48	..	487	706
1940	484	294	190	488	470	18	2,731	441	532
1941	481	279	202	482	474	8	2,690	160	572
1942	501	286	215	501	495	6	2,694	183	453
1943	496	277	219	489	483	6	3,070	332	680
1944	489	269	220	508	506	2	2,100	82	290
1945	491	268	223	490	486	4	2,177	77	279
1939 September	429	271	158	473	424	49	..	590	868
October	463	286	177	489	440	49	..	545	811
November	488	293	195	512	464	48	..	487	749
December	509	292	217	520	465	55	..	487	706
1940 January	535*	295*	240*	586*	543*	43	..	400	540
February	525	295	230	579	541	38	..	361	364
March	508	299	209	537	502	35	..	305	305
April	505	305	200	518	480	38	..	266	291
May	479*	305*	174*	469*	441*	28	..	243	362
June	468	302	166	449	440	9	..	243	438
July	463*	296*	167*	424*	420*	4	..	379	496
August	457	289	168	431	429	2	..	437	548
September	442	283	159	435	431	4	..	486	527
October	451*	282*	169*	447*	443*	4	..	517	515
November	468	284	184	481	475	6	..	463	516
December	485	279	206	487	481	6	2,731	441	532
1941 January	505*	281*	224*	520*	510*	10	..	428	450
February	505	278	227	522	518	4	..	423	370
March	496	278	218	517	506	11	..	381	313
April	481*	276*	205*	500*	490*	10	..	303	274
May	470	275	195	478	466	12	..	252	275
June	457	278	179	447	434	13	..	227	325
July	445*	276*	169*	434*	424*	10	..	198	388
August	450	274	176	444	437	7	..	160	433
September	462	278	184	419	443	6	..	143	484
October	480*	282*	198*	462*	455*	7	..	141	557
November	509	285	224	507	501	6	..	148	544
December	515	286	229	501	496	5	2,690	160	572
1942 January	534*	286*	248*	526*	520*	6	..	163	601
February	541	288	253	563	559	4	..	154	515
March	531	288	243	561	556	5	..	140	402
April	505*	286*	219*	533*	527*	6	..	130	263
May	487	285	202	462	455	7	..	124	359
June	478	283	195	472	467	5	..	131	369
July	470*	283*	187*	461*	455*	6	..	142	391
August	463	281	182	451	443	8	..	150	424
September	481*	290*	191*	466*	460*	6	..	160	481
October	495	291	204	484	480	4	..	181	497
November	517	291	226	525	521	4	..	186	452
December	520*	288*	232*	518*	516*	2	2,694	183	453

See footnotes on page 96.

Source: Ministry of Fuel and Power

5.7 Coke: Production, consumption and stocks

continued

Thousand tons

		Production[1]			Consumption			Stocks[1] (end of period)		
		Total	At coke ovens	At gas-works	Total	Inland con-sumption[2]	Overseas ship-ments[3]	Total	At coke ovens	At gas-works
1943	January	535	289	246	536	530	6	. .	184	448
	February	530	288	242	533	530	3	. .	188	432
	March	522	287	235	525	520	5	. .	194	414
	April	496*	281*	215*	479*	475*	4	. .	230	463
	May	485	278	207	458	452	6	2,836	259	540
	June	470	276	194	417	410	7	3,049	293	625
	July	462*	270*	192*	415*	408*	7	3,284	322	717
	August	453	265	188	419	411	8	3,543	369	794
	September	473*	272*	201*	419*	414*	5	3,688	355	839
	October	492	274	218	477	466	11	3,749	360	849
	November	509	275	234	551	549	2	3,583	337	812
	December	527*	275*	252*	630*	627*	3	3,070	332	680
1944	January	524	275	249	579	575	4	2,851	316	493
	February	530	276	254	648	645	3	2,379	269	320
	March	516*	266*	250*	626*	623*	3	1,830	189	180
	April	468	253	215	474	472	2	1,806	138	166
	May	479	272	207	460	459	1	1,880	98	188
	June	460*	268*	192*	420*	418*	2	2,078	74	228
	July	453	267	186	406	404	2	2,266	70	255
	August	446*	263*	183*	390*	389*	1	2,489	78	275
	September	464	267	197	431	429	2	2,655	80	301
	October	484	270	214	493	491	2	2,619	81	304
	November	516	276	240	589	587	2	2,326	75	299
	December	533*	278*	255*	578*	577*	1	2,100	82	290
1945	January	544	273	271	617	616	1	1,809	80	241
	February	535	272	263	595	594	1	1,571	88	184
	March	513*	271*	242*	544*	543*	1	1,415	78	149
	April	490	270	220	479	477	2	1,460	69	152
	May	465	262	203	434	432	2	1,584	69	170
	June	472*	271*	201*	425*	423*	2	1,819	63	180
	July	462	267	195	411	409	2	2,023	67	204
	August	435	247	188	493	489	4	2,254	79	257

1. Great Britain.
2. Including shipments to Northern Ireland.
3. Calculated from figures for calendar months. Quantities of coke breeze are included.
* Average of five weeks.

Source: Ministry of Fuel and Power

5.8 Coal tar products: Production

Great Britain

	Unit	1942	1943	1944	1945
Road tar (including refined tar)	Thousand tons	640	650	606	628
Creosote/pitch mixture	" "	530	624	591	559
Creosote oil	Thousand gallons	64,000	49,000	55,000	60,000
Pitch	Thousand tons	467	380	404	412
White naphthalene	" "	7.6	9.0	7.4	7.4
Hot-pressed naphthalene	" "	8.4	9.2	9.3	10.0
Crude naphthalene	" "	15.2	14.5	14.1	14.9
Pyridine bases	Thousand gallons	157	137	132	132
Natural phenol	Thousand tons	8.2	8.7	9.2	8.2
Refined cresylic acid (all grades)	Thousand gallons	6,176	7,242	7,056	6,990
Anthracene 40/50 per cent	Thousand tons	1.9	2.4	2.5	1.9

Source: Ministry of Fuel and Power

5.9 Gas: Production

Great Britain

	Total gas available		Gas bought from coke ovens	Gas made				Materials used for gas making	
				Total	Coal gas	Water gas	Other gas	Coal	Gas oil
	Million therms	Million cubic feet						Thousand tons	
1939	1,655	352,072	33,010	319,062	284,570	27,489	7,003	18,866	128.91
1940	1,579	343,440	36,883	306,557	268,781	30,192	7,584	17,983	152.21
1941	1,725	370,123	40,647	329,476	287,795	33,425	8,256	19,319	177.79
1942	1,813	388,755	45,693	343,062	296,363	38,097	8,602	20,634	200.22
1943	1,840	395,457	47,478	347,979	298,521	40,784	8,674	20,732	190.71
1944	1,948	414,342	49,188	365,154	296,600	60,424	8,130	20,620	353.15
1945	2,021	427,941	51,691	376,250	302,430	65,331	8,489	20,845	401.02

Source: Ministry of Fuel and Power

5.10 Gas: Sales

Great Britain

	Total		Domestic	Industrial	Commercial			Public lighting
					Shops, offices, etc	Local authority establishments	Government departments[1]	
	Million therms	Million cubic feet						
1939	1,528	320,228			310,386			9,842
1940	1,473	310,534			309,490			1,044
1941	1,558	330,725			329,204			1,521
1942	1,672	357,137			355,468			1,669
1943	1,691	362,588	212,230	103,166	30,596	7,776	7,539	1,281
1944	1,770	379,641	228,818	96,330	34,978	8,860	8,789	1,866
1945	1,821	389,850	248,974	86,782	33,773	8,496	6,312	5,513

Source: Ministry of Fuel and Power

5.11 Electricity: Production

Great Britain

	1939	1940	1941	1942	1943	1944	1945
	Million units (million kilo-watt hours)						
Electricity generated:							
Total	27,733	29,976	33,577	36,903	38,217	39,649	38,611
Authorised undertakings:							
Public authorities	14,340	15,971	17,977	19,607	20,225	21,480	20,702
Companies	12,069	12,802	14,383	16,047	16,726	16,883	16,582
Railway and transport authorities	1,324	1,203	1,217	1,249	1,266	1,286	1,327
Method of generation:							
Steam plant	26,578	29,003	32,616	35,699	36,800	38,378	37,373
Oil engines	51	57	57	46	38	45	44
Gas engines	3	3	3	2	2	3	2
Water power	982	800	831	1,097	1,329	1,176	1,144
Destructor plant, waste heat, etc	119	113	70	59	48	47	48
	Thousand tons						
Materlals used:							
Coal	15,925	18,112	20,435	22,283	22,599	24,074	23,493
Coke and coke breeze	235	258	275	320	318	337	330
Oil	19	26	20	18	14	8	20

Source: Ministry of Fuel and Power

5.12 Electricity: Sales[1,2]

Great Britain — *Million units*

	1939	1940	1941	1942	1943	1944	1945
Total	22,234	24,263	27,308	30,286	31,449	32,519	31,363
Domestic and farm premises	5,936	6,228	6,637	6,720	6,709	7,835	8,805
Shops, offlces and other commercial premises	3,117	2,997	3,266	3,256	3,062	3,510	3,482
Factories and other industrial premises	11,672	13,874	16,244	19,142	20,516	19,976	17,679
Public lighting	248	17	18	20	20	29	161
Traction	1,261	1,147	1,143	1,148	1,142	1,169	1,236

1. Authorised electricity undertakings only.
2. The figures, which are estirnates only, are based on representative samples of the returns made to the Electricity Commissioners.

Source: Ministry of Fuel and Power

5.13 Arrivals of petroleum products

Thousand tons

	Total	Refined petroleum products							Crude and process oils
		Aviation, motor and industrial spirit	White spirit	Kerosine	Gas/Diesel oils	Fuel oil	Lubricating oils		
Annual totals									
1940	11,381	3,592	64	999	1,367	3,235	578		1,546
1941	13,051	4,741	58	1,062	1,790	3,850	491		1,060
1942	10,232	4,083	103	856	1,364	2,407	565		854
1943	14,828	5,306	69	1,214	1,887	5,122	433		798
1944	20,176	9,417	111	1,334	2,210	5,336	575		1,194
1945	15,924	6,999	98	1,292	2,101	3,703	337		1,394
Weekly averages									
1940	217.7	68.7	1.2	19.1	26.1	61.9	11.1		29.6
1941	250.3	90.9	1.1	20.4	34.3	73.9	9.4		20.3
1942	196.2	78.3	2.0	16.4	26.1	46.2	10.8		16.4
1943	284.4	101.8	1.3	23.3	36.2	98.2	8.3		15.3
1944	385.9	180.1	2.1	25.5	42.3	102.1	11.0		22.8
1945	305.4	134.2	1.9	24.8	40.3	71.0	6.5		26.7
1939 September	131.4	58.1	-	4.5	17.5	24.2	3.5		23.6
* October	128.6	57.2	-	3.7	20.6	29.9	8.7		8.5
November	185.5	63.9	-	36.2	18.1	37.1	1.6		28.6
December	215.4	64.0	0.5	25.1	16.2	65.9	4.9		38.8
1940 * January	216.3	88.9	0.8	14.6	19.5	53.0	12.9		26.6
February	192.7	59.8	1.8	8.2	16.1	56.5	6.0		44.3
March	263.3	91.7	1.2	21.3	33.1	58.5	21.7		35.8
* April	221.3	76.7	1.0	19.8	36.8	56.6	5.8		24.6
May	286.2	99.9	2.2	15.1	42.5	64.6	19.9		42.0
June	326.5	91.1	1.1	21.5	30.3	94.9	15.8		71.8
* July	200.0	57.4	0.7	16.0	25.5	67.3	15.6		17.5
August	215.7	69.0	-	6.9	31.4	76.3	6.1		26.0
* September	150.0	38.3	2.6	16.8	15.9	53.2	6.9		16.3
October	132.9	46.3	0.5	24.9	10.1	34.3	5.5		11.3
November	218.2	53.5	1.9	32.3	23.3	76.3	8.1		22.8
* December	180.3	48.2	0.8	28.4	26.3	47.8	7.9		20.9
1941 January	99.9	38.2	-	9.6	3.8	30.0	3.3		15.0
February	204.3	72.4	-	11.9	30.8	60.4	2.5		26.3
* March	196.0	55.8	-	17.4	28.2	65.4	3.4		25.8
April	230.0	71.3	0.9	6.9	34.1	81.2	10.4		25.2
May	198.6	89.5	-	5.0	25.4	48.2	5.1		25.4
* June	279.9	99.7	2.8	6.3	43.1	91.1	10.8		26.1
July	275.2	91.2	1.1	24.8	44.7	83.0	18.0		12.4
August	280.1	104.4	1.4	25.2	43.4	75.1	12.1		18.5
* September	367.9	136.5	1.8	41.2	38.3	118.5	15.0		16.6
October	298.9	105.2	0.4	30.4	37.5	94.1	6.2		25.1
November	270.0	112.9	2.5	35.7	43.2	60.5	4.4		10.8
* December	280.7	108.0	1.9	27.8	38.1	68.9	19.4		16.6
1942 January	207.8	78.9	1.7	19.4	48.4	39.5	6.8		13.1
February	239.9	99.9	1.4	19.7	29.5	60.7	9.7		19.0
* March	140.3	67.5	1.6	14.8	6.1	24.0	15.6		10.7
April	209.4	93.1	3.9	14.5	27.5	31.3	12.6		26.5
May	119.8	49.9	-	8.7	17.2	19.7	13.9		10.4
* June	163.1	71.1	2.7	9.9	24.1	25.2	12.7		17.4
July	234.4	92.1	4.9	23.6	28.5	57.4	10.5		17.4
* August	180.6	47.7	3.1	12.1	23.9	52.3	18.1		23.4
September	268.1	96.8	2.4	32.5	30.8	85.1	2.9		17.6
October	173.9	48.4	1.3	25.3	21.4	50.2	13.3		14.0
* November	197.5	72.0	0.6	9.3	34.4	57.8	7.2		16.2
December	253.0	139.0	-	12.9	27.1	58.5	4.7		10.8

Source: Ministry of Fuel and Power

5.13 Arrivals of petroleum products

continued

Thousand tons

		Total	Refined petroleum products						Crude and process oils
			Aviation, motor and industrial spirit	White spirit	Kerosine	Gas/Diesel oils	Fuel oil	Lubricating oils	
1943	January	147.4	31.7	-	-	44.6	55.4	4.4	11.3
	February	236.6	74.6	0.8	15.5	40.7	79.8	12.6	12.6
	*March	197.7	60.1	1.2	23.3	22.6	70.6	4.4	15.5
	April	278.4	84.7	-	37.9	40.8	88.9	6.5	19.6
	*May	262.6	67.0	1.8	18.8	44.9	104.7	8.0	17.4
	June	372.9	122.7	1.1	34.1	52.4	144.0	6.2	12.4
	July	408.8	143.4	3.5	28.3	36.0	167.5	9.2	20.9
	*August	325.8	115.5	0.8	29.4	33.8	113.9	9.3	23.1
	September	412.4	154.5	2.7	48.4	54.2	128.4	7.6	16.6
	October	297.9	156.2	2.0	19.1	19.1	80.3	11.1	10.1
	*November	269-3	123.9	1.4	15.1	23.2	86.6	9.0	10.1
	December	233·2	100.6	0.8	11.6	28.0	66.5	12.3	13.4
1944	*January	225.2	101.2	3.4	22.4	17.1	66.2	4.9	10.0
	February	278.6	126.6	0.8	7.0	36.4	74.1	13.5	20.2
	March	348.9	167.9	2.7	17.0	30.6	87.7	5.0	38.0
	April	427.0	199.2	6.1	17.1	55.9	107.6	12.4	28.7
	*May	441.2	205.9	1.2	34.2	59.0	112.0	8.8	20.1
	June	502.1	183.6	2.1	24.9	51.0	179.5	17.0	44.0
	*July	466.7	191.5	1.7	35.4	60.8	137.1	19.0	21.2
	August	471.0	182.2	3.0	31.9	70.7	145.1	11.3	26.8
	September	492.6	267.9	2.1	44.7	41.6	98.0	15.6	22.7
	*October	357.1	189.5	0.8	23.6	44.9	72.3	10.0	16.0
	November	341.2	189.2	1.1	35.4	26.3	62.1	7.9	19.2
	December	319.8	177.3	1.0	11.1	12.7	95.4	7.5	14.8
1945	*January	315.9	190.4	0.8	13.1	27.0	59.4	4.3	20.9
	February	258.0	138.4	2.1	5.2	21.7	56.8	7.2	26.6
	March	378.4	212.9	4.5	23.9	27.9	79.1	4.9	25.2
	*April	365.5	204.3	1.7	11.4	39.1	80.7	7.4	20.9
	May	478.5	227.7	2.9	27.2	55.9	138.9	4.7	21.2
	June	485.5	186.3	2.1	36.5	62.8	147.8	12.9	37.1
	*July	296.0	115.4	1.0	30.8	45.2	74.8	8.0	20.8
	August	205.2	49.7	3.8	30.6	55.9	42.0	6.0	17.2

* Average of five weeks.

Source: Ministry of Fuel and Power

5.14 Production of petroleum products from imported crude and process oils

Thousand tons

		Total	Aviation, motor and industrial spirit	White spirit	Kerosine	Gas /Diesel oils[1]	Fuel oil[2]	Lubricating oils	Bitumen
Annual totals									
1940		1,507	280	32.3	60.9	344	275	144	370
1941		1,023	186	19.4	29.8	242	97	109	339
1942		893	275	2.0	6.9	61	156	150	243
1943		835	306	0.1	3.8	59	105	189	172
1944		1,148	470	0.1	2.4	83	131	210	251
1945		1,249	438	2.8	4.2	117	167	242	278
Weekly averages									
1940		28.8	5.3	0.6	1.2	6.6	5.3	2.7	7.1
1941		19.6	3.6	0.4	0.6	4.6	1.8	2.1	6.5
1942		17.1	5.3	-	0.1	1.2	3.0	2.9	4.6
1943		16.0	5.9	-	0.1	1.1	2.0	3.6	3.3
1944		22.0	9.0	0.1	0.1	1.6	2.5	4.0	4.8
1945		24.0	8.4	0.1	0.1	2.3	3.2	4.6	5.3
1939	September	..	..	..	1.2	3.3	11.0	3.3	9.5
	*October	32.1	6.2	0.4	1.4	3.6	9.2	4.9	6.4
	November	31.3	6.3	0.4	2.2	4.2	6.8	2.7	8.7
	December	33.5	7.2	0.3	2.1	3.3	10.6	2.9	7.1
1940	*January	30.3	4.5	0.4	1.8	3.1	11.5	3.3	5.7
	February	28.5	5.9	0.7	1.4	4.1	8.1	3.2	5.1
	March	28.4	4.9	0.7	1.9	4.0	7.1	3.4	6.4
	*April	25.5	3.7	0.5	0.9	4.6	4.4	3.4	8.0
	May	27.3	4.1	0.3	0.9	5.3	5.1	2.9	8.7
	June	30.5	5.0	0.7	1.5	3.5	7.3	3·8	8.7
	*July	26.0	4.8	0.6	1.0	3.4	5.2	3.6	7.4
	August	24.0	4.0	0.6	0.9	3.3	5.5	2.1	7.6
	*September	22.2	3.8	0.5	0.7	2.6	6.0	1.9	6.7
	October	25.9	3.4	0.6	0.7	2.9	6.6	3.3	8.4
	November	20.9	3.5	0.5	0.9	2.5	4.4	2.8	6.3
	*December	19.8	2.7	0.7	1.0	2.2	4.0	2.9	6.3
1941	January	19.7	3.3	0.3	0.9	3.1	4.5	2.5	5.1
	February	19.9	1.8	0.4	1.1	2.3	5.8	2.4	6.1
	*March	26.9	3.6	0.5	1.1	3.2	6.5	4.0	8.0
	April	25.0	2.6	0.7	0.5	3.3	6.2	3.2	8.5
	May	20.1	2.5	0.5	1.1	2.4	4.7	2.2	6.7
	*June	21.6	2.4	0.6	0.7	2.8	4.6	2.5	8.0
	July	19.0	2.2	0.5	0.5	2.3	4.2	2.7	6.6
	August	16.0	1.5	0.3	0.2	1.6	3.8	2.3	6.3
	*September	16.6	2.6	0.1	0.4	1.6	3.2	2.5	6.2
	October	15.5	2.2	0.4	0.1	1.2	3.9	1.4	6.3
	November	14.6	2.6	0.2	0.2	1.1	3.6	1.1	5.8
	*December	14.3	3.4	0.2	0.1	1.2	3.5	0.9	5.0
1942	January	12.5	3.4	0.1	0.2	0.9	2.6	1.4	3.9
	February	13.4	4.5	-	0.2	0.5	2.9	1.6	3.7
	*March	15.2	4.4	-	0.2	1.0	2.9	1.6	5.1
	April	14.9	3.2	-	0.1	0.4	3.0	3.4	4.8
	May	13.4	3.1	-	0.3	0.7	2.7	2.0	4.6
	*June	15.9	4.3	-	0.3	1.0	2.8	2.1	5.4
	July	15.6	5.1	-	-	0.5	3.1	2.2	4.7
	*August	14.6	3.5	-	0.1	1.3	2.4	3.1	4.2
	September	17.9	5.4	-	-	0.9	2.8	3.0	5.8
	October	17.6	4.5	0.2	-	1.4	3.4	2.8	5.3
	*November	17.5	3.6	-	-	1.6	2.8	5.0	4.5
	December	16.0	3.4	0.2	0.1	1.6	2.0	4.6	4.1

See footnotes on page 102.

Source: Ministry of Fuel and Power

5.14 Production of petroleum products from imported crude and process oils

continued

Thousand tons

		Total	Aviation, motor and industrial spirit	White spirit	Kerosine	Gas /Diesel oils[1]	Fuel oil[2]	Lubricating oils	Bitumen
1943	January	15.3	5.7	-	-	1.1	1.8	3.1	3.6
	February	13.7	4.7	-	-	0.9	1.9	2.6	3.6
	*March	15.1	4.6	-	0.3	1.2	1.9	3.3	3.8
	April	12.2	4.3	-	0.2	0.2	2.0	2.8	2.7
	*May	11.7	2.4	-	-	0.7	1.9	3.9	2.8
	June	12.3	5.0	-	-	0.6	1.5	3.1	2.1
	July	14.0	5.8	-	-	0.7	1.7	2.8	3.0
	*August	13.7	4.1	-	-	0.9	1.8	3.7	3.2
	September	17.6	6.2	-	0.1	0.7	2.6	4.2	3.8
	October	17.6	5.9	-	-	1.0	2.7	3.7	4.3
	*November	17.9	5.8	-	-	0.9	2.7	4.8	3.7
	December	19.5	7.1	-	-	0.8	2.5	5.1	4.0
1944	*January	18.5	7.2	-	-	0.7	2.8	4.1	3.7
	February	20.0	7.7	-	-	1.0	2.7	4.4	4.2
	March	21.5	9.0	-	-	1.1	3.5	3.1	4.8
	April	21.8	7.7	-	-	1.3	3.1	4.8	4.9
	*May	22.0	7.6	-	-	0.9	3.4	4.6	5.5
	June	22.3	6.7	-	-	1.2	3.6	4.7	6.1
	*July	24.0	9.0	-	0.1	1.2	3.8	4.1	5.8
	August	22.7	9.1	-	-	0.8	3.7	4.2	4.9
	September	23.2	8.9	-	0.1	0.9	4.4	3.0	5.9
	*October	20.6	8.4	-	-	0.8	3.7	3.8	3.9
	November	19.8	7.8	-	0.1	0.7	3.5	3.5	4.2
	December	20.5	9.6	-	-	0.9	3.1	3.4	3.5
1945	*January	20.6	9.0	-	-	0.7	3.8	4.3	2.8
	February	21.2	8.6	-	0.1	0.8	3.8	4.6	3.3
	March	21.2	7.9	-	0.1	1.2	3.5	3.4	5.1
	*April	22.0	8.6	0.1	0.1	1.4	3.5	4.1	4.2
	May	19.2	6.6	-	0.1	1.0	3.0	3.4	5.1
	June	23.9	8.6	-	0.1	1.1	3.8	3.6	6.7
	*July	22.9	9.2	-	0.1	1.1	3.3	4.2	5.0
	August	23.4	7.1	0.1	-	1.5	3.8	4.1	6.8

1. The monthly figures are not revised to take account of inter-product transfers, blending, etc., and are therefore not fully comparable with the annual figures.
2. Including the quantity of fuel oil consumed by refineries from their own production.
* Average of five weeks.

Source: Ministry of Fuel and Power

5.15 Production from indigenous materials of petroleum products and substitutes

Thousand tons

		Total	Aviation, motor and industrial spirit[1]	Gas /Diesel oils[1]	Fuel oil[2]	Lubricating oils	Bitumen
Annual totals							
1940		639	401	72.8	158	-	7.7
1941		765	350	80.8	327	-	5.0
1942		1,009	380	96.7	520	6.8	4.0
1943		1,113	385	108.7	594	20.5	5.7
1944		1,089	401	97.8	564	20.1	3.1
1945		1,002	389	84.2	514	12.0	
Weekly averages							
1940		12.2	7.7	1.4	3.0	-	0.1
1941		14.7	6.7	1.6	6.3	-	0.1
1942		19.4	7.3	1.9	10.0	0.1	0.1
1943		21.3	7.4	2.1	11.4	0.4	-
1944		20.8	7.6	1.9	10.8	0.4	0.1
1945		19.2	7.5	1.6	9.8	0.2	0.1
1939	September	5.0	2.6	1.2	0.9	-	0.3
	*October	7.4	4.8	1.2	1.3	-	0.1
	November	10.5	7.6	1.4	1.4	-	0.1
	December	10.0	7.3	1.5	1.1	-	0.1
1940	*January	9.0	6.5	1.3	1.1	-	0.1
	February	9.9	6.9	1.6	1.3	-	0.1
	March	10.3	7.8	1.4	1.1	-	-
	*April	12.1	9.1	1.2	1.8	-	-
	May	13.5	9.4	1.5	2.4	-	0.2
	June	11.4	7.5	1.3	2.5	-	0.1
	*July	12.7	6.9	1.6	4.0	-	0.2
	August	12.9	7.4	1.4	3.9	-	0.2
	*September	12.5	7.5	1.1	3.8	-	0.1
	October	13.9	7.5	1.5	4.7	-	0.2
	November	14.4	7.5	1.4	5.3	-	0.2
	*December	13.1	6.9	1.3	4.8	-	0.1
1941	January	13.6	6.9	1.5	5.1	-	0.1
	February	13.9	6.3	1.7	5.8	-	0.1
	*March	13.2	6.4	1.4	5.3	-	0.1
	April	13.1	6.3	1.6	5.1	-	0.1
	May	13.5	6.8	1.6	5.0	-	0.1
	*June	13.1	6.8	1.6	4.6	-	0.1
	July	12.9	6.5	1.6	4.7	-	0.1
	August	14.7	6.7	1.5	6.4	-	0.1
	*September	15.3	5.8	1.8	7.6	-	0.1
	October	17.2	7.2	1.6	8.3	-	0.1
	November	18.1	7.0	1.8	9.2	-	0.1
	*December	16.9	7.0	1.7	8.1	-	0.1
1942	January	17.2	7.0	1.8	8.3	-	0.1
	February	18.5	7.6	1.6	9.2	-	0.1
	*March	19.2	7.7	1.6	9.8	-	0.1
	April	18.3	7.7	2.1	8.4	-	0.1
	May	17.3	7.1	1.6	8.4	0.1	0.1
	*June	19.0	7.2	2.0	9.5	0.2	0.1
	July	19.2	6.8	2.2	9.9	0.2	0.1
	*August	17.4	6.8	2.0	8.3	0.2	0.1
	September	20.9	6.4	2.0	12.2	0.1	0.2
	October	20.1	6.7	1.5	11.2	0.6	0.1
	*November	22.9	7.6	2.0	13.1	0.1	0.1
	December	20.0	6.8	1.6	11.3	0.2	0.1

See footnotes on page 104.

Source: Ministry of Fuel and Power

5.15 Production from indigenous materials of petroleum products and substitutes

continued

Thousand tons

		Total	Aviation, motor and industrial spirit[1]	Gas /Diesel oils	Fuel oil[2]	Lubricating oils	Bitumen
1943	January	21.8	7.2	1.7	12.7	0.1	0.1
	February	23.8	7.4	2.3	13.9	0.1	0.1
	*March	22.4	7.5	2.2	11.9	0.8	-
	April	19.5	7.3	1.9	10.1	0.2	-
	*May	21.2	7.7	2.0	11.3	0.1	0.1
	June	20.2	7.3	2.1	10.5	0.2	0.1
	July	18.0	7.2	2.2	8.3	0.2	0.1
	*August	17.6	6.2	1.8	9.4	0.1	0.1
	September	19.8	7.1	1.6	10.6	0.4	0.1
	October	20.7	6.8	2.4	10.9	0.4	0.2
	*November	23.6	7.7	2.2	13.3	0.3	0.1
	December	21.6	6.6	1.8	12.3	0.8	0.1
1944	*January	22.5	7.1	1.8	13.2	0.2	0.2
	February	21.7	7.5	2.0	11.9	0.2	0.1
	March	22.4	8.4	1.9	11.5	0.5	0.1
	April	19.6	7.7	1.8	9.1	0.9	0.1
	*May	20.5	7.7	2.0	10.5	0.1	0.2
	June	20.7	7.7	2.0	10.2	0.5	0.3
	*July	19.2	7.8	1.6	9.3	0.4	0.1
	August	17.9	7.9	1.7	7.8	0.4	0.1
	September	18.7	7.2	1.7	9.5	0.1	0.2
	*October	21.2	7.5	1.7	11.4	0.6	-
	November	24.5	8.3	1.9	13.6	0.6	0.1
	December	21.9	7.9	1.6	12.0	0.4	-
1945	*January	20.2	6.6	1.5	11.6	0.4	0.1
	February	20.7	7.5	1.7	11.2	0.2	0.1
	March	21.5	7.4	1.8	11.8	0.4	0.1
	*April	19.3	7.5	1.4	10.0	0.3	0.1
	May	16.7	7.1	1.3	8.0	0.3	-
	June	17.3	7.5	1.7	7.9	0.1	0.1
	*July	15.0	6.3	1.5	6.7	0.4	0.1
	August	13.3	5.8	1.0	6.4	-	0.1

1. Including white spirit and kerosine.
2. Mainly tar oils.
* Average of five weeks.

Source: Ministry of Fuel and Power

5.16 Deliveries into consumption of petroleum products

Thousand tons

		Total	Aviation, motor and industrial spirit	White spirit	Kerosine	Gas /Diesel oils	Fuel oil[1]	Lubricating oils	Bitumen
Annual totals									
1940		11,649	3,786	82	874	1,448	4,562	517	380
1941		12,326	4,433	90	943	1,547	4,318	647	348
1942		12,603	4,367	101	1,012	1,575	4,672	628	248
1943		13,204	5,069	93	1,067	1,510	4,696	592	177
1944		19,447	8,519	106	1,134	1,745	6,981	699	263
1945		15,358	5,992	113	1,263	1,786	5,408	553	243
Weekly averages									
1940		222.8	72.4	1.5	16.7	27.7	87.2	10.0	7.3
1941		236.4	85.0	1.7	18.1	29.7	82.8	12.4	6.7
1942		241.7	83.8	1.9	19.4	30.2	89.6	12.0	4.8
1943		253.2	97.2	1.8	20.5	28.9	90.0	11.4	3.4
1944		371.9	162.9	2.0	21.7	33.4	133.5	13.4	5.0
1945		294.5	114.9	2.2	24.2	34.2	103.7	10.6	4.7
1939	September	266.2	97.8	1.6	16.8	32.6	89.0	17.1	11.3
	* October	199.3	62.4	0.7	15.2	24.9	71.8	15.6	8.7
	November	201.7	64.1	1.4	15.0	28.3	74.6	9.8	8.5
	December	205.6	59.3	1.5	15.9	29.0	80.4	12.2	7.3
1940	* January	207.2	58.2	1.6	22.5	32.0	78.0	9.9	5.0
	February	208.1	59.1	1.2	19.7	33.0	80.1	9.7	5.3
	March	209.4	64.9	1.4	17.2	29.6	79.9	9.2	7.2
	* April	245.8	72.8	1.9	18.5	28.5	104.3	11.4	8.6
	May	231.4	71.6	2.4	14.0	25.2	97.5	11.9	8.8
	June	227.6	72.7	1.8	12.2	28.2	91.7	11.4	9.6
	* July	214.3	77.3	1.9	12.1	26.9	79.7	8.9	7.5
	August	213.4	76.8	1.4	14.7	27.6	76.5	9.1	7.3
	* September	223.5	79.4	1.4	16.9	26.4	84.5	8.1	6.8
	October	223.5	78.8	1.3	17.8	29.6	77.5	10.4	8.1
	November	226.5	76.4	1.6	16.3	30.7	83.0	10.6	7.9
	* December	221.1	77.2	1.4	18.3	31.9	76.0	9.6	6.7
1941	January	221.6	71.2	1.2	20.5	32.8	81.0	9.8	5.1
	February	239.4	75.8	1.5	18.5	36.2	88.9	11.7	6.8
	* March	256.1	83.6	1.5	20.4	37.4	93.4	11.6	8.2
	April	255.6	88.8	1.5	21.8	32.2	92.5	10.5	8.3
	May	254.1	92.9	1.7	17.6	31.7	90.0	12.9	7.3
	* June	226.7	89.8	1.6	12.6	28.0	75.4	11.9	7.4
	July	226.0	88.3	1.8	13.0	27.7	74.4	13.5	7.3
	August	222.7	87.4	1.7	14.8	24.9	75.0	12.2	6.7
	* September	234.8	90.7	1.9	18.7	28.1	76.8	12.2	6.4
	October	231.2	84.6	2.1	21.6	28.7	74.8	13.2	6.2
	November	236.6	83.1	2.2	20.2	30.7	82.6	11.9	5.9
	* December	225.0	80.3	1.9	17.9	29.8	78.6	11.7	4.8
1942	January	231.6	76.1	1.9	18.7	32.5	86.7	11.7	4.0
	February	243.7	80.8	1.9	19.2	37.0	89.9	10.8	4.1
	* March	256.8	83.6	2.2	22.5	36.3	92.0	15.2	5.0
	April	248.3	85.5	2.0	25.8	31.2	86.5	12.2	5.1
	May	248.5	86.9	2.3	19.6	29.5	91.8	13.3	5.1
	* June	235.2	89.7	1.7	14.0	29.2	81.7	14.3	4.6
	July	232.0	85.0	2.0	14.0	29.3	86.2	10.8	4.7
	* August	232.9	83.9	1.9	17.5	30.4	84.1	10.4	4.7
	September	245.4	87.5	1.9	20.8	30.8	88.7	10.1	5.6
	October	265.1	87.2	2.0	23.3	33.6	101.9	11.7	5.4
	* November	232.7	83.0	2.0	20.5	33.3	76.6	12.4	4.9
	December	222.9	75.4	1.7	18.0	29.9	83.9	10.2	3.8

See footnotes on page 106.

Source: Ministry of Fuel and Power

5.16 Deliveries into consumption of petroleum products

continued

Thousand tons

		Total	Aviation, motor and industrial spirit	White spirit	Kerosine	Gas/Diesel oils	Fuel oil[1]	Lubricating oils	Bitumen
1943	January	228.9	74.4	1.7	19.0	32.3	87.7	10.2	3.6
	February	236.3	82.5	1.6	20.0	32.1	85.8	10.5	3.8
	* March	251.7	91.9	1.8	29.4	31.9	81.7	11.5	3.5
	April	234.5	88.3	1.6	23.2	28.1	80.6	10.3	2.4
	May	249.3	96.5	1.8	17.0	29.7	88.8	12.6	2.9
	June	259.8	100.2	1.6	14.4	29.4	100.2	11.5	2.5
	July	231.2	98.0	1.9	16.1	27.1	74.6	10.9	2.6
	* August	243.3	106.2	1.7	19.8	25.8	76.4	10.3	3.1
	September	259.2	109.5	1.9	22.5	29.9	79.6	11.8	4.0
	October	272.0	104.6	2.0	24.5	33.8	90.9	11.8	4.4
	November	281.8	104.4	2.1	21.1	34.4	102.7	12.7	4.4
	* December	276.6	105.1	1.6	18.4	35.2	101.5	11.3	3.5
1944	* January	305.1	117.1	1.9	21.2	38.4	108.7	13.7	4.1
	February	337.1	135.9	2.1	23.3	38.1	118.6	14.7	4.4
	March	374.8	156.6	2.2	29.5	42.1	124.0	15.2	5.2
	April	386.4	164.5	2.0	26.7	38.3	134.9	15.1	4.9
	* May	437.9	201.8	2.2	20.9	37.8	151.5	17.4	6.3
	June	447.9	212.2	2.3	17.0	35.8	156.2	18.1	6.3
	* July	392.3	181.2	1.9	16.4	31.1	141.7	13.9	6.1
	August	384.7	178.8	1.8	22.3	30.0	136.2	10.5	5.1
	September	372.2	165.9	2.0	22.5	32.0	132.4	11.5	5.9
	* October	368.4	160.5	2.2	23.1	36.4	131.4	10.3	4.5
	November	348.6	148.1	2.0	21.2	39.0	123.9	10.3	4.1
	December	329.5	137.9	1.9	18.5	36.5	120.1	11.1	3.5
1945	* January	338.6	136.9	1.9	21.4	39.4	126.8	9.5	2.7
	February	384.3	166.5	2.3	25.2	44.4	131.5	10.7	3.7
	March	411.5	186.4	2.9	38.4	39.5	126.1	13.0	5.2
	* April	370.0	157.9	2.4	30.2	35.1	129.1	10.6	4.7
	May	318.1	119.2	2.0	18.9	34.7	131.0	7.9	4.4
	June	274.7	106.9	2.4	18.0	33.3	98.5	10.2	5.4
	* July	258.2	103.3	2.4	19.5	32.3	84.0	10.6	6.1
	August	233.5	85.9	1.8	22.4	33.2	76.0	8.9	5.3

1. Including products used for refinery fuel.
* Average of five weeks.

Source: Ministry of Fuel and Power

5.17 Deliveries into civilian consumption of motor spirit[1]

Thousand tons

		Great Britain						Northern Ireland
		Total	Private cars and motor cycles		Commercial vehicles	Industrial uses	Agricultural uses	
			Basic ration[2]	Supplementary ration				
Annual totals								
1940		2,939	359	464	1,696	314	106	56
1941		3,001	336	429	1,783	347	106	68
1942		2,501	116	357	1,640	286	102	67
1943		2,139	4	296	1,545	194	100	58
1944		2,264	5	323	1,605	215	116	57
1945		2,734	217	430	1,742	204	141	66
Weekly averages[3]								
1940		56.2	6.9	8.9	32.4	6.0	2.0	1.1
1941		57.6	6.5	8.2	34.2	6.7	2.0	1.3
1942		48.0	2.2	6.8	31.5	5.5	2.0	1.3
1943		41.0	0.1	5.7	29.6	3.7	1.9	1.1
1944		43.3	0.1	6.2	30.7	4.1	2.2	1.1
1945		52.4	4.2	8.2	33.4	3.9	2.7	1.3
1940	January	50.6	7.8	8.1	29.2	3.8	1.7	1.0
	February	52.1	6.6	8.4	30.5	4.6	2.0	1.0
	March	55.1	7.0	9.0	32.2	4.8	2.1	1.0
	April	61.9	8.0	10.4	35.7	5.5	2.3	1.3
	May	59.0	7.6	10.0	34.0	5.2	2.2	1.1
	June	53.4	7.0	9.1	29.9	5.3	2.1	1.0
	July	57.6	7.6	9.9	32.2	5.7	2.2	1.2
	August	56.1	7.0	9.4	31.8	5.7	2.2	1.1
	September	55.2	6.8	9.2	31.4	5.7	2.1	11.1
	October	57.9	7.0	9.2	33.8	5.7	2.2	1.1
	November	58.9	6.7	9.0	35.5	5.5	2.2	1.1
	December	56.3	6.5	8.7	33.8	5.2	2.1	1.1
1941	January	54.8	6.5	8.6	32.8	5.0	1.9	1.1
	February	56.5	6.3	9.0	33.7	5.4	2.1	1.2
	March	58.2	6.6	9.3	34.7	5.4	2.2	1.3
	April	61.8	7.4	9.4	37.3	5.5	2.2	1.4
	May	63.5	7.6	9.7	38.2	5.7	2.3	1.5
	June	57.9	7.7	8.4	34.3	5.3	2.2	1.4
	July	59.8	7.9	8.7	35.4	5.6	2.2	1.4
	August	56.1	7.1	8.0	34.1	4.8	2.1	1.3
	September	59.0	7.6	8.4	35.6	5.2	2.2	1.4
	October	55.5	3.8	8.4	35.9	5.2	2.2	1.3
	November	52.7	6.2	7.6	32.4	4.5	2.0	1.3
	December	53.6	5.6	7.6	33.8	4.7	1.9	1.3
1942	January	50.8	5.7	7.4	31.3	4.5	1.9	1.3
	February	52.3	5.6	7.6	32.1	4.9	2.1	1.3
	March	52.3	5.6	7.6	32.1	4.9	2.1	1.3
	April	51.1	2.9	7.1	33.9	5.1	2.1	1.4
	May	48.5	2.7	6.8	32.2	4.8	2.0	1.4
	June	51.1	1.7	7.6	34.8	4.9	2.1	1.4
	July	47.7	1.6	7.1	32.4	4.6	2.0	1.3
	August	42.0	0.7	7.1	27.5	4.6	2.1	1.2
	September	46.4	0.6	7.2	32.2	4.3	2.1	1.3
	October	46.2	0.6	7.1	32.1	4.3	2.1	1.3
	November	43.7	0.1	6.8	30.6	4.2	2.0	1.2
	December	43.5	0.1	6.7	30.9	3.9	1.9	1.2

See footnotes on page 108.

Source: Ministry of Fuel and Power

5.17 Deliveries into civilian consumption of motor spirit[1]

continued

Thousand tons

			Great Britain						Northern Ireland
		Total	Private cars and motor cycles		Commercial vehicles	Industrial uses	Agricultural uses		
			Basic ration2	Supplementary ration					
1943	January	40.5	0.1	6.2	28.7	3.7	1.8		1.1
	February	42.6	0.1	6.2	30.5	3.8	2.0		1.1
	March	43.9	0.1	6.4	31.5	3.9	2.0		1.2
	April	40.9	0.1	6.0	29.2	3.7	1.9		1.1
	May	41.0	0.1	5.8	29.4	3.7	2.0		1.1
	June	40.2	0.1	5.7	28.8	3.7	1.9		1.1
	July	40.1	0.1	5.7	28.7	3.7	1.9		1.0
	August	38.7	0.1	5.5	27.5	3.5	2.1		1.0
	September	41.6	0.1	5.9	29.5	3.9	2.2		1.1
	October	40.4	0.1	5.8	28.6	3.8	2.1		1.1
	November	42.2	0.1	5.8	30.3	3.9	2.1		1.2
	December	40.3	0.1	5.6	29.0	3.6	2.0		1.1
1944	January	39.9	0.1	5.7	28.3	3.8	2.0		1.1
	February	43.5	0.1	6.2	30.9	4.1	2.2		1.1
	March	45.4	0.1	6.5	32.2	4.3	2.3		1.2
	April	40.9	0.1	5.8	29.0	4.0	2.0		1.1
	May	43.9	0.1	6.3	30.9	4.3	2.3		1.1
	June	44.4	0.1	6.4	31.4	4.2	2.3		1.1
	July	41.2	0.1	5.9	29.1	3.9	2.2		1.0
	August	42.9	0.1	6.2	30.4	3.9	2.3		1.1
	September	44.1	0.1	6.5	31.0	4.1	2.4		1.1
	October	44.4	0.1	6.5	31.2	4.2	2.4		1.1
	November	47.5	0.1	7.0	33.6	4.2	2.6		1.2
	December	40.7	0.1	6.0	28.8	3.6	2.2		1.0
1945	January	42.8	0.1	6.5	30.0	3.9	2.3		1.0
	February	45.7	0.1	6.9	32.0	4.2	2.5		1.1
	March	47.3	0.1	7.1	33.3	4.3	2.5		1.2
	April	44.8	0.1	6.8	31.5	4.0	2.4		1.1
	May	45.3	0.1	8.1	30.8	3.9	2.4		1.1
	June	51.2	5.2	8.1	31.1	4.0	2.8		1.1
	July	54.5	5.9	8.4	33.2	3.9	3.1		1.3
	August	56.8	5.8	9.5	33.9	4.2	3.4		1.4

1. Including industrial spirit. The analysis of deliveries by consumer categories is based on total coupon issues. No adjustments have been made for non-use or misuse of coupons.
2. During the period June 1942 to May 1945, the figures in this column relate to supplementary rations for domestic purposes only. The higher figures for June to October 1942 reflect the completion of the consumption of the last basic ration issue.
3. Based on calendar months.

Source: Ministry of Fuel and Power

5.18 Deliveries into consumption of fuel for diesel-engined road vehicles[1]

Thousand tons

		Total	Great Britain				Northern Ireland
			Total	Public service vehicles	Goods vehicles	Others	
Annual totals							
1940		429	426	314	103	8.8	3.6
1941		467	463	337	117	8.7	4.3
1942		473	469	338	122	8.6	4.5
1943		452	448	329	110	8.5	4.2
1944		499	495	342	143	9.7	4.4
1945		511	506	382	114	10.2	4.9
Weekly averages[2]							
1940		8.2	8.1	6.0	2.0	0.1	0.1
1941		9.0	8.9	6.5	2.2	0.2	0.1
1942		9.1	9.0	6.5	2.3	0.2	0.1
1943		8.7	8.6	6.3	2.1	0.2	0.1
1944		9.5	9.4	6.5	2.7	0.2	0.1
1945		9.8	9.7	7.3	2.2	0.2	0.1
1940	January	7.4	7.3	5.2	2.0	0.1	0.1
	February	7.7	7.6	5.7	1.7	0.2	0.1
	March	7.9	7.8	5.6	2.0	0.2	0.1
	April	8.6	8.5	6.2	2.1	0.2	0.1
	May	8.6	8.5	6.1	2.2	0.2	0.1
	June	8.2	8.1	5.6	2.4	0.1	0.1
	July	8.8	8.7	5.9	2.7	0.1	0.1
	August	8.7	8.6	6.0	2.5	0.1	0.1
	September	8.3	8.2	5.7	2.4	0.1	0.1
	October	8.4	8.3	5.6	2.6	0.1	0.1
	November	8.6	8.5	5.8	2.6	0.1	0.1
	December	8.5	8.4	5.2	2.9	0.3	0.1
1941	January	8.6	8.5	5.6	2.6	0.3	0.1
	February	8.8	8.7	6.0	2.5	0.2	0.1
	March	9.0	8.9	6.1	2.7	0.1	0.1
	April	9.1	9.0	6.4	2.4	0.2	0.1
	May	9.3	9.2	6.5	2.6	0.1	0.1
	June	8.7	8.6	6.2	2.3	0.1	0.1
	July	9.2	9.1	6.6	2.4	0.1	0.1
	August	8.7	8.6	6.3	2.2	0.1	0.1
	September	9.4	9.3	6.6	2.6	0.1	0.1
	October	9.1	9.0	6.4	2.4	0.2	0.1
	November	8.7	8.6	6.1	2.3	0.2	0.1
	December	8.9	8.8	6.2	2.4	0.2	0.1
1942	January	8.8	8.7	6.2	2.3	0.2	0.1
	February	9.2	9.1	6.3	2.6	0.2	0.1
	March	9.0	8.9	6.2	2.5	0.2	0.1
	April	9.2	9.1	6.6	2.3	0.2	0.1
	May	8.9	8.8	6.4	2.2	0.2	0.1
	June	9.3	9.2	6.5	2.5	0.2	0.1
	July	9.5	9.4	6.6	2.6	0.2	0.1
	August	8.6	8.5	5.8	2.6	0.1	0.1
	September	9.2	9.1	6.3	2.6	0.2	0.1
	October	9.2	9.1	6.3	2.6	0.2	0.1
	November	8.8	8.7	6.0	2.5	0.2	0.1
	December	8.9	8.8	6.0	2.6	0.2	0.1

See footnotes on page 110.

Source: Ministry of Fuel and Power

5.18 Deliveries into consumption of fuel for diesel-engined road vehicles

continued

Thousand tons

		Total	Great Britain				Northern Ireland
			Total	Public service vehicles	Goods vehicles	Others	
1943	January	8.7	8.6	5.7	2.7	0.2	0.1
	February	8.9	8.8	6.1	2.5	0.2	0.1
	March	9.1	9.0	6.2	2.6	0.2	0.1
	April	8.5	8.4	5.9	2.4	0.1	0.1
	May	8.4	8.3	5.9	2.2	0.2	0.1
	June	8.5	8.4	6.0	2.2	0.2	0.1
	July	8.5	8.4	6.0	2.2	0.2	0.1
	August	8.2	8.1	5.7	2.3	0.1	0.1
	September	8.7	8.6	6.0	2.5	0.1	0.1
	October	8.5	8.4	5.9	2.3	0.2	0.1
	November	9.1	9.0	6.2	2.6	0.2	0.1
	December	9.0	8.9	6.1	2.6	0.2	0.1
1944	January	8.8	8.7	5.9	2.6	0.2	0.1
	February	9.4	9.3	6.4	2.7	0.2	0.1
	March	9.9	9.8	6.6	3.0	0.2	0.1
	April	9.8	9.7	6.0	3.5	0.2	0.1
	May	10.6	10.5	6.5	3.8	0.2	0.1
	June	10.5	10.4	6.6	3.6	0.2	0.1
	July	9.1	9.0	6.1	2.7	0.2	0.1
	August	9.2	9.1	6.3	2.6	0.2	0.1
	September	9.3	9.2	6.5	2.5	0.2	0.1
	October	9.3	9.2	6.6	2.4	0.2	0.1
	November	9.7	9.6	6.9	2.5	0.2	0.1
	December	8.9	8.8	6.3	2.3	0.2	0.1
1945	January	9.4	9.3	6.8	2.3	0.2	0.1
	February	9.9	9.8	7.1	2.5	0.2	0.1
	March	9.8	9.7	7.1	2.4	0.2	0.1
	April	9.5	9.4	6.8	2.4	0.2	0.1
	May	9.7	9.6	7.0	2.4	0.2	0.1
	June	9.7	9.6	7.0	2.4	0.2	0.1
	July	9.6	9.5	6.9	2.4	0.2	0.1
	August	9.7	9.6	7.0	2.4	0.2	0.1

1. The analysis of deliveries by consumer categories is based on total coupon issues.
2. Based on calendar months.

Source: Ministry of Fuel and Power

5.19 Deliveries into consumption of gas, diesel and fuel oil

Thousand tons

		Total	Bunkers	Inland: Road vehicles[1]	Inland: Burning	Inland: Power	Inland: Manu-facture	Inland: Petroleum industry	Inland: Government depart-ments[2]
Annual totals									
1940		6,010	3,849	429			1,732		
1941		5,865	3,537	467	916	349	213	259	124
1942		6,247	3,906	473	939	330	216	287	96
1943		6,206	3,965	452	883	326	248	224	108
1944		8,726	6,279	499	843	341	405	260	99
1945		7,194	4,726	511	797	347	452	291	70
Weekly averages[3]									
1940		114.9	73.6	8.2			33.1		
1941		112.5	67.8	9.0	17.5	6.7	4.1	5.0	2.4
1942		119.8	74.9	9.1	18.0	6.3	4.2	5.5	1.8
1943		118.9	76.0	8.7	16.9	6.2	4.7	4.3	2.1
1944		166.9	120.1	9.5	16.1	6.5	7.8	5.0	1.9
1945		137.9	90.6	9.8	15.3	6.6	8.7	5.6	1.3
1940	January	107.8	64.3	7.4			36.1		
	February	115.7	65.7	7.7			42.3		
	March	106.2	66.4	7.9			31.9		
	April	128.8	88.2	8.6			32.0		
	May	121.7	86.0	8.6	15.0	7.0	2.3	2.2	0.6
	June	117.1	83.3	8.2	13.9	6.8	2.2	2.2	0.5
	July	106.6	71.5	8.8	14.5	6.8	2.0	1.9	1.1
	August	102.5	69.4	8.7	13.3	6.3	1.7	2.0	1.1
	September	106.3	72.1	8.3	13.7	6.1	2.6	2.0	1.5
	October	105.4	65.7	8.4	16.4	6.8	3.5	2.5	2.1
	November	113.3	72.1	8.6	18.2	6.5	4.0	2.1	1.8
	December	105.8	64.6	8.5	18.1	6.5	3.9	1.9	2.3
1941	January	115.4	66.6	8.6	21.1	7.0	4.8	4.7	2.6
	February	123.5	73.1	8.8	20.9	7.4	4.9	5.2	3.2
	March	129.1	81.6	9.0	19.4	7.2	4.3	4.1	3.4
	April	123.0	74.4	9.1	18.8	7.1	4.4	5.4	3.7
	May	123.0	76.8	9.3	17.7	7.3	4.5	3.7	3.7
	June	100.8	63.0	8.7	14.4	6.8	2.9	3.2	1.8
	July	104.0	64.3	9.2	13.9	7.0	3.2	4.5	1.8
	August	98.0	61.9	8.7	13.3	6.1	3.3	4.6	1.4
	September	105.8	64.0	9.4	15.7	7.0	3.7	4.6	1.4
	October	105.5	61.2	9.1	17.2	6.8	4.4	4.9	1.9
	November	111.5	65.4	8.7	19.5	6.4	4.8	5.0	1.7
	December	108.2	62.6	8.9	19.6	6.4	3.9	5.3	1.5
1942	January	120.4	69.9	8.8	22.0	6.7	5.9	5.3	1.8
	February	127.2	73.2	9.2	23.4	7.0	6.9	5.6	1.9
	March	126.1	75.8	9.0	21.0	7.0	6.7	4.8	1.9
	April	118.5	74.6	9.2	18.3	6.6	4.1	4.0	1.7
	May	120.9	80.6	8.9	16.1	6.1	3.4	4.4	1.4
	June	111.3	70.3	9.3	16.4	6.8	2.7	4.0	1.8
	July	116.3	76.9	9.5	15.1	6.4	2.5	4.0	1.9
	August	112.5	75.1	8.6	13.9	6.0	2.5	4.4	1.9
	September	121.9	80.3	9.2	15.8	6.6	3.3	4.7	2.0
	October	134.1	91.3	9.2	16.9	6.5	3.6	4.7	1.9
	November	108.3	62.5	8.8	19.6	6.5	4.6	4.3	2.0
	December	115.5	70.9	8.9	18.8	6.2	4.0	4.5	2.2

See footnotes on page 112.

Source: Ministry of Fuel and Power

5.19 Deliveries into consumption of gas, diesel and fuel oil

continued

Thousand tons

		Total	Bunkers	Inland					
				Road vehicles[1]	Burning	Power	Manu-facture	Petroleum industry	Government depart-ments[2]
1943	January	116.3	71.6	8.7	19.7	6.0	3.7	4.7	1.9
	February	119.3	72.7	8.9	19.8	6.6	3.9	5.2	2.2
	March	115.4	68.2	9.1	19.6	6.8	4.3	5.1	2.3
	April	109.6	69.7	8.5	16.5	6.0	3.1	3.8	2.0
	May	117.6	79.0	8.4	15.5	6.1	3.0	3.8	1.8
	June	130.4	91.4	8.5	14.9	6.0	3.7	3.7	2.2
	July	103.4	66.4	8.5	14.0	6.0	3.0	3.7	1.8
	August	101.7	65.6	8.2	13.5	5.6	3.5	3.4	1.9
	September	109.3	67.2	8.7	15.9	6.5	4.8	4.2	2.0
	October	121.9	76.1	8.5	15.8	6.4	8.5	4.6	2.0
	November	139.5	91.4	9.1	18.6	6.7	7.2	4.1	2.4
	December	141.3	91.4	9.0	19.6	6.5	8.3	4.2	2.3
1944	January	143.6	93.9	8.8	19.1	6.5	8.6	4.4	2.3
	February	154.2	102.4	9.4	20.3	6.9	8.6	4.4	2.2
	March	169.3	112.7	9.9	20.2	7.3	10.4	5.9	2.9
	April	171.3	123.3	9.8	15.5	6.4	7.9	5.8	2.6
	May	188.8	141.7	10.6	15.3	6.8	7.6	4.6	2.2
	June	192.1	147.2	10.5	14.3	6.8	6.6	4.6	2.1
	July	169.1	130.1	9.1	12.6	6.0	5.0	4.8	1.5
	August	170.6	131.5	9.2	12.4	6.0	5.5	4.7	1.3
	September	164.6	122.3	9.3	14.1	6.3	6.8	4.8	1.0
	October	166.5	119.6	9.3	15.7	6.3	8.8	5.2	1.6
	November	163.5	113.5	9.7	17.6	6.9	9.2	4.8	1.8
	December	156.1	110.0	8.9	16.5	6.0	8.2	4.9	1.6
1945	January	169.6	114.8	9.4	20.3	6.5	10.7	6.0	1.9
	February	174.7	120.0	9.9	19.0	7.0	10.9	5.7	2.2
	March	168.2	119.1	9.8	17.0	7.0	8.0	5.4	1.9
	April	163.9	119.1	9.5	14.3	6.5	6.4	6.5	1.6
	May	167.3	123.3	9.7	14.1	6.3	8.0	4.6	1.3
	June	132.0	87.9	9.7	13.8	6.4	7.3	5.6	1.3
	July	115.2	74.7	9.6	11.9	6.4	6.6	5.0	1.0
	August	111.7	71.1	9.7	11.5	6.2	7.3	5.0	1.0

1. Fuel for diesel-engined road vehicles.
2. Includes smoke-screens until 1 April 1943.
3. Based on calendar months. The weekly average for any given month shown in this table will not be exactly the same as the weekly average for the four or five weeks period under the same name in Table 5.16.

Source: Ministry of Fuel and Power

6 RAW MATERIALS

Before the war the supply of many vital raw materials was reliant on imports in 1939, for example, imports accounted for 98 per cent of the total supply of lead, 97 per cent of softwood, 87 per cent of zinc, 70 per cent of aluminium, and 27 per cent of iron ore and these imports accounted for approximately 26 million tons of shipping capacity, dominated by timber (9 million tons) and iron and steel and related materials (7 million tons)(Postan 1952: 158; Ford 1951: 144). Thus, the conquests of Germany and Japan in the early years of the war and the limited shipping capacity available to the British war economy placed great pressures on the raw material supplies of the nation. Despite this, it has been judged that the supply of raw materials did not act as a constraint on munitions production during the war (Hargreaves and Gowing 1952: 127). This was mainly because of the success of the state in finding alternative suppliers, increasing domestic production and decreasing non-essential uses, and its relatively efficient framework for controlling and allocating the available supplies.

The loss of European and eastern supplies due to the victories of Germany and Japan was crucial for many raw materials ; for example, more than three-quarters of the pre-war British imports of materials such as flax, ferro-alloys, bauxite, iron ore and softwood, rubber, raw silk and tungsten ore had been supplied by territories which were effectively cut off from Britain during the war (Hurstfield 1953: 158,167). Some of these lost supplies were replaced by new or increased supplies from Canada (for example, aluminium, abrasives, and paper making materials), other Empire countries (antimony, chrome and tungsten ores, bauxite, flax, and hemp) and especially the USA (iron and steel, chemicals and fertilisers, non-ferrous metals, and synthetic rubber).

6.1 Home production of iron ore

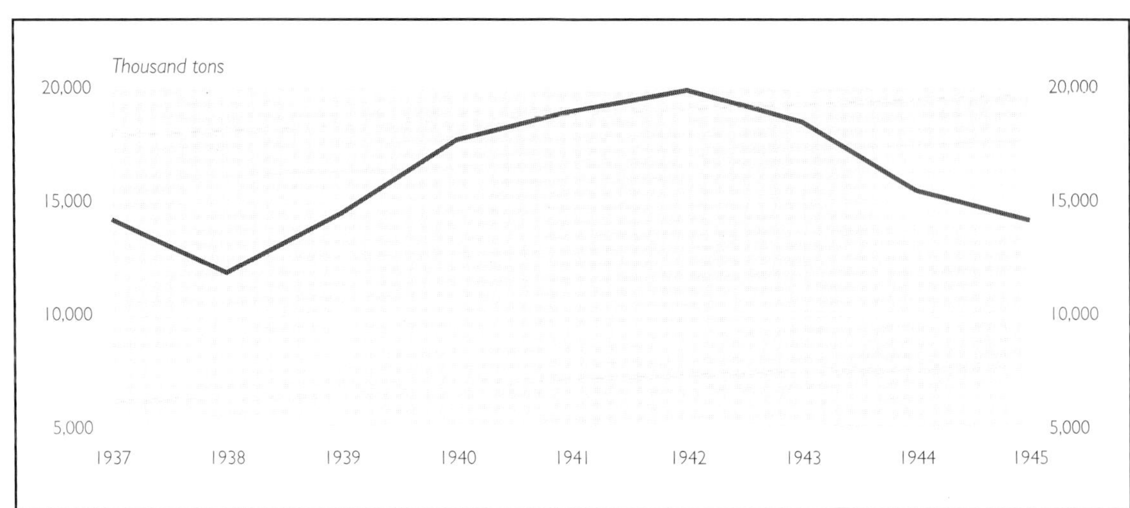

6.2 Home production of virgin aluminium

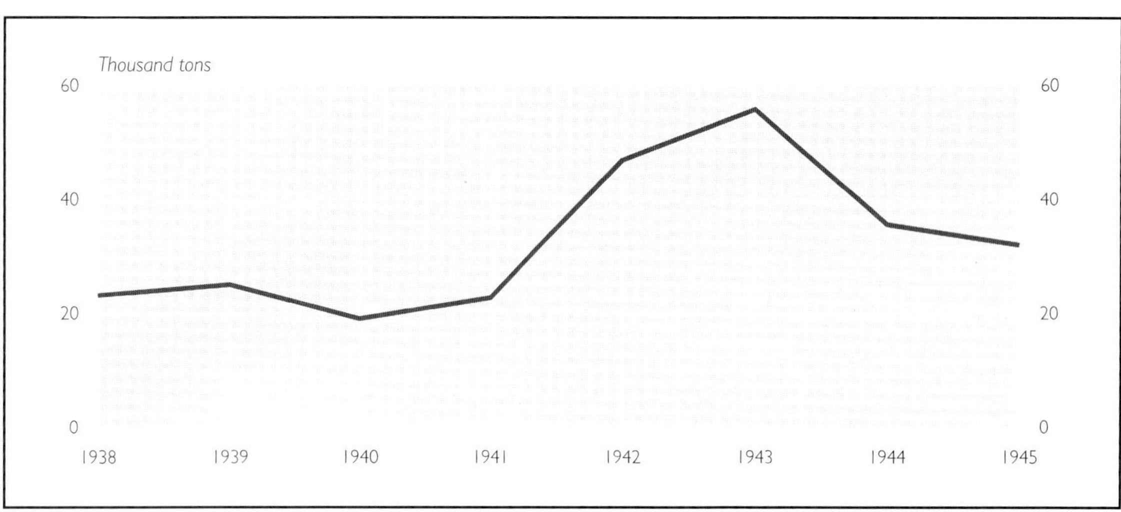

Even before the passage of the Lend-Lease Act in March 1941 the USA proved a vital source of increased supplies, raising their exports of raw materials to the UK from 1.9 million tons in 1939 to 5.4 million tons in 1940 (Hurstfield 1953: 160-4, 169-72). Despite this, the need to conserve scarce shipping capacity, and the impact of enemy action, meant that raw material imports fell from more than 22 million tons in 1940 to less than 12 million tons in 1942, although much of this loss (more than 8 million tons) was due to reductions in the import of just one material, timber (Hargreaves and Gowing 1952: 126; Ford 1951: 144; **table 6.23**).

The option of increasing the domestic production to replace the lost supplies was simply not available for many raw materials but where this was practical (for example, in the cases of iron ore, ferro-chrome, magnesium and magnesium alloys, virgin aluminium and timber) it occurred (Hurstfield 1953: 239-41; **tables 6.3 and 6.7-6.10**). In many of these industries, given that labour, capital, raw materials, energy and transport were all in short supply, increased production had to rely on a greater utilisation of the existing capacity; however, in the case of certain strategic materials (such as alloy steel and aluminium) and synthetic substitutes (rubber and plastics) there was little alternative but to build new plant (Hornby 1958: 279-84; Howlett 1994b: 527-8; **tables 6.9, 6.13, 6.16**). In the case of timber the response to the loss of imported supplies was to dramatically increase home production (from 444,000 tons in 1940 to a wartime peak of 745,000 tons for softwood, and from 496,000 tons to 1.13 million tons for hardwoods) (House 1965: 318-9; Meiggs 1949:43).

The pressure on raw material supplies was eased by the use of scrap or other recycled material (such as waste) rubber and by using substitute materials, although this latter option often merely represented an ordering of the current relative scarcity of materials (as in the case of pit props in 1940 where scarce steel was substituted for the even more scarce timber) (Hurstfield 1953:356-62; **tables 6.5 and 6.13**). The pressure was further lessened by reducing the quantity and quality of finished goods that were considered less essential to the war effort.

Thus, the production of many consumer goods (such as textiles, clothing, leather, wood and paper) was deliberately curtailed by the state and quality was sacrificed by simply using less of the raw material input (for example, reducing the height of ladies' shoe heels, which saved several thousand tons of shipping space, and slimming the thickness of coffins, which saved 0.5 million cubic feet of wood per year) or by producing a much limited and more basic range of designs (as was the case with the utility schemes in furniture and clothing) (Ford 1951: 149; Hargreaves and Gowing 1952: 335-7, 431-79, 507-10; **tables 6.17-6.22**).

The role the state played in the supply of raw materials during the war was crucial: it monitored production, imports (through a licensing system), exports (which, after 1940, were severely curtailed on state direction), stocks and distribution, and it centrally allocated most of them. This monitoring (including the collection of a vast amount of statistical information), and some of the allocation, was carried out by the raw material Controls (Hargreaves and Gowing 1952: 127-8; House 1965). The first Controls to

be created were the Iron and Steel Control and the Flax Control in October 1939 and the last to be established was the Tin Control in March 1942; typically the Head Controller was a businessman with many years of experience in the relevant industry (Hurstfield 1953: 414, 447). The most important body in this process was, however, the Materials Committee (originally a War Cabinet sub-committee and later part of the Ministry of Production) which was responsible for the allocation of scarce materials.

Government departments made bids to the Materials Committee for the amount of a particular raw material (for example steel) that they felt they needed to fulfil their production programme in the coming quarter; the Committee would then assess these bids in the light of the supply position as detailed by the relevant Control (the Iron and Steel Control) and the strategic priorities set by the War Cabinet and decide how much material (steel) each department would actually be allocated (Howlett 1993; Howlett 1994b). The process at the level of the firm was controlled by licences which were issued, depending on the raw material, either by government departments (up to an amount equal to their allocation as decided by the Materials Committee) or by the relevant material Control (Howlett 1994b: 531-2; Ford 1951: 146). Finally, with the entry of the USA into the war a Combined Raw Materials Board was established in Washington to allow the allies to assess requirements and supplies globally, although within Britain the Materials Committee still remained the linchpin of the allocation system (Duncan Hall and Wrigley 1956: 262-311).

6.3 Iron ore and manganese ore

Thousand tons

	Home iron ore					Imported iron ore					Manganese ore	
			Stocks (end of period)				Consumption		Stocks (end of period)			
	Pro-duction	Consum-ption[1]	Total	At mines	At blast furnaces and steel works	Arrivals	Total[1]	Blast furn-aces[2]	Total	At blast furnaces and steel works	Consum-ption	Stocks (end of period)
Annual totals[3]												
1937	14,215	13,943[4]	..	..	..	..	6,193[4]	5,736	..	..	..	..
1938	11,589	11,715[4]	..	..	..	..	4,632[4]	4,380	..	..	..	..
1939	14,486	..	1,988	1,464	524	..	..	..	871.1	758.9	250	..
1940	17,702	16,006	2,582	1,386	1,196	4,508	4,712	4,052	736.4	698.5	290	104.0
1941	18,974	17,826	2,475	1,200	1,275	2,241	2,085	1,596	882.3	855.6	291	115.8
1942	19,906	18,692	2,451	1,302	1,149	1,935	2,061	1,564	752.3	749.5	407	94.3
1943	18,494	17,124	2,677	1,644	1,033	1,924	1,877	1,456	787.4	756.0	307	208.1
1944	15,472	14,908	2,216	1,532	684	2,148	2,433	2,070	515.9	482.2	375	117.2
1945	14,175	13,671	2,142	1,436	706	4,191	4,020	3,656	633.8	549.1	296	120.5
Weekly averages												
1939	279.0	..	1,988	1,464	524	..	..	..	871.1	758.9	4.8	..
1940	340.0	308.0	2,582	1,386	1,196	86.7	90.6	78.0	736.4	698.5	5.6	104.0
1941	365.0	343.0	2,475	1,200	1,275	43.1	40.1	30.7	882.3	855.6	5.6	115.8
1942	376.0	353.0	2,451	1,302	1,149	36.5	39.0	29.5	752.3	749.5	7.7	94.3
1943	355.8	329.3	2,677	1,644	1,033	37.0	36.0	28.0	787.4	756.0	5.9	208.1
1944	297.6	286.7	2,216	1,532	684	41.3	46.7	39.8	515.9	482.2	7.2	117.2
1945	272.5	262.9	2,142	1,436	706	80.6	77.2	70.3	633.8	549.1	5.8	120.5
1939 October	322.0	288.0	1,947	1,437	510	..	124.2	..	..	987	4.1	..
November	323.0*	289.0*	2,031	1,461	570	..*	116.2	..	..	871	5.2*	..
December	288.0	286.0	1,988	1,464	524	..	115.0	..	..	759	6.0	..
1940 January	269.0*	270.0*	1,858	1,414	444	..	119.5*	103.0*	761.4	703.8	5.9*	183.0
February	293.0	267.0	1,932	1,421	511	..	116.9	101.2	745.8	684.7	5.9	166.0
March	335.0	304.0	1,936	1,398	565	..	107.3	91.0	780.0	716.1	5.0	166.0
April	363.0	327.0	2,054	1,399	655	..	103.6	87.3	951.0	853.6	5.2	157.0
May	365.0*	335.0*	2,076	1,373	703	..	111.0*	95.4*	1,077.2	979.7	5.3*	141.0
June	366.0	320.0	2,163	1,371	792	..	112.7	99.0	1,179.0	1,104.4	4.6	164.0
July	363.0	317.0	2,263	1,359	904	..	97.7	86.3	1,040.4	989.3	4.8	171.0
August	358.0*	306.0*	2,402	1,330	1,072	..	77.8*	68.2*	931.2	898.1	5.3*	169.0
September	356.0	303.0	2,512	1,347	1,165	..	64.2	55.4	846.0	812.3	6.6	159.0
October	344.0*	307.0*	2,608	1,388	1,220	..	61.1*	52.7*	802.5	777.4	5.5*	147.0
November	343.0	318.0	2,601	1,390	1,211	..	57.0	47.9	749.2	717.3	7.0	126.0
December	337.0	323.0	2,582	1,386	1,196	..	56.7	47.3	736.4	698.5	6.0	104.0
1941 January	326.0*	329.0*	2,444	1,347	1,097	28.6*	49.9*	40.0*	638.4	598.8	5.8*	74.9
February	346.0	339.0	2,357	1,286	1,070	30.1	39.9	30.3	608.9	578.1	5.1	53.7
March	363.0	346.0	2,336	1,254	1,083	37.2	38.4	29.6	580.1	561.7	5.1	47.6
April	366.0*	338.0*	2,352	1,212	1,140	38.4*	40.3*	31.4*	598.5	566.9	4.3*	48.2
May	368.0	339.0	2,361	1,167	1,193	61.9	37.0	28.4	707.6	678.7	3.7	62.4
June	359.0	338.0	2,347	1,161	1,185	48.2	38.2	29.0	760.5	719.5	5.4	70.4
July	369.0*	339.0*	2,380	1,182	1,198	28.0*	37.9*	28.9*	761.3	725.7	5.8*	64.3
August	368.0	343.0	2,364	1,152	1,212	55.0	40.0	31.5	788.5	768.9	6.1	71.4
September	395.0	353.0	2,428	1,157	1,271	49.0	39.5	30.1	822.4	797.5	5.7	78.3
October	379.0*	352.0*	2,462	1,156	1,306	49.2*	39.8*	29.9*	876.0	828.6	6.2*	94.5
November	379.0	350.0	2,497	1,170	1,327	44.8	41.5	31.3	881.3	853.1	6.1	90.8
December	366.0	353.0	2,475	1,200	1,275	39.8	36.4	26.6	882.3	855.6	7.4	115.8

See footnotes on page 117

Source: Ministry of Supply

6.3 Iron ore and manganese ore

continued

Thousand tons

		Home iron ore					Imported iron ore					Manganese ore	
				Stocks (end of period)				Consumption		Stocks (end of period)			
		Pro-duction	Consum-ption[1]	Total	At mines	At blast furnaces and steel works	Arrivals	Total[1]	Blast furn-aces[2]	Total	At blast furnaces and steel works	Consum-ption	Stocks[4] (end of period)
1942	January	348.5*	346.9*	2,367	1,197	1,170	43.8*	36.8*	27.7*	927.9	877.4	7.7*	117.8
	February	358.1	341.3	2,326	1,181	1,145	29.6	38.0	28.4	882.7	866.4	7.4	129.3
	March	374.9	352.7	2,315	1,195	1,120	45.9	37.4	27.0	898.3	881.8	7.5	123.9
	April	383.2*	357.4*	2,341	1,184	1,158	43.8*	43.4	33.1*	913.6	887.4	6.7*	127.4
	May	376.6	355.5	2,339	1,165	1,174	38.2	43.1	33.4	915.1	889.0	8.1	136.1
	June	397.7	356.1	2,386	1,147	1,239	56.7	44.2	33.9	947.3	906.1	7.9	136.8
	July	398.2*	353.8*	2,516	1,199	1,318	30.7*	39.8*	30.6*	887.1	882.5	8.1*	152.1
	August	376.3	343.3	2,531	1,230	1,301	59.4	41.2	32.9	967.6	945.1	8.2	142.1
	September	394.5	358.1	2,583	1,264	1,319	30.6	42.8	33.5	918.2	910.4	6.3	165.7
	October	384.3*	356.9*	2,600	1,290	1,311	34.7*	34.7*	25.9*	926.1	913.2	8.1*	157.3
	November	372.0	357.9	2,578	1,312	1,266	11.3	34.4	25.6	834.2	832.1	8.5	132..3
	December	348.9*	351.7*	2,451	1,302	1,149	16.3*	32.6*	24.2*	752.3	749.5	7.7*	94.3
1943	January	372.0	348.4	2,446	1,323	1,124	26.4	31.8	28.4	714.4	700.5	7.1	77.6
	February	367.3	343.1	2453	1,324	1,128	18.7	31.3	21.8	675.7	658.5	6.5	62.3
	March	368.3*	345.8*	2,453	1,348	1,105	383*	33.9*	24.2*	693.3	675.8	6.0*	79.2
	April	334.1	325.9	2,429	1,351	1,078	43.0	31.7	23.1	727.9	697.9	5.4	106.9
	May	371.1	337.2	2,470	1,364	1,105	14.1	29.8	21.4	682.4	682.3	4.7	129.0
	June	362.8*	328.8*	2,517	1,399	1,118	57.5*	30.3*	21.8*	819.1	813.3	5.7*	163.2
	July	353.7	318.0	2,565	1,414	1,151	33.9	38.2	29.7	804.3	801.4	5.9	180.6
	August	328.5	312.0	2,571	1,467	1,104	45.0	38.2	30.7	801.8	764.8	6.2	211.4
	September	365.3*	325.1*	2,668	1,561	1,107	35.4*	38.6*	30.5*	798.7	773.3	6.5*	222.0
	October	364.4	326.4	2,719	1,609	1,110	39.8	42.2	34.0	795.3	772.8	4.6	229.3
	November	355.3	330.6	2,706	1,625	1,080	44.5	42.9	35.1	798.6	769.9	5.4	224.8
	December	326.7*	312.2*	2,677	1,644	1,033	40.9*	44.2*	36.8*	787.4	756.0	6.9*	208.1
1944	January	339.2	311.5	2,691	1,662	1,029	45.3	41.5	34.3	791.7	766.7	7.4	194.9
	February	344.9	313.4	2,729	1,692	1,036	41.0	42.0	34.5	797.4	758.1	7.2	187.6
	March	305.1*	284.0*	2,763	1,734	1,028	40.9*	40.5*	32.2*	802.3	791.3	7.1*	183.2
	April	272.5	271.9	2,691	1,737	954	57.8	44.2	36.9	863.4	843.8	7.4	158.4
	May	286.9	284.6	2,601	1,738	863	58.6	42.1	34.7	897.7	864.0	8.1	159.1
	June	279.3*	275.4*	2,530	1,736	794	29.7*	47.9*	40.8*	831.1	814.2	7.3*	141.6
	July	293.1	269.8	2,554	1,755	799	40.1	50.7	44.0	781.2	776.9	7.8	152.0
	August	263.8*	266.0*	2,447	1,698	750	25.7*	50.0*	43.7*	671.0	660.9	7.2*	137.0
	September	302.8	290.1	2,396	1,641	755	30.1	47.6	41.1	594.4	584.3	7.7	122.7
	October	311.5	294.0	2,392	1,609	783	40.0	47.6	41.4	556.7	543.5	7.0	103.0
	November	301.7*	299.3*	2,300	1,569	732	44.6*	53.5*	46.5*	532.5	510.6	6.1*	100.2
	December	286.5	285.9	2,216	1,532	684	48.6	52.2	45.7	515.9	482.2	6.5	117.2
1945	January	279.8*	280.5*	2,117	1,520	597	46.0*	52.2*	46.7*	484.5	411.0	6.2*	108.3
	February	31.2.3	294.9	2,106	1,510	596	66.2	57.6	51.1	505.0	466.9	6.5	113.4
	March	329.6	294.8	2,164	1,507	656	54.7	60.3	53.3	531.8	502.6	6.4	119.6
	April	316.0	279.4	2,234	1,507	727	68.4	64.2	57.2	535.5	498.1	5.9	121.1
	May	290.7*	260.2*	2,299	1,506	793	68.7*	61.4*	55.1*	576.7	531.5	5.3*	114.2
	June	288.0	261.2	2,337	1,523	813	111.0	68.7	61.6	714.5	638.5	4.6	116.4
	July	274.5	252.2	2,372	1,556	816	104.0	77.5	70.8	786.5	716.6	4.9	122.4
	August	221.4*	223.5*	2,306	1,540	767	104.5*	77.9*	71.7*	896.6	855.4	5.1*	123.4

1. Raw and calcined ore as charged, except in the case of the figures of home iron ore in 1937 and 1938 which relate to raw and raw equivalent of calcined ore.
2. Including consumption in sinter plant.
3. Production and consumption figures relate to calendar years for 1937, 1938 and 1939, to a period of 53 weeks for 1942 and to periods of 52 weeks for the remaining years.
4. Including consumption of manganese ore. Excluding consumption in steel works. The average weekly consumption of both home and imported ore in steel works amounted to 15,300 tons in 1937 and 11,400 tons in 1938.

* Average of five weeks.

Source: Ministry of Supply

6.4 Pig Iron

Thousand tons

	Production			Consumption			Stocks (end of period)			
	Total[1]	Haematite	Basic	Total	Steel furnaces and convertors	Foundries, forges and iron works[2]	Total[3]	Blast furnaces	Steel works	Iron foundries
Annual totals[4]										
1937	8,493	1,866	4,689	..	6,256	..	..	..	..	..
1938	6,761	1,484	3,763	..	4,844	..	..	..	..	..
1939	7,980	1,396	5,108	..	6,673	..	..	323.4	252.4	343.1
1940	8,205	1,428	5,453	8,701	6,731	1,970	1,094	363.0	399.9	235.6
1941	7,393	906	5,182	8,038	6,311	1,727	1,417	459.2	466.4	264.0
1942	7,726	964	5,553	8,050	6,355	1,695	1,473	547.1	502.3	262.0
1943	7,187	927	5,070	7,784	6,125	1,659	1,207	496.8	364.7	270.6
1944	6,737	1,009	4,792	7,299	5,777	1,522	896	342.6	317.0	200.8
1945	7,107	1,076	4,884	7,049	5,663	1,386	1,023	441.0	392.2	243.8
Weekly averages										
1939	153.0	26.8	98.2	..	128.3	..	..	323.4	252.4	343.1
1940	158.0	27.5	104.9	167.3	129.4	37.9	1,904	363.0	399.9	235.6
1941	142.2	17.4	99.7	154.6	121.4	33.2	1,417	459.2	466.4	264.0
1942	145.8	18.2	104.8	151.9	119.9	32.0	1,474	547.1	502.3	262.0
1943	138.2	17.8	97.5	149.7	117.8	31.9	1,207	496.8	364.7	270.6
1944	129.6	19.4	92.1	140.4	111.1	29.3	896	342.6	317.0	200.8
1945	136.7	20.7	93.9	135.6	108.9	26.7	1,023	441.0	392.2	243.8
1939 September	160.0	28.0	103.0	..	..	..	..	456.5	237.4	325.0
October	167.0	30.0	107.0	180.0	..	..	..	384.8	238.8	347.0
November	166.0*	31.0*	105.0*	188.0*	..	..	..	330.9	244.3	336.3
December	162.0	31.0	102.0	175.0	..	..	927	323.4	252.4	343.1
1940 January	156.0*			170.9*	133,5*	37,4*	877	325,4	233,5	309.0
February	155.0	29.3	101.8	175.9	135.1	40.8	812	298.8	209.0	294.0
March	164.0			180.7	143.3	37.4	777	283.1	197.3	286.7
April	168.0			186.4	145.3	41.1	758	261.4	215.6	271.0
May	173.0*	30.4	115.8	186.6*	144.2*	42.4*	720	256.0	220.7	234.9
June	171.0			178.9	137.3	41.6	692	221.0	243.7	219.4
July	165.0			166.4	126.3	40.1	738	233.0	281.5	209.1
August	153.0*	27.7	100.8	149.7*	113.8*	35.9*	835	265.0	339.7	221.0
September	144.0			145.2	110.7	34.5	935	312.8	370.6	224.5
October	145.0*			153.6*	116.6*	37.0*	1,018	348.5	387.6	219.5
November	146.0	22.1	99.0	155.7	121.7	34.0	1,056	361.1	388.3	224.5
December	147.0			148.4	118.6	29.8	1,094	363.0	399.9	235.6
1941 January	142.3*	20.4*	97.9*	153.0*	119.2*	33.8*	1,108	398.8	393.6	231.3
February	141.4	18.3	96.3	156.3	122.7	33.6	1,111	404.4	375.8	237.7
March	143.3	17.4	99.8	155.5	122.9	32.6	1,158	404.9	395.1	260.7
April	142.5*	17.1*	98.5*	151.5*	118.0*	33.5*	1,239	439.3	430.5	269.1
May	140.2	16.3	97.3	152.1	118.0	34.1	1,277	454.3	449.9	274.3
June	140.2	17.5	97.7	147.9	116.4	31.5	1,317	470.0	478.1	273.4
July	140.4*	18.2*	98.5*	149.4*	116.0*	33.4*	1,369	480.5	505.4	271.2
August	139.7	17.9	98.3	143.1	113.9	29.2	1,430	489.9	529.6	279.4
September	142.8	16.3	101.7	155.2	121.7	33.5	1,471	489.7	530.7	280.7
October	142.8*	15.7*	101.9*	163.2*	127.6*	35.6*	1,460	476.0	508.6	276.0
November	142.5	17.4	100.5	163.6	130.2	33.4	1,432	469.4	481.0	266.4
December	142.8	15.9	103.3	156.8	124.1	32.7	1,417	459.2	466.4	264.0

See footnotes on page 119

Source: Ministry of Supply

6.4 Pig Iron

continued

Thousand tons

	Production			Consumption			Stocks (end of period)			
	Total[1]	Haematite	Basic	Total	Steel furnaces and convertors	Foundries forges and iron works[2]	Total[3]	Blast furnaces	Steel works	Iron foundries
1942 January	140.9*	16.0*	101.7*	153.1*	120.3*	32.8*	1,414	469.6	470.7	257.3
February	139.6	16.2	99.5	159.1	125.4	33.7	1,381	454.6	455.3	261.9
March	143.7	17.0	103.0	160.7	126.0	34.7	1,369	450.1	445.1	270.5
April	148.8*	20.2*	105.0*	153.3*	122.9*	30.4*	1,387	462.1	462.0	271.7
May	149.8	20.0	107.0	153.0	119.6	33.4	1,410	484.5	483.2	271.2
June	149.5	18.3	109.6	158.0	124.4	33.6	1,418	492.2	504.6	269.6
July	147.1*	17.2*	106.7*	144.4*	115.2*	29.2*	1,457	515.8	534.4	269.0
August	145.4	18.3	104.3	138.6	109.2	29.4	1,512	541.9	539.8	281.4
September	149.2	18.5	106.6	152.9	119.0	33.9	1,520	551.8	538.1	277.0
October	147.5*	18.0*	107.1*	153.8*	121.5*	32.3*	1,498	543.6	522.5	274.9
November	145.8	20.1	105.1	158.0	123.0	35.0	1,465	535.4	502.6	268.6
December	142.6*	18.6*	102.0*	145.5*	114.0*	31.5*	1,473	547.1	502.3	262.0
1943 January	140.3	17.0	100.2	151.7	119.1	32.6	1,443	553.3	499.1	261.8
February	140.2	16.8	100.3	157.7	124.8	32.9	1,415	536.0	482.7	268.2
March	143.4*	16.9*	102.6*	158.3*	124.7*	33.6*	1,356	519.3	464.7	266.6
April	136.8	17.0	99.1	149.0	117.0	32.0	1,334	503.7	463.0	274.5
May	137.4	16.8	97.7	153.5	120.2	33.3	1,299	483.1	454.5	275.7
June	136.3*	16.2*	95.9*	147.6*	117.9*	29.7*	1,287	477.7	451.4	271.9
July	135.8	18.0	93.4	141.1	111.1	30.0	1,303	481.1	447.9	280.5
August	131.8	17.5	91.7	134.8	105.7	29.1	1,333	501.2	449.3	287.8
September	137.7*	18.0*	95.4*	152.9*	120.9*	32.0*	1,284	495.3	411.0	281.9
October	138.8	19.4	98.4	152.6	118.8	33.8	1,254	500.2	394.0	276.2
November	142.5	20.9	100.7	153.5	119.5	34.0	1,219	493.0	370.3	273.3
December	137.3*	19.7*	94.9*	142.1*	112.4*	29.7*	1,207	496.8	364.7	270.6
1944 January	135.9	19.4	93.8	148.0	114.8	33.2	1,176	476.3	359.0	272.4
February	137.7	19.7	97.3	153.0	119.5	33.5	1,136	437.8	358.8	284.3
March	127.1*	19.2*	88.5*	145.0*	112.9*	32.1*	1,071	375.1	349.7	300.5
April	122.2	19.4	85.7	137.7	108.0	29.7	1,049	337.2	359.6	303.3
May	125.6	20.1	89.2	147.0	115.1	31.9	978	309.2	328.5	294.4
June	126.6*	19.6*	91.4*	139.2*	112.0*	27.2*	921	287.9	322.0	267.2
July	124.7	19.6	91.0	127.1	99.4	27.7	919	299.6	328.3	247.7
August	123.2*	19.7*	88.6*	126.2*	102.0*	24.2*	927	319.1	334.8	230.2
September	130.7	18.9	95.1	140.5	112.3	28.2	900	322.2	323.4	218.1
October	133.3	17.8	97.0	142.1	112.7	29.4	886	316.6	330.3	205.4
November	136.4*	20.1*	96.2*	144.8*	117.2*	27.6*	865	311.9	317.6	199.6
December	132.7	19.2	93.0	133.5	107.4	26.1	896	342.6	317.0	200.8
1945 January	127.2*	19.5*	87.8*	130.2*	104.9*	25.3*	929	373.4	317.9	193.3
February	136.7	20.7	94.9	143.1	114.8	28.3	912	363.6	308.9	196.9
March	141.5	21.5	100.2	146.9	117.9	29.0	911	351.2	314.7	205.3
April	137.6	21.3	96.8	137.6	111.6	26.0	919	332.0	334.9	215.3
May	128.2*	20.0*	87.1*	123.4*	100.1*	23.3*	956	339.2	363.3	220.9
June	133.0	20.2	89.9	135.5	107.3	28.2	952	339.3	370.1	216.2
July	134.8	19.5	91.0	125.3	99.2	26.1	986	375.3	365.4	224.6
August	125.2*	20.2*	81.6*	113.5*	92.5*	21.0*	1,035	416.5	371.2	235.8

1. Including production of blast furnace ferro-alloys and other qualities of pig iron.
2. Including refined pig iron consumed in iron foundries.
3. Including stocks at wrought iron and refined iron works and Ministry of Supply stockyards.
4. Production and consumption figures relate to calendar years for 1937, 1938 and 1939, to a period of 53 weeks for 1942 and to periods of 52 weeks for the remaining years.

* Average of five weeks.

Source: Ministry to Supply

6.5 Iron and steel scrap and steel ingots and castings

Thousand tons

	Iron and steel scrap					Steel ingots and castings	
	Receipts				Stocks[1] (end of period)	Production	
	Total	Bought	Own	Consumption[1]		Total	Alloy
Annual totals							
1935	. .	. .	2,236	5,850	. .	9,859	. .
1936	6,532	3,828	2,704	6,915	. .	11,785	. .
1937	6,240	3,172	3,068	7,477	409	12,984	. .
1938	5,304	2,652	2,652	6,128	448	10,398	. .
1939	6,439	3,016	3,423	7,404	282.3	13,221	. .
1940	6,524	2,978	3,546	7,182	482.0	12,975	825
1941	6,620	3,248	3,372	6,942	680.5	12,312	1,052
1942	7,810	3,957	3,853	7,616	835.1	12,942	1,593
1943	7,783	3,822	3,961	7,965	590.3	13,031	1,596
1944	7,350	3,609	3,741	7,367	539.3	12,142	1,126
1945	7,005	3,600	3,405	7,203	470.3	11,824	707
Weekly averages							
1939	123.8	58.0	65.8	142.0	282.3	254	. .
1940	125.5	57.3	68.,2	138.1	482.0	250	16
1941	127.3	62.5	64.8	133.5	680.5	237	20
1942	147.4	74.7	72.7	143.7	835.1	244	30
1943	149.7	73.5	76.2	153.2	590.3	251	31
1944	141.3	69.4	71.9	141.7	539.3	233	22
1945	134.7	69.2	65.5	138.5	470.3	227	14
1939 September	118.5	49.2	69.3	141.2	289.2	259	. .
October	125.5	52.9	72.6	144.7	270.8	272	. .
November	128.1*	53.8	74.3*	142.9*	270.8*	270	. .
December	118.6	48.8	69.8	128.3	282.3	249	. .
1940 January	108.5*	42.2	66.3*	120.5*	250.1*	238	13*
February	114.5	45.7	68.8	121.8	233.0	241	13
March	127.8	55.4	72.4	136.7	244.7	262	13
April	136.5	61.9	74.6	144.7	290.2	272	14
May	139.7*	65.1	74.6*	149.4*	328.9*	275	14*
June	144.0	70.1	73.9	148.3	379.8	266	16
July	139.7	69.9	69.8	145.9	458.4	253	18
August	129.6*	65.5	64.1*	133.2*	551.0*	229	18*
September	117.3	54.8	62.5	132.4	605.8	225	18
October	118.8*	53.5	65.3*	143.8*	586.6*	242	20*
November	122.8	55.7	67.1	145.3	530.2	247	19
December	109.8	49.7	60.1	129.6	482.0	230	15
1941 January	107.9*	47.3	60.6*	125.5*	428.6*	227	16*
February	120.3	54.6	65.7	129.7	430.4	233	20
March	130.1	62.8	67.3	132.4	458.4	237	21
April	125.7*	61.3	64.4*	134.0*	501.9*	234	20*
May	129.4	63.3	66.1	143.2	520.5	242	19
June	126.9	63.2	63.7	133.0	567.3	232	17
July	123.4*	62.9	60.5*	126.4*	601.9*	226	18*
August	121.7	60.2	61.5	127.7	608.6	225	20
September	136.9	70.2	66.7	137.0	635.7	241	22
October	140.5*	71.4	69.1*	137.4*	684.8*	246	23*
November	136.9	68.9	68.0	141.7	671.3	252	25
December	130.9	65.2	65.7	132.2	680.5	238	24

See footnotes on page 121.

Source: Ministry of Supply

6.5 Iron and steel ingots and castings

continued

Thousand tons

	Iron and steel scrap					Steel ingots and castings	
	Receipts			Con-sumption[1]	Stocks[1] end of period	Production	
	Total	Bought	Own			Total	Alloy
1942 * January	127.5	61.8	65.7	132.5	661.9	234	24
February	138.2	67.7	70.5	141.8	646.3	247	28
March	148.0	75.3	72.7	142.4	667.1	250	29
* April	154.5	80.2	74.3	146.1	707.4	250	30
May	152.8	79.3	73.5	143.9	743.8	244	28
June	152.7	77.4	75.3	146.1	763.0	250	31
* July	143.9	72.5	71.4	139.1	786.0	235	29
August	139.4	72.1	67.3	132.2	811.4	223	27
September	155.7	81.2	74.5	150.0	830.4	249	33
* October	158.7	80.1	78.6	154.0	844.3	255	36
November	156.2	79.6	76.6	156.1	843.5	258	35
* December	142.5	69.8	72.7	142.2	835.1	236	30
1943 January	145.9	71.9	74.0	150.8	813.9	249	31
February	156.0	77.7	78.3	161.0	789.3	264	35
* March	161.8	80.9	80.9	162.2	777.0	267	35
April	154.8	76.8	78.0	157.6	759.1	255	31
May	156.8	78.1	78.7	161.9	733.7	261	33
* June	150.8	75.1	75.7	151.7	712.0	249	30
July	140.9	70.3	70.6	140.8	709.6	234	25
August	130.6	64.7	65.9	136.6	682.8	224	28
* September	154.2	73.8	80.4	159.7	651.7	259	33
October	155.9	75.7	80.2	157.9	639.9	256	32
November	154.3	74.5	79.8	158.1	622.2	256	31
* December	133.6	62.9	70.7	139.7	590.3	232	24
1944 January	142.0	67.5	74.5	148.0	559.4	242	26
February	152.3	72.9	79.4	158.8	531.2	258	28
* March	153.1	76.6	76.5	149.9	549.3	244	25
April	139.3	67.6	71.7	133.9	571.8	224	20
May	147.0	70.9	76.1	148.7	563.2	245	24
* June	143.6	70.1	73.5	139.6	578.3	233	22
July	129.9	66.8	63.1	125.5	594.6	208	18
* August	126.0	61.7	64.3	126.3	594.0	210	21
September	141.2	69.4	71.8	143.7	574.9	236	22
October	146.1	72.6	73.5	146.9	568.1	239	20
* November	145.6	72.7	72.9	147.8	552.1	244	19
December	129.6	63.5	66.1	132.4	539.3	220	15
1945 * January	121.6	58.7	62.9	131.7	490.1	216	15
February	146.2	73.1	73.1	148.4	487.3	241	17
March	150.8	77.6	73.2	149.6	502.1	246	17
April	141.6	71.6	70.0	145.5	486.9	237	17
* May	130.2	68.1	62.1	129.3	494.9	211	14
June	147.9	75.9	72.0	151.9	485.5	238	17
July	129.5	67.9	61.6	133.3	484.3	214	13
* August	106.3	54.6	51.7	110.6	472.6	186	10
September	141.5	73.2	68.3	145.2	466.9	241	14

1 At steel works and foundries.
* Average of five weeks.

Source: Ministry of Supply

6.6 Semi-finished and finished iron and steel[1]

Thousand tons

	1935	1936	1937	1938	1939	1940	1941	1942	1943	1944	1945
Production of semi-finished and finished iron and steel											
Iron castings	..	..	..	..	..	2,769	2,444	2,468	2,408	2,150	1,971
Wrought iron:											
Total	346	424	462	317	355	302	278	275	257	226	193
Forge Production	188	232	259	177	199	178	166	164	147	130	111
Finishing mills production	158	192	203	140	156	124	112	111	110	96	82
Semi-finished steel:											
Billets, blooms and slabs[2]	5,928	7,318	8,065	6,775	..	..	5,325	5,510	6,160	6,013	5,876
Sheet bars and tinplate bars	2,080	2,388	2,650	1,663	..	..	2,293	2,270	2,070	2,001	1,984
Finished steel principal products[3]											
Bright steel bars	117	132	179	119	140	238	289	363	413	390	246
Heavy rails and sleepers	442	547	518	491	395	247	215	260	292	337	400
Heavy and medium plates	1,101	1,431	1,624	1,372	1,430	1,612	1,582	1,589	1,723	1,602	1,394
Armour and bullet proof plate	..	..	..	..	71	64	80	145	113	99	56
Other heavy steel products	..	..	..	1,543	2,007	1,725	1,382	1,462	1,416	1,444	1,431
Shell steel	..	..	..	..	111	636	1,029	1,073	702	543	313
Light rolled products	..	..	..	2,251	2,909	3,416	3,217	3,387	3,387	3,273	2,907
Cold rolled strip	91	114	130	73	110	154	163	216	231	220	225
Sheets coated and uncoated	1,097	1,163	1,272	816	1,649	1,257	1,263	1,185	1,169	1,137	1,076
Tin, terne and black plates	708	815	958	610	919	977	720	678	532	521	512
Tubes, pipes and fittings	718	..	837	665[4]	675	684	685	677	659	666	595
Steel castings	115[4]	145[4]	170[4]	142[4]	159	227	248	338	365	355	285
Steel forgings	109	136	173	250[4]	..	342	469	596	617	563	387
Wire	442	..	562	500[4]	583	648	642	694	644	639	537
Tyres, wheels and axles	155	160	158	159	131	134	89	114	122	136	158
Net deliveries of finished steel											
Total	..	..	..	..	..	..	10,497	11,387	11,006	10,270	8,922
Home produced[5]	..	..	..	..	..	..	10,127	10,647	10,282	10,010	8,865
Imported	..	..	..	..	..	..	371	739	724	261	57
Deliveries for home consumption	..	..	..	..	..	..	..	11,086	10,860	10,044	8,136
Stocks of steel[6]	..	..	..	..	..	..	2,754	2,179	2,171	1,684	1,224

1. Production and consumption figures relate to calendar years for 1935 to 1939 inclusive, to a period of 53 weeks for 1942 and to periods of 52 weeks for the remaining years. Figures for stocks are for the end of the period in all cases.
2. From 1941, excluding alloy steel.
3. Including material for further conversion.
4. Estimated.
5. Total United Kingdom production less deliveries to other steel firms for further conversion.
6. Ingots, semi-finished and finished steel. Excluding stocks held by consumers.

Source: Ministry of Supply

6.7 Chrome ore and ferro-alloys

Production and consumption: calendar years or 52 week periods[1] Stocks end of period: *Thousand tons*

	1940	1941	1942	1943	1944	1945
Chrome ore						
Home consumption: Total	..	64.4	70.0	72.1	73.3	74.1[2]
Refractory	..	31.8	36.1	34.9	30.6	34.1
Chemical	..	22.9	22.4	19.8	20.4	21.3
Metallurgical	..	9.7	11.5	17.5	22.3	18.7
Stocks: Total	52.5[3]	45.1	75.1	40.1	56.3	30.6
Refractory	..	15.9	32.4	14.6	25.8	12.4
Chemical	..	11.9	9.0	11.0	13.8	7.6
Metallurgical	..	17.2	33.7	14.5	16.7	10.6
Tungsten						
Production[4]	..	4.47	2.91	1.40	2.08	2.70
Total disposals[4]	..	4.36	2.12	1.88	2.50	2.82
Home consumption[4]	..	3.46	2.01	1.87	2.48	2.53
Stocks: Ore (metal content)	2.88	1.80	2.10	4.00	5.09	2.98
Finished product[4]		1.43	2.21	1.94	1.54	1.49
Molybdenum						
Production[4]	..	1.87	3.39	2.77	1.24	0.81
Total disposals[4]	..	2.24	3.95	2.99	1.78	1.14
Home consumption[4]	..	2.09	3.93	2.99	1.78	1.05
Stocks: Ore (metal content)	1.27	0.61	0.56	1.18	0.38	0.09
Finished product[4]		0.68	1.06	1.37	0.82	0.52
Vanadium						
Production[4]	..	0.51	0.58	0.53	0.22	0.19
Total disposals[4]	..	0.55	0.57	0.51	0.29	0.24
Home consumption[4]	..	0.53	0.53	0.45	0.28	0.21
Stocks: Ore metal content	0.40	0.21	0.17	0.29	0.41	0.30
Finished product[4]		0.19	0.21	0.22	0.16	0.12
Ferro-chrome						
Production	..	3.83	4.88	6.38	8.48	6.49
Consumption	..	24.40	27.84	28.16	20.49	16.26
Stocks	12.64	19.20	11.98	19.07	17.69	10.91
Silico-manganese						
Consumption	..	14.0	14.9	10.8	10.1	9.8
Stocks	6.5	14.0	6.3	7.1	4.5	5.5
Refined ferro-manganese						
Production	..	0.58	1.46	3.68	3.90	3.64
Home consumption	..	2.71	3.85	4.77	4.17	4.05[5]
Stocks	1.24	1.21	1.62	4.21	3.96	2.60
Ferro-silicon						
Production	..	4.9	7.2	8.0	5.0	6.0
Consumption	..	43.5	50.9	62.5	51.8	41.8
Stocks	20.4	23.9	15.0	43.6	23.5	16.8
Calcium silicide						
Consumption	..	0.70	1.03	0.80	0.54	0.58
Stocks	0.42	0.74	0.47	0.52	0.38	0.29

1. Figures for chrome ore relate to calendar years. For all other items figures relate to a calendar year in 1941 and to periods of 52 weeks in subseqeunt years.
2. In addition 7.5 thousand tons were exported in 1945.
3. Includiing stocks in transit.
4. Non-ferrous metal content of ferro-alloy and other finished products.
5. In addition 1,040 tons were exported in 1945.

Source: Ministry of Supply

6.8 Non-ferrous metals

Production and consumption: calendar years Stocks: end of period: *Thousand tons*

	1935	1936	1937	1938	1939	1940	1941	1942	1943	1944	1945
Copper											
Refined copper: Production[1]	98.3	..	..	..	..	161.5	146.1	183.0	183.3	154.5	93.2
Virgin copper: Total disposals	282.0	340.8	411.6	363.3	320.4	450.0	454.8	499.2	448.6	348.4	357.5
Home consumption	240.0	258.0	301.2	258.0	292.8	446.4	450.0	490.8	448.6	348.1	288.6
Stocks	..	..	..	..	..	134.4	160.7	114.9	169.4	282.4	123.1
Zinc											
Concentrates: Production	..	..	..	..	..	..	8.4	6.8	12.8	15.8	6.8
Consumption[2]	126.0	160.8	158.4	141.6	160.8	154.8	178.8	186.3	175.6	176.8	155.8
Stocks	..	..	..	..	..	..	215.0	172.0	101.9	108.9	113.6
Virgin zinc: Production[3]:	63.0	65.0	62.0	55.0	51.0	55.6	67.5	72.6	69.4	71.0	62.0
Total disposals	217.2	211.2	217.2	192.0	228.0	260.4	253.2	258.6	223.2	184.3	189.9
Home consumption	204.0.	207.6	208.8	184.8	223.2	260.4	252.0	258.6	222.8	184.2	173.3
Stocks	..	..	..	..	..	84.9	104.8	132.2	165.0	169.5	138.3
Lead											
Concentrates (metal content): Production	41.2	30.8	26.4	29.7	16.6	13.6	8.0	5.4	4.2	3.8	2.7
Refined lead: Production	25.1	16.2	12.0	10.8	16.1	32.2	7.7	5.3	15.7	13.6	13.5
Total disposals[4]	377.2	380.6	387.8	355.6	346.9	254.6	215.1	245.5	213.0	221.6	253.5
Home consumption[4]	350.4	354.0	345.6	324.0	336.0	253.2	214.8	245.2	212.7	221.2	236.3
Stocks[4]	..	..	..	..	..	149.7	80.9	85.5	121.0	135.7	65.3
Refined nickel											
Production	12.8	..	..	..	..	..	..	20.3	15.4	15.0	13.4
Total disposals	..	..	..	..	..	..	23.7	23.1	18.5	14.5	15.2
Home consumption	..	..	..	..	..	..	22.5	21.8	17.2	12.4	8.5
Stocks	..	..	..	..	..	11.1	10.0	9.2	6.5	7.5	5.6
Tin											
Tin ore (metal content): Production	..	..	..	..	1.6	1.6	1.5	1.4	1.4	1.2	1.2
Stocks	..	..	..	..	..	..	11.4	5.9	10.0	4.8	7.3
Virgin tin: Production	31.8	33.8	37.5	32.1	37.3	46.7	41.3	37.3	31.6	28.6	27.5
Total disposals	51.8	44.1	54.0	35.0	47.9	44.1	36.6	33.6	30.4	21.6	26.2
Home consumption	22.0	21.9	26.0	18.3	27.3	29.2	30.0	23.5	17.6	18.4	16.4
Stocks[5]	..	4.1	4.2	15.1	6.0	7.5	16.6	17.4	19.9	27.8	26.0
Bauxite[6]											
Production(in Northern Ireland)	..	..	..	..	..	..	..	49.2	45.4	28.5	..
Consumption	..	..	..	..	..	..	164.4	168.0	223.2	214.8	153.6
Stocks	..	..	..	..	..	194.4	117.1	28.4	101.6	81.5	93.5
Cryolite											
Consumption	..	..	..	..	..	1.43	2.20	3.85	2.92	1.90	..
Stocks	..	..	..	..	3.78	4.41	6.39	6.22	4.87	2.87	..
Alumina											
Production	..	..	..	..	..	..	65.73	67.06	99.11	82.46	66.05
Consumption	..	..	..	..	..	46.68	47.64	92.64	114.35	76.80	72.45
Stocks	..	..	..	..	..	42.50	62.05	38.75	22.24	31.33	24.24
Magnesium and magnesium alloys											
Production[7]	0.8	1.6	2.0	3.0	5.0	6.1	10.9	18.1	23.1	18.1	6.8
Consumption	..	..	..	..	..	8.0	13.8	20.8	36.1	36.0	8.6
Stocks	..	..	..	..	..	4.3	2.0	2.1	19.0	20.8	20.7
Magnesite											
Crude: Consumption	..	..	..	..	..	..	22.7	23.3	17.3	11.8	..
Stocks	..	..	..	..	..	46.0	67.0	38.5	24.7	18.8	10.0[8]
Calcined: Production[9]	..	..	..	..	..	..	4.4	31.9	46.7	24.9	9.6
Consumption	..	..	..	..	..	..	23.0	42.2	52.3	34.2	..
Stocks	..	..	..	..	..	11.0	9.2	13.9	55.7	53.6	46.8[8]
Dead burnt: Production[9]	..	..	..	..	..	..	8.5	10.2	17.4	11.3	28.6
Consumption	..	..	..	..	..	..	17.7	20.9	21.3	22.3	..
Stocks	..	..	..	..	..	11.4	13.6	12.9	14.5	11.6	8.4[8]

Source: Ministry of Supply

1. From 1943, including scrap refined on private account.
2. From 1942, including consumption other than for zinc production.
3. Some secondary material is included in the years 1935 to 1939.
4. English refined lead is included in consumption figures from 1942 and in stocks figures throughout.
5. From 1935 to 1940, excluding consumers' stocks. The figure for 1941 is estimated.
6. In terms of high grade bauxite.
7. Including scrap recovery.
8. Government stocks only.
9. These figures refer to magnesia extracted from sea-water.

6.9 Aluminium

Thousands tons

		Production		Consumption		Stocks (end of period)	
		Virgin aluminium	Secondary aluminium[1]	Virgin aluminium[2]	Secondary aluminium	Virgin aluminium[3]	Secondary aluminium
Annual totals							
1938		23.04	. .	44.4	. .	. .	. .
1939		24.96	. .	78.0	. .	. .	. .
1940		18.95	37.92	102.3	32.17	. .	. .
1941		22.67	53.17	116.8	49.04	82.0	14.4
1942		46.78	78.81	195.3	63.78	77.0	27.5
1943		55.66	93.48	208.2	85.49	130.5	31.0
1944		35.47	104.48	150.1	71.68	142.4	58.7
1945		31.90	81.00	99.1	51.24	92.3	92.3
Monthly averages							
1938		1.92	. .	3.7	. .	. .	. .
1939		2.08	. .	6.5	. .	. .	. .
1940		1.58	3.16	8.5	2.68	. .	. .
1941		1.89	4.43	9.7	4.08	82.0	14.4
1942		3.90	6.56	16.3	5.31	77.0	27.5
1943		4.64	7.79	17.3	7.12	130.5	31.0
1944		2.96	8.71	12.5	5.97	142.4	58.7
1945		2.66	6.75	8.3	4.27	92.3	92.3
1939	October	. .	. .	8.5	2.04	. .	. .
	November	. .	. .	8.9	2.19	. .	. .
	December	. .	. .	7.4	1.89	. .	. .
1940	January	1.57	2.85	7.7	1.87	. .	. .
	February	0.84	2.53	7.8	2.63	. .	. .
	March	1.27	2.79	7.9	2.02	. .	. .
	April	1.61	3.18	8.6	2.26	. .	. .
	May	1.78	3.24	8.1	2.35	. .	. .
	June	1.21	2.89	7.5	1.96	. .	. .
	July	0.87	3.68	7.4	2.41	. .	. .
	August	1.22	3.30	9.1	3.38	. .	. .
	September	1.48	3.17	8.3	2.85	. .	
	October	2.30	3.47	10.2	3.70	. .	. .
	November	2.24	3.39	7.5	3.52	. .	. .
	December	2.56	3.43	12.2	3.22	. .	. .
1941	January	2.71	3.61	11.6	3.83	. .	. .
	February	1.94	3.78	11.3	3.56	. .	. .
	March	1.77	5.16	10.9	4.17	33.1	12.8
	April	1.77	4.45	10.4	3.92	43.5	14.2
	May	1.92	4.90	9.3	4.03	48.3	15.4
	June	1.52	4.25	7.2	3.97	54.4	15.2
	July	0.95	4.66	5.5	3.29	66.2	15.1
	August	1.24	3.79	6.9	3.09	67.6	14.9
	September	1.67	4.37	12.6	3.75	63.2	14.3
	October	2.16	4.81	11.3	5.46	67.0	14.7
	November	2.31	4.72	7.3	4.75	72.1	14.0
	December	2.71	4.67	12.5	5.22	82.0	14.4
1942	January	4.37	5.44	19.0	4.85	78.7	14.9
	February	3.66	5.69	11.5	5.02	78.3	15.9
	March	3.95	5.99	17.3	5.22	81.7	16.7
	April	4.09	5.92	16.3	5.33	82.0	18.8
	May	3.49	5.75	14.1	5.15	86.4	18.8
	June	3.54	6.16	17.3	5.47	88.6	19.9
	July	3.22	6.63	16.6	4.99	91.5	20.9
	August	3.16	5.92	13.7	4.32	90.6	21.2
	September	3.92	7.52	13.5	5.83	89.1	22.9
	October	4.32	7.92	19.0	6.13	85.9	23.8
	November	4.35	8.03	17.3	6.03	81.3	25.2
	December	4.71	7.84	19.7	5.44	77.0	27.5

See footnotes on page 126.

Source: Ministry of Supply

6.9 Aluminium

continued

Thousand tons

		Production		Consumption		Stocks (end of period)	
		Virgin aluminium	Secondary aluminium[1]	Virgin aluminium[2]	Secondary aluminium	Virgin aluminium[3]	Secondary aluminium
1943	January	4.84	7.05	20.2	5.80	72.1	28.1
	February	4.49	6.91	14.6	6.20	65.0	27.2
	March	4.72	7.66	23.2	6.92	64.8	28.6
	April	4.52	6.99	19.3	6.73	70.8	31.3
	May	4.48	7.19	15.6	6.55	78.4	31.5
	June	4.56	7.17	11.2	6.94	87.4	30.5
	July	4.88	7.46	15.7	6.42	102.4	30.4
	August	4.50	6.90	15.1	6.97	119.5	29.8
	September	4.49	8.68	14.8	8.00	125.0	30.1
	October	4.73	9.35	17.5	8.49	122.2	27.9
	November	4.65	9.37	20.6	8.56	123.7	28.0
	December	4.80	8.75	20.4	7.91	130.5	31.0
1944	January	4.71	10.13	17.3	8.76	131.3	32.3
	February	3.48	9.57	17.8	8.83	127.1	32.4
	March	3.25	10.17	17.8	8.17	125.8	32.1
	April	2.45	7.54	16.3	5.59	126.4	33.1
	May	2.47	8.32	14.7	6.57	130.0	36.3
	June	2.72	8.42	12.9	5.38	156.0	39.3
	July	2.61	8.53	12.7	5.29	146.2	42.7
	August	2.84	7.53	7.5	4.95	142.2	45.0
	September	2.65	8.65	9.7	5.22	136.6	48.0
	October	2.66	8.90	7.0	4.81	148.1	51.0
	November	2.54	9.28	9.3	4.47	145.8	54.7
	December	3.09	7.44	7.1	3.64	142.4	58.7
1945	January	3.03	8.79	8.7	3.27	137.3	63.3
	February	2.74	7.71	9.4	3.05	130.9	66.7
	March	2.96	7.67	9.3	3.77	124.7	73.7
	April	2.66	6.53	8.7	4.06	119.6	76.9
	May	2.68	6.15	10.2	3.42	112.1	79.7
	June	2.61	7.36	11.6	3.30	103.3	84.5
	July	2.86	6.81	4.8	3.88	101.8	87.0
	August	2.32	5.12	7.9	3.06	96.9	90.5

1. Including production from crashed aircraft.
2. Including the aluminium content of virgin alloys.
3. Including virgin aluminium content of all alloys.

Source: Ministry of Supply

6.10 Softwood and hardwood

		Softwood[1]					Hardwood[1]				
		Production[2]	Consumption		Stocks (end of period)		Production[2]	Consumption		Stocks (end of period)	
			Imported	Home grown[2]	Imported	Home grown		Imported	Home grown	Imported	Home grown
		Thousand standard[3]					Million cubic feet				
Annual totals											
1939		..	..	..	511.3	..	..	..	..	23.28	..
1940		177.59	709.16	161.43	685.1	12.86	22.32	25.46	22.11	18.78	1.31
1941		280.43	630.26	224.64	427.5	39.29	29.38	19.43	26.09	16.21	3.88
1942		297.91	478.36	279.64	292.9	53.73	41.40	16.31	38.46	10.54	6.42
1943		288.18	429.59	248.85	410.7	99.05	50.83	13.13	44.97	9.38	11.60
1944		196.08	604.89	252.91	330.2	42.10	46.97	11.18	47.32	14.74	11.12
1945		130.17	752.14	168.47	440.5	4.13	41.19	16.86	43.43	14.50	8.87
Monthly averages											
1940		14.80	59.10	13.45	685.1	12.86	1.86	2.12	1.84	18.78	1.31
1941		23.37	52..52	18.71	427.5	39.29	2.46	1.61	2.17	16.21	3.88
1942		24.82	39.86	23.30	292.9	53.73	3.45	1.36	3.21	10.54	6.42
1943		24.01	35.80	20.74	410.7	99.05	4.24	1.09	3.75	9.38	11.60
1944		16.34	50.41	21.08	330.2	42.10	3.91	0.93	3.94	14.74	11.12
1945		10.85	62.68	14.04	440.5	4.13	3.43	1.41	3.62	14.50	8.87
1940	January	5.19	69.32	4.50	511.6	10.22	1.25	3.23	1.22	18.81	..
	February	5.92	67.27	6.27	479.8	10.45	1.27	3.07	1.50	17.51	1.42
	March	8.44	62.35	7.81	474.7	10.44	1.58	2.96	1.62	16.17	1.39
	April	11.62	83.23	10.91	455.4	10.57	1.92	2.95	1.83	14.96	1.40
	May	15.07	76.06	13.91	448.5	10.63	2.14	2.63	2.23	14.40	1.33
	June	17.17	75.74	14.34	450.5	10.81	2.01	3.00	1.91	13.70	1.32
	July	18.31	46.23	15.26	490.6	11.02	2.11	2.11	2.18	14.11	1.26
	August	20.24	47.22	24.09	560.3	11.17	2.11	0.87	2.19	15.85	1.21
	September	19.90	35.08	17.90	623.9	11.67	1.99	1.86	1.95	15.50	1.20
	October	20.23	42.17	17.71	659.1	12,16	2,13	0.48	1.94	17.52	1.24
	November	17.98	52.46	15.79	671.0	12.66	2.02	0.74	1.90	19.49	1.26
	December	17.53	52.02	12.94	685.1	12.86	1.80	1.56	1.63	18.78	1.31
1941	January	16.80	43.74	15.04	707.4	13.02	1.88	1.06	1.74	19.62	1.36
	February	16.66	48.29	14.59	684.9	13.56	1.87	1.12	1.72	19.97	1.41
	March	20.03	74.14	16.13	648.2	14.32	2.10	2.36	1.89	18.91	1.50
	April	21.52	49.21	18.30	637.5	15.31	2.24	1.51	2.04	18.22	1.59
	May	24.77	42.78	19.76	618.4	18.12	2.54	2.16	2.33	17.28	1.65
	June	24.28	58.35	18.87	584.6	21.23	2.39	1.53	2.42	14.94	1.69
	July	26.54	56.92	20.93	564.2	27.49	2.74	1.37	2.48	15.58	3.05
	August	25.64	53.42	19.81	535.1	31.24	2.56	1.71	2.29	15.10	3.20
	September	26.92	50.81	17.31	485.2	39.02	2.85	1.72	1.84	18.21	4.07
	October	27.45	55.56	22.16	473.8	42.33	2.86	1.71	2.59	16.44	3.71
	November	24.71	47 .56	20.46	454.2	44.86	2.72	1.72	3.08	16.10	3.21
	December	25.13	49.48	21.31	427.5	39.29	2..66	1.46	1.60	16.21	3.88
1942	January	18.07	50.56	21.95	383.,5	35.41	2.40	1.41	2.40	15.06	3.88
	February	19.62	40.45	15.97	349.7	39.06	2.54	1.26	2.08	14.73	4.33
	March	22.12	50.30	19.01	305.9	42.17	2.94	1.44	2.60	14.55	4.68
	April	26.39	41.08	22.52	270.4	46.03	3.23	1.56	3.09	13.92	4.82
	May	26.66	35.14	25.01	241.2	47.68	3.54	1.21	3.19	14.00	5.16
	June	27.53	40.09	28.14	226.3	47.08	3.71	1.48	3.56	13.26	5.31
	July	28.94	37.64	27.11	235.0	46.49	3.90	1.32	3.31	12.99	5.75
	August	26.60	34.54	25.91	236.2	45.76	3.54	1.34	3.54	12.68	5.49
	September	27.32	38.26	23.74	243.7	49.34	4.00	1.43	3.49	11.99	6.00
	October	26.90	38.70	25.01	263.2	51.23	4.25	1.43	3.91	11.58	6.34
	November	24.42	34.42	24.28	266.0	51.37	3.79	1.27	3.83	11.03	6.30
	December	23.35	37.19	21.00	292.9	53.73	3.57	1.17	3.46	10.54	6.42

See footnotes on page 128

Source: *Board of Trade*

6.10 Softwood and hardwood

continued

		Softwood[1]					Hardwood[1]				
		Pro-duction[2]	Consumption		Stocks (end of period)		Pro-duction[2]	Consumption		Stocks (end of period)	
			Im-ported	Home grown[2]	Im-ported	Home grown		Im-ported	Home grown[2]	Im-ported	Home grown
		Thousand standard[3]					*Million cubic feet*				
1943	January	22.29	34.99	21.72	290.9	54.30	3.66	1.29	3.32	9.81	6.75
	February	23.45	33.14	18.07	280.3	59.99	3.81	1.22	3.04	9.14	7.50
	March	27.50	38.71	24.15	255.6	69.34	4.39	1.24	2.77	8.81	9.37
	April	25.81	32.35	20.73	246.6	74.41	4.56	1.14	4.06	8.42	9.86
	May	25.75	33.72	22.93	254.3	77.23	4.57	1.05	4.28	8.20	10.15
	June	25.65	34.06	20.13	273.8	82.75	4.56	1.16	3.47	7.96	11.23
	July	25.47	35.16	20.24	298.3	87.67	4.51	1.02	4.41	8.24	11.17
	August	26.02	32.43	20.10	321.3	93.59	3.92	1.09	3.58	8.62	11.51
	September	26.57	33.78	20.49	371.7	99.66	4.63	1.12	4.05	9.18	12.10
	October	21.87	37.34	22.92	396.2	98.62	4.30	1.07	4.05	8.88	11.60
	November	19.16	42.87	18.45	389.9	99.33	4.20	1.00	4.19	9.08	11.60
	December	18.63	41.03	18.91	410.7	99.05	3.72	0.78	3.73	9.38	11.60
1944	January	18.21	37.58	19.47	398.0	97.79	3.78	0.73	3.81	9.20	11.57
	February	18.26	47.82	20.82	378.5	95.23	4.04	0.87	3.91	9.20	11.71
	March	19.55	55.88	22.11	347.6	92.67	4.35	0.94	4.28	9.36	11.78
	April	7.11	54.67	19.73	326.1	90.05	3.75	0.88	3.77	9.65	11.75
	May	18.44	50.17	24.76	317.4	83.73	4.20	0.98	4.53	10.02	11.43
	June	17.10	54.03	24.95	305.6	75.88	4.20	1.14	4.57	10.40	11.06
	July	14.54	53.60	21.34	276.7	69.07	3.91	0.88	3.85	10.62	11.06
	August	15.41	53.36	20.71	254.2	63.66	3.63	0.74	3.54	11.74	11.08
	September	15.74	47.73	21.33	273.5	58.06	3.97	0.91	3.65	12.66	11.39
	October	15.66	48.67	22.10	295.7	51.62	3.96	1.21	4.13	13.88	11.22
	November	13.94	51.26	19.31	328.4	46.25	3.88	1.28	3.93	14.58	11.18
	December	12.13	50.12	16.27	330.2	42.10	3.30	0.62	3.35	14.74	11.12
1945	January	9.42	55.86	17.74	324.4	35.66	3.25	1.66	3.64	14.23	10.97
	February	10.52	56.84	15.95	290.2	28.69	3.33	1.11	3.70	14.23	10.38
	March	13.40	54.75	15.66	273.1	26.48	3.77	1.33	4.18	14.08	10.19
	April	12.67	54.96	15.81	241.2	23.29	3.53	1.27	3.83	13.95	9.67
	May	12.05	60.38	15.80	228.9	19.97	3.62	1.23	3.72	13.83	9.46
	June	12.24	59.57	16.31	228.5	15.47	3.75	1.46	3.76	13.89	9.56
	July	10.44	67.58	14.85	259.4	12.00	3.55	1.41	3.96	14.42	9.40
	August	9.74	54.98	12.60	325.9	8.19	3.08	1.34	3.41	14.85	8.83

1. Excluding sleepers of all kinds except in figures for production before 1942.
2. In the figures for production after 1941 and in all figures for consumption of home-grown timber an allowance of 10 per cent. (softwood) and 5 per cent. (hardwood) has been made for conversion to square edged material.
3. Standards of 165 cubic feet.

Source: Board of Trade

6.11 Pitwood and plywood

	Production of pitwood							Plywood			
		Sawn		Round				Constructional			Technical
	Total	Trade	Home Timber Production Department	Trade	Home Timber Production Department	Consumption of sawn and round pitwood	Stocks of sawn and round pitwood (end of period)	Production	Consumption	Stocks (end of period)	Production
	Thousand standards[1]							Million square feet			
Annual totals											
1939	..	..	..	..	..	..	537.6	..	..	..	9.96
1940	597.49	132.40	4.16	305.62	155.31	895.99	658.9	4.42	107.44	141.0	24.00
1941	573.85	138.85	29.69	221.65	183.66	833.52	450.4	3.61	167.27	110.1	52.44
1942	636.77	141.61	49.64	229.54	215.98	803.58	286.7	7.31	167.60	43.0	65.76
1943	720.56	146.62	47.87	243.57	282.50	720.43	332.6	4.21	121.01	192.0	63.84
1944	602.33	153.18	51.47	184.21	213.47	737.34	251.1	4.23	304.22	190.9	68.28
1945	501.24	142.81	41.24	137.26	182.93	683.24	268.6	43.08	377.76	166.3	32.28
Monthly averages											
1940	49.79	11.03	0.35	25.47	12.94	74.67	658.9	0.37	9.0	141.0	2.00
1941	47.82	11.57	2.47	18.47	15.31	69.46	450.4	0.30	13.9	110.1	4.37
1942	53,97	11,80	4.14	19.13	18.00	66.97	286.7	0.61	14.0	43.0	5.48
1943	60.05	12.22	3.99	20.30	23.54	60.04	332.6	0.35	10.1	190.9	5.32
1944	50.20	12.77	4.29	15.35	17.79	61.45	251.1	0.35	25.4	192.0	5.69
1945	42.02	11.90	3.44	11.44	15.24	56.94	268.6	3.59	31.5	166.3	2.69
1940 January	21.27	6.71	-	12.38	2.18	77.95	498.5	..	6.92	..	..
February	25.96	8.08	-	14.12	3.76	70.49	475.0	..	11.61	..	..
March	36.19	9.79	-	21.23	5.17	85.21	441.7	..	13.19	..	..
April	42.25	10.08	-	23.90	8.27	71.14	429.5	..	11.86	..	..
May	56.04	12.74	0.01	31.16	12.14	92.56	407.9	..	9.81	..	..
June	63.85	12.32	0.10	32.91	18.52	76.48	432.4	..	9.87	..	..
July	63.89	12.48	0.20	33.44	17.77	81.50	456.1	..	9.84	..	..
August	73.65	13.55	0.61	38.50	20.99	77.98	547.9	..	9.00	..	..
September	64.75	12.29	0.63	31.47	20.35	66.30	603.2	..	3.63	..	..
October	61.50	12.49	0.80	28.92	19.29	74.01	636.7	..	5.67	..	..
November	44.15	11.22	0.91	18.41	13.61	61.43	652.1	..	7.24	..	..
December	43.99	10.65	0.90	19.17	13.27	60.94	658.9	..	8.81	141.0	..
1941 January	34.27	7.75	1.02	13.89	11.61	59.86	651.0	..	11.85	163.7	..
February	33.55	7.77	1.12	13.17	11.49	62.20	648.7	..	11.43	171.6	..
March	48.85	9.98	1.33	20.48	17.06	62.23	648.6	..	14.22	178.4	..
April	44.44	10.60	1.39	17.07	15.38	64.46	628.5	..	19.06	168.4	..
May	47.32	11.50	1.40	20.69	13.73	71.70	580.6	..	13.05	170.8	..
June	49.50	12.16	1.83	19.96	15.55	76.24	559.5	..	12.37	173.7	..
July	52.87	12.74	2.34	19.99	17.80	69.02	543.7	..	6.73	178.1	..
August	56.47	12.47	2.77	21.45	19.78	71.49	528.8	..	16.29	163.1	..
September	56.23	14.07	2.92	21.78	17.46	72.00	522.1	..	14.93	148.3	..
October	56.39	14.12	3.74	21.06	17.47	81.28	499.6	..	12.97	138.7	..
November	48.29	12.59	5.48	15.18	15.04	73.13	475.6	..	18.14	123.7	..
December	45.68	13.10	4.35	16.94	11.29	69.92	450.4	..	16.24	110.1	..

See footnote on page 130.

Source: Board of Trade

6.11 Pitwood and plywood

continued

		Production of pitwood							Plywood			
		Total	Sawn		Round		Con-sump-tion of sawn and round pitwood	Stocks of sawn and round pit-wood (end of period)	Constructional			Tech-nical
			Trade	Home Timber Produc-tion Depart-ment	Trade	Home Timber Produc-tion Depart-ment			Produc-tion	Con-sump-tion	Stocks end of period	Prod-uction
		Thousand standards[1]							Million square feet			
1942	January	37.65	9.52	4.72	13.69	9.72	72.19	414.1	0.32	22.94	84.4	..
	February	38.21	9.67	3.58	13.85	11.11	65.80	386.9	0.32	17.14	67.1	..
	March	45.13	11.39	4.58	15.95	13.21	66.80	365.3	0.51	21.56	49.8	..
	April	53.88	12.15	4.19	18.55	18.99	69.06	351.2	0.56	18.08	40.7	..
	May	58.04	12.80	4.80	20.04	20.40	67.69	340.8	0.39	9.98	41.1	..
	June	60.88	13.90	3.33	22.85	20.80	67.13	334.8	0.93	10.49	43.9	..
	July	59.47	12.03	3.37	22.17	21.90	69.67	328.0	0.61	12.04	47.7	..
	August	56.82	12.53	3.56	20.98	19.75	60.63	324.2	0.52	12.24	40.8	..
	September	62.84	13.23	4.84	22.21	22.56	66.22	320.3	0.81	13.84	43.3	..
	October	60.35	12.25	4.33	22.15	21.62	71.51	310.0	0.79	10.66	46.7	..
	November	53.17	11.33	4.84	18.81	18.19	66.31	296.4	0.85	9.73	45.2	..
	December	50.33	10.81	3.50	18.29	17.73	60.57	286.7	0.69	8.90	43.0	..
1943	January	44.47	9.74	3.51	15.37	15.85	56.46	290.3	0.50	9.20	42.3	..
	February	49.44	11.03	3.44	16.99	17.98	57.48	290.2	0.53	7.89	46.8	..
	March	66.72	11.45	3.78	23.10	28.39	62.32	293.1	0.59	9.75	51.6	..
	April	67.35	12.55	3.51	23.61	27.68	55.53	303.3	0.29	10.60	55.9	..
	May	64.66	13.04	4.51	20.45	26.66	60.31	307.0	0.33	7.72	68.8	..
	June	69.52	13.24	4.76	21.97	29.55	60.62	313.5	0.27	8.70	78.5	..
	July	68.87	12.59	4.36	23.85	28.07	63.82	317.7	0.34	9.18	94.2	..
	August	62.59	12.48	3.84	20.92	25.35	54.09	326.9	0.14	9.99	112.2	..
	September	65.34	13.41	3.65	22.07	26.21	65.04	331.3	0.45	7.84	126.2	..
	October	61.75	13.23	4.42	21.57	22.53	62.03	336.1	0.25	12.99	147.0	..
	November	52.86	12.22	4.52	17.88	18.24	61.02	331.7	0.27	12.82	173.7	..
	December	47.00	11.64	3.57	15.80	15.99	61.72	332.6	0.25	14.34	192.0	..
1944	January	45.98	11.62	4.50	14.57	15.29	53.46	326.4	0.19	14.50	217.5	..
	February	50.88	12.11	3.82	14.90	20.05	63.74	322.4	0.17	19.17	237.1	..
	March	57.47	14.10	4.22	17.61	21.54	62.82	319.5	0.20	22.93	247.6	..
	April	50.96	12.63	5.00	16.18	17.15	56.92	314.4	0.22	17.91	268.8	..
	May	57.17	13.36	4.91	18.86	20.04	65.56	312.0	0.15	21.63	284.9	..
	June	54.78	14.07	4.82	18.16	17.73	64.39	301.0	0.21	24.02	285.7	..
	July	52.42	12.33	4.05	16.74	19.30	60.96	291.0	0.09	23.24	272.2	..
	August	55.10	13.27	4.38	15.61	21.84	58.62	290.7	0.12	22.02	266.2	..
	September	50.40	13.39	4.50	15.39	17.12	63.54	284.0	0.16	28.62	253.8	..
	October	47.55	12.76	4.16	14.66	15.97	62.71	281.1	0.53	37.56	234.9	..
	November	43.03	12.11	4.27	11.44	15.21	64.11	269.6	1.14	41.66	206.5	..
	December	36.60	11.43	2.84	10.10	12.23	60.49	251.1	1.06	30.96	190.9	..
1945	January	27.73	8.32	2.20	7.58	9.63	53.32	226.1	1.68	38.5	176.8	5.50
	February	35.92	9.69	3.39	9.10	13.74	64.62	198.3	2.42	35.4	159.4	4.34
	March	49.01	12.49	3.57	13.46	19.49	59.17	195.0	2.88	40.2	142.3	5.16
	April	49.44	12.52	4.21	13.65	19.06	58.31	186.5	2.37	31.9	130.8	4.30
	May	44.42	12.31	3.41	12.52	16.18	53.19	182.1	2.18	29.9	123.0	4.20
	June	50.74	13.40	4.33	13.38	19.63	58.66	180.0	3.47	31.1	124.3	3.29
	July	47.19	12.61	3.86	13.10	17.62	56.46	183.7	3.35	26.9	133.4	3.59
	August	39.01	11.34	2.61	11.05	14.01	46.81	197.9	3.46	24.0	136.2	1.94

1. Gothenburg standards of 180 piled cubic feet

Source: Board of Trade

6.12 Hides, skins and finished leather

Production and consumption: calendar years Stocks: end of year *Thousand tons*

		1942	1943	1944	1945
Cattle hides					
Production[1]		54.9	54.3	58.6	61.5
Stocks[2]		20.6[3]	17.3[3]	21.5	26.2
Kips and calfskins					
Production		4.1	4.6	4.7	5.0
Stocks		..[3]	..[3]	2.6	3.4
Goatskins					
Stocks		0.8	1.0	1.0	0.5
Sheepskin					
Production		10.6	10.1	9.1	8.7
Stocks		6.7	6.1	8.4	8.8
Rough tanned hides and kips					
Stocks		1.4	1.1	0.9	0.7
Rough tanned goat and sheepskins					
Stocks		0.8	0.9	0.7	1.0
Finished leather					
Heavy[4]:					
Production:	Sole leather	79.3	59.5	68.1	62.7
	Other		6.4	7.2	6.8
Consumption:	Sole leather	84.7	80.2	71.4	72.0
	Other			7.1	7.1
Stocks:	Sole leather	18.7	17.8	21.6	19.5
	Other			0.8	0.7
Light[5]:					
Production:	Upper leather	28.5	26.9	14.2	14.4
	Lining leather			3.8	4.2
	Other			6.7	6.9
Consumption:	Upper leather	31.1	28.3	15.3	15.5
	Lining leather			4.0	4.3
	Other			6.7	6.9
Stocks:	Upper leather	6.4	6.1	4.4	4.0
	Lining leather			1.4	1.3
	Other			0.4	0.4

1. Wet.
2. Wet, dry and dry salted cattle and buffalo hides.
3. Kips and calfskins are included in the figures for "cattle hides".
4. Leathers sold by weight.
5. Leathers sold by area.

Source: Board of Trade

6.13 Rubber

Thousand tons

		Waste[1]			Reclaimed[1]			Natural (Including latex)[2]		Synthetic[3]	
		Production[4]	Consumption[5]	Stocks (end of period)	Production	Consumption[6, 7]	Stocks (end of period)	Consumption[7]	Stocks end of period	Consumption	Stocks (end of period)
Annual totals											
1941		..	..	..	..	..	1.93[8]	167.84	97.7	..	..
1942		..	..	58.1	18.3	23.4	9.78	97.30	62.5	..	0.80
1943		101.50	44.73	113.5	28.3	33.6	7.30	75.51	60.3	3.65	8.06
1944		81.59	32.02	116.5	28.04	27.80	9.12	49.43	47.4	43.73	55.05
1945		53.13	20.36	149.0	22.32	27.86	3.58	34.17	52.5	65.39	17.19
Weekly averages											
1941		..	..	..	..	..	1.93[8]	3.23	97.7	..	..
1942		..	..	58.1	..	0.45	9.78	1.87	62.5	..	0.80
1943		1.95	0.86	113.5	0.54	0.65	7.30	1.45	60.3	0.07	8.06
1944		1.57	0.62	116.5	0.54	0.53	9.12	0.95	47.4	0.84	55.08
1945		1.02	0.39	149.0	0.43	0.54	3.58	0.66	52.5	1.26	17.19
1941	January	..	..	..	..	..	..	3.03	96.3	..	..
	February	..	..	..	..	..	..	2.90	101.7	..	..
	March	..	..	..	..	..	..	3.03	100.8	..	..
	April	..	..	..	..	..	..	2.87	961	..	..
	May	..	..	..	..	..	..	3.25	98.2	..	..
	June	..	..	..	..	..	..	2.75	99.6	..	..
	July	..	..	..	..	0.17	1.60	3.30	100.9	..	..
	August	..	..	..	..	0.15	1.70	2.57	101.5	..	..
	September	..	..	..	..	0.19	1.75	5.46	80.8	..	..
	October	..	..	..	..	0.20	1.80	3.30	78.6	..	..
	November	..	..	..	..	0.20	1.88	3.10	82.5	..	..
	December	..	..	..	..	0.19	1.93	3.55	97.7	..	..
1942	January	..	..	..	..	0.21	2.28	2.88	100.0	..	..
	February	..	..	..	..	0.25	2.27	2.44	94.5	..	..
	March	..	..	..	..	0.36	2.53	2.35	98.0	..	..
	April	..	..	..	..	0.42	2.98	1.90	102.2	..	..
	May	..	..	..	..	0.46	3.69	1.75	94.4	..	..
	June	..	..	..	0.33*	0.53*	6.85	1.70*	88.0	..	..
	July	..	..	3.48	0.34*	0.45*	7.21	1.33*	82.3	..	..
	August	2.41	0.75	41.4	0.41	0.48	8.26	1.52	77.9	..	..
	September	2.21	0.85	46.9	0.43	0.51	7.44	1.57	73.1	..	..
	October	2.25	0.73	53.0	0.43	0.52	6.96	1.46	70.8	0.02	0.88
	November	1.73	0.77	56.8	0.43	0.56	7.20	1.49	65.4	0.02	0.78
	December	0.99*	0.73*	58.1	0.36*	0.52*	9.78	1.38*	59.4	0.02*	0.80

See footnootes on page 133.

Source: Board of Trade

6.13 Rubber

continued

Thousand tons

		Waste[1]			Reclaimed[1]			Natural (Including latex)[2]		Synthetic[3]	
		Production[4]	Consumption[5]	Stocks (end of period)	Production	Consumption[6, 7]	Stocks end of period	Consumption[7]	Stocks (end of period)	Consumption	Stocks (end of period)
1943	January	1.13	0.74	59.7	0.59	0.73	11.09	1.49	59.2	0.02	0.82
	February	2.57	0.75	65.8	0.61	0.75	11.36	1.56	58.9	0.02	0.78
	* March	2.18	0.75	72.6	0.59	0.78	11.47	1.56	59.0	0.02	0.89
	April	2.00	0.80	77.4	0.69	0.72	11.70	1.38	59.5	0.02	1.17
	May	2.02	0.90	81.8	0.78	0.85	11.44	1.58	57.3	0.03	1.27
	* June	1.83	0.83	86.8	0.71	0.85	10.65	1.42	56.5	0.03	1.60
	July	2.06	0.81	91.8	0.74	0.80	10.49	1.35	54.6	0.03	2.25
	August	1.21	0.86	93.2	0.66	0.74	10.10	1.27	56.4	0.05	2.64
	* September	2.15	0.96	99.1	0.75	0.91	9.12	1.54	57.4	0.08	3.73
	October	2.60	0.97	105.8	0.81	0.88	8.35	1.52	56.9	0.09	5.78
	November	2.00	1.04	109.7	0.88	0.87	8.36	1.52	54.1	0.16	6.39
	* December	1.68	0.91	113.5	0.65	0.77	8.09	1.25	60.3	0.26	8.06
1944	January	1.93	1.08	116.9	0.64	0.60	7.43	1.23	58.1	0.38	8.06
	February	2.28	1.12	121.6	0.65	0.61	7.60	1.20	60.0	0.53	14.58
	* March	2.01	1.01	126.6	0.60	0.59	7.74	1.11	58.1	0.62	18.91
	April	2.03	0.94	131.0	0.64	0.52	8.54	0.98	58.5	0.63	27.35
	May	2.44	1.04	136.6	0.63	0.57	9.68	1.13	55.8	0.76	31.96
	* June	1.49	0.85	139.7	0.56	0.56	9.69	0.93	54.2	0.78	41.86
	July	1.19[9]	0.24[9]	96.8[9]	0.54	0.51	9.92	0.95	53.4	0.86	52.72
	August	1.07	0.11	100.7	0.43	0.45	9.84	0.65	54.1	0.73	54.11
	* September	1.10	0.22	105.2	0.44	0.48	9.68	0.82	52.7	0.96	52.63
	October	1.37	0.35	109.2	0.51	0.54	9.53	0.90	51.6	1.11	54.41
	November	1.45	0.30	113.8	0.50	0.62	9.06	0.85	49.6	1.16	58.86
	* December	0.71	0.18	116.5	0.38	0.37	9.12	0.71	47.4	1.45	55.08
1945	January	0.89	0.28	118.6	0.43	0.62	8.36	0.67	46.2	1.19	54.15
	February	0.83	0.36	120.5	0.42	0.51	7.98	0.80	44.1	1.28	54.85
	* March	0.95	0.60	122.2	0.40	0.55	7.27	0.74	42.1	1.25	49.69
	April	1.18	0.44	125.2	0.40	0.50	6.89	0.63	41.2	1.18	45.05
	May	1.24	0.31	128.9	0.37	0.50	6.40	0.83	38.7	1.08	40.76
	* June	1.09	0.18	133.5	0.39	0.59	5.42	0.60	38.2	1.34	35.31
	July	1.24	0.38	136.9	0.44	0.55	4.95	0.49	37.0	1.24	32.41
	August	0.99	0.26	139.8	0.36	0.51	4.36	0.55	39.6	1.20	35.73

1. Crumb is included in waste rubber in 1942. In 1943 it is included in the monthly figures for reclaimed rubber but not in the annual figures. Thereafter it is excluded from the table.
2. Monthly figures for 1942 exclude latex and exports.
3. Excluding "Novoplas" and "Thiokol" from July1944 onwards.
4. Waste rubber collected.
5. Processed into reclaimed rubber.
6. Until June 1994, including direct usage of waste rubber.
7. Up to and including May1942 computed from figures relating to calendar months.
8. Excluding Government lend-lease stocks.
9. From July1944 the figures relate only to Government waste depots.

* Average of five weeks.

Source: Board of Trade

6.14 Chemicals

Production and consumption: calendar years Stocks: end of year

	Unit	1938	1939	1940	1941	1942	1943	1944	1945
Industrial alcohol[1]									
Production	Million	27.24	29.88	29.42	32.40	22.48	7.78	32.50	20.83
Consumption	bulk	27.36	30.24	30.25	35.11	40.03	34.67	40.58	27.24
Stocks	gallons	1.79	1.90	2.65	5.50	5.24	7.37	7.94	3.28
Industrial methylated spirit									
Production	"	7.84	9.40	10.94	9.03	8.55	9.63	9.48	8.65
Consumption	"	. .	. .	10.97	8.87	8.58	9.74	9.57	8.75
Stocks	"	. .	. .	0.31	0.34	0.37	0.34	0.34	0.32
Methanol									
Production	Thousand	. .	. .	. .	28.0	36.6	48.7	54.5	30.1
Consumption	tons	. .	. .	. .	23.3	36.7	46.7	53.9	40.6
Stocks	"	. .	. .	7.2	11.9	11.8	13.9	14.5	4.0
Urea									
Production	"	. .	. .	. .	4.3	4.7	4.4	4.5	7.5
Consumption	"	. .	. .	. .	4.5	5.2	5.0	4.6	7.2
Stocks	"	. .	. .	2.7	2.5	2.0	1.4	1.1	1.4
Nitric acid									
Production	"	. .	. .	. .	254.5	349.4	380.7	341.7	281.0
Consumption	"	. .	. .	. .	. .	344.0	381.0	338.7	283.2
Stocks	"	. .	. .	. .	5.6	11.4	10.3	12.1	4.8
Pyrites[2]									
Production[3]	"	. .	. .	6.4	7.6	15.4	26.9	26.0	20.1
Consumption	"	279.6	313.2	335.8	294.8	279.5	243.1	222.8	201.1
Stocks	"	. .	318.0	353.1	279.9	212..4	174.6	131.7	88.9
Sulphur (for acid)									
Production[3]	"	. .	. .	2.0	3.9	4.3	3.0	3.8	3.7
Consumption	"	74.4	92.9	127.9	153.5	170.6	159.4	171.5	173.8
Stocks	"	. .	63.6	64.4	129.6	59.0	101.2	81.2	61.8
Sulphur (regular)									
Production[4]	"	. .	. .	3.3	5.6	6.0	9.5	11.2	7.3
Consumption	"	. .	. .	. .	67.2	62.4	68.3	65.6	59.4
Stocks	"	. .	. .	28.1	49.2	26.7	37.7	35.6	30.0
Spent oxide[2]	"	. .	. .	154.1	171.4	182.4	191.7	195.4	196.8
Production[3]	"	. .	. .	16.27	150.1	153.3	192.1	190.9	187.0
Consumption	"	145.2	155.4	162.7	150.1	153.3	192.1	190.9	187.0
Stocks	"	. .	74.6	65.9	87.3	116.0	115.5	120.2	130.2
Anhydrite[2]									
Production[3]	"	. .	. .	. .	139.7	143.6	134.2	150.5	161.1
Consumption	"	. .	. .	. .	139.9	143.2	134.3	150.8	161.1
Stocks	"	. .	. .	. .	0.5	0.9	0.8	0.4	0.4
Sulphuric acid[5]									
Production	"	994.8	1,119.6	1,196.4	1,200.0	1,284.0	1,250.4	1,268.2	1,216.1
Consumption	"	. .	. .	1,206.0	1,213.7	1,284.8	1,273.4	1,281.7	1,248.9
Stocks	"	. .	. .	65.5	67.5	81.8	81.7	82.2	67.6
Calcium carbide									
Production	Thousand	. .	. .	. .	3.1	24.8	62.4	70.2	72.1
Consumption	metric	65.0	. .	. .	. .	107.9	106.3	129.0	100.6
Stocks	tons	. .	. .	17.3	24.2	22.3	44.4	37.1	27.6

1. Ethyl alcohol as 68 O.P. spirit.
2. Excluding material used for purposes other than for the manufacture of sulphuric acid.
3. Arrivals of hom-produced materials at acid works.
4. Recovered sulphur.
5. As 100 per cent. acid. Including from 1941acid made at Government factories.

Source: Board of Trade

6.15 Fertilizers, ammonia and molasses

Production and consumption: calendar year[1] Stocks: end of period *Thousand tons*

	1939	1940	1941	1942	1943	1944	1945
Nitrogenous fertilizers (nitrogen content)[2]							
Production	..	123.4	133.5	144.6	170.8	210.7	186.3
Total disposals	..	127.0	132.5	171.9	177.3	194.3	215.5
Home consumption	..	77.1	127.7	168.0	171.0	181.5	172.1
Stocks	..	24.0[5]	41.0	20.5	26.8	51.8	34.5
Total phosphatic fertilizers (P_2O_5 content)							
Production	157.2	188.7	225.0	259.4	251.9	274.9	296.9
Consumption	162.4	194.7	232.7	287.4	302.6	343.8	345.5
Stocks	19.4	14.1	8.8	10.9	20.8	23.2	15.5
Superphosphate (P_2O_5 content):							
Production	63.2	83.0	118.9	144.9	148.0	175.9	184.8
Consumption	68.9	86.8	121.4	144.1	144.3	175.4	186.7
Stocks	10.6	6.8	5.5	7.7	13.6	14.1	12.1
Ground basic slag (P_2O_5 content):							
Production	59.0	73.6	69.7	72.1	77.4	64.2	66.0
Consumption	56.3	71.6	72.6	72.6	77.3	62.4	67.8
Stocks	4.8	4.6	1.2	0.7	0.8	2.9	0.8
Ground phosphate (P_2O_5 content):							
Production	15.0	12.0	9.3	6.3	3.6	10.6	20.5
Consumption	16.6	12.3	9.3	6.1	3.8	10.6	19.7
Stocks	..	..	-	0.2	0.1	0.2	0.9
All other phosphatic fertilizers (P_2O_5 content):							
Production	20.1	20.1	27.2	36.1	22.9	24.3	25.7
Consumption	20.7	24.0	29.5	64.6	77.2	95.3	71.3
Stocks	4.0	2.7	2.1	2.3	6.3	6.0	1.7
Potash (K_2O content)[3]							
Consumption	..	..	48.0	60.0	72.9	103.7	115.0
Stocks	..	..	..	21.0	7.0	18.8	3.6
Compound fertilizers[4]							
Production	600.0[5]	739.1	773.9	952.2	1,077.8	1,185.5	1,181.2
Consumption	..[5]	714.1	804.7	929.5	1,051.2	1,147.4	1,191.1
Stocks	30.0[5]	55.0	24.2	46.9	71.0	105.2	92.8
Phosphate rock[6]							
Consumption	..	490.1	534.5	624.5	599.3	649.8	753.9
Stocks	183.9	78.8	344.3	35.4	240.7	250.7	160.1
Ammonia[7]							
Production	..	190.8	253.4	276.4	339.1	313.9	300.6
Consumption	..	..	253.4	276.2	336.6	315.8	301.7
Stocks	..	2.9	2.0	5.6[8]	7.6	5.7	5.0
Molasses[9]							
Production:							
Cane	111.6[10]	50.2	109.4	99.5	52.3	247.8	99.3
Beet		135.0	111.4	137.1	197.9	156.1	171.0
Consumption:							
Total	..	882.9	802.9	594.9	347.8	709.1	541.6
Distilling	..	526.9	550.4	332.8	116.3	492.1	315.6
Cattle food	..	..	162.0	128.2	122.4	104.4	120.0
Other uses	..	..	90.5	133.9	109.2	112.8	106.0
Stocks	426.2	370.1	419.0	351.9	292.1	316.2	317.6

1. Years ended 30 June, except for phosphate rock, ammonia and molasses.
2. For agricultural uses only except in the figures for total disposals which include exports of ammonium sulphate for all purposes.
3. Agricultural potash.
4. Total weight of product. Excluding concentrated compound fertilizers. The nitrogen, P_2O_5 and for consumption, K_2O content are included under appropriate headings above.
5. Estimated.
6. For agricultural and industrial purposes.
7. Excluding ammonia produced in by-product factories and converted directly into ammonium sulphate.
8. Including consumers' stocks.
9. In terms of blackstrap containing 52 per cent. sugars.
10. Year ended 30 September.

Source: Board of Trade

6.16 Plastics and materials for plastics

Production and consumption: calendar years Stocks: end of year *Tons*

	1941	1942	1943	1944	1945
Total synthetic resins					
Production	16,096	20,931	23,979	24,424	25,424
Total disposals	15,766	20,291	24,069	24,551	25,696
Home consumption	15,560	20,202	24,005	24,502	25,186
Stocks	1,124	1,764	1,674	1,547	1,275
Phenolic:					
Production	..	..	8,937	9,644	10,058
Total disposals	..	..	9,033	9,640	10,279
Home consumption	..	..	9,016	9,636	10,064
Stocks	..	..	912	916	695
Cresylic:					
Production	..	..	8,723	8,293	6,996
Total disposals	..	..	8,737	8,465	7,114
Home consumption	..	..	8,695	8,436	6,964
Stocks	..	..	606	434	316
Urea:					
Production	..	..	5,924	5,905	7,902
Total disposals	..	..	5,898	5,905	7,823
Home consumption	..	..	5,894	5,890	7,701
Stocks	..	..	120	120	199
Other synthetic resins:					
Production	..	..	395	582	468
Total disposals	..	..	401	541	480
Home consumption	..	..	400	540	457
Stocks	..	..	36	77	65
Moulding powders					
Phenolic and cresylic:					
Production	13,521	13,124	14,289	15,249	17,531
Total disposals	12,593	13,100	14,195	15,330	17,487
Home consumption	11,117	11,952	13,679	14,742	15,814
Stocks	2,926	2,910	3,090	3,009	1,078 [1]
Urea:					
Production	4,136	4,080	3,869	2,760	3,996
Total disposals	4,039	4,046	3,948	2,824	4,067
Home consumption	2,456	3,243	3,447	2,396	3,115
Stocks	714	748	727	663	351 [1]
Cellulose acetate:					
Production	1,207	1,343	1,489	1,307	2,162
Total disposals	1,204	1,335	1,344	1,324	1,967
Home consumption	1,063	1,279	1,326	1,262	1,784
Stocks	262	270	415	398	271 [1]

See footnotes on page 137.

Source: Board of Trade [1]

6.16 Plastics and materials for plastics

continued

Production and consumption: calendar years Stocks: end of year *Tons*

	1941	1942	1943	1944	1945
Cellulose acetate sheet, rods, tubes and film					
Production	2,335	2,718	3,059	2,623	1,133
Total disposals	2,255	2,772	2,941	2,573	1,279
Home consumption	1,938	2,041	2,928	2,571	1,215
Stocks	323	212	244	277	131
Acrylic sheet					
Production	1,463	2,507	3,796	4,718	1,832
Total disposals	1,182	2,594	3,629	4,370	1,851
Home consumption	1,011	1,102	2,764	3,407	1,798
Stocks	358	260	424	772	753
Celluloid					
Production	1,719	1,531	1,486	1,572	1,976
Total disposals	1,723	1,651	1,544	1,450	1,857
Home consumption	1,019	1,518	1,501	1,331	1,391
Stocks	281	165	112	234	353
Polyvinyl chloride (unplasticised)					
Production	..	..	745	3,365	4,122
Consumption	..	..	3,875	5,892	5,122
Stocks	..	..	1,118	1,834	4,227
Polyvinyl chloride (plasticised)					
Production	..	..	..	10,082	8,463
Consumption	..	..	..	10,025	8,736
Stocks	..	..	894	951	678
Casein plastic materials					
Production	1,480	1,724	1,523	1,433	2,051
Total disposals	2,018	1,851	1,566	1,443	1,899
Home consumption	1,801	1,735	1,530	1,370	1,421
Stocks	266	139	96	86	238
Laminated material[2]					
Production	..	..	7,672	8,474	5,929
Consumption	..	..	7,422	8,446	5,895
Stocks	..	..	359	387	421

1. Excluding consumers' stocks.
2. Sheet, rod, tube and other forms.

Source: Board of Trade

6.20 Rayon, rayon yarn and woven fabrics

continued

		Production					Consumption of rayon yarn	Looms running[1]
		Rayon		Spun rayon and mixture yarns (including waste)	Woven fabrics			
		Continuous filament yarn (single)	Staple fibre		Cotton	Rayon and mixtures		
		Million lb			Million linear yards		Million lb	Thousands
1943	January	5.91	4.62	0.67 *	34.0 *	5.4*	1.42 *	230.2
	February	5.73	4.06	0.73	35.7	5.7	1.46	230.1
	March	6.47	4.57	0.77 *	36.1 *	5.7*	1.48 *	231.3
	April	5.84	4.17	0.69	32.7	5.3	1.36	231.3
	May	6.10	4.58	0.78	36.2	5.8	1.48	234.2
	June	5.88	4.06	0.70 *	33.8 *	5.4*	1.32 *	227.2
	July	6.00	4.65	0.77	29.2	5.0	1.25	196.3
	August	4.85	3.29	0.73	34.0	5.3	1.28	219.4
	September	6.32	4.67	0.76 *	32.9 *	5.3*	1.28 *	227.6
	October	6.15	4.60	0.79	36.1	5.7	1.41	230.7
	November	6.87	4.85	0.73	34.7	5.6	1.37	227.6
	December	5.92	4.20	0.63 *	29.9 *	4.9*	1.21 *	215.0
1944	January	6.37	4.55	0.70	33.2	5.4	1.37	225.8
	February	6.40	4.92	0.72	34.3	5.6	1.47	225.7
	March	6.89	4.93	0.74 *	33.3 *	5.7*	1.49 *	227.5
	April	5.61	4.06	0.67	31.5	5.3	1.41	227.1
	May	6.53	4.82	0.70 *	32.2 *	5.4*	1.41 *	221.0
	June	6.71	4.48	0.65	33.4	5.8	1.51	224.0
	July	6.76	5.05	0.63	26.2	4.8	1.31	217.3
	August	5.48	3.58	0.60 *	30.5 *	5.4*	1.38 *	222.1
	September	6.53	4.99	0.64	29.8	5.6	1.49	223.5
	October	7.12	4.83	0.69	33.6	6.3	1.63	226.4
	November	6.98	4.92	0.64 *	32.5 *	6.2*	1.60 *	224.7
	December	6.24	3.91	0.57	29.4	5.5	1.45	208.3
1945	January	7.08	5.26	0.61 *	29.3 *	5.7*	1.50 *	211.3
	February	6.89	4.73	0.63	31.6	6.3	1.66	218.2
	March	7.60	4.96	0.59	30.6	6.2	1.62	216.5
	April	6.63	4.28	0.62	31.0	6.1	1.62	220.0
	May	6.14	3.91	0.57 *	27.9 *	5.4*	1.42 *	218.5
	June	7.47	4.73	0.63	32.1	6.4	1.69	218.7
	July	7.96	5.09	0.57	25.3	5.2	1.40	214.6
	August	5.63	3.00	0.51 *	26.1 *	5.2*	1.40 *	216.6

1. Up to December 1943, weekly averages; from January 1944, number running at end of period. Annual figures for 1944 and 1945 are monthly averages.
2. Million square yards.
* Average of five weeks.

Source: Board of Trade

6.21 Wool and silk

Production and consumption: calendar years[1] Stocks: end of period

	Unit	1937	1938	1939	1940	1941	1942	1943	1944	1945
Wool										
Raw wool:										
Production:	Million									
Actual weight, mainly greasy	lb	107	110	111	127	112	101	89	84	81
Estimated clean weight	"	66	68	69	91	80	72	62	59	58
Consumption[2]: Total	"	..	..	..	536	381	333	269	258	331
Home	"	..	..	..	481	365	329	269	257	272
Export	"	..	..	..	11	16	4	-	1	11
Re-export	"	..	..	..	44	-	-	-	-	48
Stocks[2,3]	"	..	..	342	378	406	367	284	436	453
Wool tops:										
Production[4]:	Million									
Total	lb	278.5	..	..	334.9[5]	236.3[5]	206.4[5]	152.3	133.6	135.3
Merino	"	141.5	..	..	171.1[5]	118.7[5]	116.2[5]	80.8	83.5	85.3
Crossbred	"	124.0	..	..	151.9[5]	108.6[5]	85.8[5]	66.8	46.9	46.4
Hair	"	13.0	..	..	11.9[5]	9.0[5]	4.4[5]	4.7	3.2	3.6
Worsted yarn (wool content):										
Production	"	224.2[6]	..	..	..	..	152.3	130.5	123.1	126.9
Woven wool fabrics (excluding blankets):	Mn linear									
Production	yds	316.7	..	..	..	..	..	236.4[5]	194.5	193.1
Blankets: Production	"	..	..	..	..	..	..	34.4[5]	29.7	28.4
Silk										
Raw silk:	Thousand									
Consumption	lb	5,832	5,493	..	..	1,982	1,625	393	345	332
Stocks	"	..	..	..	2,062	1,754	506	452	578	804
Silk noils:										
Production	"	..	..	..	..	300	345	262	280	202
Consumption	"	..	..	..	..	1,551	625	194	63	397
Stocks	"	..	..	..	445	406	488	630	797	609

Source: Board of Trade

1. Series for wool tops relate to period of 52 weeks.
2. Estimated clean weight.
3. Figures relate to beginning of September in 1939 and to 31 July in other years.
4. Clean scoured weight.
5. Years ended August.
6. Production of yarn wholly or mainly of wool, including admixtures amounting to about 5 per cent.

6.22 Jute, flax and hemps

Production and consumption: calendar years[1] Stocks: end of year *Thousand tons*

	1940	1941	1942	1943	1944	1945
Raw jute						
Total disposals	158.37	112.22	102.68	83.35	79.10	86.98
Home consumption	150.04	111.57	100.86	82.21	75.32	71.99
Stocks	59.93	42.88	45.80	65.24	71.35	84.37
Imported jute goods[2]						
Total disposals	..	56.94	59.85	63.03	93.84	93.72
Home consumption	..	..	59.44	62.73	90.22	83.92
Stocks	..	..	42.14	41.59	55.00	42.95
Flax						
Production[3]:						
Line and machine tow	..	7.00	12.73	14.17	21.91	22.67
Low grade tow	..	3.38	7.09	8.03	9.42	11.71
Total disposals	..	28.62	26.11	33.74	37.81	39.12
Home consumption:						
Line and machine tow	..	28.62	18.45	21.10	23.50	25.11
Low grade tow	..		7.67	12.65	14.30	11.40
Stocks:						
Line and machine tow	23.90	8.46	11.09	16.52	21.28	29.58
Low grade tow		2.78	6.96	10.63	14.00	17.71
Soft hemps						
Consumption:						
All varieties	24.17	19.72	22.48	20.64	19.53	24.31[4]
True hemp	9.43	3.70	4.58	5.38	5.81	5.67
Indian hemp						
Spinning	14.74	16.02	17.90	15.26	5.74	6.17
Paper-making					7.98	7.15
Stocks:						
All varieties	13.56	10.75	11.27	13.99	15.20	11.49
True hemp	5.44	5.76	5.00	6.87	4.48	3.04
Indian hemp	8.12	4.99	6.27	7.12	10.72	8.45
Hard hemps						
Total disposals - all varieties	97.60	76.30	78.04	72.91	68.46	77.27
Home consumption:						
All varieties	94.20	75.48	78.04	69.58	65.95	65.30
Sisal fibre and tow	61.80	50.28	66.15	60.32	58.49	61.17
Manila and other	32.40	25.20	11.89	9.26	7.46	4.13
Stocks:						
All varieties	49.02	55.52	49.67	25.49	37.06	25.92
Sisal fibre and tow	24.52	37.17	30.43	11.76	29.43	21.84
Manila and other	24.50	18.35	19.24	13.73	7.63	4.08

1. Raw jute figures for 1942 and 1944 are for periods of 53 weeks and those for other years for periods of 52 weeks.
2. Including home produced goods from Control stocks.
3. Including from April 1944 imports from Eire.
4. Including exports of Indian hemp amounting to 5.33 thousand tons.

Source: Board of Trade

6.23 Losses of raw materials at sea[1]

Monthly averages or calendar months — *Thousand tons*

		Total	Iron ore, iron and steel and allied materials	Non-ferrous metals and ores	Textiles	Timber	Hides, skins, etc.	Paper and paper-making materials	Materials for sulphuric acid and fertilizers	Miscel-laneous
1941		75.1	49.1	5.4	3.4	4.3	1.0	3.4	5.8	2.7
1942		48.8	16.2	6.7	7.5	6.4	1.5	2.4	4.1	4.0
1943		35.8	18.1	6.2	2.6	2.5	0.9	0.7	2.6	2.2
1944		4.5	0.8	1.0	0.6	0.8	0.2	..	0.7	0.4
1941	January	88.4	54.4	15.5	3.0	7.2	0.9	0.4	0.6	6.4
	February	126.5	96.3	1.0	6.2	8.3	2.8	1.7	6.9	3.3
	March	141.2	96.4	10.8	5.1	1.5	4.4	13.0	3.9	6.1
	April	89.1	50.1	2.0	6.9	10.6	1.0	3.5	12.7	2.3
	May	56.8	30.5	6.2	2.1	0.8	0.2	11.2	-	5.8
	June	69.5	57.4	7.0	3.1	0.7	0.9	0.4	-	-
	July	57.2	43.8	5.8	3.3	-	-	2.2	-	2.1
	August	21.1	18.4	-	-	0.3	1.0	-	-	1.4
	September	93.5	48.7	10.3	-	15.7	-	0.9	17.9	-
	October	89.3	52.5	3.2	7.2	2.8	0.3	1.2	19.6	2.5
	November	34.0	23.8	1.8	2.7	2.8	0.3	1.1	-	1.5
	December	34.8	17.0	0.7	1.9	1.0	-	4.6	8.2	1.4
1942	January	18.9	6.4	1.0	0.2	1.8	0.1	0.5	5.4	3.5
	February	25.2	8.5	5.2	2.6	2.6	0.5	1.0	3.6	1.2
	March	40.4	13.0	6.3	5.2	5.6	1.3	1.3	0.5	7.2
	April	49.0	15.9	4.8	6.2	1.4	0.2	3.0	15.3	2.2
	May	30.7	12.0	6.2	1.0	5.4	0.1	4.7	-	1.3
	June	29.5	3.1	8.0	3.1	8.9	-	-	2.0	4.4
	July	10.4	1.7	0.8	3.6	1.0	0.7	0.1	0.5	2.0
	August	94.5	26.5	16.6	14.3	10.2	3.8	4.8	11.2	7.1
	September	63.7	26.2	6.9	11.6	10.4	2.2	0.7	0.5	5.2
	October	79.7	28.5	5.9	15.5	8.2	5.1	7.1	4.4	5.0
	November	117.8	44.4	13.4	20.6	19.1	3.8	5.1	5.9	5.5
	December	26.6	8.5	5.2	6.0	2.4	0.6	-	0.2	3.7
1943	January	29.8	17.2	-	-	0.6	..	3.5	8.0	0.5
	February	34.3	16.9	4.0	0.2	7.9	..	1.0	-	4.3
	March	144.1	90.8	28.6	4.0	9.5	0.4	1.4	1.3	8.1
	April	76.7	26.8	14.9	6.0	7.7	3.4	1.1	12.9	3.9
	May	56.7	28.0	8.2	10.3	3.0	4.1	-	0.6	2.5
	June	11.0	2.1	3.6	1.0	0.3	-	0.1	3.1	0.8
	July	3.2	0.6	-	1.6	0.1	-	0.2	-	0.7
	August	25.0	13.9	4.6	4.5	0.4	..	0.7	-	0.9
	September	7.5	-	-	0.5	0.5	2.9	-	0.1	3.5
	October	16.0	1.2	7.2	3.0	0.1	0.4	0.1	4.0	-
	November	14.2	14.2	-	-	-	-	-	-	-
	December	13.1	5.2	3.3	0.6	0.5	0.1	0.9	1.7	0.8
1944	January	1.2	-	1.0	-	0.2	-	-	-	..
	February	6.4	0.2	-	0.9	-	-	-	3.2	2.1
	March	1.8	-	-	-	1.2	-	-	0.5	0.1
	April	9.3	1.2	-	-	3.5	-	-	4.6	-
	May	1.2	-	-	..	..	-	0.2	-	1.0
	June	8.7	8.7	-	-	-	-	-	-	-
	July	6.0	-	2.5	0.5	-	2.6	-	-	0.3
	August	6.0	-	5.5	..	-	-	-	-	0.5
	September	3.4	-	-	-	3.4	-	-	-	-
	October	0.7	-	-	-	-	0.2	-	0.2	0.3
	November	5.4	-	-	5.3	-	-	-	-	0.1
	December	4.1	-	2.5	..	1.1	-	-	-	0.5
1945	January	-	-	-	-	-	-	-	-	-
	February	5.7	5.7	-	-	-	-	-	-	-
	March	9.0	-	0.6	-	8.4	-	-	-	-
	April	0.5	-	0.4	-	-	0.1	-	-	-

1. Before October 1941 the coverage was not complete and the figures given are partly estimated.

Source: Ministry of Supply and Board of Trade

7 PRODUCTION

The dramatic transformation of the British economy in the Second World War, both in terms of the displacement of a market economy by a centrally administered economy and in terms of the temporary change in the industrial structure, was the result of one objective - to fight the war successfully. To do this the strategic priorities of the conflict on land, sea and air had to be turned into production programmes and fighter aircraft, battleships and tanks had to be produced by the factories and shipyards of the nation. The government departments responsible for those production programmes (the Ministry of Supply, the Ministry of Aircraft Production, the production arm of the Admiralty, and the coordinating Ministry of Production which was created in February 1942) came to dominate the economy and firms working on their contracts had priority with regard to scarce resources (Howlett 1993).

There was a massive increase in the output of munitions, as tables 7.3 to 7.26 testify: for example, the tonnage of major combat naval vessels increased more than threefold between 1938 and 1942, the production of light bombers and fighter aircraft increased by more than tenfold, tank production by twentyfold, mortar production rose from 158 in 1938 to more than 29,000 in 1942, and from producing a mere 12,000 .303 rifles in 1938 the economy was producing more than 900,000 by 1943.

These crude measures of output almost certainly underestimate the scale of the achievement of the munitions industries because much of what they produced increased in complexity and often also in weight (for example, in 1939 the heaviest bomber produced was the Wellington which weighed 30,000 pounds and had a wing span of 86 feet but by 1944 the Lancaster bomber weighed in at 68,000 pounds and had a wing span of 102 feet); another important feature that should not be

7.1 Wartime aircraft production

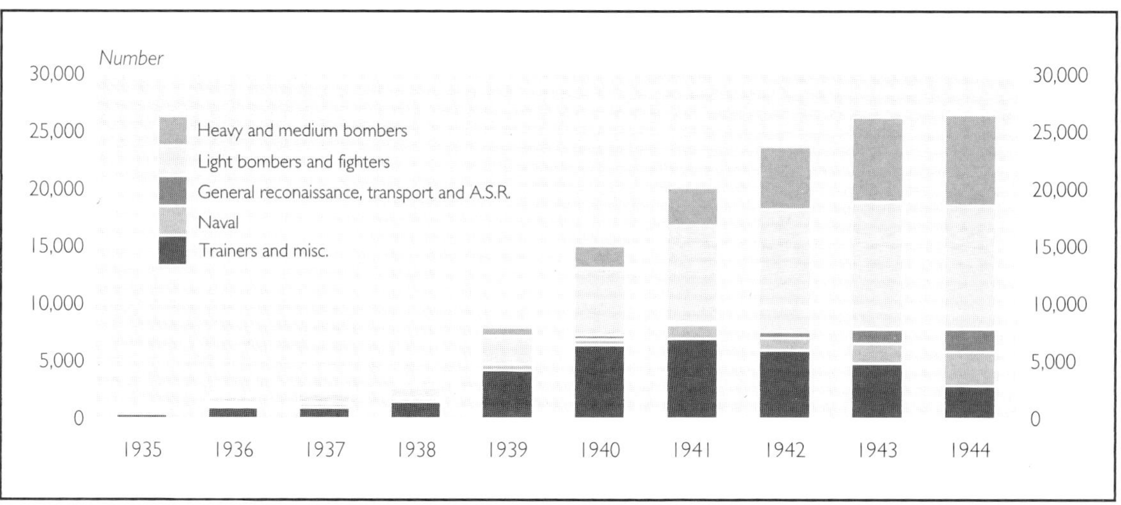

underestimated was the output from repairs in both the shipbuilding and aircraft industries (Kohan 1952: 283; **tables 7.23, 7.7-7.8 and 7.25**). Furthermore this expansion occurred despite the constant modifications in weapons design and the disruption caused by air raids and the relocation of factories (Postan 1952: 164-6; 339-45). A related success story was that of machine tool production: this industry had a poor interwar record but its output increased from less than 20,000 machines prior to the start of rearmament in 1935 to 37,000 in 1939 to a wartime peak of nearly 100,000 in 1942; and small tool production increased from 17,000 in 1940 to more than 42,000 in 1943. However, imports from the USA still remained crucial for several groups of machine tools, such as automatic lathes and vertical drillers (Hornby 1958: 330-1).

The corollary of the expansion of munition sector was the contraction of the consumer orientated sector of the economy. This was engineered by the state by squeezing both demand (through such measures as rationing) and supply (through limiting access to raw materials; import and export restrictions; setting quantity ceilings on the amount wholesalers could sell and then progressively reducing those ceilings; and, more directly, by promoting a concentration of production drive in many consumer industries to release resources to the munitions and related industries, at least for the duration of the war) (Allen 1951; Hargreaves and Gowing: 202-33; **tables 7.32, 6.16-6.22**). Munitions output peaked in the first quarter of 1944 but its expansion during the war was not a smooth process but one of continual 'ebb and flow' whereby production expanded until it met a resource limit or a production or administrative bottleneck and was temporarily checked, then overcame this constraint and expanded again until the next constraint was encountered (Harrison 1990: 665; Postan 1952). The 'ebb and flow' of munitions production also reflected the changing strategic priorities of the war. Although the military and political leaders were committed to a policy of 'armament in depth' (that is building up the long term strength of the army, navy and air force in order to eventually launch successful counter campaigns against Germany and Japan) the unpredictable nature of warfare meant that in the short term strategic priorities could change abruptly and in such cases the munitions industries had to respond rapidly to the new demands these made. An example of this was the Battle of Britain. One of the consequences of the collapse of France and the Dunkirk evacuation in May 1940 was that a German invasion was highly likely; a precondition for this was air supremacy and thus the overriding priority of the British economy in the Summer of 1940, as the Battle of Britain raged, was to produce fighter aircraft (Churchill 1949: 61). Thus, between the first and third quarters of 1940 the quarterly rate of aircraft produced increased by 93 per cent (and the official index of production increased from 569 in May 1940 to a level in excess of 700 between June and August, a level that was not reached again until February 1941) whilst the rate for the light bomber and fighter aircraft category increased by 170 per cent, with their share of the total output rising from 30 per cent to 41 per cent (**tables 7.22 and 7.24**).

The impressive increase in the domestic production of munitions should not mask the importance of munitions supplied by the USA (nor indeed those supplied by Canada) (Duncan Hall 1955; Duncan Hall and Wrigley 1956). The Lend-Lease Act of March 1941 released Britain, and her allies, from the financial burden of immediate payment for goods received (payment being postponed

7.2 Index of Ministry of Supply munitions production

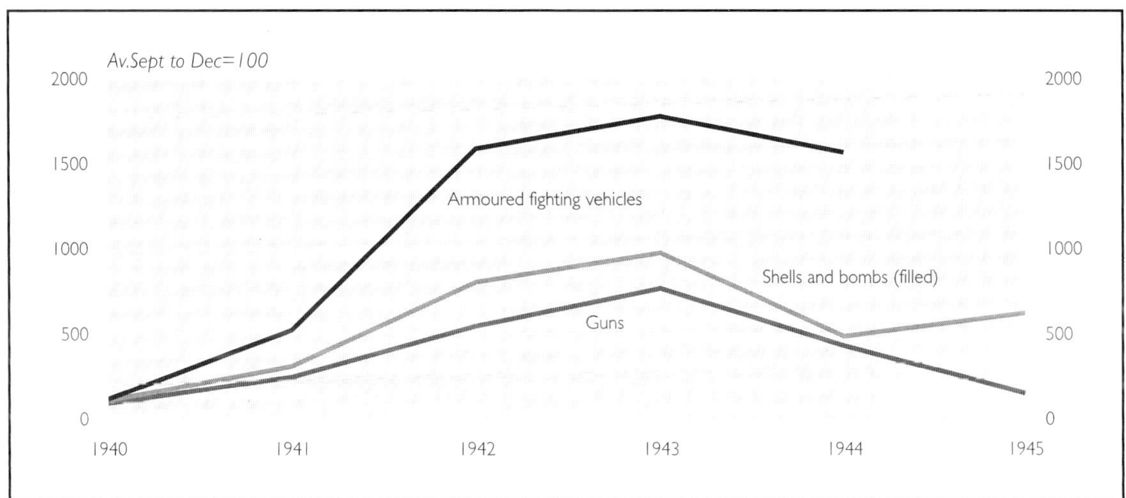

British needs to supplying its own armed forces. Neither should it be forgotten they Britain itself supplied munitions to another ally: between October 1941 and June 1942 Britain supplied the USSR with 1,800 aircraft, 2,250 tanks, 1,800 Bren-gun carriers and 1,210 machine tools, as well as large quantities of other machinery, raw materials, foodstuffs and medical supplies (Postan 1952: 119).

until after the war). Total Lend-Lease aid provided 17 per cent of all British empire munitions during war, and included the equivalent of 150 per cent of the domestic production of transport aircraft, 24 per cent of combat aircraft, 104 per cent of tanks, 67 per cent of small arms ammunition and 60 per cent of landing crafts and ships (Allen 1946: 268; Postan 1952: 247; **tables 7.27-7.28**). The only blip in this supply of munitions came, paradoxically, when the USA finally entered the war in December 1941 and needed to divert some of its capacity from supplying

7.3 Shipbuilding

Naval vessels : Major combat[1]

Number and displacement in thousand tons

	Battleships		Aircraft carriers		Monitors		Cruisers		Destroyers		Submarines	
	Number	S.D.	Number	S.D.	Number	S.D.	Number	S.D.	Number	S.D.	Number	S.D.
1936/37[2]	-	-	-	-	-	-	4	30.3	10	13.7	3	3.7
1937 April-December	-	-	-	-	-	-	4	32.5	8	11.1	1	0.7
1938	-	-	1	22.0	-	-	2	18.8	12	21.9	6	5.0
1939	-	-	-	-	-	-	3	29.6	22	38.6	7	8.1
1940	1	35.0	2	46.0	-	-	7	45.9	27	31.3	15	12.0
1941	2	70.0	2	46.0	1	7.6	6	37.9	39	50.6	20	14.1
1942	2	70.0	-	-	-	-	6	40.4	73	99.5	33	24.0
1943	-	-	2	30.0	1	7.9	7	47.0	37	61.6	39	27.7
1944	-	-	4	74.5	-	-	2	13.8	31	53.7	39	29.0
1938 1st Quarter	-	-	-	-	-	-	-	-	1	1.4	-	-
2nd Quarter	-	-	-	-	-	-	-	-	2	3.7	1	0.7
3rd Quarter	-	-	1	22.0	-	-	1	9.4	2	3.7	2	2.1
4th Quarter	-	-	-	-	-	-	1	9.4	7	13.09	3	2.2
1939 1st Quarter	-	-	-	-	-	-	1	9.6	5	9.4	-	-
2nd Quarter	-	-	-	-	-	-	-	-	5	8.6	2	2.6
July-August	-	-	-	-	-	-	2	20.0	3	5.2	1	1.1
September-December	-	-	-	-	-	-	-	-	9	15.4	4	4.4
1940 1st Quarter	-	-	-	-	-	-	-	-	4	5.1	3	3.3
2nd Quarter	-	-	1	23.0	-	-	2	13.5	5	5.8	2	2.2
3rd Quarter	-	-	-	-	-	-	5	32.4	6	6.0	4	2.7
4th Quarter	1	35.0	1	23.0	-	-	-	-	12	14.4	6	3.8
1941 1st Quarter	1	35.0	-	-	-	-	2	13.5	8	10.5	3	2.2
2nd Quarter	-	-	1	23.0	-	-	1	5.5	9	11.1	4	2.7
3rd Quarter	-	-	-	-	-	-	-	-	9	12.9	7	4.9
4th Quarter	1	35.0	1	23.0	1	7.6	3	18.9	13	16.1	6	4.3
1942 1st Quarter	-	-	-	-	-	-	1	8.0	14	18.6	3	1.8
2nd Quarter	1	35.0	-	-	-	-	3	18.9	19	24.3	10	6.7
3rd Quarter	1	35.0	-	-	-	-	2	13.5	18	25.4	8	6.7
4th Quarter	-	-	-	-	-	-	-	-	22	31.2	12	8.8
1943 1st Quarter	-	-	-	-	-	-	2	16.0	8	11.9	7	4.9
2nd Quarter	-	-	-	-	1	7.9	-	-	9	15.0	11	7.7
3rd Quarter	-	-	-	-	-	-	3	19.5	11	19.3	8	5.4
4th Quarter	-	-	2	30.0	-	-	2	11.5	9	15.4	13	9.7
1944 1st Quarter	-	-	1	14.5	-	-	1	5.8	9	15.4	9	7.3
2nd Quarter	-	-	1	23.0	-	-	1	8.0	6	10.3	11	7.9
3rd Quarter	-	-	1	23.0	-	-	-	-	8	14.3	7	4.9
4th Quarter	-	-	1	14.0	-	-	-	-	8	13.7	12	8.9
1945 1st Quarter	-	-	2	28.0	-	-	-	-	1	1.7	5	4.2
2nd Quarter	-	-	1	14.0	-	-	1	8.0	3	5.7	6	5.4
3rd Quarter	-	-	1	14.0	-	-	-	-	9	9.2	3	2.5

1. Vessels completed in the United Kingdom, including ships built for Dominion Governments but excluding ships built for other Governments.
2. Year ended 31 March 1937.

Source : Admiralty

7.4 Shipbuilding

Naval vessels : Ocean and coastal convoy vessels, mosquito craft and landing craft[1]

Number and displacement in thousand tons

	Sloops		Corvettes and frigates		Minelayers		Minesweepers, trawlers and boom defence vessels		Mosquito craft		Landing craft		Transport ferries (L.S.T.)	
	Number	S.D.	Number	S.D.	Number	S.D.	Number	S.D.	Number	W.L.D.	Number	W.L.D.	Number	S.D.
1936/37[2]	8	7.3	-	-	-	-	-	-	5	0.09	-	-	-	-
1937 April-December	-	-	2	1.1	1	0.8	4	2.8	3	0.05	-	-	-	-
1938	3	3.6	1	0.5	3	1.5	21	15.2	9	0.2	-	-	-	-
1939	2	2.5	3	1.7	1	0.4	19	12.8	14	0.3	4	0.1	-	-
1940	1	1.3	48	47.5	3	1.1	44	26.2	121	6.94	158	9.94	-	-
1941	4	5.3	70	70.1	5	11.1	87	51.9	395	37.7	246	34.9	-	-
1942	2	2.7	28	32.3	2	1.1	93	57.0	403	46.1	521	108.3	-	-
1943	17	22.7	40	50.4	5	5.1	74	51.3	337	44.4	1,459	250.7	3	10.8
1944	5	6.8	68	81.4	4	4.4	35	24.4	234	24.5	1,305	268.6	1	2.3
1938 1st Quarter	1	1.2	-	-	-	-	2	1.6	-	-	-	-	-	-
2nd Quarter	-	-	1	0.5	1	0.5	6	4.2	4	0.1	-	-	-	-
3rd Quarter	-	-	-	-	-	-	5	3.6	4	0.07	-	-	-	-
4th Quarter	2	2.4	-	-	2	1.0	8	5.8	1	0.02	-	-	-	-
1939 1st Quarter	1	1.2	-	-	-	-	2	1.3	4	0.07	-	-	-	-
2nd Quarter	-	-	-	-	-	-	9	6.3	4	0.07	-	-	-	-
July-August	-	-	-	-	-	-	4	2.9	4	0.07	-	-	-	-
September-December	1	1.3	3	1.7	1	0.4	4	2.3	2	0.07	4	0.1	-	-
1940 1st Quarter	1	1.3	-	-	2	0.7	7	4.2	1	0.04	2	0.04	-	-
2nd Quarter	-	-	10	10.1	-	-	15	9.0	20	0.8	23	0.4	-	-
3rd Quarter	-	-	21	20.6	-	-	9	5.0	41	1.9	15	0.2	-	-
4th Quarter	-	-	17	16.8	1	0.4	13	8.0	59	4.2	118	9.3	-	-
1941 1st Quarter	-	-	28	28.0	-	-	13	7.6	75	6.3	92	4.4	-	-
2nd Quarter	3	3.9	15	15.0	4	8.4	25	14.2	118	10.8	72	6.6	-	-
3rd Quarter	1	1.4	15	15.1	1	2.7	25	15.4	112	11.4	33	11.0	-	-
4th Quarter	-	-	12	12.0	-	-	24	14.7	90	9.2	49	12.9	-	-
1942 1st Quarter	-	-	6	5.9	-	-	20	12.3	70	8.1	72	13.3	-	-
2nd Quarter	-	-	9	10.1	1	0.4	29	17.6	105	10.9	122	34.6	-	-
3rd Quarter	-	-	5	6.1	-	-	25	15.0	110	13.0	154	22.5	-	-
4th Quarter	2	2.7	8	10.2	1	0.7	19	12.1	118	14.1	173	37.9	-	-
1943 1st Quarter	5	6.8	5	6.6	1	0.7	16[3]	12.3	78	8.9	395	47.7	1	3.6
2nd Quarter	7	9.3	10	14.0	2	1.0	21	15.3	103	12.4	375	64.1	2	7.2
3rd Quarter	2	2.6	14	17.9	1	0.7	19	11.6	88	13.4	329	62.5	-	-
4th Quarter	3	4.0	11	11.9	1	2.7	18	12.1	68	9.7	360	76.4	-	-
1944 1st Quarter	1	1.4	19	22.3	2	3.1	12	7.8	52	7.0	368	82.4	-	-
2nd Quarter	4	5.4	19	22.4	-	-	7	4.5	74	6.6	391	86.5	-	-
3rd Quarter	-	-	14	16.0	-	-	8	6.2	57	5.4	284	46.3	-	-
4th Quarter	-	-	16	20.7	2	1.3	8	5.9	51	5.5	262	53.4	1	2.3
1945 1st Quarter	-	-	7	9.5	-	-	7	4.5	35	4.8	236	40.7	4	9.2
2nd Quarter	2	2.7	7[4]	9.5	-	-	10	6.3	24	2.8	204	38.7	14	32.2
3rd Quarter	1	1.4	7[4]	9.8	-	-	6	4.7	24	2.4	160	20.2	9	20.7

1. See footnote 1 to Table 7.3.
2. Year ended 31 March 1937.
3. Including three vessels of 3,420 tons deep displacement.
4. Including the following A.A. escorts, each of 1,400 tons S.D. :April, 1; May, 2; June, 2; July, 2.

Source: Admiralty

7.5 Shipbuilding

Merchant vessels built in the United Kingdom[1]

Vessels of 100 gross tons and over

Thousand gross tons

	Total			100-1,599 gross tons			1,600 gross tons and over: Non-tankers			1,600 gross tons and over: Tankers		
	Laid down	Under construct-tion end of period	Completed[2]	Laid down	Under construc-tion end of period	Completed	Laid down	Under construc-tion end of period	Completed	Laid down	Under construc-tion end of period	Completed
1940	1,073	1,184	810	31	31	38	811	836	741	231	317	31
1941	1,201	1,229	1,156	32	25	38	898	887	847	271	317	271
1942	1,345	1,271	1,301	38	29	34	1,076	1,007	956	230	235	312
1943	990	1,062	1,204	35	32	32	743	791	959	212	239	208
1944	941	990	1,014	74	47	59	665	677	779	202	266	175
1940 4th Quarter	279	1,184	219	7	31	10	206	836	184	66	317	24
1941 1st Quarter	271	1,236	219	6	28	9	180	858	158	85	349	53
2nd Quarter	279	1,263	252	10	31	7	209	871	196	60	361	48
3rd Quarter	330	1,266	327	10	32	9	258	892	237	62	341	82
4th Quarter	321	1,229	358	6	25	13	251	887	256	64	317	88
1942 1st Quarter	277	1,234	272	13	30	8	208	873	222	58	333	42
2nd Quarter	353	1,253	334	10	31	9	286	920	239	57	304	86
3rd Quarter	390	1,337	306	6	27	10	318	1,035	203	65	276	93
4th Quarter	325	1,271	389	9	29	7	264	1,007	292	50	235	91
1943 1st Quarter	262	1,304	229	6	27	8	189	1,007	189	67	269	32
2nd Quarter	266	1,264	306	5	20	12	127	998	226	44	245	68
3rd Quarter	254	1,285	233	8	22	6	189	980	207	57	282	20
4th Quarter	208	1,062	431	16	32	6	148	791	337	44	239	88
1944 1st Quarter	223	1,078	207	21	43	10	174	817	148	28	218	49
2nd Quarter	215	1,054	239	17	43	17	164	783	198	34	228	24
3rd Quarter	245	1,082	217	14	46	11	153	769	167	78	267	39
4th Quarter	258	990	350	22	47	21	174	677	266[3]	62	266	63
1945 1st Quarter	225	1,077	138	29	63	13	145	717	105	51	297	20
2nd Quarter	362	1,216	223	23	66	20	251	840	128	88	310	75
3rd Quarter	269	1,334	151	11	60	17	168	908	100	90	366	34

Source: Admiralty

This table does not incorporate certain revisions which have been made to figures since the end of the war as the revisions cannot be made in the full detail required by this table.
In addition to vessels built in the United Kingdom, the following vessels were built on British account in the Commonwealth and United States of America:-

	Number	Thousand gross tons
1941: Total	11	77.3
Canada	1	7.2
Hong Kong	5	34.3
United States of America	5	35.9
1942: Total	56	401.8
Canada	1	7.2
United States of America	55	394.6

2. Including merchant-type vessels built for the Navy as follows: In 1941 4,000 gross tons non-tanker (all of 100-1,599 gross tons); 20,000 gross tons tanker (all of over 1,600 gross tons); in 1942 8,000 gross tons non-tanker (all of 100 1,599 gross tons); and in 1943 1,000 gross tons tanker and 63,000 gross tons non-tanker.
3. Including two suction dredgers of 3,944 and 1,747 gross tons.

7.6 Shipbuilding

Merchant vessels built in the United Kingdom

Non-tankers of 1,600 gross tons and over[1]

Thousand gross tons

	Cargo liners						Tramps of 3,500 gross tons and over[2]			Colliers and tramps of 1,600-3,499 gross tons[3]		
	Fully refrigerated			Others								
	Laid down	Under construct-tion end of period	Com-pleted	Laid down	Under construc-tion end of period	Com-pleted	Laid down	Under construc-tion end of period	Com-pleted	Laid down	Under construc-tion end of period	Com-pleted
1940	37	95	_	124	152	193	601	539	406	49	50	44
1941	63	130	28	91	145	98	686	562	663	58	50	58
1942	99	134	95	200	273	72	696	549	709	81	51	80
1943	36	105	65	223	279	217[4]	436	373	612	48	34	65
1944	48	74	79	180[5]	261	198	400	312	461	37	30	41
1941 3rd Quarter	9	117	7	35	151	16	208	588	206	6	37	10
4th Quarter	34	130	21	33	145	39	162	562	188	22	50	9
1942 1st Quarter	10	114	26	38	178	5	142	530	174	18	51	17
2nd Quarter	33	133	14	41	201	18	190	534	186	22	53	20
3rd Quarter	38	163	9	51	218	34	209	598	145	20	58	15
4th Quarter	18	134	46	70	273	15	155	549	204	21	51	28
1943 1st Quarter	_	127	7	61	309	25	113	515	147	15	56	10
2nd Quarter	10	109	28	54	333	30	136	503	148	17	53	20
3rd Quarter	8	107	10	73	372	34	92	448	147	16	53	16
4th Quarter	18	105	20	35	279	128	95	373	170	_	34	19
1944 1st Quarter	8	104	9	53	316	16	107	367	113	6	31	9
2nd Quarter	10	84	30	34	323	27	111	347	131	9	30	10
3rd Quarter	9	75	18	36	296	63	99	366	80	9	32	7
4th Quarter	21	74	22	57[5]	261	92	83	312	137	13	30	15
1945 1st Quarter	44	110	8	53	287	27	33	280	65	15	40	5
2nd Quarter	70	171	9	101	357	31	37	241	76	27	55	12
3rd Quarter	14	177	8	143	483	17	5	180	66	6	52	9

1. In addition to the classes of vessel shown below, passenger liners of 98,000 gross tons were completed in 1940.
2. These vessels are mostly of about 7,000 gross tons and 10,000 deadweight tons.
3. Including dredgers from May 1943.
4. Including four vessels totalling 56,800 gross tons handed over to the Royal Navy.
5. Including one cable ship.

Source: Admiralty

7.7 Merchant vessels undergoing or awaiting repair in United Kingdom ports

Vessels of 100 gross tons asnd over, British and foreign — *Thousand gross tons*

	All vessels[1]					Vessels of 1,600 gross tons and over						Troop-ships and hospital ships
				Cause of damage		Non-tankers			Tankers			
	Total	Under-going repairs while working cargo	Immo-bilised by reason of repair	Enemy action	Other causes	Total	Under-going repairs while working cargo	Immo-bilised by reason of repair	Total	Under-going repairs while working cargo	Immo-bilised by reason of repair	
1941 February 27	2,593	1,008	1,585	453	2,140	2,031	971	1,060	421	23	397	..
March 27	2,306	860	1,447	567	1,740	1,819	821	999	364	30	334	..
April 24	2,025	681	1,345	612	1,413	1,573	641	932	322	24	298	..
May 29	2,070	935	1,135	592	1,478	1,615	874	741	338	44	294	..
June 26	1,922	1,100	822	461	1,460	1,525	1,003	522	282	57	225	..
July 31	1,618	735	883	428	1,189	1,264	691	573	246	12	234	..
August 28	1,691	907	784	392	1,299	1,279	807	473	319	67	252	..
September 25	1,694	1,051	643	306	1,388	1,309	910	399	282	111	172	..
October 30	1,857	1,116	742	236	1,621	1,392	970	422	349	95	254	..
November 27	1,668	972	696	254	1,414	1,181	814	367	378	114	264	..
December 25	1,891	1,155	736	210	1,682	1,394	1,006	388	401	118	283	..
1942 January 29	1,768	926	841	176	1,592	1,245	776	468	415	104	311	198
February 26	1,846	1,002	844	182	1,664	1,396	880	516	345	82	263	198
March 26	1,567	919	648	139	1,428	1,200	816	384	277	76	201	223
April 30	1,570	871	699	116	1,455	1,190	769	421	272	64	209	390
May 28	1,508	851	658	146	1,362	1,190	809	381	223	10	213	320
June 25	1,460	857	602	80	1,379	1,164	779	385	189	47	142	124
July 30	1,402	731	671	48	1,354	968	626	342	317	75	241	246
August 27	1,438	768	671	47	1,392	1,078	674	404	254	61	193	206
September 24	1,701	905	796	71	1,630	1,279	828	452	314	52	262	307
October 29	1,628	939	689	74	1,555	1,255	863	392	277	49	228	266
November 26	1,597	868	728	81	1,516	1,200	777	423	300	63	237	215
December 31	1,606	846	759	97	1,509	1,265	809	456	251	18	233	526
1943 January 28	1,781	938	843	89	1,692	1,371	861	510	299	50	249	342
February 25	1,698	869	829	85	1,613	1,331	801	529	267	39	228	389
March 25	1,759	837	922	92	1,667	1,386	787	600	267	22	245	350
April 29	2,004	1,031	973	117	1,888	1,658	971	687	242	28	214	287
May 27	1,846	1,027	820	87	1,759	1,536	962	574	209	38	171	464
June 24	1,601	851	750	99	1,502	1,329	817	512	169	18	151	495
July 29	1,531	956	576	83	1,449	1,236	843	393	198	84	114	534
August 26	1,477	870	607	98	1,379	1,124	736	388	240	110	130	404
September 30	1,609	985	624	89	1,520	1,263	876	387	236	70	166	426
October 28	1,798	1.025	774	92	1,706	1,454	972	482	232	29	203	254
November 25	1,536	806	729	88	1,448	1,211	770	442	220	14	205	363
December 30	1,736	1,006	731	96	1,640	1,470	968	502	181	14	167	448
1944 January 27	1,753	1,005	748	98	1,656	1,479	968	512	182	17	165	446
February 24	1,768	989	779	60	1,708	1,436	917	520	209	44	165	469
March 30	1,506	747	759	72	1,434	1,167	681	486	237	39	199	319
April 27	1,807	1,010	797	53	1,753	1,468	929	539	220	47	173	540
May 25	1,723	991	731	47	1,676	1,446	940	506	185	33	152	246
June 29	1,515	904	611	66	1,449	1,258	830	428	173	49	124	305
July 27	1,510	863	647	74	1,436	1,184	811	373	236	36	200	309
August 31	1,619	805	814	91	1,527	1,318	759	558	198	29	169	466
September 28	1,618	806	812	111	1,507	1,325	749	576	183	35	148	522
October 26	1,995	1,123	872	93	1,902	1,681	1,057	623	202	41	160	551
November 30	2,053	1,100	952	84	1,969	1,684	1,054	630	241	21	220	577
December 28	1,989	1,142	847	67	1,922	1,660	1,074	586	183	34	149	515
1945 January 25	2,127	1,121	1,006	67	2,060	1,705	1,009	696	254	71	183	412
March 1	2,179	1,242	937	78	2,101	1,824	1,154	670	225	62	163	560
March 29	1,860	947	913	65	1,795	1,536	902	634	197	23	174	274
April 26	1,983	1,087	897	71	1,913	1,683	1,042	641	163	18	146	556
May 31	2,047	1,049	998	125	1,922	1,695	970	725	208	54	154	480
June 28	2,184	1,130	1,055	120	2,065	1,774	1,087	687	271	18	253	525
July 26	2,076	902	1,174	125	1,951	1,502	791	711	413	87	327	455
August 30	2,410	1,247	1,163	94	2,317	1,834	1,193	641	419	24	395	410

1. Excluding troopships, hospital ships, naval and commissioned vessels, Royal Fleet auxiliaries and vessels undergoing conversion to or from naval or military purposes.

Source: Admiralty

7.8 Merchant vessels repaired in United Kingdom ports

Vessels of 100 gross tons and over, British and foreign weekly averages — *Thousand gross tons*

	Total	Vessels of 100 to 1,599 gross tons	Vessels of 1,600 gross tons and over	
			Non-tankers	Tankers
1942	728	62	544	122
1943	728	50	562	116
1944	847	60	701	85
1941 February	768	40	639	89
* March	934	61	755	117
April	760	53	609	98
May[1]	788	52	654	83
* June	881	59	706	116
July	743	54	584	105
August	749	57	592	99
* September	797	54	613	130
October	752	70	566	117
November	815	73	635	107
* December	789	62	575	153
1942 January	800	65	607	128
February	825	74	572	179
* March	756	68	566	123
April	730	67	555	108
May	737	69	546	122
* June	675	61	521	93
July	742	64	570	107
* August	640	61	471	108
September	736	55	532	149
October	782	55	585	142
* November	674	55	519	101
December	679	52	505	122
1943 January	674	55	518	101
February	771	58	592	121
* March	753	51	583	119
April	756	54	583	119
* May	744	55	568	121
June	811	50	633	129
July	692	46	514	132
* August	681	48	493	139
September	775	46	594	135
October	667	48	529	90
* November	710	46	565	99
December	707	42	577	89
1944* January	750	43	620	88
February	796	49	678	70
March	804	51	668	85
April	713	51	551	110
* May	918	59	758	100
June	854	62	695	97
* July	798	63	669	66
August	848	64	697	87
September	811	57	676	77
* October	926	71	779	76
November	987	80	836	70
December	955	70	785	100
1945* January	924	74	748	102
February	984	74	842	68
March	1,088	67	913	107
* April	923	64	781	78
May	843	62	709	73
June	858	56	699	103
* July	918	51	774	93
August	720	44	602	74

1. Figures for two weeks have been omitted as unreliable on account of disorganisation following air raids.

* Average of five weeks.

Source: Admiralty

7.9 Munitions

Index of Ministry of Supply munitions production[1]

Average September to December 1939=100

	Guns, small arms and instruments				Ammunition								
					Shells and bombs		Small arms ammunition	Propellants and high explosives	Armoured fighting vehicles	Wheeled vehicles	Signal	Radar and searchlight	Engineer and transportation
	Total	Guns	Small arms	Instruments	Filled	Empty components							
1939 September-December	100	100	100	100	100	100	100	100	100	100	100	100	100
1940 Ist Quarter	106	104	116	105	120	153	214	96	128	242	112	102	224
2nd Quarter	185	184	186	188	194	213	336	147	247	337	167	89	318
3rd Quarter	212	222	165	253	214	298	358	161	324	343	180	124	391
4th Quarter	207	214	143	293	263	374	356	186	361	290	199	139	383
1941 Ist Quarter	242	259	141	352	322	459	499	202	533	290	210	153	370
2nd Quarter	270	301	149	332	426	549	701	246	689	299	222	136	380
3rd Quarter	332	375	197	365	560	612	911	338	1,010	302	244	121	427
4th Quarter	441	487	302	442	717	769	1,198	423	1,336	328	269	174	443
1942 Ist Quarter	541	557	477	528	815	920	1,832	478	1,597	323	347	165	459
2nd Quarter	668	654	688	601	983	1,052	2,331	553	1,772	354	433	181	539
3rd Quarter	701	646	812	645	1,009	1,037	2,679	513	1,727	341	523	198	593
4th Quarter	797	744	907	715	1,051	1,175	3,648	573	1,702	361	644	184	735
1943 Ist Quarter	857	778	1,026	773	986	994	4,010	529	1,787	342	688	139	796
2nd Quarter	825	708	1,059	803	774	769	4,676	533	1,807	344	748	120	900
3rd Quarter	689	589	867	721	574	519	5,000	483	1,596	319	841	123	1,030
4th Quarter	637	505	886	695	544	487	5,427	467	1,494	338	980	165	1,276
1944 Ist Quarter	557	443	732	688	498	429	5,142	450	1,577	320	927	142	1,851
2nd Quarter	457	335	671	564	501	418	4,766	451	1,276	316	918	132	1,841
3rd Quarter	385	291	584	389	529	394	4,188	480	..	280	670	94	1,547
4th Quarter	313	193	502	489	624	397	4,331	513	..	333	713	90	1,300
1945 Ist Quarter	263	164	392	464	634	461	3,254	585	..	328	745	78	1,159
2nd Quarter	166	108	202	372	561	436	1,686	545	..	314	662	36	1,071
3rd Quarter	99	57	128	241	185	211	473	157	..	284	452	16	815

1. Ministry of Supply production in the United Kingdom only.

Source: Ministry of Supply

7.10 Munitions

Artillery equipments and instruments and tank and anti-tank guns[1]

Number

	Artillery: Field	Artillery: Medium and heavy	Artillery: Coast[2]	Anti-aircraft: Light	Anti-aircraft: Heavy[3]	Predictors	Searchlight equipment: A.A. projectors	Searchlight equipment: Sound locators	Tank and anti-tank guns[4]: Light	Tank and anti-tank guns[4]: Medium
1936/37[5]	-	-	-	-	-		196	127	29	-
1937 April-December	-	-	4	-	-	185	358	441	100	-
1938	-	-	12	-	203		1,043	1,114	360	-
1939	-[6]	-	11	30	776[6]		3,116	3,151	1,000	-
1940	1,359	35	38	1,082	1,090	1,180	1,537	1,315	1,773	-
1941	3,173	218	61	2,680	1,555	2,467	2,703	793	9,361	-
1942	3,389	730	52	5,262	2,146	5,134	1,077	56	36,324	691
1943	2,021	952	90	5,570	1,308	4,685	1,577	-	21,633	8 125
1944	1,995	813	69	838	239	891	504	-	2,613	8,073
1938 1st Quarter	-	-	2	-	3	..	102	195	51	-
2nd Quarter	-	-	-	-	37	..	242	260	76	-
3rd Quarter	-	-	-	-	63	..	312	255	98	-
4th Quarter	-	-	10	-	100	..	387	404	135	-
1939 1st Quarter	-	-	3	-	111	..	648	1,327	114	-
2nd Quarter	-	-	4	-	176	..	1,049	885	248	-
July-August	-	-	-	-	150	..	622	273	226	-
Sept-December	-	-	4	30	339	75	797	666	412	-
1940 1st Quarter	20	-	2	100	223	135	..	272	297	-
2nd Quarter	196	23	14	261	309	249	..	291	395	-
3rd Quarter	525	7	12	364	302	363	..	424	498	-
4th Quarter	618	5	10	357	256	433	..	328	583	-
1941 1st Quarter	653	31	11	492	270	523	1,249	397	887	-
2nd Quarter	792	38	12	642	329	496	908	208	1,383	-
3rd Quarter	892	57	18	713	427	620	452	133	2,539	-
4th Quarter	836	92	20	833	529	828	94	55	4,552	-
1942 1st Quarter	976	114	10	1,031	484	1,019	38	31	6,757	-
2nd Quarter	936	219	6	1,204	539	1,184	110	25	9,911	8
3rd Quarter	685	197	22	1,367	554	1,332	376		10,570	128
4th Quarter	792	200	14	1,660	569	1,599	553		9,086	555
1943 1st Quarter	876	214	23	1,662	526	1,622	444		7,985	413
2nd Quarter	738	261	22	1,559	407	1,441	405		6,327	1,266
3rd Quarter	207	220	25	1,300	236	969	352		4,430	2,625
4th Quarter	200	257	20	1,049	139	653	376		2,891	3,821
1944 1st Quarter	507	314	29	460	109	402	260		2,141	1,935
2nd Quarter	797	238	17	240	76	258	185		393	1,624
3rd Quarter	610	166	16	110	30	134	36		68	2,162
4th Quarter	81	95	7	28	24	97	23		11	2,352
1945 1st Quarter	124	88	12		26	64	45		3	2,716
2nd Quarter	109	74	3		9	48	16		1	1,944
3rd Quarter	89	43	5		3	34	10		5	685

1. The figures for artillery equipments relate to mountings.
2. Excluding A.A./C.A. dual purpose equipments.
3. Including A.A./C.A. dual purpose equipments.
4. Excluding A.F.V. machine guns.
5. Year ended 31 March.
6. In addition there was an extensive reconditioning and conversion programme in operation immediately before the outbreak of war.

Source: Ministry of Supply

7.11 Munitions

Naval guns[1]

Number

	Other than anti-aircraft	Anti-aircraft		Machine guns	
		Long range	Short range	·5-in. Vickers	·303-in. Hefah
1936/37[2]	56	148	180	228	-
1937 April-December	54	112	200	156	-
1938	41	364	396	448	-
1939	82	551	624	440	-
1940	59	676	747	1,450	-
1941	61	1,098	1,490	2,491	-
1942	171	1,797	1,830	3,507	39
1943	172	1,253	1,737	1,738	2,935
1944	139	407	399	-	-
1938 Ist Quarter	7	60	84	136	-
2nd Quarter	5	73	66	123	-
3rd Quarter	7	110	114	121	-
4th Quarter	22	121	132	68	-
1939 Ist Quarter	21	126	168	60	-
2nd Quarter	15	146	144	137	-
July-August	22	138	144	63	-
September-December	24	141	168	180	-
1940 Ist Quarter	21	140	144	200	-
2nd Quarter	21	178	168	321	-
3rd Quarter	11	165	193	459	-
4th Quarter	6	193	242	470	-
1941 Ist Quarter	10	182	347	568	-
2nd Quarter	20	263	361	516	-
3rd Quarter	11	293	357	619	-
4th Quarter	20	360	425	788	-
1942 Ist Quarter	57	288	454	868	-
2nd Quarter	42	484	431	844	2
3rd Quarter	40	476	443	799	37
4th Quarter	32	549	502	996	-
1943 Ist Quarter	47	518	537	818	171
2nd Quarter	48	331	405	498	855
3rd Quarter	30	190	407	322	1,302
4th Quarter	47	214	388	100	607
1944 Ist Quarter	44	130	192	-	-
2nd Quarter	36	89	147	-	-
3rd Quarter	41	88	46	-	-
4th Quarter	18	100	14	-	-
1945 Ist Quarter	19	142	166	-	-
2nd Quarter	17	105	262	-	-
3rd Quarter	-	93	286	-	-

1. Excluding 20 mm. guns.
2. Year ended 31 March.

Source: Admiralty

7.12 Munitions

Aircraft and light guns

Number

	Aircraft guns			Light guns 20mm.		
	·303-in. Vickers G.O.	·303-in. Browning	40 mm. Vickers	Hispano-Suiza (Aircraft)	Oerlikon (Naval)	Polsten (Army)
1936/37[1]	-	-	-	-	-	-
1937 April-December	725	532	-	-	-	-
1938	2,525	9,139	-	-	-	-
1939	5,705	22,387	-	387	-	-
1940	11,364	55,352	-	3,319	-	-
1941	15,177	128,952	4	11,927	1,512	-
1942	19,892	167,820	655	43,398	9,651	-
1943	28,227	70,218	1,311	56,950	16,861	240
1944	13,725	51,082	344	46,800	16,529	13,548
1938 Ist Quarter	675	1,194	-	-	-	-
2nd Quarter	250	2,070	-	-	-	-
3rd Quarter	1,075	1,659	-	-	-	-
4th Quarter	525	4,216	-	-	-	-
1939 Ist Quarter	766	4,811	-	-	-	-
2nd Quarter	1,330	5,392	-	45	-	-
July-August	1,120	3,533	-	102	-	-
September-December	2,489	8,651	-	240	-	-
1940 Ist Quarter	2,019	8,229	-	539	-	-
2nd Quarter	2,990	14,420	-	809	-	-
3rd Quarter	2,862	16,786	-	775	-	-
4th Quarter	3,493	15,917	-	1,196	-	-
1941 Ist Quarter	3,479	16,787	-	1,329	6	-
2nd Quarter	3,510	30,179	-	1,449	146	-
3rd Quarter	3,739	36,211	-	3,095	440	-
4th Quarter	4,449	45,775	4	6,054	920	-
1942 Ist Quarter	4,358	44,383	47	7,205	1,386	-
2nd Quarter	4,786	45,845	133	10,403	1,899	-
3rd Quarter	5,206	38,830	187	12,412	2,829	-
4th Quarter	5,542	38,762	288	13,378	3,537	-
1943 Ist Quarter	5,612	25,062	325	14,972	3,923	-
2nd Quarter	6,294	19,111	356	13,878	4,207	-
3rd Quarter	7,311	14,186	347	13,267	3,996	-
4th Quarter	9,010	11,859	283	14,833	4,735	240
1944 Ist Quarter	7,428	11,296	173	14,888	5,037	1,720
2nd Quarter	3,746	13,372	125	13,350	4,814	4,104
3rd Quarter	1,479	12,723	46	10,444	3,696	4,367
4th Quarter	1,072	13,691	-	8,118	2,982	3,357
1945 Ist Quarter	66	3,704	-	8,936	2,010	1,164
2nd Quarter	-	-	-	5,915	1,221	3
July-August	-	-	-	3,103	6	-

1. Year ended 31 March.

Source: Admiralty and Ministry of Supply

7.13 Munitions

Other weapons

Number

	Projectors							
	U.P. and Rocket	Livens	Northover	P.I.A.T.	Flame throwers	Bomb throwers	Smoke dischargers	Mortars
1936/37[1]	-	-	-	-	-	-	-	-
1937 April-December	-	-	-	-	-	-	-	-
1938	-	6	-	-	-	-	] 3,443	[158
1939	-	1,150	-	-	-	-		2,822
1940	6,369	12,415	-	-	554	-	1,618	7,559
1941	1,881	11,847	19,171	-	1,445	2,384	10,229	21,725
1942	5,711	790	1,829	7,908	1	10,773	10,429	29,162
1943	1,264	-	-	98,326	4,326	10,504	31,196	17,121
1944	844	-	-	9,067	6,412	3,460	15,378	19.046
1939 September-December	-	673	-	-	-	-	756	1,317
1940 Ist Quarter	-	481	-	-	-	-	..	1,363
2nd Quarter	-	220	-	-	-	-	..	2,111
3rd Quarter	1,051	5,602	-	-	-	-	..	1,742
4th Quarter	5,318	6,112	-	-	554	-	..	2,343
1941 Ist Quarter	1,719	6,759	3,963	-	1,299	128	1,551	2,505
2nd Quarter	29	3,586	4,472	-	143	439	2,500	2,104
3rd Quarter	1	1,126	3,850	-	3	620	3,209	5,195
4th Quarter	132	376	6,886	-	-	1,197	2,969	11,921
1942 Ist Quarter	1,381	63	1,678	-	1	1,742	827	14,099
2nd Quarter	2,048	526	151	-	-	2,113	1,223	7,013
3rd Quarter	534	201	-	377	-	2,905	1,519	3,201
4th Quarter	1,748	-	-	7,531	-	4,013	6,860	4,849
1943 Ist Quarter	968	-	-	30,612	21	4,060	14,321	6,932
2nd Quarter	296	-	-	33,614	562	3,164	11,594	5,439
3rd Quarter	-	-	-	22,279	1,395	1,970	3,164	2,788
4th Quarter	-	-	-	11,821	2,348	1,310	2,117	1,962
1944 Ist Quarter	83	-	-	8,737	2,380	1,176	2,318	6,620
2nd Quarter	76	-	-	330	3,005	326	2,849	6,021
3rd Quarter	637	-	-	-	448	1,113	4,833	4,903
4th Quarter	48	-	-	-	579	845	5,378	1,502
1945 Ist Quarter	36	-	-	-	501	905	4,017	2,371
2nd Quarter	64	-	-	-	589	682	1,707	1,697
3rd Quarter	2	-	-	-	301	274	574	1,447

1. Year ended 31 March.

Source: Ministry of Supply

7.14 Munitions

Small arms[1]

Number

	Rifles ·303-in.	Anti-tank rifles	Machine carbines 9mm.	Machine guns ·303-in.	A.F.V. machine guns[2]	Pistols ·38-in.
1936/37[3]		-	-			
1937 April-December	3,448	296	-	12	438	1,978
1938	12,028	5,364	-	5,418	886	3,919
1939	34,416	9,603	-	16,405	1,838	13,437
1940	80,763	14,027	-	30,179	3,548	38,777
1941	78,533	7,313	6,404	39,340	7,405	55,377
1942	594,889	22,643	1,438,336	68,167	24,446	83,557
1943	909,785	9,608	1,572,445	81,030	19,293	107,333
1944	547,382	-	671,490	53,368	7,095	87,719
1938 Ist Quarter	1,510	718	-	308	237	627
2nd Quarter	1,693	953	-	442	209	769
3rd Quarter	3,974	1,768	-	1,868	92	1,087
4th Quarter	4,851	1,925	-	2,860	348	1,436
1939 Ist Quarter	3,766	2,078	-	3,313	392	1,779
2nd Quarter	8,529	2,133	-	3,378	489	1,922
July-August	3,866	1,290	-	2,727	228	2,251
September-December	18,255	4,102	-	6,987	729	7,485
1940 Ist Quarter	17,349	3,539	-	5,513	400	4, 630
2nd Quarter	21,348	5,426	-	8,546	1,077	12,915
3rd Quarter	26,317	4,214	-	9,059	1,060	11,269
4th Quarter	15,749	848	-	7,061	1,011	9,963
1941 Ist Quarter	8,454	-	-	8,998	1,237	12,599
2nd Quarter	11,914	1,037	-	9,467	1,395	13,217
3rd Quarter	12,586	2,537	-	10,080	2,064	14,148
4th Quarter	45,579	3,739	6,404	10,795	2,709	15,413
1942 Ist Quarter	86,485	5,291	130,364	14,558	4,666	14,453
2nd Quarter	126,202	6,519	323,776	16,791	5,946	20,904
3rd Quarter	168,086	5,251	503,447	18,813	6,718	22,030
4th Quarter	214,116	5,582	480,749	18,005	7,116	26,170
1943 Ist Quarter	233,018	3,458	561,676	21,086	6,039	28,425
2nd Quarter	245,275	3,940	508,515	19,779	5,826	27,781
3rd Quarter	217,498	2,210	232,684	19,792	4,194	26,110
4th Quarter	213,994	-	269,570	20,373	3,234	25,017
1944 Ist Quarter	180,443	-	211,703	18,191	1,853	23,305
2nd Quarter	139,281	-	184,224	15,596	1,510	21,453
3rd Quarter	120,721	-	140,481	14,756	1,669	22,210
4th Quarter	106,937	-	135,082	4,825	2,063	20,751
1945 Ist Quarter	92,720	-	110,963	4,680	2,097	18,842
2nd Quarter	74,389	-	68,487	4,067	1	17,635
3rd Quarter	60,344	-	51,866	100	-	7,741

1. All services.
2. 7·92 mm. Besa, 15 mm. Besa and ·303-in. and 5-in Vickers.
3. Year ended 31 March.

Source: Ministry of Supply

7.15 Munitions

Filled ammunition: Army[1]

Thousands

	Artillery				Anti-aircraft		Tank and anti-tank	Mines	Grenades	Mortar bombs	P.I.A.T.
	Field	Medium	Heavy	Coast	Light	Heavy					
1936/37[2]	-	..	..	..	-	143	41	-	..	39	-
1937 April-December	474	..	..	..	-	514	169	-	..	117	-
1938	1,034	..	..	..	180	1,108	296	-	..	191	-
1939 January-August	771	..	..	..	550	1,333	165	14	..	111	-
September-December	758	28	7.70	39	160	677	135	151	180	223	-
1940	6,175	626	..	76	2,338	2,138	836	1,043	15,812	2,127	-
1941	11,763	1,744	84.00	70	4,648	4,413	5,534[4]	2,361	15,502	13,784	-
1942	20,146	2,117	357.60	120	10,582[3]	4,452	17,143[4]	6,480	22,098	35,017	357
1943	9,152	1,784	259.02	205	13,574[3]	2,030	15,886[4]	9,611	21,510	23,772	4,113
1944	8,180	1,918	1.25	243	8,982	837	5,177	3,099	16,872	12,192	4,806
1938 1st Quarter	190	..	..	..	-	214	47	-	..	81	-
2nd Quarter	338	..	..	..	15	235	95	-	..	56	-
3rd Quarter	291	..	..	..	82	245	82	-	..	32	-
4th Quarter	215	..	..	..	83	414	72	-	..	22	-
1939 1st Quarter	316	..	..	..	110	503	48	-	..	-	-
2nd Quarter	265	..	..	..	196	477	20	7	..	52	-
July-August	190	..	..	..	244	353	97	7	..	59	-
September-December	758	28	7.70	39	160	677	135	151	180	223	-
1940 1st Quarter	1,068	90	..	35	80	574	90	..	299	155	-
2nd Quarter	1,516	189	..	19	542	530	156	..	1,478	278	-
3rd Quarter	1,901	108	..	10	713	404	278	..	6,498	895	-
4th Quarter	1,690	239	..	12	1,003	630	312	..	7,537	799	-
1941 1st Quarter	2,580	349	..	3	585	773	279	306	5,195	1,291	-
2nd Quarter	2,302	466	..	24	542	1,079	772	648	3,683	2,446	-
3rd Quarter	3,091	470	..	15	1,545	1,115	1,522	437	3,023	4,335	-
4th Quarter	3,790	459	..	28	1,976	1,446	2,961	970	3,601	5,712	-
1942 1st Quarter	4,560	469	50.00	45	2,323	1,332	3,560	1,158	3,359	7,915	-
2nd Quarter	5,388	517	93.00	29	2,682	1,029	4,068	1,717	5,357	9,701	-
3rd Quarter	5,114	536	106.44	19	2,321	995	4,727	1,489	6,144	9,901	-
4th Quarter	5,084	595	108.15	27	3,256	1,096	4,788	2,116	7,238	7,500	357
1943 1st Quarter	5,351	579	136.80	42	3,126	1,034	4,755	1,854	6,438	7,537	939
2nd Quarter	2,399	585	95.90	39	3,491	598	4,834	2 382	4 441	6,472	1,112
3rd Quarter	783	336	25.50	35	3,230	209	3,338	2 990	4 575	5,254	1,023
4th Quarter	619	284	0.82	89	3,727	189	2,959	2,385	6,057	4,509	1,039
1944 1st Quarter	1,038	285	1.15	71	2,724	110	2840	1,854	5,444	3,994	1,292
2nd Quarter	920	362	0.10	45	2,084	152		1,200	3,705	2,445	1,374
3rd Quarter	2,486	392	-	43	2,294	345	1,037	45	3,724	2,147	1,176
4th Quarter	3,736	879	-	84	1,880	230	1,300	-	3,999	3,606	964
1945 1st Quarter	4,222	776	-	5	1,718	138	949	16	3,593	3,096	820
2nd Quarter	3,420	759	-	26	1,296	206	721	-	3,026	1,815	231
3rd Quarter	678	77	-	6	629	168	212	-	1,155	648	78

1. Despatches ex factory. Before September 1939 figures are for unfilled ammunition.
2. Year ended 31 March.
3. In addition 58 thousand rounds were produced in 1942 and 139 thousand in 1943 for which no quarterly figures are available.
4. In addition 349 thousand rounds were produced during the years 1941 to 1943 which cannot be allocated to individual years.

Source: Ministry of Supply

7.16 Munitions

Filled ammunition: Naval and aircraft

	Naval[1]				Aircraft bombs[2]					
					H.E., A.P. and A.S.				Incendiary	Smoke
	Shell	Depth charges	Mine and minecharge cases	Torpedoes	Total		H.E.	A.P. and A.S.		
					Weight filled	Weight of explosive	Weight filled			
	Thousands			*Number*	*Short tons*					
1936/39[3]	2,781[4]	..	..	..	..[5]	..	..	..	..	..
1940	..	..	..	939	51,093	6,389	41,252	9,841	..	-
1941	5,674.0	87.7	62.5	1,926	147,848	34,149	132,487	15,361	..	-
1942	7,154.8	55.9	40.6	3,883	211,048	73,610	184,250	26,798	52,373	483
1943	6,505.8	101.3	35.3	7,288	223,807	104,844	204,746	19,061	102,138	3,858
1944	3,607.6	110.2	13.0	6,825	309,366	168,248	307,978	1,388	106,740	4,166
1939 September-December	..	..	..	362	5,055	1,078	3,864	1,191	..	-
1940 Ist Quarter	..	..	..	231	5,504	..	4,673	831	..	-
2nd Quarter	..	..	..	241	11,303	..	8,043	3,260	..	-
3rd Quarter	..	..	..	194	13,120	..	10,687	2,433	..	-
4th Quarter	..	..	..	273	21,166	..	17,849	3,317	..	-
1941 Ist Quarter	1,304.3	9.0	40.8	350	26,673	4,179	23.794	2,879	..	-
2nd Quarter	1,353.2	24.8	16.1	411	45,020	8,562	41.365	3,655	..	-
3rd Quarter	1,462.5	33.0	1.4	505	37,641	8,764	32,842	4,799	..	-
4th Quarter	1,554.0	20.9	4.2	660	38,514	12,644	34,486	4,028	..	-
1942 Ist Quarter	1,586.4	9.5	5.9	711	39,959	..	34,946	5,013	..	-
2nd Quarter	1,832.3	11.4	11.1	864	48,309	..	41,848	6,461	..	160
3rd Quarter	1,901.8	13.1	14.9	985	58,218	..	51,137	7,081	..	183
4th Quarter	1,834.3	21.9	8.7	1,323	64,562	..	56,319	8,243	..	140
1943 Ist Quarter	1,683.1	15.2	16.0	1,490	50,601	20,717	41,401	9,200	..	404
2nd Quarter	1,604.1	21.6	9.7	1,830	38,511	15,963	32,930	5,581	..	600
3rd Quarter	1,760.6	28.6	6.1	2,030	53,342	25,585	50,570	2,772	..	783
4th Quarter	1,458.0	35.9	3.5	1,938	81,353	42,579	79,845	1,508	..	2,071
1944 Ist Quarter	853.0	21.5	4.5	2,097	71,453	39,490	70,795	658	32,977	1,638
2nd Quarter	1,000.9	27.7	3.4	1,574	71,880	41,237	71,202	678	33,045	1,626
3rd Quarter	1,012.1	30.2	0.1	1,715	74,871	40,774	74,846	25	25,646	891
4th Quarter	741.6	30.8	5.0	1,439	91,162	46,747	91,135	27	15,072	11
1945 Ist Quarter	475.4	29.4	8.2	1,143	103,640	52,290	103,580	60	5,710	45
2nd Quarter	403.4	23.1	15.6	575	90,703	44,470	90,693	10	3,402	582
3rd Quarter	170.2	0.7	0.8	401	50,155	20,542	50,145	10	-	423

1. Factory output from December 1941.
2. Despatches ex factory.
3. April 1936 to August 1939.
4. Unfilled shell.
5. Estimated weight filled under the Rearmament Programme to 31 May 1939 was 57,000 tons.

Source: Admiralty and Ministry of Supply

7.17 Munitions

Rocket ammunition, small arms and 20 mm. ammunition, propellants and high explosives[1]

	Rocket (U.P.) ammunition[2,3]	Small arms and 20 mm. ammunition ·22-in. to ·455-in[4]	·5-in. to 15mm.	20mm.	Propellants[2]	High explosives[2,5]
	Thousands	*Millions*			*Short tons*	
1936/37[6]	-	..	-	-	2,914	1,291
1937 April-December	-	..	0.205	-	5,851	2,905
1938	-	..	0.713	-	14,479	7,593
1939	-	..	12.053	-	23,989	41,555
1940	14	..	9.775	3.168	30,513	74,206
1941	301	1,266.513	16.492	15.454	58,525	112,558
1942	2 ,386	2,263.253	40.730	91.264	112,442	190,562
1943	1,932	3,078.380	88.202	167.502	89,222	220,717
1944	2,253	2,334.500	28.881	217.611	61,668	206,648
1938 Ist Quarter	-	..	0.002	-	3,132	1,497
2nd Quarter	-	..	0.286	-	3,905	1,247
3rd Quarter	-	..	0.078	-	3,702	1,433
4th Quarter	-	..	0.346	-	3,740	3,416
1939 Ist Quarter	-	..	0.301	-	5,292	2,827
2nd Quarter	-	..	6.110	-	4,021	3,329
July-August	-	..	2.124	-	6,470	24,833
September-December	-	..	3.518	-	8,206	10,566
1940 Ist Quarter	-	..	1.907	0.768	..	11,641
2nd Quarter	-	..	3.354	0.915	..	16,439
3rd Quarter	-	..	2.521	0.738	..	22,210
4th Quarter	14	..	1.993	0.747	..	23,916
1941 Ist Quarter	24	234.887	3.319	1.082	9,529	21,835
2nd Quarter	32	312.678	4.008	2.028	11,462	25,003
3rd Quarter	79	347.038	4.556	4.625	16,408	28,610
4rd Quarter	166	371.910	4.609	7.719	21,126	37,110
1942 Ist Quarter	341	498.713	5.162	13.756	24,821	46,063
2nd Quarter	630	571.944	7.736	19.014	30,767	44,743
3rd Quarter	709	549.913	12.197	24.454	27,524	44,880
4th Quarter	706	642.683	15.635	34.040	29,330	54,876
1943 Ist Quarter	609	742.845	20.344	32.079	26,103	57,545
2nd Quarter	682	742.565	24.806	39.993	24,081	53,679
3rd Quarter	367	786.592	21.655	43.855	21,678	51,198
4th Quarter	274	806.378	21.397	51.575	17,360	57,895
1944 Ist Quarter	460	697.856	12.191	56.180	15,300	53,191
2nd Quarter	570	631.547	3.783	54.038	14,135	47,652
3rd Quarter	558	526.147	7.202	48.225	15,280	47,063
4th Quarter	665	478.950	5.705	59.168	16,953	58,742
1945 Ist Quarter	566	270.757	3.593	44.835	15,481	67,097
2nd Quarter	464	221.921	2.124	19.790	16,501	61,156
3rd Quarter	285	94.581	1.282	5.825	4,172	38,973

1. All Services.
2. Deliveries ex factory.
3. Including motor rockets aircraft.
4. Including 7·92 mm. and 9 mm.
5. Excluding small quantities of aluminium powder produced before October 1943 and a small quantity of picric acid produced in 1941.
6. Year ended 31 March.

Source: Admiralty and Ministry of Supply

7.18 Munitions
Armoured fighting vehicles

	Tanks[1]			Armoured carriers, armoured cars, scout cars and armoured command vehicles	
	United Kingdom production		Supplies from overseas	United Kingdom production	Supplies from overseas
	Number	*Thousand tons*[2]		*Number*	
1936/37[3]	42	0.23	-	26	-
1937 April-December	32	0.18	-	83	-
1938	419	2.55	-	681	-
1939	969	7.44	-	1,920	-
1940	1,399	23.73	-	6,070	-
1941	4,841	109.24	1,390	10,681	4,550
1942	8,611	203.99	9,253	19,317	13,399
1943	7,476	186.19	15,933	24,375	23,534
1938 Ist Quarter	-	-	-	14	-
2nd Quarter	75	0.41	-	46	-
3rd Quarter	146	0.89	-	258	-
4th Quarter	198	1.25	-	363	-
1939 Ist Quarter	145	0.95	-	406	-
2nd Quarter	394	2.42	-	514	-
July-August	116	1.03	-	367	-
September-December	314	3.05	-	633	-
1940 Ist Quarter	218	2.65	-	618	-
2nd Quarter	340	5.50	-	1,617	-
3rd Quarter	392	7.17	-	1,985	-
4th Quarter	449	8.40	-	1,850	-
1941 Ist Quarter	653	12.98	300	2,338	..
2nd Quarter	943	18.47		2,281	..
3rd Quarter	1,368	31.59	349	2,764	..
4th Quarter	1,877	46.20	741	3,298	..
1942 Ist Quarter	2,118	51.70	1,384	3,704	2,440
2nd Quarter	2,220	52.84	2,118	4,701	3,014
3rd Quarter	2,200	50.78	3,020	5,304	3,650
4th Quarter	2,073	48.68	2,731	5,608	4,295
1943 Ist Quarter	2,041	49.46	2,934	5,965	5,402
2nd Quarter	2,147	53.33	6,285	5,629	5,357
3rd Quarter	1,878	45.91	3,633	5,441	5,881
4th Quarter	1,410	37.48	3,081	7,340	6,894
1944 Ist Quarter	1,400	40.59	2,575	7,741	6,097
2nd Quarter	1,074	33.11	4,095	6,216	4,614

1. Including special purpose tanks and self-propelled artillery on tank chassis.
2. Weight in action.
3. Year ended 31 March.

Source: Ministry of Supply

7.19 Munitions

Wheeled vehicles[1]

Number

	Tank transporters	Lorries 10 ton and over	Lorries 6 ton	Lorries 1-3 ton	Trucks 15 cwt.	Ambulances	Heavy cars	Tractors Heavy	Tractors Light	Light cars and vans	Motor cycles	Trailers
1940	5	447	569	60,445	28,121	3,938	13,173	1,539	4,108	21,232	68,532	14,098
1941	41	266	962	53,181	33,752	4,540	8,914	1,956	5,910	17,324	70,804	20,275
1942	440	88	1,834	57,449	28,128	1,269	11,955	1,768	5,997	15,963	75,081	17,303
1943	553	348	1,305	58,943	27,207	2,201	5,312	1,956	6,493	17,306	78,633	29,039
1944	193	617	2,807	53,316	23,984	1,450	3,093	2,605	2,268	12,511	74,576	33,061
1939 September-December	2	22	6	3,705	4,635	378	1,838	89	387	2,000	11,679	1,088
1940 1st Quarter	-	..	..	..	..	..	..	279	704	..	..	..
2nd Quarter	-	..	..	..	..	..	..	497	1,134	..	..	..
3rd Quarter	1	..	..	..	..	..	..	455	1,167	..	..	..
4th Quarter	4	..	..	..	..	..	..	308	1,103	..	..	..
1941 1st Quarter	8	142	166	13,686	8,383	1,268	1,867	334	1,432	6,907	17,122	5,152
2nd Quarter	10	39	262	14,393	8,737	1,714	2,367	430	1,547	4,937	18,335	6,010
3rd Quarter	11	35	280	12,256	8,538	1,150	2,186	634	1,402	2,594	16,527	4,502
4th Quarter	12	50	254	12,846	8,094	408	2,494	558	1,529	2,886	18,820	4,611
1942 1st Quarter	13	20	259	12,688	7,397	362	2,475	465	1,519	3,599	16,420	3,605
2nd Quarter	53	1	325	15,843	7,303	361	3,511	401	1,657	3,954	17,778	4,510
3rd Quarter	129	30	655	14,813	6,619	239	2,921	380	1,450	3,795	19,501	4,063
4th Quarter	245	37	595	14,105	6,809	307	3,048	522	1,371	4,615	21,382	5,125
1943 1st Quarter	214	43	359	14,411	6,283	364	1,946	476	1,728	4,604	20,508	5,244
2nd Quarter	190	60	241	15,101	6,686	386	1,553	589	1,804	4,138	17,843	7,437
3rd Quarter	99	67	324	14,527	6,893	583	1,034	485	1,470	3,896	18,931	7,907
4th Quarter	50	178	381	14,904	7,345	868	779	406	1,491	4,668	21,351	8,451
1944 1st Quarter	49	150	508	13,550	6,848	630	1,143	451	765	4,639	20,322	9,487
2nd Quarter	48	114	642	13,445	6,446	212	817	681	665	3,583	18,336	9,127
3rd Quarter	42	119	690	12,990	4,605	281	359	693	481	2,984	17,267	6,191
4th Quarter	54	234	967	13,331	6,085	327	774	780	357	1,305	18,651	8,256
1945 1st Quarter	37	513	886	13,385	4,877	407	765	662	142	1,727	15,597	9,387
2nd Quarter	31	532	690	11,051	3,357	236	945	482	76	2,549	14,703	13,313
3rd Quarter	15	527	390	8,990	1,975	124	694	309	73	2,807	11,434	13,506

1. For 1939, War Office only; for 1940, War Office and Air Ministry; from January 1941, all Services.
Deliveries of wheeled vehicles to the War Office under the Rearmament Programme amounted to 34,918 during the period April 1936 to August 1939.

Source: Ministry of Supply

7.20 Munitions

Signal equipment[1]

Number

	Wireless sets	Reception sets	Mine detectors	Charging sets	Telephones	Tele-printers	Switch-boards
1936-39[2]	3,567	133	-	192	35,730	118	859
1940	19,616	140	-	1,470	58,243	444	6,416
1941	26,015	1,623	-	1,964	100,064	962	6,079
1942	101,145	5,848	2,026	3,603	112,767	939	8,283
1943	193,076	24,619	17,606	11,529	136,041	2,376	9,360
1944	144,161	21,099	33,802	14,077	111,367	3,308	6,157
1939 September-December	3,044	188	-	265	13,271	176	1,899
1940 1st Quarter	..	..	-	142	12,008	107	1,603
2nd Quarter	..	..	-	315	20,791	149	1,994
3rd Quarter	..	..	-	489	12,219	85	1,523
4th Quarter	..	..	-	524	13,225	103	1,296
1941 1st Quarter	..	..	-	660	21,892	267	2,152
2nd Quarter	..	..	-	416	23,721	285	1,881
3rd Quarter	..	..	-	495	29,210	254	1,498
4th Quarter	..	..	-	393	25,241	156	548
1942 1st Quarter	11,921	1,018	-	552	26,389	134	1,880
2nd Quarter	17,227	1,032	-	863	23,645	127	2,147
3rd Quarter	29,268	1,362	494	807	29,867	138	1,804
4th Quarter	42,729	2,436	1,532	1,381	32,866	540	2,452
1943 1st Quarter	43,208	..	2,629	2,165	38,332	228	2,580
2nd Quarter	42,352	..	3,671	2,399	35,545	772	2,057
3rd Quarter	50,615	..	4,445	3,398	32,922	727	1,968
4th Quarter	56,901	..	6,861	3,567	29,242	649	2,755
1944 1st Quarter	50,950	4,620	7,461	4,291	32,440	876	2,417
2nd Quarter	44,759	5,026	7,466	3,216	33,367	750	1,423
3rd Quarter	24,731	4,947	8,961	3,168	18,882	638	1,058
4th Quarter	23,721	6,506	9,914	3,402	26,678	1,044	1,259
1945 1st Quarter	23,437	12,733	7,229	3,002	25,726	960	1,475
2nd Quarter	24,643	9,903	11,523	3,128	26,614	1,408	2,524
3rd Quarter	17,673	10,863	7,220	3,258	15,246	1,048	2,988

1. For War Office only.
2. April 1936 to August 1939.

Source: Ministry of Supply

7.21 Munitions

Engineer stores

	Boats[1] and tugs	Bridging equipment: Pontoons	Bridging equipment: Inglis bridges (complete)	Bridging equipment: Bailey bridges (panels)	Airfield track	"Mulberry" harbour: Pierheads	"Mulberry" harbour: Breakwaters
	Number				Mn. sq. yds.	Number	
1936-1939[2]	2,206	681	-	-	-	-	-
1940	4,432	1,058	-	-	-	-	-
1941	2,999	980	21	-	-	-	-
1942	8,091	3,025	144	88,356	7.15	-	-
1943	14,998	15,662	31	261,730	27.38	-	-
1944	21,531	29,145	-	220,768	25.76	23	146
1939 September-December	1,047	467	-	-	-	-	-
1940 Ist Quarter	1,008	405	-	-	-	-	-
2nd Quarter	1,583	314	-	-	-	-	-
3rd Quarter	1,251	158	-	-	-	-	-
4th Quarter	590	181	-	-	-	-	-
1941 Ist Quarter	496	89	-	-	-	-	-
2nd Quarter	524	204	-	-	-	-	-
3rd Quarter	602	332	-	-	-	-	-
4th Quarter	1,377	355	21	-	-	-	-
1942 Ist Quarter	1,522	585	7	2,450	0.26	-	-
2nd Quarter	2,042	712	36	10,292	0.42	-	-
3rd Quarter	1,477	1,064	36	22.153	1.37	-	-
4th Quarter	3,050	664	65	53.461	5.10	-	-
1943 Ist Quarter	2,449	1,783	31	60,099	6.49	-	-
2nd Quarter	3,531	3,072	-	65,788	6.78	-	-
3rd Quarter	4,284	4,720	-	66,314	7.10	-	-
4th Quarter	4,734	6,087	-	69,529	7.01	-	-
1944 Ist Quarter	5,100	6,084	-	41,067	7.91	6	22
2nd Quarter	5,970	7,414	-	59,774	8.73	17	124
3rd Quarter	5,446	7,493	-	56,297	6.67	-	-
4th Quarter	5,015	8,154	-	63,630	2.45	-	-
1945 Ist Quarter	2,783	7,039	-	49,584	2.25	-	-
2nd Quarter	883	5,322	-	49,952	5.05	-	-
3rd Quarter	172	3,064	-	25,463	7.79	-	-

1. Assault, reconnaissance and storm boats and motor tugs.
2. April 1936 to August 1939.

Source: Ministry of Supply

7.22 Aircraft

Production by main groups

Number

		Total	Heavy bombers	Medium bombers	Light bombers and fighters	General recon-naissance	Transport and A.S.R.	Naval	Trainers and miscellaneous
1935		893	-	-	214	196	-	89	394
1936		1,830	-	-	468	222	-	181	959
1937		2,218	-	34	799	159	-	302	924
1938		2,828	-	160	909	38	-	286	1,435
1939		7,940	-	758	2,403	61	-	509	4,209
1940		15,049	41	1,926	5,804	387	-	476	6,415
1941		20,094	498	2,777	8,457	196	-	1,232	6,934
1942		23,672	1,976	3,463	10,663	546	-	1,082	5,942
1943		26,263	4,615	2,737	11,103	1,054	209	1,720	4,825
1944		26,461	5,507	2,396	10,730	1,123	889	2,939	2,877
1938	Ist Quarter	511	-	29	209	6	-	86	181
	2nd Quarter	534	-	17	157	10	-	75	275
	3rd Quarter	738	-	20	240	13	-	71	394
	4th Quarter	1,045	-	94	303	9	-	54	585
1939	Ist Quarter	1,736	-	163	542	9	-	109	913
	2nd Quarter	2,017	-	168	634	9	-	141	1,065
	3rd Quarter	2,044	-	168	591	11	-	143	1,131
	4th Quarter	2,143	-	259	636	32	-	116	1,100
1940	Ist Quarter	2,381	-	253	703	84	-	64	1,277
	2nd Quarter	3,951	2	552	1,409	153	-	108	1,727
	3rd Quarter	4,607	8	619	1,901	97	-	146	1,836
	4th Quarter	4,110	31	502	1,791	53	-	158	1,575
1941	Ist Quarter	4,515	75	601	1,933	50	-	224	1,632
	2nd Quarter	4,865	104	675	2,116	53	-	311	1,606
	3rd Quarter	5,376	148	722	2,278	29	-	353	1,846
	4th Quarter	5,338	171	779	2,130	64	-	344	1,850
1942	Ist Quarter	5,639	266	827	2,460	94	-	290	1,702
	2nd Quarter	5,945	432	879	2,765	122	-	202	1,545
	3rd Quarter	5,940	576	898	2,706	151	-	226	1,383
	4th Quarter	6,148	702	859	2,732	179	-	364	1,312
1943	Ist Quarter	6,407	984	766	2,831	224	-	346	1,256
	2nd Quarter	6,604	1,198	704	2,801	311	3	385	1,202
	3rd Quarter	6,515	1,151	643	2,750	285	62	442	1,182
	4th Quarter	6,737	1,282	624	2,721	234	144	547	1,185
1944	Ist Quarter	7,419	1,447	653	2,909	302	227	712	1,169
	2nd Quarter	7,188	1,442	637	2,847	293	249	821	899
	3rd Quarter	6,145	1,382	586	2,566	259	215	722	415
	4th Quarter	5,709	1,236	520	2,408	269	198	684	394
1945	Ist Quarter	5,264	1,073	384	2,334	186	299	657	331
	2nd Quarter	4,092	596	264	1,822	243	266	683	218
	3rd Quarter	2,714	400	95	1,289	171	131	485	143

Source: Ministry of Supply

7.23 Aircraft

Production by structure weight

Million lb.

	Total	Heavy bombers	Medium bombers	Light bombers and fighters	General reconnaissance transport and A.S.R.	Naval	Trainers and miscellaneous
1935	1.91	-	-	0.52	0.64	0.20	0.55
1936	3.75	-	-	0.87	0.77	0.50	1.61
1937	6.54	-	0.36	2.81	0.57	0.85	1.95
1938	9.82	-	1.56	3.38	0.54	0.84	3.50
1939	28.89	-	6.83	8.33	0.79	1.63	11.29
1940	58.83	0.75	18.54	18.39	2.65	1.90	16.63
1941	87.25	9.29	27.96	26.69	1.69	4.41	17.19
1942	133.38	37.96	37.21	34.75	4.62	3.61	15.24
1943	185.25	88.96	29.30	38.16	9.95	6.29	12.60
1944	208.52	100.95	25.30	39.63	23.64	11.46	7.54
1938 1st Quarter	1.77	-	0.32	0.75	0.03	0.24	0.43
2nd Quarter	1.90	-	0.17	0.66	0.16	0.22	0.69
3rd Quarter	2.47	-	0.19	0.86	0.20	0.20	1.02
4th Quarter	3.68	-	0.88	1.11	0.15	0.18	1.36
1939 Ist Quarter	6.13	-	1.46	1.86	0.16	0.35	2.30
2nd Quarter	6.93	-	1.48	2.09	0.16	0.45	2.75
3rd Quarter	7.50	-	1.52	2.14	0.19	0.46	3.19
4th Quarter	8.33	-	2.37	2.24	0.28	0.37	3.05
1940 Ist Quarter	8.86	-	2.32	2.29	0.57	0.23	3.46
2nd Quarter	15.67	0.04	5.20	4.42	0.98	0.42	4.60
3rd Quarter	18.23	0.16	6.10	5.94	0.67	0.60	4.77
4th Quarter	16.07	0.55	4.92	5.74	0.43	0.65	3.80
1941 Ist Quarter	18.70	1.38	5.91	6.18	0.40	0.85	3.97
2nd Quarter	20.90	1.88	6.70	6.81	0.43	1.10	3.96
3rd Quarter	23.51	2.76	7.34	7.23	0.33	1.25	4.60
4th Quarter	24.14	3.27	8.01	6.47	0.53	1.21	4.66
1942 Ist Quarter	27.51	5.12	8.68	7.69	0.80	1.05	4.17
2nd Quarter	32.41	8.28	9.48	8.82	1.22	0.75	3.87
3rd Quarter	35.46	11.23	9.73	8.90	1.22	0.70	3.68
4th Quarter	38.00	13.33	9.32	9.34	1.38	1.11	3.52
1943 Ist Quarter	42.64	18.71	8.26	9.59	1.63	1.13	3.31
2nd Quarter	46.61	23.09	7.54	9.61	1.89	1.36	3.13
3rd Quarter	46.11	22.39	6.91	9.49	2.58	1.68	3.06
4th Quarter	49.89	24.77	6.59	9.47	3.85	2.12	3.10
1944 Ist Quarter	56.47	27.09	6.90	10.58	6.13	2.76	3.01
2nd Quarter	55.31	26.52	6.72	10.18	6.34	3.19	2.36
3rd Quarter	50.40	25.14	6.18	9.61	5.58	2.83	1.06
4th Quarter	46.34	22.20	5.50	9.26	5.59	2.68	1.11
1945 Ist Quarter	42.87	19.39	4.06	9.30	6.49	2.59	1.05
2nd Quarter	31.95	10.83	2.78	7.51	7.53	2.61	0.68
3rd Quarter	19.80	7.41	1.00	5.31	3.67	1.78	0.63

Source: Ministry of Supply

7.24 Aircraft

Index of aircraft production[1]

January 1942 = 1,000

	January	February	March	April	May	June	July	August	September	October	November	December
1939	181	238	278	234	285	279	282	248	335	323	341	277
1940	333	300	373	463	569	736	735	731	581	609	635	563
1941	527	748	807	721	810	792	808	857	930	915	897	829
1942	1,000	958	1,046	1,129	1,190	1,175	1,236	1,139	1,348	1,425	1,277	1,282
1943	1,369	1,452	1,597	1,510	1,701	1,562	1,504	1,507	1,744	1,732	1,726	1,636
1944	1,852	1,823	2,081	1,808	1,922	1,926	1,630	1,725	1,800	1,762	1,673	1,285
1945	1,199	1,600	1,598	1,158	1,036	1,083	995	704				

1. Based on airframe structure weight and man-hours per airframe.
Figures for the years immediately preceding the war were as follows: 1935 (year), 18; 1936 (year), 40; 1937 (year), 66; 1938- 1st Quarter, 71; 2nd Quarter, 73; 3rd Quarter, 96; 4th Quarter, 138.

Source: Ministry of Supply

7.25 Aircraft

Aircraft undergoing and awaiting repair and repaired

Number

	Undergoing and awaiting repair (end of period)	Repaired							
		Total	Heavy bombers	Medium bombers	Light bombers and fighters	General recon-naissance	Transport and A.S.R.	Naval	Trainers and miscel-laneous
Annual totals									
1941	2,354	13,560	..	..	..	..	..	..	..
1942	2,385	16,636	711	3,097	6,659	784	-	433	4,952
1943	2,625	17,932	1,971	3,336	5,976	779	10	1,164	4,696
1944	2,368	18,400	3,285	2,135	6,678	705	453	1,477	3,667
Monthly averages									
1940 2nd Quarter	..	177	..	..	..	..	..	..	..
3rd Quarter	..	660	..	..	..	..	..	..	..
4th Quarter	1,785	738	..	..	..	..	..	..	..
1941 1st Quarter	1,773	809	..	..	..	..	..	..	..
2nd Quarter	2,149	1,063	..	..	..	..	..	..	..
3rd Quarter	2,646	1,336	..	..	..	..	..	..	..
4th Quarter	2,354	1,312	17	227	583	53	-	31	401
1942 1st Quarter	2,263	1,197	22	226	486	65	-	33	366
2nd Quarter	2,537	1,395	48	272	555	77	-	25	418
3rd Quarter	2,610	1,508	74	272	599	62	-	34	466
4th Quarter	2,385	1,445	93	262	580	57	-	53	400
1943 1st Quarter	2,602	1,360	111	259	491	59	-	56	385
2nd Quarter	2,744	1,586	166	306	563	67	-	91	393
3rd Quarter	2,774	1,567	194	304	507	64	-	103	395
4th Quarter	2,625	1,464	187	243	430	70	3	139	392
1944 1st Quarter	2,678	1,426	203	195	465	66	17	114	365
2nd Quarter	2,733	1,642	279	193	593	57	38	149	333
3rd Quarter	2,672	1,676	330	176	661	65	41	111	292
4th Quarter	2,368	1,390	283	147	507	47	55	118	233
1945 1st Quarter	2,493	1,256	233	109	476	56	44	117	221
2nd Quarter	1,945	1,106	156	93	399	55	33	168	202
3rd Quarter	1,880	644	62	52	198	22	29	107	173

Source: Ministry of Supply

7.26 Aircraft

Aircraft engines: Production, imports and repairs

		Piston types				Turbine types
		Production		Imports	Repaired	Production
		Number	*Thousand horsepower*		*Number*	
1936 April-December		2,248	1,580	..	..	-
1937		3,440	2,710	..	..	-
1938		5,431	4,037	..	..	-
1939		12,499	8,340	..	..	-
1940		24,074	17,398	..	..	-
1941		36,551	31,416	2,704	20,082	-
1942		53,916	59,447	3,145	27,563	-
1943		57,985	72,784	9,441	35,832	9
1944		56,931	80,042	11,327	44,594	98
1938	1st Quarter	823	630	..	..	-
	2nd Quarter	1,154	890	..	..	-
	3rd Quarter	1,176	869	..	..	-
	4th Quarter	2,278	1,648	..	..	-
1939	1st Quarter	2,947	2,092	..	..	-
	2nd Quarter	2,971	2,026	..	..	-
	3rd Quarter	3,078	1,980	..	..	-
	4th Quarter	3,503	2,242	..	..	-
1940	1st Quarter	3,940	2,555	..	..	-
	2nd Quarter	6,644	4,619	..	..	-
	3rd Quarter	7,162	5,205	..	3,174	-
	4th Quarter	6,328	5,019	..	3,552	-
1941	1st Quarter	7,271	5,963	698	4,299	-
	2nd Quarter	8,441	6,901	1,034	4,413	-
	3rd Quarter	9,603	8,273	583	5,233	-
	4th Quarter	11,236	10,279	389	6,137	-
1942	1st Quarter	11,955	12,542	184	5,743	-
	2nd Quarter	13,316	14,177	435	6,547	-
	3rd Quarter	13,657	15,361	1,476	7,442	-
	4th Quarter	14,988	17,367	1,050	7,831	-
1943	1st Quarter	14,463	17,489	1,264	7,990	-
	2nd Quarter	13,953	17,401	1,524	8,470	-
	3rd Quarter	13,780	17,644	3,028	8,803	-
	4th Quarter	15,789	20,250	3,625	10,569	9
1944	1st Quarter	16,458	21,364	2,892	11,520	13
	2nd Quarter	15,185	20,552	3,522	11,183	24
	3rd Quarter	13,477	19,298	2,124	11,359	43
	4th Quarter	11,811	18,828	2,789	10,532	18
1945	1st Quarter	10,091	16,441	1,228	10,299	102
	2nd Quarter	8,292	13,700	3,300	9,146	179
	3rd Quarter	4,438	7,290	..	7,244	186

Source: Ministry of Supply

7.27 Aircraft

Arrivals in United Kingdom from North America[1]

Number

		Total	Heavy bombers	Medium bombers	Light bombers and general reconnaissance	Fighters	Transports	Naval	Trainers and miscellaneous
1940		1,069	-	-	395	578	-	71	25
1941		1,712	98	-	974	467	6	57	110
1942		2,394	147	243	451	1,099	5	207	242
1943		2,418	188	171	381	470	71	593	544
1944		5,667	453	335	502	495	702	1,638	1,542
1940	1st Quarter	13	-	-	13	-	-	-	-
	2nd Quarter	74	-	-	74	-	-	-	-
	3rd Quarter	596	-	-	256	280	-	44	16
	4th Quarter	386	-	-	52	298	-	27	9
1941	1st Quarter	330	1	-	38	262	3	-	26
	2nd Quarter	477	42	-	350	6	-	32	47
	3rd Quarter	541	3	-	443	65	3	22	5
	4th Quarter	364	52	-	143	134	-	3	32
1942	1st Quarter	492	5	-	25	404	1	32	25
	2nd Quarter	924	62	131	217	419	3	31	61
	3rd Quarter	568	58	97	49	200	1	67	96
	4th Quarter	410	22	15	160	76	-	77	60
1943	1st Quarter	302	45	1	164	46	7	7	32
	2nd Quarter	555	62	43	167	110	19	122	32
	3rd Quarter	573	33	44	23	44	19	185	225
	4th Quarter	988	48	83	27	270	26	279	255
1944	1st Quarter	1,189	80	111	69	102	231	374	222
	2nd Quarter	1,891	133	60	197	127	264	530	580
	3rd Quarter	1,550	131	86	132	146	157	342	556
	4th Quarter	1,037	109	78	104	120	50	392	184
1945	1st Quarter	884	155	46	119	289	118	75	82
	2nd Quarter	1,115	212	10	216	204	135	249	89

1. Arrivals on pre-war contracts are excluded. Between September 1939 and February 1940 214 such aircraft despatched from the United States arrived in the United Kingdom. These were general reconnaissance aircraft and trainers.

Source: Ministry of Supply

7.28 Aircraft

Arrivals overseas direct from the United States[1]

Number

	Total[2]	Heavy bombers	Medium bombers	Light bombers and general reconnaissance	Fighters	Transports	Naval	Trainers[2] and miscellaneous
1941	2,761	-	-	408	922	42	30	1,359
1942	3,504	5	181	1,103	1,066	52	120	977
1943	4,292	146	350	1,218	648	227	180	1,523
1944	5,747	734	574	677	1,041	954	771	996
1941 1st Quarter	421	-	-	48	143	8	-	222
2nd Quarter	808	-	-	122	267	11	-	408
3rd Quarter	699	-	-	54	273	23	27	322
4th Quarter	833	-	-	184	239	-	3	407
1942 1st Quarter	792	5	2	264	307	-	-	214
2nd Quarter	713	-	28	259	297	-	19	110
3rd Quarter	937	-	107	307	253	33	19	218
4th Quarter	1,062	-	44	273	209	19	82	435
1943 1st Quarter	967	-	29	409	149	1	11	368
2nd Quarter	841	3	11	307	104	91	52	273
3rd Quarter	996	-	63	322	210	71	7	323
4th Quarter	1,488	143	247	180	185	64	110	559
1944 1st Quarter	1,317	110	189	198	141	243	217	219
2nd Quarter	1,576	272	217	184	298	146	11	448
3rd Quarter	1,434	152	85	196	275	261	205	260
4th Quarter	1,420	200	83	99	327	304	338	69
1945 1st Quarter	1,074	147	72	29	192	259	332	43
2nd Quarter	620	128	13	-	68	171	240	-

1. To British overseas commands and other governments, including Canada.
2. 284 trainer aircraft which were delivered to Canada before June 1942 are excluded from the table as their exact dates of arrival are not available.
3. Including amendments to earlier figures.

Source: Ministry of Supply

7.29 Machine tools, welding sets and electric motors: Deliveries

	Unit	1935	1942	1943	1944	1945
Machine tools[1]	Thousand	. .	95.8	76.2	59.1	47.5
Metal-working	Value £ million	6.1	33.5	31.3	25.8	20.7
	Thousands	. .	9.0	11.3	10.7	9.4
Wood-working	Value £ million	0.6	1.3	1.5	1.7	1.5
Engineers' small tools[2]	"	. .	35.8	42.4	40.2	23.3
Welding sets:						
Arc	Thousands	. .	. .	. .	8.6	6.6
	Value £ million	0.22[3]	. .	. .	1.47	1.20
	Thousands	. .	. .	2.8	2.4	2.5
Resistance	Value £ million	. .	. .	0.73	0.51	0.59
Electric motors 1-300 horse-power:						
A.C.	"	. .	. .	6.5	6.2	12.5
D.C.	"	. .	. .	6.5	7.7	

1. Excluding, except in 1935, machine tools of low value.
2. From January 1943 the figures include roller box tools, and from January 1944 they include balancing and testing machines.
3. Including resistance.

Source: Ministry of Supply

7.30 Agricultural machinery: Production

Number

	1938	1939	1940	1941	1942	1943	1944	1945
Tractors:								
Total	10,679	15,733	19,316	24,401	27,056	25,059	23,022	23,296
Tracklayers:								
Full and half track	48	30	19	-	48	87	133	45
Market-garden type	198	211	327	339	411	440	557	630
Three-and four-wheeled	9,981	14,632	17,906	22,168	24,099	21,595	18,716	17,455
Two-wheeled market-garden type[1]	452	860	1,064	1,894	2,498	2,937	3,616	5,166
Mouldboard ploughs:								
Total	12,580	16,665	23,172	24,657	21,414	19,246	23,701	30,227
Horse-drawn	7,424	9,541	14,492	14,162	12,485	10,939	13,963	17,345
Tractor-drawn	5,156	7,124	8,680	10,495	8,929	8,307	9,738	12,882
Disc harrows	1,260	2,108	3,905	5,696	8,343	9,791	10,521	12,940
Cultivators or grubbers	6,405	7,668	11,087	16,763	9,878	11,485	11,710	9,642
Toolbars	1,342	1,734	2,296	3,417	4,358	5,144	7,244	7,773
Corn drills[2]	352	664	1,567	1,452	1,262	1,176	1,353	1,743
Mowing machines	4,641	5,587	7,087	5,896	5,910	5,611	5,802	6,297
Binders	687	708	954	1,010	798	1,567	2,957	2,722
Threshing machines	486	489	842	998	1,149	1,149	1,160	1,083
Potato spinners	1,496	1,253	2,108	5,226	7,534	9,831	5,586	6,021
Milking machines	. .	. .	. .	. .	4,582	5,623	4,888	4,807

1. Including motor hoes and self-propelled grass cutters (not lawn mowers).
2. Including combined seed and fertilizer drills.

Source: Ministry of Agriculture and Fisheries

7.31 Locomotives and motor vehicles: Production

	1940	1941	1942	1943	1944	1945
			Number			
Steam locomotives[1]:						
Main line types	272	234	350	797	1,050	754
Industrial types[2]	84	110	110	58	45	43
Motor vehicles:						
Public service vehicles:						
Total	-	164	1,260	2,217	2,017	2,914
Single deck buses	-	1	624	1,172	606	791
Double deck buses	-	163	636	1,045	1,411	2,123
Other heavy type vehicles[3]						
Total	112,531	124,574	136,079	125,496	111,234	99,709
For the Services	112,345	109,522	108,928	104,308	90,333	60,385
For other users[4]	186	15,052	27,151	21,188	20,901	39,324
Light cars and vans[5]						
Total	21,338	20,692	23,183	21,605	19,704	36,782
For the Services	21,232	17,324	15,963	17,306	12,511	9,197
For other users[4]	106	3,368	7,220	4,299	7,193	27,585
			Thousands			
Motor cycles:						
Total[6]	70.0	73.0	77.0	81.7	77.4	50.0
For the services	68.5	70.8	75.1	78.6	74.6	42.6
For other users [4, 6]	1.5	2.2	1.9	3.1	2.8	7.4

1. Production by the railway companies and by private makers.
2. Including shunters for docks.
3. Goods vehicles of 15 cwt. and over and passenger cars of over 16 horse-power.
4. For Government Departments and other essential users.
5. Goods vehicles of under 15 cwt. and passenger cars of 16 horse-power and less.
6. Estimated.

Source: Ministry of Transport and Ministry of Supply

7.32 Woven cloth, household textiles, hosiery and footwear

Supplies for home civilian use

	Unit	1935	1942	1943	1944	1945
Woven cloth for clothing						
Total	Mn.sq.yds.	. .	173	162	159	166
Utility	"	. .	128	119	104	133
Non-utility	"	. .	45[1]	43	55	33
Woven non-wool cloth:						
Total	"	. .	371	454	404	403
Utility	"	. .	299	358	336	330
Non-utility	"	. .	72[2]	96	68	73
Wool hand-knitting yarn	Million lb.	. .	. .	8.7	9.4	11.1
Household textiles						
Blankets[3]:						
Wool	Millions	6.49	. .	2.26	2.70	3.80
Cotton	"	. .	. .	4.40	4.76	5.02
Sheets	"	. .	. .	3.00	3.87	7.06
Pillowcases	"	. .	. .	5.82	7.56	10.78
Towels:						
Hand and bath	"	. .	. .	18.5	15.1	12.5
Other	"	. .	. .	14.7	10.7	9.8
Hosiery						
Men's and youths':						
Socks and stockings	Mn.pairs	90[4]	35.4	33.4	20.1	23.9
Pullovers and cardigans	Millions	. .	1.8	1.9	2.3	2.8
Vests	"	. .	8.4	10.9	8.4	8.8
Pants and trunks	"	. .	10.1	13.9	9.1	9.6
Women's and maids':						
Stockings and socks	Mn.pairs	280[4,5]	160.4	140.6	131.3	134.2
Jumpers and cardigans	Millions	. .	6.6	5.3	6.0	6.2
Vests	"	. .	19.6	17.8	15.8	17.1
Children's:						
Socks and stockings	Mn.pairs	90[4,6]	51.0	66.0	61.8	61.7
Underwear	Mn. pieces	. .	23.2	31.4	26.9	26.8
Footwear[7]						
Total production for all uses	Mn. pairs	132.5	108.2	102.7	99.7	99.8
Production for home civilian use:						
Total	"	129.0	90.3	89.4	87.4	87.7
Leather uppers:						
Total	"	105.0	74.7	75.5	74.1	73.7
Men's	"	29.3	16.7	14.7	12.6	12.9
Women's	"	46.4	31.2	29.6	28.1	28.2
Children's	"	29.3	26.9	31.2	33.3	32.6
Fabric uppers	"	5.5	5.9	5.0	4.1	4.4
Slippers	"	18.4	9.7	9.0	9.2	9.6

1. Total for 11 months converted to yearly rate.
2. Total for 5 months converted to yearly rate.
3. Including cot size.
4. Approximate figures for 1937.
5. Stockings only.
6. Including women's and maids' socks.
7. Excluding rubber footwear.

Source: Board of Trade

7.33 Pottery, hollow-ware and brushes

Production and supplies for home civilian use

Millions

	1943		1944		1945	
	Production	For home civilian use	Production	For home civilian use	Production	For home civilian use
Pottery						
Cups, mugs and beakers	138.7	108.9	125.9	94.9	108.8	80.2
Saucers and small plates	83.8	52.8	80.1	49.4	78.9	47.1
Large plates	53.7	25.1	51.2	26.8	46.7	23.9
Teapots and coffee pots	8.7[1]	7.3[1]	8.8	7.4	8.1	6.4
Cooking ware (all types)	4.1[2]	3.6[2]	4.3	3.7	4.7	4.2
Hollow-ware						
Kettles	5.8	5.2	5.7	5.1	7.6	7.2
Saucepans and stewpans	11.7	10.9	13.3	12.6	18.0	16.9
Dustbins	1.18	0.71	1.11	0.97	1.47	1.37
Brushes and brooms						
Household type	45.9	34.7[3]	43.3	32.4	43.6	35.6
Paint and paste	17.9	10.5[3]	17.2	10.8	20.1	14.2
Toilet	38.0	22.9[3]	38.1	23.9	43.2	28.0

1. Coffee pots included from March 1943 only.
2. Until February 1943 including pie and baking dishes only.
3. First three months of 1943 include exports.

Source: Board of Trade

8 TRANSPORT

The transport sector of the economy came under great strain in the war as it bore the brunt of enemy action, from shipping sunk by German submarines to the railway and road system having to cope with the relocation of factories and the vast troop and equipment movement that was prompted by the D-Day build up. The loss of shipping capacity was one of the key constraints facing the wartime economy and problems with the inland transport system, and particularly the railways, posed major problems in 1940-41 (Robinson 1951: 37; Savage 1957: 191-256).

In the 1930's foreign shipping had carried between 40 and 50 per cent of British imports but with the onset of war Britain had problems chartering neutral shipping and by the end of March 1940 a mere 55 non-tanker foreign ships, amounting to 361,000 deadweight tons, had been chartered (Behrens 1955: 58-64; **tables 8.3 and 8.5**). The situation changed radically with the German conquests of the second quarter of that year which forced the major shipping nations of Holland, Norway and Greece out of neutrality and into the Allied arms of the British: by the end of September Britain had at its disposal more than 3.5 million deadweight tons of non-tanker foreign shipping and indeed the importance of foreign vessels to British shipping capacity increased during the war, rising to over 6.5 million deadweight tons by mid-1944 (Behrens 1955: 91-118; **table 8.5**). This increase in the available foreign shipping helped to compensate for the marked decline in the UK and Colonies non-tanker shipping (from 17.7 million deadweight tons in September 1939 to a low of 11.5 million tons in mid-1943) although the total dry cargo merchant shipping under British control fell by more than 3 million tons (or approximately 15 per cent) between 1940 and 1943 (**table 8.5**). The deadweight tonnage of tankers under British control actually increased from 5 million deadweight tons to almost 7 million tons by the end of 1941 before declining to a level of about 5.5 million tons

8.1 Merchant shipping under British control (at September of each year)

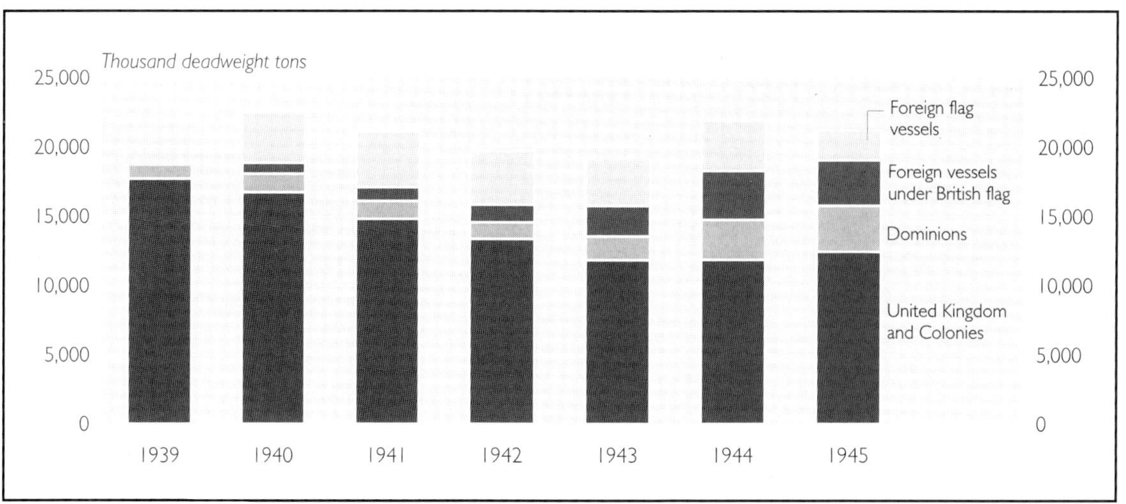

from 1943 onwards, although here again it was a story of British losses being made good by foreign additions, with American shipping being particularly important (Hancock and Gowing 1949: 257; **table 8.5**). The shipping problems were compounded by two other features: first, as the war progressed the proportion of non-tanker shipping under British control that was unavailable at any one time because of repairs or other reasons increased from 8.5 per cent of the total in September 1939 to a peak of 15.6 per cent in December 1942; second, the entry of the Italians into the war closed the Mediterranean to merchant shipping and greatly increased the length of the journey to Suez and to India (Behrens 1955: 109; **table 8.6**).

The greatest threat to British shipping, however, came from enemy action (especially in the Battle of the Atlantic) with total losses of 2.4 million gross tons in 1940 and 2.9 million gross tons in 1941; it reached its peak in the fifteen months from January 1942 to March 1943 when 4.1 million gross tons was sunk, 81 per cent of it by submarine (**table 9.10**). The impact on government import programmes was as dramatic: monthly non-tanker imports fell from 2.68 million tons in December 1941 (which was itself far below the April 1940 peak of 4.2 million tons) to a low of 1.18 million tons in January 1943; between 1941 and 1942 imports of food and raw materials declined, respectively, by 4 million tons (28 per cent) and 3.5 million tons (24 per cent) (**tables 8.13-8.15**). Although the increased effectiveness of the convoy escort ships (many provided by the USA) helped to dent the German campaign the decisive factor in the Battle of the Atlantic was a technological one: the invention and success of radar greatly reduced the threat from the U-boats and after July 1943 total losses due to enemy action fell dramatically so that by 1944 the total losses had been reduced to 490,000 tons and imports recovered (Duncan Hall and Wrigley 1956:36; Hancock and Gowing 1949: 417-35; **tables 8.10 and 8.13-8.15**).

The importance of the inland transport sector is illustrated by the fact that the state felt it was necessary for it to administer all four of its branches (rail, road, canal and coastal shipping), road haulage being the last to be brought into the fold in 1943 (Savage 1957: 119-29, 155-9, 446-8, 538-5). At the apex of the state administrative organisation was the Ministry of War Transport which was formed by the amalgamation of the Ministries of Shipping and Transport in May 1941 (Savage 1957: 279-83). The volume of traffic carried on the inland transport system increased during the war years but all of this increased burden fell on the railways: compared to their pre-war loads road, canal and coastal shipping all experienced a decline but railway freight traffic rose from 16.3 million ton-miles in 1938 to a wartime peak of 24.4 million ton-miles in 1944 whilst passenger traffic in the same period increased from 19 to 32 million passenger miles (Savage 1957: 634; **tables 8.17 and 8.22-8.23**).

The railway system was placed under great strain by various wartime pressures, including: the diversion of shipping form east to west coast ports; the transfer onto rail of freight normally carried by coastal shipping (which faced the threat of German attack) and road (to conserve petrol, rubber and manpower); the switch of Anglo-Scottish freight to the east coast route to release the west coast route for the movement of American troops (who disembarked in the Clyde) and later the transfer of troops and their supplies to Southampton and the South-West for the D-Day build-up (Kohan 1952: 345; Savage 1957).

8.2 Losses of merchant shipping due to enemy action

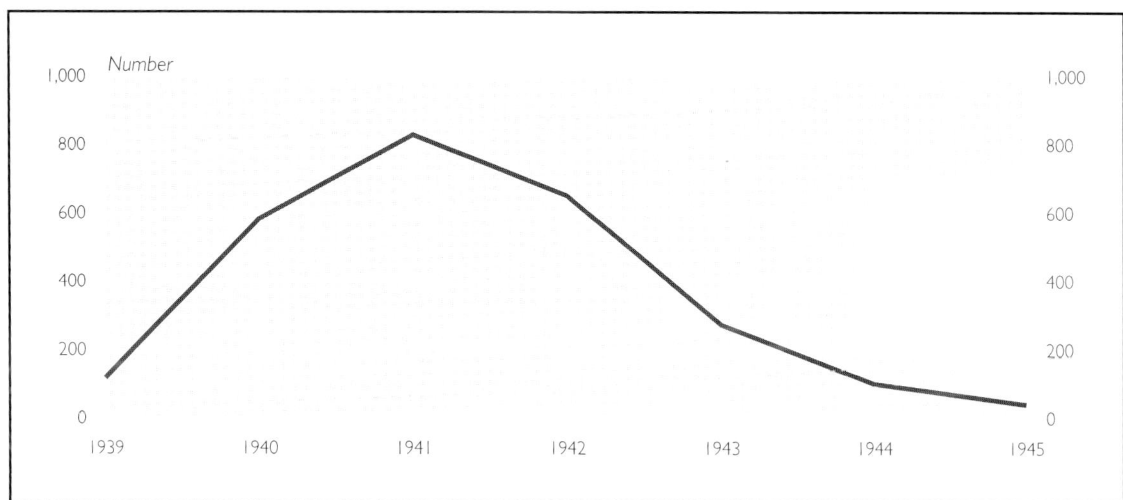

8.4 Merchant shipping under British control[1]

(ii) Vessels of 1,600 gross tons and over: Gross Tonnage

Thousand gross tons

	Total	British flag					Foreign flag vessels[2]
		Total	United Kingdom and Colonies	Dominions	Foreign vessels		Time-chartered to United Kingdom
					Bareboat charter	Requisitioned	
Non-tankers							
1939 September 3	14,352	14,352	13,452	900	-	-	-
December 31	14,264	14,143	13,181	957	5	-	121
1940 March 31	14,484	14,242	13,263	954	25	-	242
June 30	15,926	14,559	13,235	1,075	51	198	1,367
September 30	16,910	14,512	12,779	1,124	34	575	2,398
December 31	16,507	14,136	12,425	1,103	35	573	2,371
1941 March 31	16,337	13,900	12,093	1,100	66	641	2,437
June 30	15,780	13,223	11,414	1,076	99	634	2,557
September 30	15,925	13,221	11,355	1,090	112	664	2,704
December 31	16,083	13,329	11,400	1,094	148	687	2,754
1942 March 31	15,829	13,017	11,114	1,046	175	682	2,812
June 30	15,560	12,709	10,766	1,030	245	668	2,851
September 30	15,047	12,392	10,387	1,006	351	648	2,655
December 31	14,299	11,822	9,686	999	581	556	2,477
1943 March 31	14,112	11,685	9,450	958	742	535	2,427
June 30	14,207	11,804	9,103	1,170	1,002	529	2,403
September 30	14,631	12,249	9,299	1,349	1,067	534	2,382
December 31	15,272	12,962	9,323	1,678	1,436	525	2,310
1944 March 31	15,777	13,478	9,395	1,766	1,779	538	2,299
June 30	16,682	14,051	9,487	1,962	2,073	529	2,631
September 30	16,704	14,097	9,402	2,134	2,057	504	2,607
December 31	16,905	14,330	9,542	2,267	2,035	486	2,575
1945 March 31	16,939	14,387	9,565	2,337	2,011	474	2,552
June 30	16,907	14,532	9,746	2,365	2,017	404	2,375
September 30	16,274	14,675	9,907	2,428	2,075	265	1,599
Tankers							
1939 September 3	3,432	3,172	3,007	165	-	-	260
December 31	3,508	3,248	3,079	169	-	-	260
1940 March 31	3,716	3,192	3,021	171	-	-	524
June 30	4,551	3,177	2,937	198	-	42	1,374
September 30	4,463	3,078	2,778	202	-	98	1,385
December 31	4,347	3,018	2,727	203	-	88	1,329
1941 March 31	4,546	2,928	2,615	201	-	112	1,618
June 30	4,351	2,802	2,530	179	-	93	1,549
September 30	4,627	2,944	2,671	180	-	93	1,683
December 31	4,610	2,955	2,688	180	-	87	1,655
1942 March 31	4,291	2,755	2,528	147	-	80	1,536
June 30	4,063	2,585	2,383	122	-	80	1,478
September 30	3,909	2,532	2,329	123	-	80	1,377
December 31	3,823	2,486	2,296	123	-	67	1,337
1943 March 31	3,680	2,436	2,251	117	-	68	1,244
June 30	3,651	2,429	2,244	117	-	68	1,222
September 30	3,594	2,453	2,268	117	-	68	1,141
December 31	3,667	2,544	2,336	140	-	68	1,123
1944 March 31	3,751	2,632	2,369	195	-	68	1,119
June 30	3,788	2,669	2,386	204	-	79	1,119
September 30	3,798	2,678	2,415	197	-	66	1,120
December 31	3,821	2,720	2,463	197	-	60	1,101
1945 March 31	3,795	2,710	2,445	197	-	68	1,085
June 30	3,703	2,762	2,507	197	-	58	941
September 30	3,176	2,836	2,594	196	7	39	340

See footnotes to Table 8.3.

Source: Ministry of Transport

8.5 Merchant shipping under British control[1]

(iii) Vessels of 1,600 gross tons and over: Deadweight tonnage

Thousand deadweight tons

	Total	British flag					Foreign flag vessels[2]
		Total	United Kingdom and Colonies	Dominions	Foreign vessels: Bareboat charter	Foreign vessels: Requisitioned	Time chartered to United Kingdom
Non-tankers							
1939 September 3	18,710	18,710	17,691	1,019	-	-	-
December 31	18,579	18,418	17,314	1,096	8	-	161
1940 March 31	18,764	18,403	17,258	1,102	43	-	361
June 30	21,096	18,911	17,264	1,276	68	303	2,185
September 30	22,459	18,831	16,718	1,343	45	725	3,628
December 31	21,963	18,453	16,362	1,330	46	715	3,510
1941 March 31	21,622	18,050	15,858	1,305	81	806	3,572
June 30	20,858	17,037	14,828	1,282	131	796	3,821
September 30	21,115	17,085	14,807	1,302	153	823	4,030
December 31	21,324	17,221	14,851	1,316	206	848	4,103
1942 March 31	20,994	16,809	14,452	1,272	245	840	4,185
June 30	20,505	16,336	13,921	1,250	346	819	4,169
September 30	19,722	15,826	13,333	1,219	488	786	3,896
December 31	18,758	15,135	12,411	1,225	826	673	3,623
1943 March 31	18,449	14,937	12,059	1,168	1,066	644	3,512
June 30	18,528	15,067	11,514	1,480	1,456	617	3,461
September 30	19,163	15,725	11,810	1,746	1,548	621	3,438
December 31	20,082	16,738	11,801	2,232	2,093	612	3,344
1944 March 31	20,765	17,426	11,892	2,364	2,546	624	3,339
June 30	21,967	18,245	11,996	2,650	2,997	602	3,722
September 30	21,962	18,282	11,841	2,901	2,971	569	3,680
December 31	22,225	18,597	12,000	3,104	2,945	548	3,628
1945 March 31	22,228	18,638	11,996	3,202	2,910	530	3,590
June 30	22,143	18,844	12,234	3,246	2,918	446	3,299
September 30	21,210	19,043	12,426	3,345	2,977	295	2,167
Tankers							
1939 September 3	5,044	4,654	4,429	225	-	-	390
December 31	5,052	4,662	4,435	227	-	-	390
1940 March 31	5,368	4,581	4,351	230	-	-	787
June 30	6,638	4,560	4,225	271	-	64	2,078
September 30	6,523	4,427	4,002	276	-	149	2,096
December 31	6,365	4,344	3,932	278	-	134	2,021
1941 March 31	6,658	4,224	3,776	277	-	171	2,434
June 30	6,406	4,082	3,694	246	-	142	2,324
September 30	6,894	4,371	3,975	254	-	142	2,523
December 31	6,860	4,378	3,991	254	-	133	2,482
1942 March 31	6,386	4,083	3,753	208	-	122	2,303
June 30	6,040	3,825	3,530	173	-	122	2,215
September 30	5,813	3,746	3,450	174	-	122	2,067
December 31	5,692	3,684	3,407	174	-	103	2,008
1943 March 31	5,468	3,604	3,338	163	-	103	1,864
June 30	5,430	3,590	3,324	163	-	103	1,840
September 30	5,334	3,620	3,354	163	-	103	1,714
December 31	5,431	3,743	3,447	193	-	103	1,688
1944 March 31	5,545	3,863	3,493	267	-	103	1,682
June 30	5,596	3,914	3,518	278	-	118	1,682
September 30	5,614	3,932	3,558	274	-	100	1,682
December 31	5,647	3,991	3,626	274	-	91	1,656
1945 March 31	5,602	3,972	3,595	274	-	103	1,630
June 30	5,453	4,041	3,679	274	-	88	1,412
September 30	4,653	4,145	3,802	272	12	59	508

See footnotes to Table 8.3.

Source: Ministry of Transport

8.8 Merchant shipping under the British flag

Analysis of gains and losses: Non-tankers of 1,600 gross tons and over[1]

Thousand gross tons

		Gains					Losses				Net gain (+) or loss (-)
		Total	New vessels	Foreign tonnage: Bareboat charter	Foreign tonnage: Requisitioned	Other[2]	Total	War[3]	Marine	Other[4]	
1939 to 1945[5]		11,799	6,831	2,402	931	1,635	11,476	9,449	833	1,194	+323
1939[6]		280	162	-	-	118	380	346	28	6	-100
1940		2,202	757	65	604	776	2,261	1,968	216	77	-59
1941		1,694	905	114	264	411	2,591	2,332	119	140	-897
1942		1,834	1,313	473	9	39	3,341	2,906	181	254	-1,507
1943		2,784	1,757	994	30	3	1,609	1,332	123	154	+1,175
1944		2,175	1,422	712	24	17	809	427	96	286	+1,366
1939	September[6]	37	35	-	-	2	106	106	-	-	-69
	4th Quarter	243	127	-	-	116	274	240	28	6	-31
1940	1st Quarter	277	189	25	-	63	262	145	87	30	+15
	2nd Quarter	835	216	30	198	391	405	346	29	30	+430
	3rd Quarter	652	159	4	382	107	726	693	19	14	-74
	4th Quarter	438	193	6	24	215	868	784	81	3	-430
1941	1st Quarter	490	148	27	105	210	822	763	54	5	-332
	2nd Quarter	351	201	33	48	69	1,028	916	16	96	-677
	3rd Quarter	452	256	18	65	113	465	420	6	39	-13
	4th Quarter	401	300	36	46	19	276	233	43	-	+125
1942	1st Quarter	313	259	32	7	15	642	459	68	115	-329
	2nd Quarter	474	367	87	-	20	767	642	46	79	-293
	3rd Quarter	469	346	119	-	4	778	717	28	33	-309
	4th Quarter	578	341	235	2	-	1,154	1,088	39	27	-576
1943	1st Quarter	413	224	187	-	2	557	495	41	21	-144
	2nd Quarter	598	508	68	22	-	476	373	41	62	+122
	3rd Quarter	811	478	327	5	1	361	294	26	41	+450
	4th Quarter	962	547	412	3	-	215	170	15	30	+747
1944	1st Quarter	685	282	380	14	9	169	137	26	6	+516
	2nd Quarter	749	422	309	10	8	178	104	27	47	+571
	3rd Quarter	356	339	17	-	-	310	128	21	161	+46
	4th Quarter	385	379	6	-	-	152	58	22	72	+233
1945	1st Quarter	191	191	-	-	-	134	101	25	8	+57
	2nd Quarter	273	182	13	-	78	128	37	38	53	+145
	3rd Quarter	366	142	31	-	193	223	-	7	216	+143

1. Recorded by date of notification. For this reason the figures for war losses differ from those given in Table 8.10 which are analysed by date of occurrence.
2. Including prizes, transfers of flag, etc.
3. Including overdue and presumed lost.
4. Including transfers of flag, etc.
5. 3 September 1939 to 30 September 1945.
6. From 3 September.

Source: Ministry of Transport

8.9 Merchant shipping under the British flag

Analysis of gains and losses: Tankers of 1,600 gross tons and over[1]

Thousand gross tons

		Gains					Losses				Net gain (+) or loss (-)
		Total	New vessels	Foreign tonnage: Bareboat charter	Foreign tonnage: Requisi-tioned	Other[2]	Total	War[2]	Marine	Other[4]	
1939 to 1945 [5]		1,727	1,298	7	143	279	2,063	1,828	44	191	-336
1939 [6]		117	42	-	-	75	81	67	8	6	+36
1940		178	44	-	98	36	395	385	-	10	-217
1941		402	285	-	26	91	488	446	10	32	-86
1942		277	266	-	-	11	693	646	-	47	-416
1943		273	271	-	-	2	217	160	24	33	+56
1944		273	259	-	12	2	98	67	2	29	+175
1939	September[6]	13	-	-	-	13	43	43	-	-	-30
	4th Quarter	104	42	-	-	62	38	24	8	6	+66
1940	1st Quarter	18	8	-	-	10	73	73	-	-	-55
	2nd Quarter	66	7	-	42	17	68	60	-	8	-2
	3rd Quarter	65	-	-	56	9	166	166	-	-	-101
	4th Quarter	29	29	-	-	-	88	86	-	2	-59
1941	1st Quarter	68	44	-	24	-	170	167	-	3	-102
	2nd Quarter	78	65	-	2	11	199	170	-	29	-121
	3rd Quarter	154	85	-	-	69	40	36	4	-	+114
	4th Quarter	102	91	-	-	11	79	73	6	-	+23
1942	1st Quarter	34	34	-	-	-	213	202	-	11	-179
	2nd Quarter	89	78	-	-	11	250	214	-	36	-161
	3rd Quarter	67	67	-	-	-	131	131	-	-	-64
	4th Quarter	87	87	-	-	-	99	99	-	-	-12
1943	1st Quarter	76	76	-	-	-	124	93	15	16	-48
	2nd Quarter	55	53	-	-	2	66	54	8	4	-11
	3rd Quarter	39	39	-	-	-	15	8	-	7	+24
	4th Quarter	103	103	-	-	-	12	5	1	6	+91
1944	1st Quarter	118	116	-	-	2	30	22	-	8	+88
	2nd Quarter	46	34	-	12	-	10	7	-	3	+36
	3rd Quarter	49	49	-	-	-	40	26	2	12	+9
	4th Quarter	60	60	-	-	-	18	12	-	6	+42
1945	1st Quarter	23	16	-	7	-	33	33	-	-	-10
	2nd Quarter	85	58	-	-	27	33	24	-	9	+52
	3rd Quarter	99	57	7	-	35	25	-	-	25	+74

See footnotes. to Table 8.8.

Source: Ministry of Transport

8.10 Merchant shipping under the British flag: Losses from enemy action[1]

	Vessels lost						Cause of loss				
	Total	Under 1,600 gross tons	1,600 gross tons and over	Under 1,600 gross tons	1,600 gross tons and over	Total	Sub-marine	Mine	Surface craft	Aircraft	Cause unknown or other cause
	Number			*Thousand gross tons*							
1939 to 1945[2]	2,627	731	1,896	440.6	10,956.4	11,396.9	7,622.4	823.0	965.4	1,589.3	396.1
1939	122	49	73	30.2	400.1	430.3	266.3	99.4	55.1	2.2	7.3
1940	587	192	395	123.4	2,323.4	2,446.8	1,359.7	342.8	343.0	310.8	90.6
1941	833	320	513	182.7	2,681.2	2,863.8	1,562.6	191.4	312.4	574.6	222.7
1942	656	105	551	60.4	3,394.0	3,454.4	2,761.7	45.1	192.5	398.7	56.4
1943	278	28	250	15.9	1,505.7	1,521.6	1,175.3	44.0	27.1	273.3	2.1
1944	106	22	84	13.7	475.9	489.6	365.5	53.2	25.1	29.7	16.1
1945[3]	45	15	30	14.3	176.1	190.4	131.2	48.0	10.2	-	0.9
1939 September	37	10	27	5.4	154.6	160.0	137.1	11.4	5.1	-	6.4
October	23	4	19	3.2	102.4	105.5	74.9	3.2	27.4	-	-
November	29	19	10	14.7	44.5	59.2	22.9	35.6	0.7	-	-
December	33	16	17	7.0	98.6	105.6	31.4	49.2	22.0	2.2	0.9
1940 January	28	11	17	7.9	90.6	98.4	11.3	63.4	-	23.7	-
February	25	7	18	3.4	112.0	115.4	73.0	42.1	-	0.2	-
March	15	8	7	7.2	32.5	39.7	19.1	15.2	-	5.4	-
April	19	4	15	4.2	70.7	74.8	14.6	13.1	5.2	-	41.9
May	33	18	15	13.8	68.8	82.6	25.0	23.2	6.9	23.3	4.2
June	67	25	42	6.6	276.8	283.4	134.9	39.4	39.3	54.7	15.1
July	68	26	42	20.0	255.7	275.7	139.2	33.3	56.6	42.2	4.3
August	59	11	48	9.3	269.8	279.1	188.2	11.3	28.5	49.6	1.5
September	66	12	54	9.3	315.5	324.8	223.0	3.7	45.7	45.1	7.3
October	68	23	45	14.4	288.0	302.4	257.4	23.2	10.3	4.6	6.9
November	76	23	53	11.6	301.5	313.1	110.7	39.7	106.5	54.0	2.2
December	63	24	39	15.9	241.5	257.4	163.3	35.1	44.0	7.9	7.1
1941 January	45	12	33	7.4	202.2	209.6	105.1	16.8	40.0	47.2	0.5
February	80	25	55	18.8	297.5	316.3	171.7	13.2	67.9	51.9	11.7
March	98	38	60	18.9	348.0	366.8	174.3	16.1	104.0	70.3	2.1
April	79	20	59	13.4	349.1	362.5	188.6	23.3	25.1	122.5	3.0
May	100	34	66	7.9	380.0	387.8	234.0	23.2	15.0	115.6	-
June	63	11	52	8.1	260.5	268.6	203.8	9.6	13.6	39.3	2.4
July	36	17	19	8.5	87.0	95.5	71.9	8.6	5.8	6.1	3.1
August	31	12	19	7.8	89.2	97.0	60.7	1.4	15.6	19.0	0.2
September	61	21	40	18.6	196.6	215.2	156.6	14.9	7.7	34.2	1.8
October	32	6	26	7.0	144.8	151.8	106.4	15.8	1.5	27.4	0.6
November	29	10	19	5.5	85.8	91.4	55.2	1.1	15.7	19.4	-
December	179	114	65	60.8	240.5	301.3	34.4	47.4	0.5	21.7	197.3
1942 January	38	9	29	4.0	143.9	147.9	124.4	10.1	-	11.0	2.5
February	60	11	49	8.0	306.2	314.2	207.5	-	-	85.8	20.8
March	67	30	37	11.5	239.2	250.7	195.5	12.3	5.6	21.4	15.8
April	52	4	48	3.1	289.8	292.9	151.5	11.1	70.3	59.9	0.1
May	58	11	47	4.5	253.8	258.3	203.1	7.0	7.1	40.7	0.3
June	50	11	39	7.7	226.0	233.7	182.4	2.0	16.9	32.2	0.2
July	43	7	36	4.0	228.8	232.7	192.7	-	27.1	12.9	-
August	58	6	52	2.2	342.6	344.8	245.2	-	38.8	60.5	0.2
September	50	3	47	2.5	272.4	275.0	249.4	-	10.4	15.1	-
October	59	2	57	2.1	402.3	404.4	389.8	1.3	7.6	5.7	-
November	76	4	72	4.2	470.4	474.6	403.7	1.0	7.5	50.4	12.0
December	46	8	38	5.2	227.1	232.3	216.5	0.3	12.6	2.9	-

See footnotes on page 191.

Source: Admiralty

8.10 Merchant shipping under the British flag: Losses from enemy action[1]

continued

		Vessels lost					Cause of loss				
		Total	Under 1,600 gross tons	1,600 gross tons and over	Under 1,600 gross tons	1,600 gross tons and over	Total	Sub-marine	Mine	Surface craft	Aircraft	Cause unknown or other cause
		Number			*Thousand gross tons*							
1943	January	18	3	15	0.2	90.8	91.1	66.9	0.1	-	24.0	-
	February	29	2	27	2.3	164.7	166.9	148.0	14.1	4.9	-	-
	March	62	3	59	2.5	382.5	384.9	327.9	0.9	-	56.1	-
	April	33	2	31	0.8	193.4	194.3	185.1	7.4	1.7	-	-
	May	31	3	28	2.5	144.0	146.5	119.1	1.6	4.9	20.9	-
	June	12	4	8	2.8	42.2	45.0	38.7	0.1	-	6.1	-
	July	30	3	27	0.4	187.4	187.8	101.7	-	-	85.9	-
	August	14	2	12	-	62.8	62.9	47.0	-	-	14.0	2.0
	September	12	1	11	0.2	60.3	60.5	42.2	4.4	-	13.9	-
	October	11	-	11	-	57.6	57.6	35.8	10.9	-	10.9	-
	November	15	4	11	3.6	57.9	61.6	21.8	4.3	8.5	26.7	0.2
	December	10	1	9	0.6	55.0	55.6	40.9	-	-	14.7	-
1944	January	14	3	11	1.4	65.4	66.8	51.7	-	5.0	9.9	0.2
	February	11	-	11	-	63.2	63.2	53.8	-	2.1	7.3	-
	March	10	-	10	-	49.6	49.6	41.8	-	7.8	-	-
	April	3	-	3	-	21.4	21.4	13.5	-	-	7.9	-
	May	5	-	5	-	27.3	27.3	24.4	-	-	2.0	-
	June	16	6	10	3.7	50.9	54.6	24.9	15.4	1.8	1.8	10.7
	July	11	4	7	1.2	39.3	40.5	25.1	8.1	7.2	-	-
	August	17	2	15	1.2	79.3	80.6	68.2	7.2	-	-	5.2
	September	4	1	3	1.3	25.1	26.4	26.4	-	-	-	-
	October	1	1	-	1.2	-	1.2	-	1.2	-	-	-
	November	4	2	2	1.4	9.8	11.3	10.1	-	1.1	-	-
	December	10	3	7	2.3	44.4	46.7	25.5	21.3	-	-	-
1945	January	9	2	7	1.7	44.0	45.7	30.0	13.3	2.4	-	-
	February	13	6	7	5.5	38.1	43.6	26.8	12.0	3.9	-	0.9
	March	12	3	9	3.5	42.4	45.9	27.6	14.3	4.0	-	-
	April	10	4	6	3.6	48.7	52.3	43.9	8.4	-	-	-
	May	1	-	1	-	2.9	2.9	2.9	-	-	-	-

1. The difference between the figures for losses of vessels of 1,600 gross tons and over given in this table and those given in Tables 8.8 and 8.9 is explained in footnote 1 to Table 8.8.
2. 3 September 1939 to 2 September 1945.
3. To 2 September 1945. There were no sinkings of merchant ships anywhere between 8 May and 2 September 1945.

Source: Admiralty

8.11 Shipping movement at United Kingdom ports: Entrances and clearances in the foreign trade

Monthly averages or calendar months — *Thousand net tons*

	Entered with cargo		Cleared with cargo		Entered in ballast		Cleared in ballast	
	British vessels[1]	Foreign vessels	British vessels[1]	Foreign vessels	British vessels[1]	Foreign vessels	British vessels[1]	Foreign vessels
1939	2,903	1,926	2,474	1,851	876	978	1,262	1,070
1940	2,110	633	1,303	456	452	276	1,294	405
1941	1,467	542	668	185	92	23	984	386
1942	1,176	592	530	155	175	97	904	536
1943	1,201	1,064	489	147	195	90	955	995
1944	1,345	1,321	458	141	930	1,148	1,834	2,327
1945	1,527	885	855	260	1,206	1,018	1,904	1,627
1939 September	1,813	1,141	1,518	1,100	1,014	745	1,646	624
4th Quarter	2,224	833	1,676	1,267	697	876	1,081	480
1940 1st Quarter	2,381	684	1,600	878	610	577	1,432	336
2nd Quarter	2,512	756	1,728	570	877	446	1,710	501
3rd Quarter	1,984	593	1,055	199	208	47	1,181	445
4th Quarter	1,562	500	829	178	115	36	854	338
1941 1st Quarter	1,348	420	690	181	71	20	909	340
2nd Quarter	1,430	532	702	180	95	14	939	357
3rd Quarter	1,559	598	654	178	113	34	1,130	453
4th Quarter	1,533	618	627	203	88	26	957	393
1942 1st Quarter	1,234	467	575	160	82	54	894	416
2nd Quarter	1,207	552	579	177	126	93	879	485
3rd Quarter	1,240	711	541	147	119	93	750	609
4th Quarter	1,022	640	424	136	372	149	1,093	634
1943 1st Quarter	980	580	445	135	327	129	906	625
2nd Quarter	1,231	974	479	137	177	58	1,054	908
3rd Quarter	1,314	1,390	485	161	128	62	942	1,244
4th Quarter	1,280	1,313	548	157	148	109	918	1,202
1944 1st Quarter	1,234	1,291	518	167	163	220	927	1,370
2nd Quarter	1,369	1,523	368	115	533	887	1,464	2,249
3rd Quarter	1,312	1,333	409	118	1,794	2,158	2,752	3,405
4th Quarter	1,466	1,139	537	162	1,232	1,326	2,193	2,283
1945 1st Quarter	1,365	916	629	189	1,330	1,392	2,157	2,096
2nd Quarter	1,523	1,130	730	244	1,268	993	2,042	1,829
July	1,662	1,011	868	250	1,111	795	2,108	1,403
August	1,723	725	907	261	1,181	900	1,915	1,423

1. Including, from the end of 1943, the tonnage of certain foreign vessels transferred temporarily to the British flag.

Source: Board of Trade

8.12 Arrivals of shipping at United Kingdom ports

Monthly averages or calendar months | *Thousand net tons*

		Total	Foreign trade						Coasting trade	
				With cargo		In ballast				
			Total	West coast ports	East and South coast ports	West coast ports	East and South coast ports		With cargo	In ballast
1939		13,833	8,742	2,322	3,757	951	1,712		2,268	2,822
1940		8,126	4,186	1,904	1,152	620	510		1,776	2,163
1941		6,362	2,665	1,617	593	326	128		1,825	1,873
1942		6,296	2,446	1,584	328	475	59		1,934	1,916
1943		6,778	2,954	1,908	543	406	97		1,928	1,896
1944		9,297	5,405	2,373	736	857	1,438		1,787	2,105
1945		8,541	4,933	1,585	971	767	1,611		1,682	1,925
1939	September	11,030	5,904	1,767	1,814	737	1,586		1,988	3,138
	4th Quarter	9,513	5,648	1,751	1,809	813	1,275		1,755	2,109
1940	1st Quarter	8,684	5,062	1,716	1,759	691	896		1,639	1,984
	2nd Quarter	9,858	5,397	2,009	1,605	864	920		1,913	2,547
	3rd Quarter	7,558	3,482	2,082	741	532	128		1,904	2,172
	4th Quarter	6,403	2,804	1,811	503	395	95		1,649	1,951
1941	1st Quarter	5,887	2,526	1,448	547	351	180		1,618	1,744
	2nd Quarter	6,462	2,602	1,573	609	287	132		1,924	1,936
	3rd Quarter	6,721	2,773	1,716	629	315	113		1,953	1,995
	4th Quarter	6,379	2,758	1,729	588	351	89		1,804	1,816
1942	1st Quarter	5,886	2,254	1,524	337	328	65		1,814	1,818
	2nd Quarter	6,270	2,372	1,550	344	418	60		1,943	1,955
	3rd Quarter	6,464	2,526	1,756	344	380	46		2,008	1,931
	4th Quarter	6,563	2,630	1,507	285	773	64		1,972	1,961
1943	1st Quarter	6,033	2,400	1,384	302	631	82		1,841	1,792
	2nd Quarter	6,553	2,793	1,860	474	360	99		1,915	1,844
	3rd Quarter	7,281	3,288	2,187	723	291	88		1,987	2,005
	4th Quarter	7,244	3,335	2,201	671	343	118		1,968	1,941
1944	1st Quarter	7,642	3,605	2,276	660	509	159		1,949	2,088
	2nd Quarter	9,169	5,025	2,605	758	674	988		1,803	2,342
	3rd Quarter	11,113	7,323	2,464	734	1,072	3,053		1,734	2,056
	4th Quarter	9,265	5,667	2,146	794	1,174	1,553		1,663	1,935
1945	1st Quarter	8,824	5,340	1,799	673	1,069	1,799		1,610	1,875
	2nd Quarter	8,870	5,229	1,900	928	837	1,564		1,710	1,930
	July	8,813	4,911	1,794	1,056	540	1,522		1,790	2,112
	August	8,268	4,789	1,501	1,036	558	1,665		1,619	1,859

Source: Board of Trade

8.13 Imports into the United Kingdom[1]

Thousand tons

	Non-tanker imports under Departmental programmes					Tanker imports[3]	Imports from Eire
	Total	Ministry of Food	Ministry of Supply	Munitions[2]	Miscellaneous		
1941[4]	30,478	14,654	15,046	778		13,603	505
1942[4]	22,891	10,606	11,505	780		10,710	489
1943[4]	26,372	11,525	12,834	1,455	558	15,118	346
1944[4]	25,147	10,996	11,753	1,913	485	20,532	414
1939 September	2,831	1,063	1,678	90		625	. .
October	3,091	1,368	1,634	89		652	. .
November	3,529	1,576	1,867	86		933	. .
December	3,690	1,845	1,757	88		883	. .
1940 January	3,811	2,010	1,703	98		1,171	. .
February	3,598	1,817	1,680	100		923	. .
March	3,856	1,894	1,832	131		1,186	. .
April	4,207	1,949	2,132	127		1,181	. .
May	4,177	2,035	2,021	120		1,406	. .
June	4,054	2,019	1,940	95		1,320	. .
July	3,389	1,419	1,895	75		1,006	. .
August	3,936	1,694	2,161	81		956	. .
September	2,974	1,220	1,699	55		717	43
October	3,208	1,282	1,876	50		834	57
November	2,602	947	1,612	43		773	54
December	2,547	1,012	1,500	36		980	43
1941 January	2,413	1,094	1,277	42		541	36
February	2,152	915	1,202	35		842	26
March	2,386	1,123	1,227	37		953	30
April	2,360	1,038	1,219	103		877	32
May	2,767	1,331	1,369	68		1,186	29
June	2,776	1,557	1,150	69		1,208	30
July	2,648	1,544	1,041	63		1,227	40
August	2,712	1,360	1,278	74		1,416	36
September	2,816	1,279	1,464	73		1,711	40
October	2,930	1,239	1,632	59		1,465	48
November	2,140	954	1,100	86		1,282	73
December	2,680	1,320	1,279	81		1,259	81
1942 January	2,006	984	960	62		1,037	57
February	1,867	956	866	45		1,139	34
March	1,943	1,015	870	57		724	39
April	2,099	1,099	950	51		896	38
May	2,214	1,162	989	63		623	31
June	2,091	1,047	970	74		774	41
July	2,167	958	1,128	37	43	988	42
August	1,919	674	1,180	35	30	916	39
September	2,149	882	1,189	39	39	1,075	39
October	2,023	723	1,217	33	50	942	48
November	1,300	602	636	37	26	903	43
December	1,235	551	630	30	25	943	42

See footnotes on page 195.

Source: Ministry of Transport

8.13 Imports into the United Kingdom[1]

continued

Thousand tons

	Non-tanker imports under Departmental programmes					Tanker imports[3]	Imports from Eire
	Total	Ministry of Food	Ministry of Supply	Munitions[2]	Miscellaneous		
1943 January	1,177	531	598	29	20	857	30
February	1,267	633	551	61	22	895	26
March	2,015	874	1,017	88	37	996	31
April	2,378	1,173	1,020	135	49	1,071	26
May	2,064	1,022	874	121	48	1,281	26
June	2,723	1,173	1,312	188	49	1,467	33
July	2,748	1,235	1,292	170	51	1,966	26
August	2,368	889	1,267	160	52	1,519	24
September	2,661	1,058	1,358	185	60	1,760	28
October	2,569	1,170	1,209	128	62	1,293	35
November	2,186	859	1,179	90	57	1,141	31
December	2,327	969	1,212	101	45	1,138	29
1944 January	1,966	843	964	127	31	977	35
February	2,126	758	1,155	179	33	1,273	33
March	2,073	900	1,003	136	34	1,537	35
April	1,992	789	987	177	39	1,641	31
May	2,345	1,000	1,104	198	44	2,031	22
June	2,352	1,123	948	234	47	2,291	28
July	2,060	1,035	816	173	36	2,024	31
August	2,102	1,010	882	168	43	2,326	36
September	2,000	998	817	148	37	2,123	36
October	2,216	913	1,104	149	50	1,745	46
November	2,371	1,044	1,155	123	48	1,541	45
December	1,923	776	985	122	40	1,473	36
1945 January[5]	1,841	801	900	100	40	1,480	29
February[5]	1,830	805	877	101	48	1,097	27
March[5]	2,013	938	922	113	41	1,544	44
April[5]	1,926	874	911	103	38	1,598	37
May[5]	2,130	998	982	107	43	2,109	32
June[5]	2,658	1,357	1,171	75	55	2,166	32
July[5]	2,608	1,124	1,408	31	45	1,447	36
August[5]	2,438	979	1,377	22	61	1,088	37

1. The monthly and quarterly figures of imports given in this and in the next two tables represent the estimated weights of the commodities included in the Trade and Navigation Accounts for each month, and are unadjusted for small revisions subsequently made in the cumulative totals given in the Accounts for later months. From September 1939 to August 1940, imports from Eire are included under Departmental programmes.
2. Including imports of munitions on Canadian Government account from January 1943.
3. Petroleum products, molasses, unrefined whale oil and industrial alcohol. From January 1943 acetone is included. From January to May 1945, a further 760,000 tons of petroleum products were shipped direct to the Continent under this programme.
4. Adjusted for revisions.The figures for 1944 exclude approximately 36,000 tons of food and 23,000 tons of munitions destined for Europe and 104,000 tons of timber as a replacement of supplies delivered to the United States Army, since these amounts were not provided for in the United Kingdom import programme.
5. The figures of actual imports in 1945 exclude about 179,000 tons of cereals and oilseeds which have been shipped direct to the Continent, a corresponding amount having been transferred to United Kingdom stocks form S.H.A.E.F. emergency reserves held in this country. On the other hand, about 58,000 tons of foodstuffs intended for relief stockpile and 22,000 tons of softwood imported in repayment of a loan to the United States Army are included.

Source: Ministry of Transport

8.14 Imports of food under the Ministry of Food programme[1]

Non-tanker imports (excluding imports from Eire)

Thousand tons

		Total	Grain and pulses	Animal feeding-stuffs	Meat	Oilseeds, oils and fats[2]	Sugar	Dairy produce vegetables	Fruit	Beverages and other foods
1941		14,654	7,315	325	1,433	1,948	1,658	665	462	847
1942		10,606	4,162	74	1,583	1,905	773	789	458	862
1943		11,525	4,299	12	1,658	2,154	1,458	655	327	963
1944		10,996	3,843	98	1,768	1,975	1,156	664	646	846
1940	4th Quarter	3,241	1,684	133	305	336	339	107	125	215
1941	1st Quarter	3,132	1,560	163	253	403	302	159	69	226
	2nd Quarter	3,927	2,349	113	313	447	286	149	76	193
	3rd Quarter	4,183	2,089	35	430	577	559	157	135	203
	4th Quarter	3,513	1,342	15	448	531	560	207	185	227
1942	1st Quarter	2,955	906	47	349	571	318	250	196	318
	2nd Quarter	3,308	1,528	11	466	598	223	160	86	237
	3rd Quarter	2,514	1,004	13	446	493	134	185	77	162
	4th Quarter	1,876	730	3	323	248	129	194	102	145
1943	1st Quarter	2,038	730	-	302	371	210	161	69	195
	2nd Quarter	3,368	1,552	-	404	525	373	201	71	241
	3rd Quarter	3,182	1,373	3	440	511	397	146	69	242
	4th Quarter	2,998	643	8	519	750	523	153	115	286
1944	1st Quarter	2,501	776	9	429	557	161	149	217	202
	2nd Quarter	2,912	1,055	3	534	444	338	141	157	238
	3rd Quarter	3,043	1,082	34	466	566	413	157	130	196
	4th Quarter	2,733	991	52	378	412	323	220	151	207
1945	1st Quarter[3]	2,544	840	44	355	437	189	149	322	208
	2nd Quarter[3]	3,229	1,500	64	291	360	491	129	177	217
	July and August[3]	2,103	1,156	30	162	175	251	118	67	145

Source: Ministry of Transport

1. See footnote 1 to Table 8.13.
2. Excluding unrefined whale oil.
3. See footnote 5 to Table 8.13.

8.15 Imports of food under the Ministry of Supply programme[1]

Non-tanker imports (excluding imports from Eire)

Thousand tons

		Total	Iron ore	Iron and steel and allied materials	Non-ferrous ores and metals	Textiles	Wood and timber	Paper and paper-making materials	Materials for sulphuric acid and fertilizers	Mis-cellaneous materials
1941		15,046	2,298	5,176	1,463	785	1,976	588	1,683	1,077
1942		11,505	1,923	3,092	1,400	1,112	1,365	657	984	972
1943		12,834	1,895	3,358	1,671	891	1,932	573	1,557	956
1944		11,753	2,167	2,215	1,479	964	2,068	614	1,404	842
1940	4th Quarter	4,988	665	1,747	426	211	1,123	223	289	302
1941	1st Quarter	3,706	385	1,277	378	200	714	157	321	274
	2nd Quarter	3,738	698	1,383	309	136	416	133	375	288
	3rd Quarter	3,783	627	1,321	366	147	337	161	523	302
	4th Quarter	4,011	602	1,253	406	306	478	142	519	305
1942	1st Quarter	2,696	523	675	392	312	173	129	224	270
	2nd Quarter	2,909	609	641	349	349	264	193	244	260
	3rd Quarter	3,497	518	1,144	327	317	463	217	272	239
	4th Quarter	2,483	313	649	341	147	467	122	237	207
1943	1st Quarter	2,166	361	479	323	112	315	73	344	158
	2nd Quarter	3,206	525	990	476	178	325	116	366	228
	3rd Quarter	3,917	487	1,070	472	306	624	255	421	282
	4th Quarter	3,600	520	843	405	295	677	145	428	289
1944	1st Quarter	3,122	586	743	437	269	437	101	331	218
	2nd Quarter	3,039	626	444	430	231	510	158	433	207
	3rd Quarter	2,515	389	459	286	197	469	184	323	209
	4th Quarter	3,244	566	590	341	273	765	177	324	208
1945	1st Quarter	2,699	733	289	289	239	513	158	307	171
	2nd Quarter	3,064	1,051	200	234	270	450	261	421	178
	July and August	2,785	814	138	190	185	717	342	256	143

See footnote 1 to Table 8.13.

Source: Ministry of Transport

8.16 Repair and availability of railway rolling stock

Great Britain — End of year — *Thousands*

	1937	1938	1939	1940	1941	1942	1943	1944	1945
Locomotives									
Operating stock	19.8	19.7	19.5	19.5	19.5	19.6	20.6	20.3	20.3
Available for traffic[1]	16.3	16.2	..	..	..	16.1	16.8	16.7	16.4
Under or awaiting repair or otherwise not available[1]	3.4	3.5	..	..	..	3.5	3.8	3.6	3.9
Passenger carrying vehicles[2]									
Operating stock	43.7	43.5	43.1	42.3	42.0	41.7	41.1	40.6	40.4
Available	41.0	40.8	40.6	39.6	39.6	39.2	38.4	37.1	35.5
Under or awaiting repair	2.7	2.7	2.5	2.7	2.5	2.5	2.7	3.5	4.9
Trucks and wagons									
Operating stock	1,294.5	..	1,269.2	1,276.8	1,276.0	1,280.2	1,292.4	1,298.3	1,289.0
Available[3]	..	..	..	1,204.7	1,199.2	1,199.7	1,208.2	1,182.9	1,138.7
Under or awaiting repair[3]	..	..	..	44.6	48.8	52.9	57.3	89.0	124.3
Railway owned:									
Operating stock	656.8	663.6	664.1	670.3	671.6	677.6	683.4	686.6	677.8
Available	636.7	644.8	645.3	647.9	650.3	650.3	654.3	637.1	609.3
Under or awaiting repair	20.1	18.8	18.7	22.5	21.3	27.2	29.1	49.5	68.5
Privately owned (requisitioned):									
Operating stock	-	-	583.8	578.9	576.4	575.1	582.1	585.3	585.2
Available	-	-	..	556.8	548.9	549.4	553.9	545.8	529.4
Under or awaiting repair	-	-	..	22.1	27.4	25.7	28.2	39.5	55.7
Privately owned (not requisitioned):									
Operating stock	637.7[4]	..	21.3	27.5	28.0	27.6	26.9	26.4	26.0

1. The figures for 1937 and 1938 are not completely comparable with those for the period 1942 to 1945 owing to differences in the method of recording locomotives undergoing boiler washing, etc.
2. Including rail motors.
3. Excluding privately owned (not requisitioned).
4. July 1937.

Source: Ministry of Transport

8.17 Passenger and goods traffic

Great Britain

	Unit	1937	1938	1939	1940	1941	1942	1943	1944	1945
Passenger traffic										
Number of passenger journeys:										
Total	Millions	1,295.4	1,237.2	1,225.5	966.6	1,023.3	1,218.2	1,334.6	1,345.3	1,371.8
Full fare	"		77.8	77.2	64.9	62.6	81.4	103.8	110.7	116.0
Monthly return, excursion, weekend, etc.	"	659.1	474.5	463.2	284.3	297.4	359.1	372.8	370.5	405.9
Service or Government journeys, etc.	"		53.6	53.4	77.7	116.1	163.7	227.4	250.5	256.9
Workmen	"	247.0	244.2	251.2	264.2	302.2	340.1	332.6	307.4	276.9
Season tickets (on basis of 600 journeys per annum)	"	389.3	387.1	380.5	275.5	245.0	273.9	298.0	306.2	316.1
Average receipt:										
Per passenger journey:										
Total	Pence	..	11.38	12.55	16.37	21.05	22.99	24.65	25.83	27.63
Ordinary	"	17.04	18.47	21.29	30.47	39.20	41.15	42.20	43.16	44.70
Workmen	"	3.55	3.68	3.80	4.54	5.08	5.13	5.02	4.99	4.99
Season	"	5.02	5.19	5.51	6.00	6.17	6.07	6.15	6.38	6.39
Per train mile	Shillings	5.25	5.17	5.75	7.83	10.25	12.83	14.75	15.83	16.00
Estimated passenger miles[1]:										
Total	Millions	..	18,993[3]	..	..	..	..	32,273	32,052	35,248
Ordinary[2]	"	..	12,550[3]	..	..	..	..	25,613	25,531	28,827
Workmen	"	..	1,737[3]	..	..	..	..	3,015	2,791	2,548
Season tickets	"	..	4,706[3]	..	..	..	..	3,645	3,730	3,873
Goods traffic										
Goods, mineral and livestock traffic[4]:	Million									
Total	tons	298.7	265.7	288.3	294.4	286.7	295.1	300.8	292.6	266.4
Merchandise and livestock	"	51.8	45.6	52.0	58.9	61.8	71.0	82.0	87.4	73.5
Minerals	"	58.7	47.4	51.3	58.2	61.6	61.3	62.1	54.5	49.8
Coal, coke and patent fuel	"	188.1	172.8	185.0	177.3	163.3	162.8	156.7	150.7	143.1
Estimated net ton miles[1]										
Total	Millions	17,935	16,266	..	..	..	23,822	24,358	24,444	22,023
Merchandise and livestock	"	5,442	4,980	..	..	..	8,591	9,659	10,275	8,850
Minerals	"	3,789	3,182	..	..	..	5,280	5,356	4,902	4,303
Coal, coke and patent fuel	"	8,703	8,104	..	..	..	9,951	9,343	9,267	8,870

1. Main line companies.
2. All passenger travel (including Service travel) except workmen's and season tickets.
3. September 1938 to August 1939 inclusive.
4. Excluding freehauled traffic.

Source: Ministry of Transport

8.18 Operating statistics of railways

Great Britain

	Unit	1937	1938	1939	1940	1941	1942	1943	1944	1945
Train-miles										
Loaded:										
Coaching	Millions	272.62[1]	277.01[2]	245.96	190.45	191.78	193.16	194.05	191.08	204.79
Freight	"	125.03[1]	119.52[2]	123.70	133.23	130.86	135.10	135.50	133.47	123.05
Empty	"	24.68[1]	23.99[2]	..	28.42	27.97	28.29	28.45	30.51	27.80
Wagon-miles										
Loaded: Total	"	3,252	3,003	..	..	3,838	3,983	4,052	4,064	3,683
Merchandise and livestock	"	..	..	..	..	..	2,402	2,537	2,604	2,331
Minerals	"	..	..	..	..	..	532	534	489	428
Coal, coke and patent fuel	"	..	..	..	..	..	1,048	981	971	925
Empty	"	1,591	1,492	..	..	1,446	1,412	1,392	1,427	1,257
Average length of haul per ton[3,4]										
Total	Miles	57.86	59.00	..	..	..	75.90	76.16	78.64	77.73
Merchandise and livestock	"	103.21	107.49	..	..	..	115.45	112.45	112.16	114.92
Minerals	"	62.37	63.49	..	..	..	79.95	79.93	83.44	80.13
Coal, coke and patent fuel	"	44.29	45.21	..	..	..	57.39	55.97	57.75	58.11

1. Fifty-two weeks ended 25 December.
2. Fifty-two weeks ended 24 December.
3. Main line companies.
4. Including freehauled traffic.

Source: Ministry of Transport

8.19 Traffic receipts

Main line railway companies and London Passenger Transport Board (including joint lines)[1]

Great Britain — *£ thousand*

	1939	1940	1941	1942	1943	1944	1945
Total traffic receipts	204,227	242,987	289,517	339,147	375,844	388,985	378,410
Passenger receipts: Total	102,081	103,842	131,286	162,897	185,378	193,212	209,480
Passengers	85,929	87,819	113,640	143,648	164,325	169,662	187,142
Parcels, etc[2]	16,152	16,023	17,646	19,249	21,053	23,550	22,338
Goods receipts: Total	102,146	139,145	158,231	176,250	190,466	195,773	168,930
Merchandise	48,265	67,610	78,830	96,399	114,052	123,541	101,030
Minerals	13,750	18,557	23,423	24,067	24,057	20,353	18,469
Coal, coke and patent fuel	38,810	51,226	54,633	54,471	51,040	50,710	48,113
Livestock	1,321	1,752	1,345	1,313	1,317	1,169	1,318

1. Including road services of the London Passenger Transport Board.
2. Including parcels and other merchandise by passenger train, mails and parcels post.

Source: Ministry of Transport

8.20 Vehicles with licences current[1]

Great Britain — *Thousands*

	1937	1938	1939	1940	1941	1942	1943	1944	1945
Total[2]	2,938	3,094	3,157	2,332	2,484	1,847	1,544	1,599	2,559
Private cars, etc.	1,798	1,944	2,034	1,423	1,503	858	718	755	1,487
Cycles and tricycles	488	462	418	278	317	306	124	124	309
Vehicles for public conveyance:									
Total	95	97	98	88	92	92	93	97	105
Buses, coaches, taxis, private hire cars, etc.	84	85	90	81	85	85	87	90	99
Trolleybuses	2	3							
Tramcars	10	9	8	7	7	6	6	6	6
Goods vehicles:									
Total	481	497	492	447	453	455	452	452	477
General Haulage:									
Petrol, heavy oil, etc.	459	473	466	418	423	422	415	411	434
Other	4	5	6	7	7	7	7	8	8
Agricultural vans and lorries	12	13	14	18	19	22	24	26	28
Showmen's special vehicles[3]	3	3	3	1	1	1	2	3	3
Local authorities vehicles (watering and cleansing)	1	1	1	1	1	1	1	1	1
Tractors for general haulage	2	2	2	2	2	2	3	3	3
Agricultural tractors and engines	26	29	32	50	66	90	106	118	126
Vehicles exempt from duty[2]:									
Total	50	64	84	47	55	46	51	55	56
Owned by Government authorities	34	47	..	..	..	..	..	..	..
Other	17	18	..	..	..	..	..	..	..

1. For the years 1937 and 1937, licences current at any time during the September quarter. Other years relate to 31 August.
2. From 1940 excluding vehicles exempt from duty operating under defence permits.
3. Including showmen's tractors.

Source: Ministry of Transport

8.21 New vehicle registrations[1]

Great Britain | *Number*

	1937	1938	1939	1940	1941	1942	1943	1944	1945
Total	486,269	419,154	381,627	99,234	61,657	79,512	58,381	58,248	77,880
Cars, etc:									
Total	..	..	..	..	..	4,664	1,108	1,063	9,238
Private cars, etc.	320,239	272,192	231,042	31,396	3,083	3,164	267	416	7,708
Other cars (exempt from licence duty)[2]	..	..	..	..	..	1,500	841	647	1,530
Cycles and tricycles[3]:									
Total	..	..	..	..	..	7,399	2,888	3,115	13,372
Privately owned	57,060	45,041	47,210	22,709	8,980	5,157	1,641	1,676	12,929
Other (exempt from licence duty)[2]	..	..	..	..	..	2,242	1,247	1,439	443
Vehicles for public conveyance:									
Total	8,377	8,990	6,988	2,492	596	1,332	2,075	2,011	2,170
Buses, coaches, taxis, etc.	7,827	8,264	..	..	..	1,216	2,007	1,919	2,055
Trolleybuses	550	726	..	..	..	64	57	84	115
Vehicles exempt from licence duty[2]	-	-	..	..	..	52	11	8	-
Goods vehicles:									
Total	..	..	..	..	..	30,858	26,379	30,747	35,260
General haulage:									
Petrol, heavy oil, etc.	77,555	67,3033	60,258	16,200	11,595	22,153	16,251	18,502	27,586
Other	910	918	..	..	..	-	323	342	372
Agricultural vans and lorries	1,115	1,022	1,060	287	15	704	775	852	1,330
Showmen's special vehicles[4]	3	3	8	-	-	-	-	3	4
Local authorities vehicles (watering and cleansing)	106	107	90	21	12	28	31	48	26
Vehicles exempt from licence duty[2]	..	..	..	..	..	7,716	8,828	10,842	5,812
Tractors for general haulage	231	243	201	191	257	257	171	158	130
Agricultural tractors and engines, etc.:									
Total	..	..	..	..	..	30,268	23,546	19,856	16,846
Privately owned	7,261	7,343	12,059	20,005	23,959	27,101	20,643	17,587	15,537
Exempt from licence duty[2]	..	..	..	..	..	3,167	2,903	2,269	1,309
Miscellaneous vehicles exempt from licence duty:									
Total	13,412	15,962	22,711	5,933	13,160	4,991	2,385	1,456	994
Owned by government authorities[2]	12,154	14,542	20,893	2,929	9,476	-	-	-	-
Other	1,258	1,420	..	..	..	4,991	2,385	1,456	994

1. Before 1939 figures are for years ended 30 September.
2. Before 1942 details of exempt vehicles by types are not available. From 1942 Government owned vehicles are included with other exempt vehicles under the appropriate headings. From 1940 vehicles operating under defence permits are excluded.
3. Including pedestrian controlled delivery vans.
4. Including showmen's tractors.

Source: Ministry of Transport

8.22 Canal traffic originating[1]

Thousand tons

	1937	1938	1939[2]	1940	1941	1942	1943	1944	1945
Total	14,358	12,952	6,307	11,005	11,241	11,043	11,315	11,047	10,060
Coal, coke and patent fuel	6,803	6,158	3,196	5,234	5,272	5,450	5,411	5,381	4,983
Liquids in bulk	1,259	1,329	576	1,254	1,353	1,563	1,616	1,814	1,491
Other merchandise	6,297	5,465	2,536	4,517	4,617	4,031	4,288	3,852	3,585

1. Great Britain.
2. Total for six months January-June.

Source: Ministry of Transport

8.23 Coasting trade

(i) Cargoes of coal: Analysis by areas of discharge

	Total[1]	Thames ports	East coast		West coast		South coast	Northern Ireland	Other areas
			England	Scotland	England	Scotland			
Cargoes delivered (Thousand tons)									
Years ended December 15:									
1942	20,936	11,760	284	444	1,807	85	2,866	2,517	1,150
1943	20,170	11,832	271	414	1,544	93	2,422	2,556	1,027
1944	19,087	11,568	327	407	1,100	108	2,129	2,473	974
1945	18,159	11,385	278	376	718	77	1,957	2,506	857
Tonnage employed (Thousand deadweight tons)									
At December 15:									
1941	795.7	502.2	8.0	15.3	57.9	3.5	144.0	44.2	20.6
1942	832.9	537.7	8.7	10.5	96.0	3.0	108.1	45.0	23.9
1943	779.8	504.7	12.8	9.8	70.1	4.4	110.0	53.0	15.0
1944	628.0	415.6	4.8	7.0	53.0	2.5	90.8	42.1	12.2
1945	553.0	388.3	9.2	7.2	24.0	1.8	74.4	35.1	13.0

1. The total includes a small quantity of coal carried in liners.

Source: Ministry of Transport

(ii) Cargoes other than coal: Analysis by areas of discharge

	Total	East coast				West coast			South coast	Northern Ireland
		London to Dover	Humber	Berwick	Scotland	Silloth to North of Milford Haven	Milford Haven to Land's End	Scotland		
Cargoes delivered (Thousand tons)										
Years ended December 15:										
1942	8,923[1]	1,068	531	761	1,004	1,683	1,294	1,111	205	1,267
1943	9,025	1,204	830	725	993	1,491	1,276	1,102	312	1,092
1944	7,599[1]	1,170	537	541	673	1,369	1,179	959	205	966
1945	6,136	953	447	402	578	1,225	655	793	160	924
Tonnage employed (Thousand deadweight tons)										
At December 15:										
1941	384.0	82.1	22.8	30.2	45.2	58.1	50.2	38.0	10.9	46.5
1942	336.6	60.7	43.5	19.4	44.5	44.3	31.7	34.4	10.2	47.9
1943	402.5	57.0	33.0	42.7	40.1	71.3	56.1	42.6	7.5	52.2
1944	290.6	58.1	15.9	9.8	37.0	61.0	32.2	29.9	4.1	42.6
1945	250.1	41.0	18.1	16.6	41.3	35.2	19.5	30.8	7.5	40.1

1. In addition the following cargoes were delivered but cannot be analysed by area of discharge: January 1942, 30.7 thousand tons; January 1944, 11.5 thousand tons.

Source: Ministry of Transport

9 EXTERNAL TRADE

The war disrupted trade and trading patterns: Britain was fighting a war against former trading partners (for example, in 1938 Germany provided 3.3 per cent of British imports and took 4.4 per cent of British exports) other trading partners would come under enemy control either directly (such as France, the Netherlands and Malaya) or indirectly (as was the case with Sweden), and enemy action would interfere with the routes to other trading areas (such as North America and Asia) and destroy shipping capacity (tables 9.6-9.7). The war also brought inflation with export prices rising by 85 per cent between 1938 and 1945 (almost half of the increase occurring between 1939 and 1941) and import prices rising by 98 per cent (with more than half the increase coming in the first two years of the war) (Feinstein 1972:T139). The net result was that between 1938 and 1942 the volume of imports fell by 30 per cent whilst the cost of importing this reduced volume had risen by 16 per cent (and in 1944 Britain was paying 51 per cent more than in 1938 for a volume of imports that was 20 per cent less); exports, meanwhile, were a mere 29 per cent of their 1938 volume in 1943 although the fall in value terms was less steep at 50 per cent (**table 9.3**).

In 1938 Britain ran a trade deficit in food, drink and tobacco and the war did not aid the situation: in value terms imports of food, drink and tobacco increased by 22 per cent between 1938 and 1943 whilst exports fell by 47 per cent; and the cumulative deficit in these goods for the war years amounted to £2.9 billion (**tables 9.4-9.5**). A similar situation prevailed with raw materials: between 1938 and 1943 the value of raw material imports rose by 21 per cent whilst the value of exports, which were dominated by coal, fell by 84 per cent; and the accumulated wartime deficit was £1.7 billion (**tables 9.4-9.5**). However, possibly

9.1 Volume of imports and exports

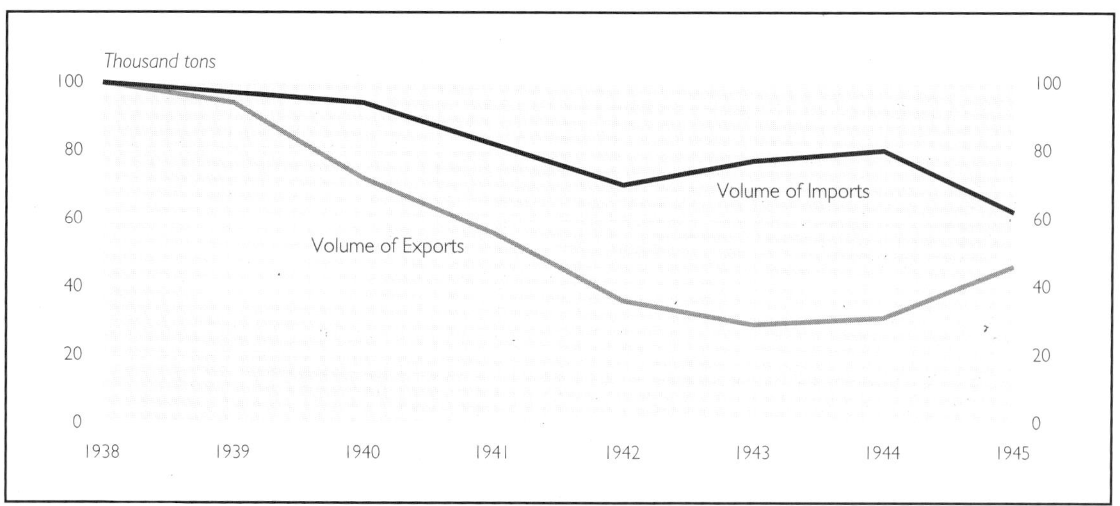

9.2 Export and import prices

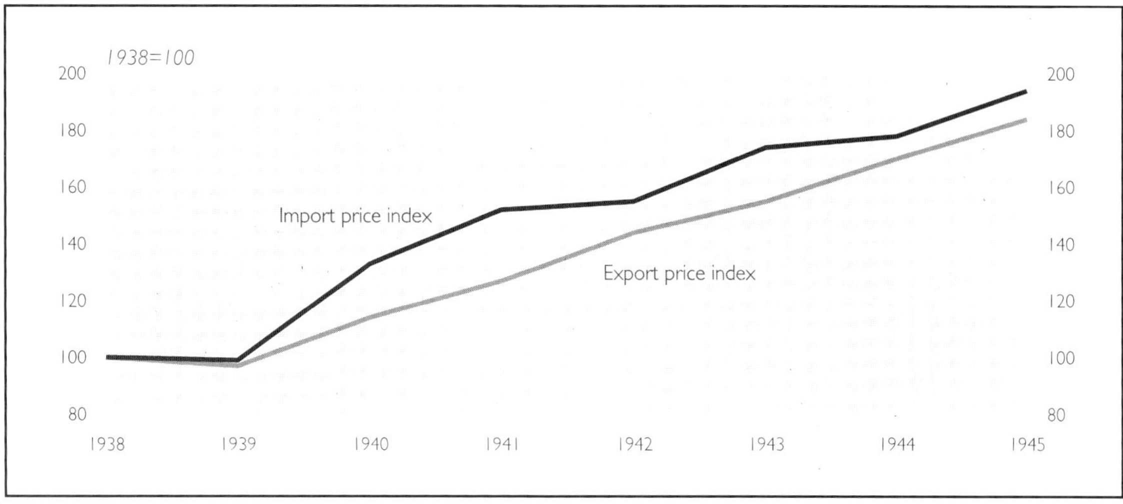

the most worrying aspect of the war from the trade position was the deterioration of the pre-war surplus in manufactures (which stood at £150 million in 1938) to a wartime deficit (peaking at £245 million in 1944 and amounting to a cumulative wartime deficit of £640 million). Although manufacturing exports fell by 45 per cent between 1938 and 1943 the main culprit in this deterioration was the rise in imports by 104 per cent in the same period (this included a rise in the value of iron and steel manufactures of over 300 per cent, a rise in oils and related manufactures of 255 per cent, and of non-ferrous metals by 163 per cent) (**tables 9.4-9.5**). The silver lining to this particular cloud was that by 1945 a small surplus in manufactures had again emerged.

Given the conditions of the war the trade deficits that were encountered were not unexpected, especially after the state abandoned its ill-conceived export drive of early 1940 (Sayers 1956: 257). This had been launched to help finance the war, and in particular to bolster hard currency reserves, but merely served to increase the pressure on the nation's scarce resources. Once a decision was taken that it was not possible to finance the war through maintaining high levels of exports resources were diverted from the export sector to the domestic war effort (in the case of manpower, for example, the 9.5 per cent of the pre-war labour engaged on exports had shrunk to 2 per cent by 1945 (Pollard 1983: 217). Thus, the squeeze on exports was not simply the result of enemy action but also reflected domestic political and economic

9.5 Value of retained imports

Analysis by classes and groups

£ million

	1938	1939	1940	1941	1942	1943	1944	1945
I. Food, drink and tobacco								
Total	417.8	387.5	412.3	419.4	433.7	511.0	510.4	464.1
A. Grain and flour	72.9	54.5	93.3	89.6	53.5	66.0	64.3	76.7
B. Feeding-stuffs for animals	11.4	8.9	8.3	2.5	0.8	0.2	1.5	2.9
C. Animals, living, for food	9.2	11.0	10.9	7.1	13.1	11.4	11.6	12.6
D. Meat	90.1	92.8	96.8	118.7	148.8	166.8	161.7	107.8
E. Dairy produce	79.3	75.3	62.2	66.3	84.4	85.3	91.1	75.7
F. Fresh fruit and vegetables	36.3	33.8	26.8	4.4	5.4	2.3	8.2	15.9
G. Beverages and cocoa preparations	40.4	34.9	40.3	41.1	36.3	49.9	49.3	48.7
H. Other food	55.7	63.6	64.9	71.8	70.9	87.5	90.1	72.0
I. Tobacco	22.5	12.7	8.7	17.9	20.5	41.6	32.6	51.8
II. Raw materials and articles mainly unmanufactured								
Total	218.0	216.5	326.3	224.7	236.1	262.7	278.3	279.9
B. Other non-metalliferous mining and quarry products	4.6	5.0	7.3	6.5	7.0	10.4	10.0	7.8
C. Iron ore and scrap	11.2	9.7	16.6	14.2	7.7	7.9	9.3	15.4
D. Non-ferrous metalliferous ores and scrap	15.4	17.3	24.4	22.4	24.6	26.5	20.7	19.5
E. Wood and timber	42.6	36.9	37.7	24.8	20.4	32.6	35.9	45.7
F. Raw cotton and cotton waste	28.3	33.0	49.8	35.8	52.6	53.7	42.0	46.5
G. Wool, raw and waste, and woollen rags	30.1	31.8	62.5	21.9	27.4	19.0	35.7	29.2
H. Silk, raw and waste, and artificial silk waste	2.0	2.5	4.4	1.4	0.7	1.0	1.9	2.1
I. Other textile materials	9.3	11.1	18.2	8.4	10.0	10.8	10.7	11.2
J. Seeds and nuts for oil, oils, fats, resins and gums	30.0	30.4	44.4	39.5	39.8	55.3	53.4	46.1
K. Hides and skins, undressed	8.7	7.7	12.1	8.3	12.4	10.4	11.5	14.2
L. Paper-making materials	17.7	16.4	14.4	8.6	11.6	10.2	10.0	17.1
M. Rubber	8.8	5.9	22.6	21.0	9.1	13.1	24.9	10.8
Other Class II	9.3	8.8	11.9	11.9	12.8	11.8	12.3	14.3
III. Articles wholly or mainly manufactured								
Total	215.2	228.9	381.5	480.4	308.9	438.8	474.7	289.7
B. Pottery, glass, abrasives, etc	7.1	4.9	1.3	1.3	2.6	2.0	0.7	0.7
C. Iron and steel and manufactures thereof	14.6	18.5	48.1	69.0	47.0	58.9	32.9	6.2
D. Non-ferrous metals and manufactures thereof	31.8	36.0	58.8	56.6	60.3	83.7	65.7	16.6
E. Cutlery, hardware, implements and instruments	6.3	5.1	3.8	5.2	9.2	13.9	10.4	5.8
F. Electrical goods and apparatus	3.0	2.7	4.1	2.6	2.7	8.2	23.9	18.7
G. Machinery	20.3	22.4	38.5	49.6	32.3	40.6	39.4	18.3
H. Manufactures of wood and timber	6.1	4.9	3.9	2.5	2.4	6.5	8.5	13.7
I. Cotton yarns and manufactures	2.9	2.2	2.8	1.6	1.3	2.4	2.5	1.8
L. Manufactures of other textile materials	4.5	6.9	16.1	4.2	5.7	4.4	10.2	7.4
M. Apparel	7.6	5.3	1.1	0.5	0.6	0.7	5.6	4.8
O. Chemicals, drugs, dyes and colours	13.1	15.4	16.9	15.4	18.8	22.0	23.7	18.6
P. Oils, fats and resins, manufactured	43.0	44.7	70.7	93.0	100.3	152.5	220.4	142.8
Q. Leather and manufactures thereof	5.5	7.2	8.4	3.6	4.1	6.2	4.5	4.4
R. Paper, cardboard, etc	14.8	15.6	16.3	5.0	4.6	4.6	6.4	11.5
S. Vehicles (including locomotives, ships and aircraft)	4.7	8.9	46.3	106.2	5.7	16.3	7.9	5.4
Other Class III	29.9	28.2	44.4	64.1	11.3	15.9	12.0	13.0
IV. Animals not for food	2.6	2.5	2.2	0.8	2.9	2.2	2.7	3.9
V. Parcel post	4.3	4.0	3.8	7.1	10.7	13.1	27.6	15.1

Source: Board of Trade

9.6 Value of exports of the produce and manufactures of the United Kingdom

Analysis by classes and groups

£ million

	1938	1939	1940	1941	1942	1943	1944	1945
I. Food, drink and tobacco								
Total	35.9	35.7	33.4	27.8	18.4	19.0	22.9	55.7
A. Grain and flour	1.7	1.2	0.6	0.3	0.1	0.2	1.3	2.0
D. Meat	1.2	1.2	0.7	0.3	0.1	0.2	0.2	0.4
E. Dairy produce	1.1	1.1	0.9	0.2	0.1	0.3	0.6	2.9
G. Beverages and cocoa preparations	13.8	15.9	19.6	17.0	11.5	11.0	10.7	15.2
I. Tobacco	4.9	5.0	4.8	5.6	4.3	5.2	5.1	12.1
Other food	13.2	11.3	6.8	4.4	2.3	2.1	5.0	23.1
II. Raw materials and articles mainly unmanufactured								
Total	57.0	54.5	36.2	15.7	10.2	9.4	8.1	15.1
A. Coal	37.4	38.3	25.3	8.0	6.0	6.4	5.0	6.6
B. Other non-metalliferous mining and quarry products	1.1	1.2	0.8	0.6	0.5	0.3	0.3	0.7
D. Non-ferrous metalliferous ores and scrap	2.3	1.6	0.2	0.1	-	-	-	-
G. Wool, raw and waste, and woollen rags	6.3	4.7	3.3	2.8	0.9	0.2	0.2	1.7
J. Seeds and nuts for oil, oils, fats, resins and gums	2.9	2.0	2.0	0.6	0.2	0.1	0.1	1.3
K. Hides and skins, undressed	1.1	1.0	1.2	1.2	1.1	1.0	1.1	1.0
L. Paper-making materials	1.2	0.9	0.3	0.2	-	-	-	0.2
Other Class II	4.7	4.8	3.1	2.2	1.5	1.4	1.4	3.6
III. Articles wholly or mainly manufactured								
Total	365.2	338.1	334.1	316.1	236.6	201.4	229.9	306.8
A. Coke and manufactured fuel	3.3	4.0	2.2	1.2	0.8	1.1	0.4	0.5
B. Pottery, glass, abrasives, etc	9.6	9.4	11.5	13.5	11.4	9.0	9.5	13.0
C. Iron and steel and manufactures thereof	41.7	32.9	31.2	19.0	9.9	6.1	8.6	20.9
D. Non-ferrous metals and manufactures thereof	12.3	12.7	12.4	7.6	7.0	6.7	4.7	12.1
E. Cutlery, hardware, implements and instruments	9.0	8.7	9.4	9.1	7.9	6.7	7.7	10.0
F. Electrical goods and apparatus	13.6	11.3	13.2	11.4	11.2	11.1	12.6	13.8
G. Machinery	57.2	47.0	36.2	30.9	29.9	27.9	40.9	46.2
H. Manufactures of wood and timber	1.2	1.1	0.8	0.5	0.4	0.2	0.2	0.5
I. Cotton yarns and manufactures	49.7	49.1	49.3	44.7	40.1	34.2	37.1	42.7
J. Woollen and worsted yarns and manufactures	26.8	26.7	28.7	29.8	25.1	18.5	15.3	21.6
K. Silk and artificial silk yarns and manufactures	5.5	5.9	8.7	11.8	16.4	12.7	16.4	17.3
L. Manufactures of other textile materials	10.7	11.1	12.4	9.6	8.9	6.3	5.2	7.1
M. Apparel	8.5	8.3	7.5	8.1	7.7	3.4	4.7	11.2
N. Footwear	2.0	1.9	1.8	5.4	1.4	0.7	0.7	1.2
O. Chemicals, drugs, dyes and colours	22.2	22.7	27.6	25.0	24.0	27.9	29.4	38.2
P. Oils, fats and resins, manufactured	5.4	4.7	3.0	2.2	0.7	0.7	1.3	3.0
Q. Leather and manufactures thereof	3.9	4.1	3.7	2.8	3.0	1.7	1.2	1.8
R. Paper, cardboard, etc	6.9	6.7	9.8	7.2	5.0	4.1	4.1	5.2
S. Vehicles (including locomotives, ships and aircraft)	45.1	40.0	31.5	35.7	9.2	8.8	13.4	20.2
T. Rubber manufactures	1.6	1.5	1.9	1.3	0.8	0.3	0.3	0.7
U. Miscellaneous articles wholly or mainly manufactured	28.8	28.4	31.4	39.4	15.9	13.4	16.3	19.8
IV. Animals not for food	0.7	0.7	0.8	0.3	0.2	0.1	0.3	0.7
V. Parcel post	12.0	10.5	6.7	5.5	5.8	3.6	5.2	21.0

Source: Board of Trade

9.7 Value of imports

Analysis by source

£ million

	1938	1939	1940	1941	1942	1943	1944	1945
Total	919.5	885.5	1,152.1	1,145.1	996.7	1,233.9	1,309.3	1,103.7
British countries[1]	371.5	358.1	548.5	515.0	456.3	479.8	517.2	522.6
Foreign countries	548.0	527.4	603.6	630.1	540.4	754.1	792.1	581.1
France and Northern Europe	262.2	240.6	109.0	46.0	49.7	42.7	52.2	98.7
Rest of Europe	46.0	42.7	40.8	18.4	17.1	17.3	29.8	31.1
Africa	63.4	68.7	95.7	86.6	102.4	106.4	122.5	101.4
India and Western Asia	79.4	76.5	101.6	75.2	73.2	88.1	91.6	90.4
Rest of Asia	44.2	38.8	63.4	50.3	14.5	0.3	0.6	3.2
Oceania	120.7	105.6	154.0	103.6	100.4	82.4	98.0	111.4
North America	199.3	199.4	428.3	602.8	505.0	739.4	745.7	526.8
Central America and West Indies	34.7	34.3	46.2	71.9	49.5	58.0	54.6	50.7
South America	69.6	78.9	113.1	90.3	84.9	99.3	114.3	90.0
Argentine Republic	38.5	46.8	61.4	52.2	49.4	58.3	80.7	47.6
Australia	71.8	62.0	96.8	46.4	40.0	32.7	45.9	50.5
Belgium	18.6	18.8	9.4	-	-	-	2.8	3.1
Brazil	7.7	8.8	16.8	14.2	16.2	17.9	18.0	21.4
Canada	78.7	80.0	147.1	190.8	150.2	200.2	208.0	199.9
Ceylon and Dependencies	12.4	10.7	12.4	12.0	9.6	25.1	16.2	15.2
Denmark including Faroe Islands	37.9	36.4	11.4	0.7	0.6	0.5	0.5	8.2
Dutch East Indies	6.4	5.9	15.2	10.5	3.8	-	-	-
Dutch West Indies	14.7	13.9	25.2	50.5	35.1	28.7	25.0	21.0
Egypt	11.6	12.1	13.4	9.0	15.6	11.0	13.1	13.9
Eire	23.0	25.3	31.7	32.1	34.0	28.4	30.8	35.0
Finland	19.3	14.6	1.3	0.1	-	-	-	4.4
France	23.6	26.9	14.7	0.1	0.1	-	0.1	2.1
Germany[2]	30.1	19.4	-	-	-	-	-	2.1
India	49.9	48.5	72.9	57.3	60.1	59.8	69.3	66.8
Burma	6.0	5.1	7.2	9.2	2.7	0.1	-	-
Malaya (British)[2]	12.2	9.9	20.2	20.6	6.3	-	-	2.0
Netherlands	29.3	30.2	11.8	-	-	-	-	1.3
New Zealand	46.9	41.8	55.8	56.4	60.3	49.8	52.2	60.9
Nigeria (including Cameroons under British mandate)	6.3	7.2	13.6	14.0	18.2	18.7	21.1	17.5
Northern Rhodesia	4.1	6.0	9.8	10.2	10.5	12.5	13.6	6.3
Soviet Union	19.5	8.2	1.3	1.1	3.2	1.8	2.2	3.8
Sweden	24.5	25.6	10.2	1.3	0.4	0.7	0.9	22.4
United States of America	118.0	117.3	275.3	409.0	352.6	535.2	532.5	320.8
Union of South Africa	14.6	15.9	23.3	15.9	16.6	12.3	14.3	14.5

1. Including protectorates, mandated territories and territories under condominium
2. Including Austria in 1939 and 1945.
3. Straits Settlements and Dependencies (including Labuan) and Federated and Unfederated Malay States.

Source: Board of Trade

9.8 Value of exports of the produce and manufactures of the United Kingdom

Analysis by destination

£ million

	1938	1939	1940	1941	1942	1943	1944	1945
Total	470.8	439.5	411.2	365.4	271.3	233.5	266.3	399.3
British countries(1)	234.8	216.6	247.4	232.2	175.0	149.2	169.8	213.9
Foreign countries	236.0	222.9	163.8	133.2	96.3	84.3	96.5	185.4
France and Northern Europe	140.0	132.9	69.3	47.0	34.5	24.2	46.4	120.2
Rest of Europe	32.2	25.7	26.0	19.5	11.5	13.4	12.3	22.6
Africa	73.6	68.5	69.0	70.4	60.9	56.7	65.9	83.4
India and Western Asia	48.2	41.4	44.5	40.4	31.8	25.3	35.9	52.9
Rest of Asia	29.9	26.7	28.4	27.2	4.1	1.2	1.2	3.3
Oceania	58.2	48.8	63.3	53.1	45.1	40.1	46.6	49.6
North America	44.0	51.9	66.3	70.9	49.9	43.1	41.2	42.7
Central America and West Indies	10.5	9.1	9.9	9.6	8.9	8.2	6.7	8.7
South America	34.2	34.5	34.5	27.3	24.6	21.3	10.1	15.9
Argentine Republic	19.3	20.4	17.8	15.5	13.3	9.6	4.1	6.4
Australia	38.2	32.3	46.3	38.0	32.3	26.9	32.1	35.2
Belgium	8.2	7.2	3.0	-	0.4	-	0.9	31.0
Brazil	5.2	4.6	5.0	3.5	3.6	4.1	2.3	3.4
Canada	22.5	22.4	32.2	38.4	25.5	23.2	21.8	23.7
Ceylon and Dependencies	3.5	3.2	3.3	2.5	2.0	2.0	3.3	5.8
Denmark including Faroe Islands	15.8	17.6	4.6	0.7	0.8	0.8	0.7	2.9
Dutch East Indies	3.6	3.9	4.3	7.6	1.7	-	-	-
Dutch West Indies	0.6	0.3	0.4	0.4	1.1	1.3	1.4	2.1
Egypt	8.7	9.7	9.0	9.0	8.8	4.5	5.9	11.3
Eire	20.3	22.9	23.2	19.0	17.9	11.5	11.9	18.6
Finland	5.5	4.1	4.0	-	-	-	-	0.3
France	15.1	13.6	16.4	-	-	-	6.8	25.7
Germany2	20.5	12.3	-	-	-	-	-	2.8
India	33.8	29.7	33.3	31.6	22.3	17.6	23.5	33.1
Burma	2.6	2.9	3.2	3.5	0.6	-	-	1.2
Malaya (British)2	11.1	10.3	11.7	10.2	1.0	-	-	0.9
Netherlands	13.1	13.5	5.8	-	-	0.3	0.5	5.9
New Zealand	19.2	16.0	16.5	14.8	12.6	12.9	14.2	14.0
Nigeria (including Cameroons under British mandate)	4.2	3.7	3.9	3.6	4.4	6.2	7.5	7.5
Northern Rhodesia	1.3	0.7	0.7	0.6	0.6	0.8	1.2	1.1
Soviet Union	6.5	4.6	0.5	23.4	9.9	9.8	23.9	16.3
Sweden	11.7	14.1	4.8	0.7	0.5	0.5	0.3	2.7
United States of America	20.5	28.4	33.0	31.8	23.8	19.5	18.9	18.6
Union of South Africa	39.5	36.2	38.2	39.2	31.5	21.7	24.8	35.7

1. Including protectorates, mandated territories and territories under condominium.
2. Including Austria in 1939 and 1945.
3. Straits Settlements and Dependencies (including Labuan) and Federated and Unfederated Malay States.

Source: Board of Trade

9.9 Quantity of imports

Principal articles of food, drink and tobacco imported

	Unit	1938	1939	1940	1941	1942	1943	1944	1945
Wheat	Mn. tons	5.1	5.3	5.8	5.4	3.5	3.3	2.8	3.6
Barley	Th. tons	993.8	687.0	457.3	63.8	-	-	-	101.8
Maize	Mn. tons	2.9	2.3	2.1	0.7	0.1	0.1	0.1	0.5
Rice	Th. tons	133.7	143.2	191.3	178.6	53.4	131.1	41.9	25.2
Peas and beans, not fresh	"	145.1	135.1	146.7	157.9	48.1	69.5	71.5	66.1
Wheat meal and flour	"	383.8	366.7	577.4	707.9	374.4	717.5	791.5	542.8
Feeding-stuffs for animals	Mn. tons	1.9	1.7	1.1	0.3	0.1	-	0.1	0.2
Cattle, living, for food	Thous.	646.7	705.8	560.3	287.8	547.8	409.4	401.6	447.5
Meat:									
Other than tinned or canned:									
Beef	Th. tons	613.3	610.4	566.4	551.5	489.7	321.4	352.2	207.5
Veal	"	17.4	17.9	11.9	9.0	5.6	13.4	16.3	14.9
Mutton	"	82.5	69.0	124.2	51.0	57.3	58.3	102.1	111.9
Lamb	"	274.4	270.1	291.6	282.9	326.0	371.0	282.8	266.0
Bacon and ham	"	376.6	394.8	238.6	274.2	326.0	334.5	399.8	243.5
Pork and other pig products	"	70.7	60.3	68.6	93.3	108.4	225.2	389.4	201.7
Tinned and canned meat of all descriptions	"	72.9	102.9	123.3	230.9	281.9	298.0	213.5	97.4
Poultry and game, dead (including tinned and canned)	"	23.5	21.8	11.6	10.3	13.1	10.7	12.0	9.7
Dairy products:									
Butter	"	475.9	436.8	264.4	218.1	134.3	151.6	153.2	190.1
Cheese	"	146.4	142.3	156.2	203.4	315.2	207.0	251.9	191.2
Eggs in shell	"	191.0	195.4	102.7	61.3	23.3	15.8	23.1	47.6
Eggs dried whole[1]	"	0.3	0.1	0.4	7.5	56.0	73.4	80.0	24.4
Condensed milk	"	81.7	70.0	70.4	139.7	192.0	137.3	93.2	65.4
Milk powder	"	17.8	15.1	15.8	26.6	65.0	81.1	83.0	30.0
Fruit, fresh or raw:									
Apples	"	353.4	234.2	92.0	16.2	20.6	8.0	20.1	30.3
Bananas	"	305.0	287.6	193.1	0.1	-	-	-	1.1
Oranges	"	538.3	563.3	413.1	84.2	104.7	45.3	165.7	305.9
Other fresh fruit	"	280.3	236.2	92.7	10.1	1.0	2.1	18.9	54.0
Nuts used as fruit	"	70.6	59.9	35.9	4.0	4.9	2.9	8.9	5.4
Vegetables fresh:									
Potatoes	"	146.2	146.2	104.9	28.5	18.0	6.7	8.1	7.9
Onions	"	228.6	249.3	138.8	9.9	5.0	0.1	27.9	46.2
Tomatoes	"	143.3	142.0	58.2	1.8	-	-	-	7.4
Other fresh vegetables	"	50.5	43.9	10.3	0.8	0.7	0.5	0.6	0.4
Cocoa, raw	"	131.5	128.8	120.2	148.8	164.4	172.2	145.3	95.3
Coffee, not kiln dried, roasted or ground[1]	"	13.9	26.3	55.4	6.1	22.2	39.9	37.6	42.3
Tea[1]	"	205.6	158.1	171.8	209.9	154.3	206.1	189.8	170.9
Wine[1]	Mn. galls	15.4	16.8	14.6	1.8	0.9	1.1	1.3	3.8
Fish (not of British taking):									
Fresh or frozen	Th. tons	81.8	97.6	163.6	144.6	162.1	175.9	209.3	229.1
Canned	"	77.1	84.8	97.7	79.6	135.6	148.6	62.7	38.7
Fruit dried:									
Currants and raisins	"	136.0	148.2	87.4	133.2	89.2	109.4	164.8	89.1
Plums, prunes and prunellos	"	23.9	18.8	16.7	33.9	54.0	44.9	38.9	9.9
Fruit tinned or bottled in syrup	"	199.9	255.1	126.3	21.6	6.6	6.1	22.2	13.1
Dates	"	21.9	18.0	15.1	25.1	38.0	10.4	26.7	40.3
Edible oils and fats, refined:									
Lard	"	72.0	79.6	34.7	96.6	218.5	218.4	189.2	90.7
Other	"	65.6	51.6	43.6	39.8	34.0	42.3	50.1	19.4
Sugar, unrefined	Mn. tons	2.4	2.1	1.4	1.6	0.8	1.4	1.2	1.1
Tobacco, unmanufactured	Mn. lb.	344.9	211.5	141.4	213.7	264.9	354.1	229.9	368.8

1. Retained imports.

Source: Board of Trade

9.10 Quantity of imports

Principal raw materials imported

	Unit	1938	1939	1940	1941	1942	1943	1944	1945
Asbestos, raw and fibre	Th. tons	50.9	54.8	87.8	50.4	66.6	53.3	69.5	66.7
Magnesite	"	57.1	48.5	89.0	80.3	28.6	55.9	22.5	3.9
Mica, slabs and splittings[1]	"	1.5	1.7	2.4	0.9	2.2	2.8	1.8	1.5
Sulphur	"	131.5	160.2	217.1	293.6	125.0	268.9	197.2	198.2
Iron ore, other than manganiferous	Mn. tons	5.1	5.2	4.5	2.3	1.9	1.9	2.2	4.1
Iron and steel scrap	"	0.6	0.6	0.9	0.5	-	..	-	0.2
Bauxite	Th. tons	249.6	302.1	112.4	87.2	47.8	241.8	172.1	162.6
Chromium ore (chromite or chrome iron ore)	"	37.6	50.6	87.6	56.0	99.6	36.6	93.8	50.4
Copper ore (including regulus and matte) and precipitate and cement copper; nickel ore, concentrates and matte	"	29.6	34.1	32.7	27.7	26.5	20.3	21.8	19.4
Cryolite	"	5.3	4.7	1.3	3.6	4.9	1.6	0.1	0.8
Manganese ore	"	192.7	325.0	247.1	314.2	421.2	444.6	315.3	314.9
Molybdenum ore	"	1.9	4.9	2.4	4.1	7.2	6.5	0.5	1.1
Tin ore and concentrates	"	55.5	54.0	83.9	65.5	43.9	52.0	32.9	44.9
Tungsten (including tin-tungsten ores)	"	10.9	9.9	13.4	12.6	7.6	6.6	6.2	3.7
Vanadium ores (lead vanadate)	"	..	..	..	..	2.6	2.6	0.6	1.3
Zinc ore and concentrates	"	157.3	177.5	226.2	201.5	142.7	97.1	179.0	156.6
Timber:									
Softwoods:									
Sawn, not further prepared	Mn. standards	1.5	1.2	0.7	0.5	0.3	0.5	0.4	0.7
Planed or dressed, excluding box-boards	Th. standards	297.9	317.9	141.0	17.8	12.3	39.7	54.8	56.6
Hardwoods:									
Hewn	Mn. cu ft	4.2	3.2	5.5	4.1	3.5	4.1	4.9	4.8
Sawn, not further prepared	"	30.7	27.3	21.4	10.4	8.7	8.3	11.3	11.4
Pitprops	Th. Standards	821.7	634.1	433.2	74.9	11.4	28.3	74.4	193.5
Sleepers	"	117.2	69.6	13.1	25.0	41.7	14.7	51.0	60.7
Veneers	Th. tons	12.3	10.9	16.6	17.6	25.4	44.6	31.5	13.8
Cotton, raw (except linters)[1]	"	518.3	552.4	627.8	364.1	525.9	440.8	360.3	385.7
Wool, raw:									
Sheep's and lambs'[1]	Mn. lb.	624.6	730.5	1,005.3	330.3	411.4	269.5	508.5	428.4
Other	"	9.1	12.0	15.1	5.5	3.2	2.6	1.9	9.1
Silk, raw	"	5.3	4.4	5.5	1.6	0.3	0.4	0.5	0.6
Flax (excluding tow or codilla)	Th. tons	40.7	46.2	17.3	5.4	6.9	12.2	12.9	17.7
Hemp (excluding tow or codilla)	"	80.5	100.4	152.9	101.8	88.7	70.1	97.3	83.0
Jute, raw[1]	"	160.2	142.0	192.0	94.8	106.1	103.1	82.8	86.6
Seeds, nuts and kernels for expressing oil	Mn. tons	1.6	1.6	1.6	1.5	1.4	1.6	1.5	1.1
Gums and resins[1]	Th. tons	90.6	106.2	96.3	54.9	70.8	82.5	33.1	67.3
Oils, fats and greases:									
Tallow, technical	"	24.3	23.8	43.2	28.6	34.7	18.7	30.4	20.9
Whale oil unrefined	"	225.7	251.9	212.4	61.4	58.3	23.4	8.1	46.2
Other fish oil, unrefined including liver oil	"	21.3	16.4	36.5	37.1	33.6	29.0	35.6	18.9
Crude petroleum	Mn. galls.	568.0	541.4	375.4	234.3	141.9	126.5	164.1	227.7
Vegetable oils, other than essential[1]	Th. tons	210.1	246.2	201.7	231.4	217.8	233.5	200.6	153.0
Hides and skins, undressed:									
Cattle hides and calfskins:									
Wet[1]	"	41.3	49.9	80.5	57.1	79.5	60.6	84.8	76.6
Dry and dry salted[1]	"	19.0	23.8	27.9	22.4	23.1	15.3	12.8	14.0
Sheep and lamb skins[1]	"	17.4	18.0	25.9	10.1	14.5	12.4	16.0	17.0
Fur skins, undressed, except rabbit	"	3.8	2.5	1.5	0.2	0.3	0.1	0.1	1.0
Rubber, raw, including crepe and latex[1]	"	132.0	69.2	199.8	168.0	66.5	69.5	33.9	36.4
Synthetic rubber	"	-	-	-	0.1	0.9	9.7	91.1	27.6
Mineral phosphate of lime	"	410.5	462.5	413.5	799.2	287.3	788.8	675.8	642.7

1. Retained imports

Source: Board of Trade

9.11 Quantity of imports

Principal imports of articles wholly or mainly manufactured

	Unit	1938	1939	1940	1941	1942	1943	1944	1945
Iron and steel:									
Pig iron	Th .tons	395.1	354.4	676.0	971.5	356.2	361.8	285.0	107.9
Ferro-alloys: Total	"	47.6	72.6	94.2	99.9	67.4	135.0	55.6	46.9
Ferro-chromium	"	10.5	14.7	19.6	27.3	17.1	28.3	11.3	3.2
Ferro-manganese refined	"	2.8	4.3	4.4	2.1	2.5	2.3	0.1	-
Other ferro-manganese and spiegeleisen	"	0.1	0.2	0.1	0.3	0.2	1.6	-	-
Ferro-silicon	"	24.6	36.3	55.2	49.0	38.3	88.4	34.6	32.2
Silico-manganese	"	9.2	16.5	14.7	21.0	7.7	11.8	8.7	10.9
Ingots and semi-finished steel:									
Total	"	373.5	830.4	2,072.2	2,296.0	1,599.0	1,463.1	998.9	116.6
Steel ingots (non-alloy)	"	22.6	23.5	488.2	561.5	480.4	498.1	297.9	36.4
Steel blooms, billets and slabs (non-alloy)	"	315.0	369.9	1,254.3	1,362.3	884.2	845.8	693.5	79.7
Sheet bars and tinplate bars (non-alloy)	"	33.9	433.9	262.6	209.5	25.6	28.0	1.7	-
Finished steel and wrought iron: Total	"	459.4	509.1	795.2	761.2	472.3	834.5	394.2	32.8
Wire rods (non-alloy)	"	60.0	66.3	150.6	118.2	118.3	132.3	90.8	17.8
Plates and sheets (uncoated)	"	71.6	88.5	196.1	180.1	24.1	319.1	136.4	1.7
Iron and steel manufacturers	"	68.7	54.8	51.5	48.7	14.5	19.9	30.5	9.2
Aluminium and aluminium alloy ingots, blocks, slabs, billets, etc.[1]	"	41.0	57.7	66.1	132.7	131.6	213.0	149.7	21.1
Copper, unwrought, including rough[1]	"	259.6	307.6	472.8	449.4	441.0	494.8	451.5	143.7
Lead, unwrought[1]	"	382.1	334.3	336.5	139.3	235.5	226.5	224.9	165.4
Magnesium	"	1.6	1.6	0.6	1.0	3.1	33.6	20.4	1.1
Nickel and nickel alloys[1]	"	9.2	7.7	11.1	7.3	5.4	5.0	3.5	1.3
Zinc or spelter, unwrought	"	165.0	167.3	204.6	209.8	211.7	187.6	119.3	97.1
Watches, complete and complete movements	Millions	8.1	4.8	1.8	1.0	0.5	0.6	0.9	1.2
Wireless apparatus and valves	£ million	0.8	1.0	0.9	0.4	0.6	3.3	16.4	12.3
Other electrical goods and apparatus	"	2.4	1.8	3.3	2.3	2.1	4.9	7.5	6.4
Machinery:									
Agricultural	Th. tons	8.2	10.5	21.8	29.5	25.1	30.6	19.6	17.6
Machine tools, new, complete	"	23.9	30.4	72.1	77.5	41.2	39.5	15.0	6.5
Other machinery and parts	"	85.4	67.9	33.8	19.1	18.1	47.3	101.8	35.6
Wood and timber manufactures:									
Plywood	Mn. cu. ft.	10.9	8.8	4.7	2.6	2.7	6.3	8.2	8.4
Other	£ million	2.9	2.3	1.2	0.6	0.6	0.7	0.9	6.8
Cotton yarns and manufactures:									
Woven piece goods[1]	Mn. sq. yds.	45.7	30.3	26.5	16.3	10.2	34.2	17.4	12.8
Jute manufactures:									
Piece goods	Th. tons	55.2	56.0	90.0	34.1	37.2	25.8	67.0	43.3
Sacks and bags	"	39.6	84.1	131.5	28.5	39.0	35.7	42.9	29.0
Apparel, not of fur:									
Outer and under garments	£ million	2.2	1.5	0.3	0.1	0.2	0.3	4.4	3.4
Gloves	Mn. doz. prs.	1.7	1.4	0.3	0.1	0.1	0.1	0.1	0.2
Hosiery	£ million	2.5	1.7	0.4	0.2	0.2	0.3	1.0	0.8
Footwear	Mn. doz. prs.	1.5	1.6	1.0	0.7	0.2	0.1	..	0.1

1. Retained imports

Source: Board of Trade

9.11 Quantity of imports

Principal imports of articles wholly or mainly manufactured

continued

	Unit	1938	1939	1940	1941	1942	1943	1944	1945
Superphosphates	Th. tons	14.4	15.4	-	30.7	73.3	134.1	60.9	70.7
Potassium chloride	"	89.2	119.0	77.1	87.6	110.1	144.3	213.8	165.6
Drugs and medicines	£ million	1.7	1.8	1.7	1.3	1.1	0.8	2.5	3.3
Dyes and dyestuffs (including extracts for tanning)	Th. tons	53.8	75.5	92.6	68.7	71.3	67.6	72.5	68.5
Essential oils, other than turpentine	"	2.1	2.3	2.7	1.5	1.2	0.6	1.1	1.1
Petroleum refined:									
Kerosene	Mn. galls.	206.4	208.0	272.6	291.6	235.2	330.9	367.3	342.1
Motor and other spirit	"	1,474.8	1,390.5	1,098.5	1,435.1	1,278.3	1,689.1	2,921.9	2,151.1
Lubricating oil[1]	"	103.9	97.9	150.1	122.4	135.6	105.4	139.1	75.5
Gas oil	"	157.9	181.4	204.1	262.5	267.1	428.2	617.5	482.0
Fuel oil and diesel oil	"	687.3	574.5	926.0	1,115.7	727.2	1,316.2	1,334.9	1,009.4
Paraffin wax	Th. tons	40.5	43.6	67.0	56.5	59.1	37.8	28.6	33.4
Leather, undressed:									
Cattle hides and calf hides[1]	"	14.8	23.5	27.7	14.3	13.7	23.4	12.6	8.8
Skin leather[1]	"	4.7	5.7	5.3	2.3	3.1	2.8	2.5	4.0
Leather, dressed	"	4.0	4.7	3.1	0.8	0.8	0.7	0.7	0.5
Newsprint in rolls	"	446.3	423.1	238.6	121.9	66.9	95.4	135.2	186.1
Packing and wrapping paper	"	202.0	255.7	125.5	9.9	11.3	11.2	13.7	33.4
Boards	"	360.2	379.7	275.3	54.3	61.5	30.4	42.0	101.8
Other paper	"	62.2	70.2	38.8	7.4	6.2	6.5	9.3	18.0
Motor vehicles complete and chassis for motor vehicles[1]	Thousands	10.6	6.6	10.0	25.5	0.3	-0.3[1]	0.1	0.1
Tractors	"	2.9	5.3	6.1	11.2	7.8	6.1	6.3	2.4
Rubber tyres and tubes	Millions	0.5	0.6	0.2	0.3	0.5	1.7	2.4	1.8
Books, printed[1]	Th. tons	16.1	12.8	4.3	2.6	1.9	2.2	2.3	2.6
Starch, not for food	"	242.1	200.0	201.7	80.4	56.3	39.3	24.6	31.8
Animals not for food									
Cows and heifers for breeding	Thousands	71.6	81.0	82.1	13.4	78.7	45.0	42.4	42.9
Horses and ponies[1]	"	9.3	10.1	6.7	8.1	8.0	6.2	3.3	13.5

1. Retained imports.
2. And other printed matter for reading purposes (other than music), manuscripts and typescripts.
3. Re-exports exceeded imports.

Source: Board of Trade

9.12 Quantity of exports of the produce and manufactures of the United Kingdom

Principal articles exported

	Unit	1938	1939	1940	1941	1942	1943	1944	1945
Food, drink and tobacco									
Wheat, meal and flour	Th. tons	106.3	80.8	14.1	5.8	2.5	4.0	4.6	26.9
Beer	Th. bulk barrels	281.3	284.0	266.8	225.6	94.8	107.0	77.6	130.4
Spirits, home made	Mn. proof gallons	9.1	10.5	12.4	9.5	7.1	5.7	4.7	5.3
Fish: Fresh or frozen	Th. tons	53.8	29.6	1.3	-	-	-	-	0.1
Cured, salted or canned	"	165.0	71.3	23.0	0.9	4.0	0.2	-	10.1
Sugar, refined, including candy	"	362.1	314.3	16.9	44.4	25.7	3.7	8.3	79.9
Cigarettes	Mn. lb.	26.5	25.1	22.2	24.6	15.0	17.0	16.3	34.0
Raw materials and articles mainly unmanufactured									
Coal	Mn. tons	35.9	36.9	19.6	5.1	3.6	3.6	2.6	3.3
Bunker coal[1]	"	10.5	9.6	7.0	4.3	3.5	3.2	2.4	3.1
Wool, raw, sheeps' and lambs':									
British wool	Mn. lb.	30.1	25.9	12.4	20.9	5.4	0.7	1.1	11.4
Imported wool treated in United Kingdom	"	12.3	8.0	2.8	0.2	-	-	-	2.9
Wool waste	"	16.8	13.1	5.1	3.6	1.5	0.2	0.2	1.0
Artificial silk waste	"	19.9	37.3	17.2	20.4	6.5	6.8	6.5	16.3
Oils, vegetable, other than essential	Th. tons	75.0	36.6	11.7	3.9	0.9	0.3	0.2	4.0
Tar and pitch	"	504.3	463.5	398.0	32.0	77.7	82.0	79.0	197.5
Articles wholly or mainly manufactured									
Cement	"	760.1	690.1	441.5	319.5	186.7	167.7	323.6	593.3
Pig iron and ferro-alloys	"	100.7	77.9	25.4	20.6	5.4	5.1	3.3	34.1
Ingots and semi-finished steel	"	22.1	10.7	10.5	0.5	1.3	2.4	0.8	2.2
Finished steel and wrought iron	"	1,338.3	1,138.5	817.5	347.0	175.0	73.6	156.5	463.4
Copper and copper manufactures	"	32.4	28.2	20.4	20.9	9.7	5.7	5.1	19.4
Brass and alloys of copper other than nickel	"	21.6	20.1	12.9	9.2	8.4	6.0	5.7	13.1
Machinery:									
Agricultural machinery	"	8.6	7.0	6.7	3.8	3.6	4.0	5.2	15.8
Boilers and boiler house plant	"	56.0	42.0	22.7	21.8	15.4	12.3	20.0	22.6
Cranes, hoists, etc	"	19.2	16.3	6.9	5.2	4.2	4.4	5.7	8.2
Electrical machinery	"	44.6	33.7	29.1	25.7	23.7	28.5	57.8	56.8
Machine tools, metal-working and parts	"	24.1	27.5	11.4	7.3	20.3	12.7	32.3	19.8
Mining machinery	"	25.6	27.1	18.9	10.7	5.4	4.4	4.3	5.2
Prime movers	"	28.6	22.4	16.1	9.5	6.5	6.9	7.0	11.5
Pumps	"	8.2	6.8	4.9	4.4	5.5	3.3	3.7	4.1
Sewing machines and parts	"	11.7	14.7	9.6	5.2	1.7	0.7	1.2	2.1
Textile machinery	"	70.8	47.5	34.1	27.4	19.2	13.0	14.3	16.8
Other machinery and parts	"	151.9	114.9	85.8	64.3	51.8	45.3	40.4	60.5
Cotton yarns and manufactures:									
Cotton yarns	Mn. lb.	123.0	113.7	66.7	28.9	18.8	19.2	19.6	16.1
Cotton woven piece goods	Mn. sq. yds.	1,368.5	1,373.2	952.8	764.6	467.5	359.1	415.6	423.9
Finished thread for sewing, etc	Mn. lb.	13.5	14.3	14.6	13.6	14.2	13.3	12.0	13.8
Woollen and worsted yarns and manufactures:									
Wool tops	"	32.5	33.8	28.2	16.2	11.7	8.2	5.0	16.1
Woollen and worsted yarns	"	27.8	26.3	14.4	11.4	9.4	7.9	7.6	7.9
Woollen and worsted woven tissue[2]	Mn. sq. yds.	90.4	93.3	82.1	86.2	73.0	44.2	34.2	40.6

1. Coal shipped for the use of steamers, etc, engaged in the foreign trade (including fishing vessels). This item is not an "export" and the value is accordingly excluded from the total of exports shown in Tables 9.4, 9.6 and 9.8.
2. Excluding "tissues wholly of mohair, alpaca and cashmere", "damasks, tapestries, brocades and the like", "wool and mohair plushes and other pile fabrics" and "flannels and delaines".

Source: Board of Trade

9.12 Quantity of exports of the produce and manufactures of the United Kingdom

Principal articles exported

continued

	Unit	1938	1939	1940	1941	1942	1943	1944	1945
Articles wholly or mainly manufactured (continued)									
Artificial silk:									
Yarns	Mn. lb.	8.0	6.9	15.0	20.2	16.3	13.8	15.6	14.2
Tissues[1]	Mn. sq. yds.	60.7	72.8	83.3	88.1	114.3	75.0	90.2	93.4
Cordage and cordage manufactures of hemp, cotton, etc.	Th. tons	21.4	20.1	15.0	9.2	6.2	14.7	8.7	11.5
Linen and hemp manufactures:									
Piece goods	Mn. sq. yds.	51.8	67.4	45.4	27.8	22.6	10.5	6.2	8.8
Jute manufactures, other than cordage	Th. tons	74.8	62.4	39.0	23.7	13.0	8.1	6.2	10.3
Footwear, wholly or mainly of leather	Th. doz. prs.	374.0	335.1	263.8	454.5	181.6	89.5	82.3	218.7
Chemical manufactures and products:									
Ammonium sulphate	Th. tons	313.4	286.2	166.3	10.2	39.2	6.1	133.1	252.3
Copper sulphate	"	30.9	31.8	34.4	31.3	24.8	35.5	20.3	44.3
Disinfectants and insecticides	"	18.9	20.4	23.6	19.1	15.9	21.6	15.4	23.7
Sodium compounds	"	356.5	450.4	479.0	441.1	470.7	413.6	345.3	442.6
Dyes and dyestuffs	"	14.8	15.8	13.0	10.3	10.0	10.4	7.3	9.2
Petroleum, refined:									
Lubricating oil	Mn. galls.	17.5	16.4	4.7	3.3	1.6	0.9	1.4	4.0
Other sorts	"	116.2	99.2	13.6	2.3	1.0	0.2	5.9	1.1
Soap	Th. tons	36.7	37.3	33.2	30.3	3.4	4.0	9.0	40.4
Paper and board:									
Printing paper, not coated	Th. tons	94.7	70.5	40.4	10.3	6.1	4.3	4.7	8.3
All other paper and board	"	81.7	85.9	108.0	62.1	31.3	23.4	21.5	26.9
Railway equipment:									
Carriages, wagons, trucks and parts thereof	"	56.5	27.4	9.1	11.0	6.1	7.8	8.5	11.8
Road vehicles:									
Motor cars, new	Thousands	44.1	43.2	20.7	3.8	0.1	-	-	2.0
Commercial vehicles, new:									
Tractors	"	7.0	4.8	2.8	0.3	0.1	0.5	1.8	5.5
Others[2]	"	3.4	2.3	3.9	2.0	0.3	1.1	3.7	5.4
Chassis for motor vehicles with engines	"	35.0	31.9	15.4	1.0	-	-	0.2	1.3
Motor cycles and tri-cars	"	19.8	18.9	14.4	5.2	0.8	0.5	1.7	4.0

1. Excluding "pile fabrics", "damasks, tapestries, brocades and the like", "ribbons" and "lace and lace net of all kinds".
2. Including industrial trucks.

Source: Board of Trade

10 PUBLIC FINANCE

Although the war economy was run on the basis of physical planning rather than financial planning the state could not ignore financial matters. Given its increased expenditure on war activities and the adverse movements in the balance of payments the state had to ensure that it could finance both its own expenditure and current account deficit and the external debt.

Information on central government finance is presented in two batches of tables: **tables 10.3-10.4** provide information on revenue and expenditure by financial year (that is, 1939/40 represents 1 April 1939 to 31 March 1940) and **tables 11.7-11.8** provide information on a calendar year basis (the sum of the total revenue from table 11.6 and the total deficit on the current account in table 11.7 gives total expenditure). The rise in central government expenditure was dramatic: between 1938/39 and 1940/41 it increased from £1 billion to almost £4 billion and by 1944/5 was in excess of £6 billion; on a calendar year basis it increased from £0.8 billion in 1938 to a peak of £5.6 billion in 1943 (**tables 10.4 and 11.7-11.8**). This rise was almost wholly attributable to increases in expenditure on defence which had accounted for less than £4 in every £10 of ordinary expenditure in 1938 but accounted for more than £9 out of every £10 spent by 1944 (**table 10.4**). The rapid expansion of expenditure meant that in the early stages of the war the state had to rely on borrowing rather than taxation to finance it: between 1938 and 1940 tax revenue increased from £0.7 billion to £1.2 billion whilst borrowing (as measured by the deficit on the current account) exploded from £0.1 billion to £2.1 billion (**tables 11.7-11.8**; see also **table 10.3**). Thereafter tax revenue increased more rapidly than borrowing although it did not exceed the latter until 1944. Thus, between 1939 and 1945 the burden of financing government expenditure was roughly shared between tax revenue and increases in the central government current account deficit (**tables 11.7-11.8**).

10.1 Total central government expenditure

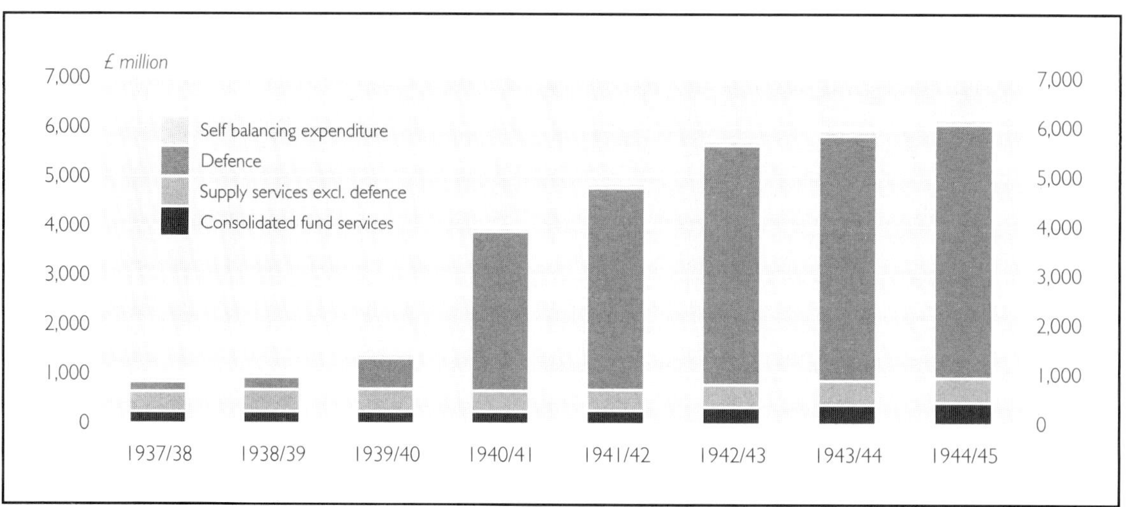

10.2 State borrowing

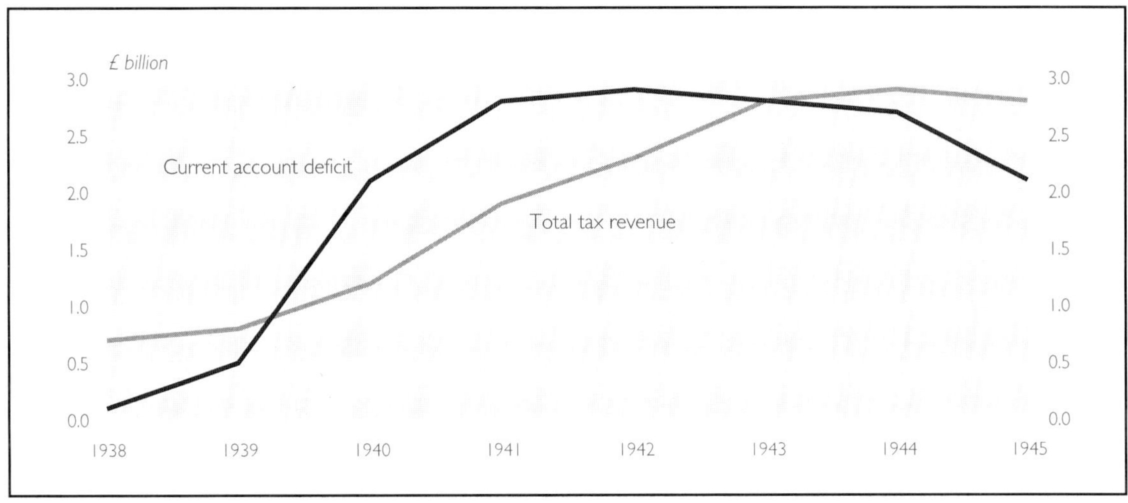

Income tax was throughout the war the most important source of tax revenue (accounting for over 40 per cent of the total): the standard rate of income tax doubled from 5 shillings in 1938 to ten shillings in 1942 (that is, from 25 per cent to fifty per cent) and the tax base itself was greatly widened through such measures as the Pay-As-You-Earn scheme (introduced in 1943) (Sayers 1956: 112-3; **table 11.6**). An important new source of tax revenue was the Excess Profits Tax which was an attempt to stop wartime profiteering by taxing profits in excess of peacetime levels; it was initially set at a rate of 60 per cent but was raised in 1940 to 100 per cent. At its peak in 1944 the Excess Profits Tax yielded 15 per cent of the total tax revenue (**table 11.7**).

Government borrowing was dominated by borrowing at home and since the state wished to keep its wartime debt as illiquid as possible, it focused on accumulating long term debt rather than short term (or floating) debt; during the war the ratio of long term to short term debt was approximately two to one (**table 11.8**). The state pursued a policy of 'forced savings' by using direct controls and financial inducements to mop up excess money in the economy and this served not only to provide funding for its expenditure but to also restrain inflationary pressures. Direct controls were used to limit investment opportunities and to force the clearing banks to make available their idle balances whilst financial inducements included old and new instruments geared towards both the small investor (the National Savings Certificate and Defence Bonds) and to the large investor and firms (the National War Bonds, Savings Bonds and the Tax Reserve Certificate) (Sayers 1956: 163-218; **tables 10.3, 10.5 and 11.8**) .

The other serious financing problem facing the British war economy was that of the external debt. Total wartime current account debits amounted to £16.9 billion whilst credits came to only £6.9 billion leaving a deficit of $10 billion to be financed (Sayers 1956: 499). It was partly financed though the disposal of overseas wealth: by selling overseas assets, accumulating external liabilities and running down gold and hard currency reserves (**table 10.8**). Britain pursued the policy of selling overseas assets vigorously (indeed, in the first year of the war the pressure on the British economy was so great that assets in North America were sold off cheaply) and by the end of the war £1.1 billion of overseas assets had been disposed of (**table 10.8**). Initially, gold and dollar reserves were also depleted rapidly: within eighteen months they were reduced by £531 million and driven to the point of exhaustion, although thereafter they recovered and between 1941 and the end of the war they increased by £3.9 million (Sayers 1956: 438-64; **table 10.8**).

The combined impact of selling both overseas assets and gold and dollar reserves did not match that of the accumulation of external liabilities: in June 1939 the total British overseas debt had stood at £0.5 billion but by June 1945 it had increased to £3.4 billion, of which £2.7 billion was held in the form of sterling balances (Sayers 1956: 439, 497). Sterling balances were credits of other countries which were held in blocked accounts in London and their wartime accumulation was the way Britain effectively paid for the large volume of wartime supplies from Sterling Area countries. While they helped to finance Britain's war effort their rapid accumulation (by countries such as India, Egypt and Sudan) left the country with a large postwar

burden, not least because interest and service charges would have to be paid on them thus depressing invisible earnings (Milward 1984: 68-9; Pollard 1983: 218-9).

Despite all these measures, however, the pressure on the external account was only relieved by the intervention of the USA which through the Lend-lease arrangements effectively gave Britain a grant for the duration of the war (Allen 1946). The total amount of Lend-lease aid by the USA to the whole of the British Empire came to $30 billion, of which the British government received $27 billion (£5 billion); against this must be set the reciprocal aid that Britain provided to the USA which came to $5.7 billion (£1.2 billion) which thus yields a net figure of approximately $21 billion (Allen 1946: 256-63; **tables 10.9-10.10**). Taking into account other aid from the USA and other countries net wartime grants financed 54 per cent of the £10 billion gap in the external account between total debits and credits, compared to 35 per cent accounted for by the accumulation of overseas debt and 12 per cent by the sale of overseas assets (Howlett 1994b: 18-21).

10.3 Central Government revenue (Exchequer receipts)

Years ended 31 March — *£ million*

	1937/38	1938/39	1939/40	1940/41	1941/42	1942/43	1943/44	1944/45
Ordinary and self-balancing revenue								
Total	948.7	1,006.2	1,132.2	1,495.3	2,174.6	2,922.4	3,149.2	3,354.7
Ordinary revenue: Total	872.6	927.3	1,049.2	1,408.9	2,074 1	2,819 9	3,038.5	3,238.1
Inland Revenue:								
Income tax and surtax	355.1	398.4	459.9	600.0	844.6	1,082.2	1,259.6	1,390.3
Death	89.0	77.4	459.9	600.0	90.9	15.3	1,259.6	17.0
Stamp duties	24.2	21.0	17.1	13.7	14.1	15.3	17.7	17.0
National defence contribution and excess profits tax	1.4	21.9	26.9	96.2	269.1	377.5	500.1	510.4
Other Inland Revenue duties	1.7	1.6	1.3	1.0	0.9	1.0	1.0	0.8
Customs and Excise:								
Customs	221.6	226.3	262.1	304.9	378.4	459.5	560.8	579.4
Excise	113.7	114.2	137.9	224.1	325.7	425.3	482.2	496.9
Motor vehicle duties	34.6	35.6	34.1	38.0	38.4	28.5	27.3	29.0
Post Office (net receipt)	10.5	9.5	3.8	15.3	13.7	12.4	0.4	-
Post Office fund								
Broadcast receiving licences	-[1]	-[1]	-[1]	-[1]	-[1]	4.6	4.8	4.8
Miscellaneous[2]	20.0	19.9	26.5	34.8	98.4	320.3	85.3	98.5
Self-balancing revenue[3]	76.1	79.0	83.1	86.4	100.6	102.5	110.6	116.6
Other receipts, repayments, etc.								
Total	267.6	190.2	808.9	2,518.2	2,748.1	2,852.5	2,797.5	2,866.4
Receipts under various Acts:								
Applicable to interest outside the permanent debt charge[4]	-	1.9	5.8	20.6	20.7	20.8	20.1	20.0
Other[5]	-	10.0	-	-	20.0	-	-	-
Money raised by the creation of debt:								
For capital expnditure issues	17.0	22.6	22.1	11.9	9.8	9.9	9.1	6.8
For other issues (net)	248.9	22.6	22.1	1,939.6	2,596.9	2,238.3	2,224.0	2,168.7
Ways and Means advances (net)	-	14.8	33.6	429.5	22.9	93.9	1.05.5	469.5
Treasury deposits by banks (net)								
Repayments in respect of issues under various Acts, etc.[6]	1.6	2.1	2.4	5.7	10.8	17.2	18.0	19.5

1. Included in Post Office self-balancing revenue
2. Including Crown lands and receipts from sundry loans. The figure for 1942/1943 includes £224 7 million Canadian Government contribution.
3. Post Office.
4. Defence Loans Act, 1937, and Overseas Trade Guarantees Act, 1939.
5. Eire (Confirmation of Agreements) Act, 1938 and War Damage Act, 1941.
6. Land Settlement (Facilities) Acts, 1919 and 1921; Tithe Act, 1936; Overseas Trade Guarantees Act, 1939; North Atlantic Shipping Act, 1934; Defence Loans Acts, 1937 and 1939. Net repayments of bullion advances are also included.

Source: Treasury

10.4 Central Government expenditure (Exchequer issues)

Years ended 31 March — £ million

	1937/38	1938/39	1939/40	1940/41	1941/42	1942/43	1943/44	1944/45
Ordinary and self-balancing expenditure								
Total	919.9	1,018.9	1,408.2	3,970.7	4,876.3	5,739.9	5,909.3	6,179.5
Ordinary expenditure: Total	843.8	940.0	1,325.1	3,884.3	4,775.7	5,637.4	5,798.7	6,062.9
Consolidated Fund services	238.8	244.3	246.9	247.2	274.1	341.6	391.2	437.3
Supply services: Total	605.0	695.7	1,078.3	3,637.1	4,501.6	5,295.8	5,407.5	5,625.6
Defence[1]	197.3	254.4	626.4	3,220.0	4,085.0	4,840.0	4,950.0	5,125.0
Civil votes: Total	394.1	427.2	437.4	402.3	400.6	437.7	438.8	474.4
Education and Broadcasting	59.9	61.6	63.1	63.3	65.6	77.5	79.5	85.3
Health, Labour and Insurance	161.6	165.7	167.2	164.7	170.0	185.6	198.7	208.4
Other	172.6	199.9	207.1	174.3	165.0	174.6	160.6	180.7
Customs and Excise	5.9	6.0	6.1	6.2	6.3	6.0	5.6	5.8
Inland Revenue	7.8	8.2	8.3	8.6	9.7	12.1	13.1	13.7
Post Office services	-	-	-	-	-	-	-	6.8
Self-balancing expenditure[2]	76.1	79.0	83.1	86.4	100.6	102.5	110.6	116.6
Other issues								
Total	296.3	177.5	532.9	42.6	46.5	35.0	37.4	41.5
Interest outside the permanent debt charge[3]	-	1.9	5.8	20.6	20.7	20.8	20.4	20.0
Issues to meet capital expenditure	17.0	22.6	22.1	11.9	9.8	9.9	9.1	6.8
Issues for the redemption of debt:								
Ways and Means advances (net)	10.4	-	-	-	-	-	-	-
Sinking funds	-	-	4.2	-	12.2	0.2	5.2	10.9
Issues under various Acts								
Defence Loans Acts, 1937 and 1939	64.9	128.1	491.8	-	-	-	-	-
Other[4]	204.4	24.7	9.1	9.9	3.9	3.8	3.2	4.0
Increase in Exchequer balances	-0.3	0.1	-0.1	0.2	-0.2	0.4	-0.4	-

1. Including votes of credit from 1939/40.
2. Post Office and, up to March 1942, broadcasting.
3. Issues under the Defence Loans Act, 1937 and the Overseas Trade Guarantees Act, 1939.
4. Finance Act, 1908, Section 9; North Atlantic Shipping Act, 1934- Tithe Act, 1936; Exchange Equalisation Account Act, 1937; Eire (Confirmation of Agreements) Act, 1938; Anglo-Turkish (Armaments Credit) Agreement Act, 1938; Czecho-Slovakia (Financial Assistance) Act, 1939; Overseas Trade Guarantees Act, 1939. Bullion advances are also included.

Source: Treasury

10.5 Floating debt

Averages of the weekly amounts outstanding — £ million

	1938	1939	1940	1941	1942	1943	1944	1945
Advances from the Bank of England								
January	1.8	0.2	-	12.4	3.6	13.1	5.9	-
February	-	-	-	10.1	8.3	10.6	12.5	0.7
March	-	1.2	-	11.1	7.9	31.5	22.9	7.3
April	1.6	-	-	6.9	15.8	3.9	20.5	4.8
May	2.0	1.1	-	12.4	0.6	-	0.4	13.3
June	8.7	7.6	-	22.4	14.1	15.9	18.5	26.3
July	-	-	4.1	4.6	5.4	4.3	4.6	4.0
August	-	-	6.6	2.5	1.6	6.8	11.9	5.6
September	-	1.0	18.6	20.4	12.8	7.1	12.1	14.4
October	1.0	-	11.9	20.5	29.1	13.5	10.7	4.7
November	0.8	-	10.8	21.4	22.9	18.4	14.8	4.6
December	1.1	-	19.3	30.2	38.0	43.8	28.5	10.8
Advances from Government Departments								
January	34.2	38.7	53.8	108.7	179.9	222.7	379.8	543.3
February	34.0	38.6	49.0	165.4	193.6	228.5	324.9	541.6
March	31.9	39.9	58.6	161.8	212.9	273.5	386.1	596.7
April	30.7	39.9	49.2	155.8	241.1	239.3	395.1	572.8
May	39.4	43.8	48.0	137.7	244.3	237.1	463.4	560.1
June	42.5	43.9	46.2	160.3	164.5	261.1	427.4	577.5
July	41.9	44.4	50.0	168.8	166.3	286.3	463.6	533.5
August	44.0	46.3	61.4	190.2	200.1	330.1	447.8	569.4
September	47.5	48.8	81.0	226.7	227.3	294.0	427.8	605.4
October	45.1	49.2	87.4	237.9	228.5	302.3	483.3	625.6
November	44.7	56.8	78.8	202.0	259.8	369.9	515.0	640.0
December	47.1	56.6	85.9	167.0	186.0	394.3	586.2	570.2
Treasury bills								
January	908.2	963.0	1,468.3	2,184.1	2,560.5	2,789.0	3,117.6	3,801.7
February	827.6	878.8	1,436.1	2,209.7	2,535.6	2,812.8	3,107.6	3,751.0
March	808.6	866.5	1,434.8	2,224.3	2,554.6	2,800.5	3,122.4	3,705.5
April	826.9	902.8	1,376.1	2,224.6	2,648.1	2,843.1	3,192.5	3,650.7
May	846.8	942.7	1,413.3	2,269.7	2,729.3	2,913.2	3,436.2	3,633.1
June	880.5	1,004.2	1,573.9	2,339.6	2,629.2	3,020.0	3,517.3	3,743.3
July	872.0	1,058.7	1,700.3	2,425.2	2,646.2	3,081.1	3,560.4	3,980.3
August	859.7	1,083.1	1,809.7	2,473.2	2,655.2	3,061.4	3,605.1	3,984.7
September	872.5	1,150.9	1,889.3	2,547.7	2,688.3	3,038.6	3,673.7	4,021.3
October	905.8	1,240.2	1,950.0	2,549.5	2,709.7	3,055.0	3,718.9	4,020.7
November	924.6	1,312.4	2,046.0	2,555.1	2,751.4	3,075.8	3,760.9	4,036.5
December	976.6	1,437.9	2,135.6	2,540.0	2,809.3	3,079.4	3,793.7	4,171.5
Treasury deposits by banks								
January	-	-	-	361.3	797.9	1,008.6	1,409.6	1,816.8
February	-	-	-	356.4	704.4	988.3	1,367.4	1,775.9
March	-	-	-	396.1	597.6	953.9	1,425.8	1,817.1
April	-	-	-	468.5	480.9	1,035.1	1,405.6	1,952.4
May	-	-	-	525.9	517.1	1,020.0	1,437.6	2,048.9
June	-	-	-	508.3	569.0	941.3	1,375.2	2,075.0
July	-	-	25.0	517.6	647.1	959.9	1,404.4	2,135.0
August	-	-	30.0	511.8	689.0	1,018.1	1,443.8	2,148.0
September	-	-	81.0	556.5	729.4	1,092.3	1,921.4	2,174.4
October	-	-	171.3	641.3	802.6	1,210.8	1,669.8	2,111.3
November	-	-	244.8	683.3	863.5	1,256.6	1,664.1	1,904.6
December	-	-	312.4	793.8	943.9	1,377.9	1,780.1	1,712.3

Source: Treasury

10.6 Currency circulation and bank clearings

£ million

	Currency circulation					Bank clearings[1]		
	Notes and coin outstanding			Held by banks[4]	Average estimaqted circulation with the public	Total	London Bankers' Clearing House	Provincial clearing houses
	Total	Notes[2]	Estimated coin[3]					
1935	549	480.2	69	187.1	362	126.9	122.7	4.19
1936	582	511.7	70	188.4	394	136.4	131.9	4.53
1937	626	552.4	74	186.1	440	144.3	139.5	4.81
1938	635	558.3	77	189.3	446	133.1	129.0	4.10
1939	658	578.3	80	199.1	459	124.3	120.1	4.16
1940	731	644.5	86	206.2	525	133.6	129.1	4.54
1941	823	730.4	93	215.0	608	144.4	139.6	4.78
1942	1,004	902.7	101	234.9	769	163.3	158.5	4.82
1943	1,184	1,072.6	112	250.4	933	189.8	186.0	3.80
1944	1,364	1,244.0	120	259.0	1,105	207.8	204.7	3.08
1945	1,519	1,391.4	128	256.0	1,263	223.6	220.2	3.35

1. Averages of working days. Figures are not strictly comparable throughout, owing in particular to changes in the composition of the clearing while the clearing banks' emergency operations were in force from September 1939.
2. Averages of Wednesdays for Bank of England notes and averages of Saturdays for Scottish and Northern Irish bank notes.
3. Excluding coin other than gold coin in the Bank of England Issue Department.
4. Averages of Wednesdays for Bank of England reserve and London clearing banks' holdings of notes and coin and averages of Saturdays for Scottish and Northern Irish bank holdings of notes and coin. Ten London clearing banks in 1935 and subsequently eleven.

Sources: Bank of England and Bankers' Clearing House

10.7 Prices and yields of British Government securities[1]

	Short dated[2]		Medium dated[2]		3½ % War Loan		2½ % Consols	
	Price	Yield	Price	Yield	Price	Yield	Price	Yield
1935	120.1	2.46	116.8	3.03	105.6	3.08	86.4	2.89
1936	118.1	2.45	117.0	2.99	106.0	3.03	85.1	2.94
1937	112.9	2.92	111.4	3.27	100.9	3.42	74.1	3.38
1938	112.2	2.73	111.4	3.27	100.9	3.42	74.1	3.38
1939	107.6	3.31	104.9	3.66	93.0	3.76	67.2	3.72
1940	108.0	2.81	110.7	3.26	99.3	3.52	73.5	3.40
1941	100.1	2.48	100.5	2.95	104.0	3.08	80.0	3.13
1942	100.5	2.33	101.2	2.89	104.8	2.96	82.6	3.03
1943	100.3	2.45	99.7	3.02	103.8	3.04	80.7	3.10
1944	100.6	2.37	99.6	3.02	103.3	3.05	79.6	3.14
1945	100.4	2.44	100.2	2.99	103.7	2.94	85.6	2.92

1. Averages of working days, allowing for accrued interest. In calculating the yields for short-dated and medium-dated securities redemption is assumed at the later date if price is below par and at the earlier date if price is above par. For 3½ % War Loan a flat yield is taken if price is below par and redemption is assumed in 1952 if price is above par. For 2½ % Consols a flat yield is taken throughout. Income tax is neglected in calculating the yields.
2. Representative securities changed from time to time, namely: Short-dated: 5% Conversion Loan 1944-64 in 1935 to 1940; 2½ % National War Bonds 1945-47 in 1941 and 1942; 2½ % National War Bonds 1949-51 in 1943 and 1944; 2½ % National War Bonds 1952-54 in 1945. Medium-dated: 4% Funding Loan 1960-90 in 1935 to 1940; 3% War Loan 1955-59 in 1941 and 1942; 3% Savings Bonds 1960-70 in 1943 to 1945.

Source: Bank of England

10.8 External disinvestment

£ million

	Total	1939 September to December	1940	1941	1942	1943	1944	1945 January to June
Total	4,198	212	811	820	674	689	663	329
Realisation of external capital assets	1,118	58	164	274	227	189	143	63
Increase in external liabilities[1] [2]	2,879	80	179	564	519	647	608	282
Decrease or increase (-) in gold and U.S. dollar reserves[2] [3]	152	57	474	-23	-75	-150	-99	-32
Unallocated	49	17	-6	5	3	3	11	16

1. Comprising banking liabilities, less assets, and funds held in the United Kingdom as cover for overseas currencies, etc.
2. After deduction of outstanding liabilities to provide gold against sterling liabilities and of liabilities to convert U.S.A. holdings of sterling into dollars on demand.
3. Gold valued at 172s. 3d. per ounce fine and dollars at £1 = $4 03.

Source: Treasury

10.9 United States lend-lease aid to the British Empire

$ million

	Total	1941 March to December	1942	1943	1944	1945 January to June	1945 July to August
Total aid to British Empire	30,073	1,082	4,757	9,031	10,766	3,604	833
Ships (sail-away)	2,107	65	195	1,078	540	160	69
Munitions destined for:							
United Kingdom	8,648	86	987	2,797	3,807	822	149
Australia	899	8	152	280	225	180	54
New Zealand	144	-	52	58	21	8	5
South Africa	194	-	40	88	55	10	1
India	1,422	8	230	371	555	227	31
Colonies	325	8	74	129	89	23	2
Other war theatres	3,902	76	610	1,205	1,349	493	169
Other goods destined for:							
United Kingdom	7,442	576	1,404	1,782	2,405	1,094	181
Australia	483	6	83	165	167	52	10
New Zealand	95	1	17	35	28	11	3
South Africa	67	-	20	29	18	-	-
India	766	1	87	175	295	157	51
Colonies	235	2	20	32	75	97	9
Services	3,344	245	786	807	1,137	270	99

Sources: Reports to Congress on lend-lease operations, and Professor R. G. D. Allen's paper " Mutual Aid between the U.S. and the British Empire, 1941-45 " read before the Royal Statistical Society, 1946.

10.10 United Kingdom reciprocal aid

£ million

	Total	To 30 June 1943	Year ended 30 June 1944	Year ended 30 June 1945	1 July to 1 September 1945
Total reciprocal aid	1,896.0	..	..	..	..
Aid to United States:					
Total	1,201.2	229.7	420.9	481.6	69.0
In United Kingdom:					
Military stores	189.6	46.3	61.6	74.1	7.6
Petroleum	213.6	5.4	58.9	135.1	14.2
Food	19.1	0.1	8.1	8.9	2.0
Services	297.5	41.9	108.3	128.8	18.5
Construction	218.9	92.0	100.9	19.6	6.4
In United States:					
Military stores	25.2	17.6	5.6	1.5	0.5
Food and materials	65.2	2.3	19.4	37.1	6.4
Miscellaneous and Services	7.3	4.5	2.5	0.2	0.1
In overseas theatres:					
Military stores	72.9	16.7	29.2	24.5	2.5[1]
Petroleum, India	60.7	2.4	12.0	38.3	8.0[1]
Petroleum, other	22.5	-	6.5	13.2	2.8
Construction	8.7	0.5	7.9	0.3	-
Aid to U.S.S.R.	312.0	187.7	93.3	27.0	4.0
Aid to other countries	382.8[2]	..	..	..	..

1. Estimated.
2. Incomplete.

Sources: Treasury and Professor R. G. D. Allen's paper " Mutual Aid between the U.S. and the British Emplre, 1941-45" read before the Royal Statistical Society, 1946.

11 NATIONAL INCOME

Although economists such as Clark and Kuznets had done extensive work in the 1930s on the concept and measurement of national income the first time they were estimated and used by a sovereign state as part of its budgetary policy was in Britain in 1941. The wartime estimates of national income were primarily the result of the work of two economists, James Meade (who created the necessary double-entry framework for the accounts) and Richard Stone (who filled in many of the numbers) (Meade and Stone 1941; Stone 1951). Given that this was the first attempt to provide such comprehensive national income accounts for the state and given that the work was carried out in the midst of a war it is not surprising that the estimates were rudimentary .

Statistical information was crucial to the running of the British war economy, in terms of monitoring the strength of the armed forces and of labour supply available to industry, in assessing the shipping capacity that was available at any point in time, in providing the basis for departmental bids for centrally allocated materials from steel to hemp, and in helping the central allocators making informed decisions about those bids (Howlett 1993). Probably the most important and innovative statistical development in the war was, however, the development and use of national income statistics (Booth 1989: 67).

The April 1941 budget which first utilised these national income estimates was also innovative in that it adopted some of the ideas of the economist John Maynard Keynes. He had argued that the traditional approach taken by the Treasury, which based government expenditure on 'what the taxpayer could bear' and whose main objective was achieving a balanced budget, was wrong (Keynes 1940). He said that in the war the state faced two problems: first, it had no choice but to greatly expand expenditure and therefore the old formula was redundant (relying on 'what the taxpayer could bear' would yield only half the

11.1 National income during the war

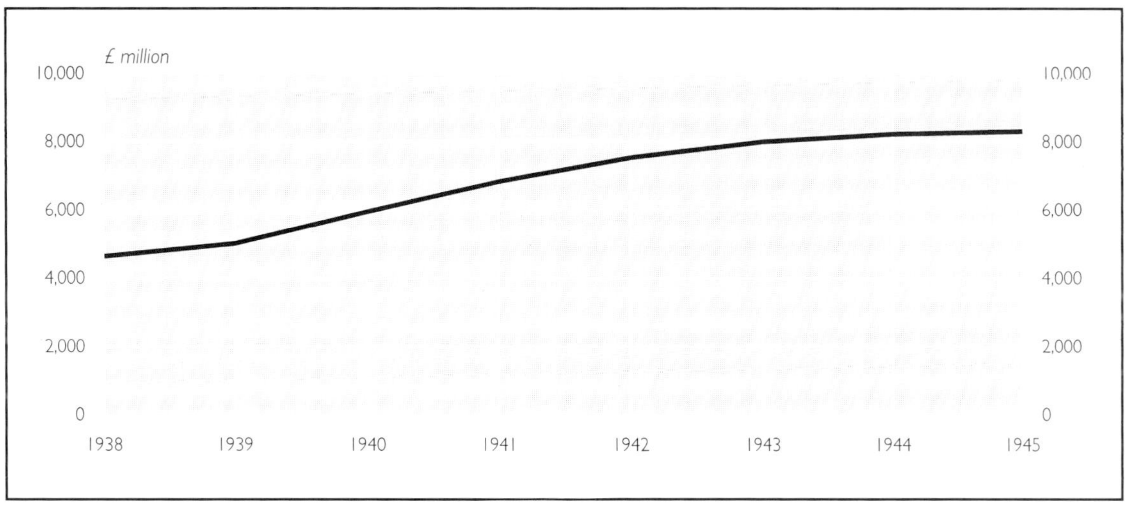

necessary expenditure); and second, there were immense potential inflationary pressures within the war economy and the state needed to take pre-emptive action against such latent de-stabilising forces. Thus, in devising its budgetary policy the state first needed to assess what the potential of the economy was, which involved the calculation of national income and its main components; then, it could calculate what level of taxation and forced savings were necessary to dampen inflationary pressures within the economy, and which would also provide finance for government expenditure. The 1941 budget adopted this approach (utilising the work of Meade and Stone) and at the same time transformed the budget speech from a bland statement of government revenue and expenditure into the comprehensive survey of the economy that we are now used to. It also transformed budgetary policy from a merely reactive tool into a pro-active one in that price and income stabilisation became explicit goals, albeit within a simplified framework in which trade and capital were both tightly controlled by the state (Sayers 1956: 108-10; Booth 1989: 68-9).

The wartime trends in nominal national income reveal rapid growth: national income increased by two-thirds between 1939 and 1945, with the most rapid period of growth occurring between 1939 and 1945 (**table11.3**). There was also a marked shift in the distribution of national expenditure as wartime commitments caused the government sector to expand rapidly: in 1938 the government sector had accounted for an eighth of total national expenditure, by 1940 its share was 42 per cent, in the following year it had reached half the total, and it peaked at 52 per cent in 1943 (**table 11.3**). The growth of the government sector was at the expense of consumption, whose share of national expenditure fell from 75 per cent in 1938 to 54 per cent in 1943 (expenditure on non-essential household goods, private motoring and clothing were affected most), and investment (there was substantial negative non-war capital formation throughout this period) (**tables 11.3 and 11.9**). Given the wartime inflation and the increased size of the working population the performance in real terms was less impressive: real Gross Domestic Product (GDP) at its wartime peak was 25 per cent higher than it had been in 1939 and real GDP per person employed was 15 per cent higher (which almost certainly still overstates the true position since the average hours worked per employee also increased sharply in the first half of the war), and both had fallen back to below their 1940 level by 1945 (Howlett 1994b: 4-7). However, compared to the other major combatant nations the wartime increase in real GDP was still impressive with only the powerhouse of the USA economy (whose real GDP increased by 65 per cent between 1939 and 1944) performing better (Howlett 1994b: 7-10).

11.3 National income, depreciation and expenditure

£ million

	1938	1939	1940	1941	1942	1943	1944	1945
National income								
Wages	1,735	1,835	2,100	2,400	2,655	2,800	2,815	2,810
Salaries	1,110	1,150	1,220	1,350	1,390	1,450	1,515	1,580
Pay and allowances of the Armed Forces	78	124	386	621	805	999	1,175	1,223
Professional earnings	84	82	78	80	86	94	98	105
Income from farming	60	80	143	191	217	231	208	194
Profits of other sole traders and partnerships	440	460	490	545	580	585	610	690
Trading profits of companies	543	715	965	1,105	1,260	1,290	1,280	1,225
Operating profits of public enterprises	25	22	22	33	77	91	72	22
Rent of land and buildings	395	404	408	404	400	400	401	403
Income arising in the United Kingdom	4,470	4,872	5,812	6,729	7,470	7,940	8,174	8,252
Net income from abroad	168	140	140	110	70	60	50	50
National income	4,638	5,012	5,952	6,839	7,540	8,000	8,224	8,302
Provision for depreciation	450	470	490	490	505	510	515	535
National income and provision for depreciation	5,088	5,482	6,442	7,329	8,045	8,510	8,739	8,837
National expenditure								
Consumption								
Personal expenditure on consumers' goods and services	4,304	4,422	4,661	4,933	5,210	5,291	5,562	6,027
Public authorities' current expenditure on goods and services	724	1,198	3,100	4,239	4,715	5,054	5,076	4,217
Additions to assets:								
Gross domestic capital formation[1]	770	(808)	(345)	(87)	(8)	(137)	(44)	(693)
Net lending abroad and purchase of assets and financial claims from overseas	-70	-250	-804	-816	-663	-680	-659	-875
Gross national expenditure at market prices	5,728	6,178	7,302	8,443	9,270	9,802	10,023	10,062
Subsidies	37	47	102	176	209	241	258	302
Less Indirect taxes	-677	-743	-962	-1,290	-1,434	-1,533	-1,542	-1,527
Gross national expenditure	5,088	5,482	6,442	7,329	8,045	8,510	8,739	8,837

1. The figures given for this item are residuals, not direct estimates.

Source: Central Statistical Office

11.4 Revenue account of persons

£ million

	1938	1939	1940	1941	194 2	1943	1944	1945
Receipts								
Wages	1,735	1,835	2,100	2,400	2,655	2,800	2,815	2,810
Salaries 1,110	1,150	1,220	1,350	1,390	1,450	1,555	1,580	
Pay and allowances of the Armed Forces	78	124	386	621	805	999	1,175	1,223
Mixed incomes	584	622	711	816	883	910	916	989
Rent, dividends and interest	1,111	1,139	1,167	1,153	1,205	1,234	1,291	1,335
Transfer incomes	272	263	266	280	300	32	325	503
Personal income	4,890	5,133	5,850	6,620	7,238	7,718	8,068	8,440
Payments								
Expenditure on consumers' goods and services	4,304	4,422	4,661	4,933	5,210	5,291	5,562	6,027
Direct taxes:								
On income	364	382	565	730	875	1,108	1,254	1,301
On capital	78	77	79	163	160	151	156	158
Additions to tax reserves	5	30	63	192	146	71	21	34
Net saving	139	222	482	602	847	1,097	1,075	920
Personal outlay and saving	4,890	5,133	5,850	6,620	7,238	7,718	8,068	8,440

Source: Central Statistical Office

11.5 Revenue account of public authorities

£ million

	1938	1939	1940	1941	1942	1943	1944	1945
Receipts								
Direct taxes:								
On income	441	494	688	1,048	1,338	1,739	1,937	1,965
On capital	78	77	79	163	160	151	156	158
Indirect taxes	677	743	962	1,290	1,434	1,533	1,542	1,527
Miscellaneous income from property	54	53	49	66	113	132	118	70
Less Debt interest	-291	-302	-314	-342	-397	-453	-511	-555
Revenue	959	1,065	1,464	2,225	2,648	3,102	3,242	3,165
Payments								
Expenditure on goods and services	724	1,198	3,100	4,239	4,715	5,054	5,076	4,217
Subsidies	37	47	102	176	209	241	258	302
Transfers to:								
Revenue account of persons	272	263	266	280	300	325	356	503
Private capital account	7	12	52	263	221	190	117	170
Surplus on current account	-81	-455	-2,056	-2,733	-2,797	-2,708	-2,565	-2,027
Current expenditure and surplus	959	1,065	1,464	2,225	2,648	3,102	3,242	3,165

Source: Central Statistical Ofmce

11.6 Combined capital account

£ million

	1938	1939	1940	1941	1942	194 3	1944	1945
Receipts								
Net saving by:								
Persons	139	222	482	602	847	1,097	1,075	920
Companies	170	175	175	175	215	235	235	245
Public authorities	-81	-455	-2,056	-2,733	-2,797	-2,708	-2,565	-2,027
Additions to tax reserves by:								
Persons	5	30	63	192	146	71	21	34
Companies	10	104	335	282	208	62	-13	-59
Provision for depreciation by:								
Enterprises	360	385	410	415	425	430	435	450
Public authorities	90	85	80	75	80	80	80	85
Transfers from public authorities	7	12	52	263	221	190	117	170
Total sums set aside	700	558	-459	-729	-655	-543	-615	-182
Payments								
Gross capital formation at home(1)	770	(808)	(345)	(87)	(8)	(137)	(44)	(693)
Net lending abroad and purchase of assets and financial claims from overseas	-70	-250	-804	-816	-663	-680	-659	875
Gross capital formation at home and abroad	700	558	-459	-729	-655	-543	-615	-182

1. The figures given for this item are residuals, not direct estimates.

Source: Central Statistical Office

11.7 Central government revenue

£ million

	1938	1939	1940	1941	1942	1943	1944	1945
Direct taxes								
Income tax and surtax	371	410	551	741	921	1,184	1,353	1,426
National defence contribution	15	28	24	23	27	33	35	34
Excess profits tax	-	-	44	211	318	453	482	440
Death duties	78	77	79	88	94	97	107	119
War damage premiums	-	-	-	75	66	54	49	39
Miscellaneous	-	-	8	5	-	-2	-3	-4
Total	464	515	706	1,143	1,426	1,819	2,023	2,054
Indirect taxes								
Customs and excise duties	337	382	474	676	851	992	1,088	1,092
Motor vehicle duties	35	34	37	38	32	27	28	35
Stamp duties	21	19	14	14	16	17	17	23
Post Office surplus	11	8	19	25	31	36	39	37
War risks insurance premiums	-	14	124	239	199	152	58	14
Miscellaneous	8	8	8	8	8	9	9	10
Total	412	465	676	1,000	1,137	1,233	1,239	1,211
Total tax revenue	876	980	1,382	2,143	2,563	3,052	3,262	3,265
Income from property								
Miscellaneous	20	22	18	33	79	93	80	33
Less National Debt interest	-223	-231	-242	-271	-328	-386	-445	-492
Total revenue	673	771	1,158	1,905	2,314	2,759	2,897	2,806

Source: Central Statistical Office

11.8 The finance of the central government deficit on current account

£ million

	1938	1939	1940	1941	1942	1943	1944	1945
Public borrowing at home								
Small savings	4	62	466	602	600	719	702	668
Other public issues (net)	73	10	567	1,031	1,047	1,059	896	1,176
Floating debt	-179	280	517	903	476	1,017	1,081	557
Tax reserve certificates	-	-	-	17	453	177	113	41
Total	-102	352	1,550	2,553	2,576	2,972	2,792	2,442
Finance through government agencies								
Extra-budgetary receipts, etc.	254	185	598	217	210	-100	-60	298
Less Sinking funds	-11	-14	-12	-17	-13	-15	-16	-16
Total	243	171	586	200	197	115	-76	314
Gifts and loans from abroad								
Canadian Government interest-free loan	-	-	-	-	157	-4	-13	-14
Reconstruction Finance Corporation Loan	-	-	-	87	4	-7	-11	-10
Credit granted by the United States Government as part of the Lend-Lease settlement	-	-	-	-	-	-	-	161
Total	-	-	-	87	161	-11	-24	137
Less Lending and net capital formation	-33	-33	-21	-18	-25	-20	-20	-134
Total deficit on current account	108	490	2,115	2,882	2,909	2,826	2,672	2,131

Source: Central Statistical Office

11.9 Personal expenditure on consumers' goods and services

(i) at current market prices

£ million

	1938	1939	1940	1941	1942	1943	1944	1945
Food	1,305	1,350	1,400	1,454	1,506	1,441	1,532	1,583
Alcoholic beverages	285	310	376	464	543	625	665	689
Tobacco	177	204	260	317	415	492	509	564
Rent, rates and water charges	491	510	519	515	509	511	516	534
Fuel and light	197	200	224	240	242	238	246	267
Durable household goods	234	223	212	197	174	141	127	172
Other household goods	54	56	59	57	53	52	55	56
Clothing	446	458	496	452	487	429	494	514
Books, newspapers and magazines	64	63	48	68	73	79	85	91
Private motoring	127	114	48	41	23	11	11	37
Travel	163	156	147	175	206	220	223	255
Communication services	29	29	32	37	39	48	54	52
Entertainments	.64	61	61	87	118	140	149	161
Other services	483	473	477	480	452	439	449	509
Other goods	177	181	187	189	184	190	201	229
Income in kind of the armed forces	17	29	81	135	146	185	206	204
Less Foreign tourists' expenditure in the United Kingdom	-43	-35	-10	-15	-30	-70	-125	-60
Personal expenditure in the United Kingdom	4,270	4,382	4,631	4,893	5,140	5,171	5,397	5,857
Personal expenditure abroad	34	40	30	40	70	120	165	170
Total	4,304	4,422	4,661	4,933	5,210	5,291	5,562	6,027

Source: Central Statistical Office

(ii) re-valued at 1938 prices

£ million

	1938	1939	1940	1941	1942	1943	1944	1945
Food	1,305	1,310	1,145	1,082	1,114	1,076	1,137	1,154
Alcoholic beverages	285	296	276	288	267	269	274	297
Tobacco	177	182	178	196	206	204	205	225
Rent, rates and water charges	491	504	508	502	497	498	503	506
Fuel and light	197	199	203	205	199	187	193	197
Durable household goods	234	219	164	115	81	67	60	82
Other household goods	54	55	52	48	42	40	40	40
Clothing	446	444	372	275	273	247	275	279
Books, newspapers and magazines	64	63	59	61	63	67	73	77
Private motoring	127	113	38	30	17	8	8	25
Travel	163	156	137	155	181	193	196	224
Communication services	29	29	27	27	31	37	42	40
Entertainments	64	61	53	75	87	89	90	94
Other services	483	467	432	411	373	350	343	369
Other goods	177	177	162	131	109	110	113	120
Income in kind of the armed forces	17	28	66	97	105	135	151	147
Less Foreign tourists' expenditure in the United Kingdom	-43	-34	-8	-11	-21	-48	-84	-39
Personal expenditure in the United Kingdom	4,270	4,269	3,864	3,687	3,624	3,529	3,619	3,837
Personal expenditure abroad	34	38	24	28	45	73	92	85
Total	4,304	4,307	3,888	3,715	3,669	3,602	3,711	3,922

Source: Central Statistical Office

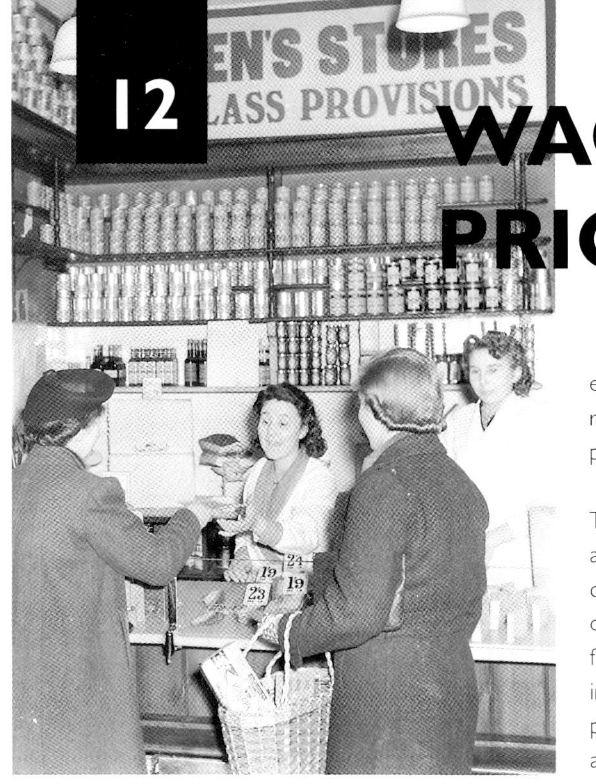

12 WAGES AND PRICES

The war brought about shortages of both goods and labour (the latter spreading from a shortage of skilled labour in the early years of the war to a shortage of all forms of labour by 1943) and it was therefore inevitable that both wages and prices would rise. This posed problems for the state as it desired neither wage nor price inflation (at the very least such inflation would increase the cost to the state of fighting the war) but it had to be careful not to alienate labour by imposing wage controls that were seen to be too strict or punitive. Thus, the state evolved a series of measures, including food subsidies and rationing, to try and minimise the effects of these pressures.

The increased demand from the armed forces for men and, from the munitions industries, for labour, was the cause of the rise in wages: the increase in the weekly wages of all manual workers in all industries and services in the first year of the war (13.8 per cent) exceeded the total increase over the previous five years; over the whole period of the war wages rose by almost 50 per cent, although the increase was most rapid between 1939 and 1941, and after 1942 the annual increase in weekly wages never exceeded five per cent (Department of Employment and Productivity 1971: 53). The pressure in the labour market can be further illustrated by conditions in the key industry of engineering where the minimum rates for skilled workers increased by 42-45 per cent from 1938 to 1945 whilst those for labourers increased by 57-60 per cent (Inman 1957: 341).

Changes in wage rates, however, do not tell the whole story of the wartime remuneration of manual workers because the war also brought many changes in work practices: more overtime was worked; working at

12.1 Average weekly earnings during wartime (at July of each year)

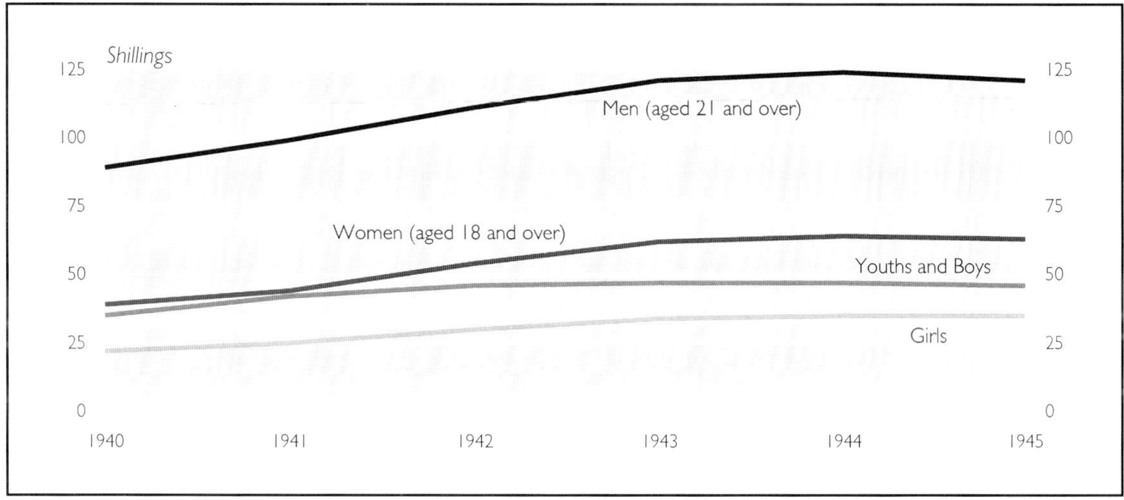

12.2 The cost of living index

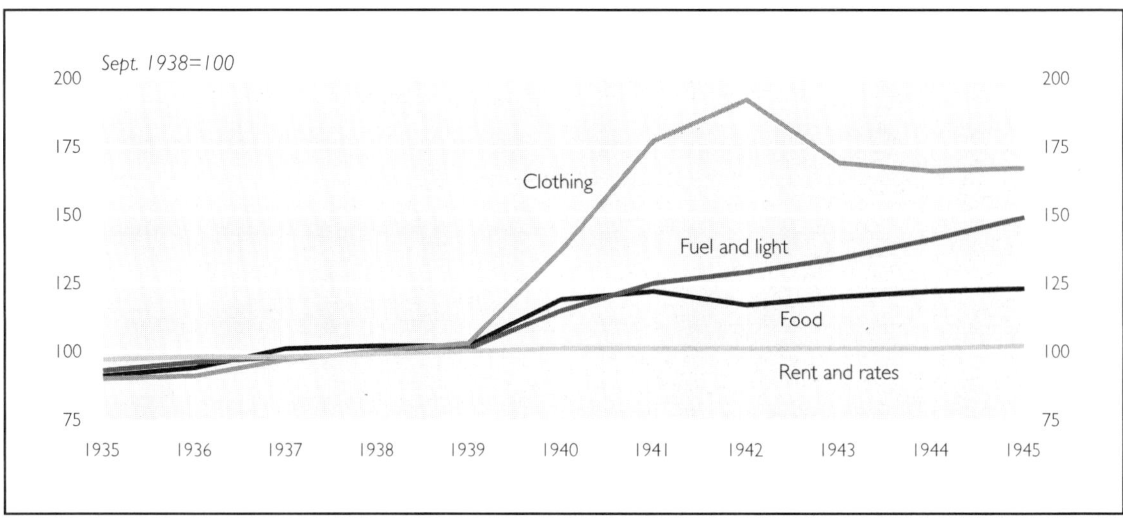

weekends became more common, as did night shift work; there was an extension of schemes based on payment-by results in some industries; and the composition of both the workforce (in terms of gender and of skill differentiation) and industrial structure changed. In the engineering and allied industries sector (which formed the core of the munitions industries), for example, the number of firms using a two shift pattern of work had increased from less than one sixth in January 1941 to a third in December 1942 and those using three shifts had increased from 2 per cent to six per cent; also, the general trend was for the proportion of workers being paid at skilled and unskilled rates to fall whilst those being paid at semi-skilled rates rose (overall in these industries the proportion of workers paid at semi-skilled rates increased from 31 per cent in June 1940 to 38 per cent by June 1943); and examples of the increased employment of women included marine engineering (where the proportion of women employed increased from 2 per cent in 1938 to 16 per cent in 1944), motor vehicles, cycle and aircraft manufacture and repair (10 per cent to 37 per cent), and electrical cables, apparatus, etc. (41 per cent to 61 per cent); finally, the percentage of all male wage-earners paid under a payment-by-results scheme increased from 18 per cent in 1938 to 24 per cent in 1947 (Inman 1957: 79-80, 424; Department of Employment and Productivity 1971: 157).

The impact of such changes is better captured by changes in average earnings rather than wages. Average weekly male earnings in industry displayed a similar, if more pronounced, trend to wages: between 1938 and 1945 they increased by 76 per cent (from 69 shillings to 121 shillings) with the most rapid increases coming in the early years of the war (by July 1941 they had already increased by 44 per cent) (**table 12.3**). Female average earnings followed a different pattern with the most rapid rises occurring between 1941 and 1943, which reflected the later timing of female industrial mobilisation and subsequent tightening of the female labour supply (**table 12.3**). Although female average earnings increased more rapidly during the war than male average earnings, this did little to erode the wide gender differential and in 1945 the average male worker still earned twice as much as the average female worker; the situation is slightly better if the changes in average hours worked is taken into account because the average amount of hours worked per week by female workers increased less rapidly than that of male workers, and thus on the basis of average earnings per hour female earnings increased from 52 per cent of male earnings in 1938 to 60 per cent of male earnings in 1945 (**table 12.3-12.4**).

The cost of living index measures the cost of maintaining a fixed standard of living in working class families (in effect, the change in cost to such a family over time of buying a fixed basket of goods). Sharp rises in the cost of living index often lead to increased wage demands and can therefore offer a crude indicator of potential wage inflation pressure. Thus, the state could help to moderate wartime wage inflation by manipulating the cost of living index. This it did through the use of price controls and the subsidising

of key items in the cost of living index; rationing also helped to reduce wage pressure. The impact of the actions taken by the state were dramatic both on prices and on the cost of living index itself, with sharp rises in the period 1939-41 (of 18 per cent in the latter) followed by much more moderate increases between 1941 and 1945 (indeed the monthly cost of living index was virtually stable between April 1941 and the end of the war) (Department of Employment and Productivity 1971: 170; **tables 12.6-12.9**). The explicit manipulation of the cost of living index by the state was an important reason why the tightening of the labour market in the second half of the war was matched, somewhat paradoxically, by falling rates of wage increases.

12.3 Average weekly earnings in manufacturing and certain other industries[1]

	All operatives			Men (aged 21 and over)			Youths and boys			Women (aged 18 and over			Girls		
	Earnings		Percentage increase over 1938	Earnings		Percentage increase over 1938	Earnings		Percentage increase over 1938	Earnings		Percentage increase over 1938	Earnings		Percentage increase over 1938
	s.	d.		s.	d.		s.	d.		s.	d.		s.	d.	
1938 October	53	3	-	69	0	-	26	1	-	32	6	-	18	6	-
1940 July	69	2	30	89	0	29	35	1	35	38	11	20	22	4	21
1941 July	75	10	42	99	5	44	41	1	61	43	11	35	25	0	35
1942 January	77	9	46	102	0	48	42	6	63	47	6	46	26	10	45
July	85	2	60	111	5	61	46	2	77	54	2	67	30	3	64
1943 January	87	11	65	113	9	65	45	1	73	58	6	80	32	1	73
July	93	7	76	121	3	76	47	2	81	62	2	91	33	10	83
1944 January	95	7	79	123	8	79	46	10	80	63	9	96	34	3	85
July	96	8	82	124	4	80	47	4	81	64	3	98	34	11	89
1945 January	93	9	76	119	3	73	44	1	69	63	2	94	33	8	82
July	96	1	80	121	4	76	45	6	74	63	2	94	35	1	90

1. The figures represent the average earnings including bonus, overtime, etc., and before deduction of income-tax or insurance contributions, in one week in the months indicated. Administrative and clerical workers and other salaried persons have been excluded.

Source: Ministry of Labour and National Service

12.4 Average weekly hours worked[1]

	All operatives	Men (aged 21 and over)	Youths and boys	Women (aged 18 and over)	Girls
1938 October	46.5	47.7	46.2	43.5	44.6
1943 July	50.0	52.9	48.0	45.9	45.1
1944 January	49.2	52.0	47.1	45.2	44.6
July	48.6	51.2	46.7	44.6	44.2
1945 January	47.0	49.4	45.2	43.1	43.0
July	47.4	49.7	45.6	43.3	43.5

1. The figures include overtime, but exclude time lost, and correspond with those for average earnings in Table 12.3.

Source: Ministry of Labour and National Service

12.5 Average weekly earnings in certain industries[1]

	Chemicals, explosives, paints and oils		Metals, engineering and shipbuilding		Textiles		Clothing[2]		Food, drink and tobacco		Building and contracting		Transport storage etc.[3]	
Men aged 21 and over	s.	d.	s.	d.	s.	d.	s.	d.	s.	d.	s.	d.	s.	d.
1938 October	69	3	75	0	57	3	64	3	65	0	66	0	70	0
1940 July	87	9	102	5	75	10	71	10	76	4	84	11	85	2
1941 July	98	5	112	2	81	6	83	7	87	4	97	1	92	2
1942 January	100	2	119	2	84	6	85	0	88	3	84	2	92	10
July	107	11	128	1	90	5	91	4	93	1	102	0	99	1
1943 January	110	9	131	6	93	5	95	0	96	9	94	8	99	9
July	116	3	138	3	96	11	98	9	101	8	108	4	104	2
1944 January	120	2	141	10	97	8	101	2	104	0	101	6	108	3
July	120	5	139	1	101	10	105	3	106	6	107	11	114	3
1945 January	118	0	131	2	100	4	106	5	106	7	104	5	110	10
July	122	10	133	0	104	7	110	8	110	4	111	4	114	10
Women aged 18 and over														
1938 October	32	8	33	4	31	9	32	9	32	11	..		34	11
1940 July	37	3	43	10	40	5	36	3	35	4	..		43	6
1941 July	44	11	48	1	42	0	41	2	40	3	..		59	6
1942 January	48	2	53	7	43	4	41	2	41	6	46	1	60	7
July	56	5	60	7	48	5	47	1	45	11	51	8	67	5
1943 January	61	4	66	5	50	3	48	4	47	11	52	5	67	2
July	63	7	69	10	52	11	50	3	50	10	61	5	71	5
1944 January	65	3	71	8	53	8	50	10	53	1	60	4	74	8
July	64	11	71	0	55	7	53	4	53	11	61	11	79	1
1945 January	62	1	70	4	53	9	53	0	54	8	59	6	78	7
July	62	10	69	1	58	2	55	7	56	7	60	5	81	7

1. See footnote 1 to Table 12.3.
2. Including laundries and dry cleaning.
3. Excluding railways.

Source: Ministry of Labour and National Service

12.6 Wage rates and cost of living

Annual averages

	Index of weekly wage rates[1]	Working-class cost of living index					
		All items included in the index		Food	Clothing	Fuel and light	Rent and rates
	1 September 1939 = 100	July 1914 = 100	1 September 1939 = 100	1 September 1939 = 100			
1935	91-92	143	92	91	90	93	97
1936	94	147	95	94	91	96	98
1937	97	154	99	101	97	98	98
1938	99-100	156	101	102	100	99	99
1939	101	158	102	102	103	101	100
1940	111-112	184	119	119	137	115	101
1941	121-122	199	128	122	177	125	101
1942	130	200	129	117	192	129	101
1943	135-136	199	128	120	169	134	101
1944	142-143	201	130	122	166	141	101
1945	149-150	203	131	123	167	149	102

1. The estimates cover most of the principal industries and a proportion of the smaller industries.

Source: Ministry of Labour and National Service

12.7 Agricultural price indices[1]

England and Wales 1936-1938 = 100

	1938	1939	1940	1941	1942	1943	1944	1945
All products	102	103	143	172	183	186	190	196
Cereals and farm crops	93	99	138	169	199	195	192	198
Live stock and live stock products[2]	104	106	143	161	177	178	184	192
Fruit,vegetables and glass house produce	111	94|	153	239	198	215	215	204
Wheat[3]	100	104	128	149	164	182	195	202
Barley	90	113	194	270	381	293	254	242
Oats	99	99	189	198	204	213	221	220
Potatoes[4]	79	75	98	129	134	136	137	143
Sugar beet	109	118	154	161	204	201	192	211
Hops	100	104	133	169	198	205	227	241
Fruit:								
Total	126	82	140	249	192	191	200	183
Dessert and cooking apples	128	83	162	229	222	229	228	188
Pears	111	87	166	623	300	344	314	302
Plums	153	63	90	253	138	152	150	168
Cherries	123	90	136	445	205	205	211	173
Blackcurrants	125	91	151	150	129	138	195	140
Gooseberries	129	89	156	92	207	185	220	198
Strawberries	109	98	135	210	159	165	156	170
Raspberries	123	96	149	86	111	121	130	130
Vegetables:								
Total	100	101	150	208	207	239	235	229
Carrots	129	121	197	159	140	162	204	208
Onions	128	169	795	546	506	466	381	448
Cabbage	94	100	142	219	148	225	207	225
Caulifl ower and broccoli	93	101	148	200	247	173	151	151
Brussels sprouts	92	93	149	195	265	170	183	172
Peas	96	102	133	218	182	375	340	337
Beans	122	92	107	197	227	368	444	274
Glasshouse produce[5]	101	101	194	303	190	195	187	182
Hay:								
Clover	93	108	151	193	225	229	230	230
Meadow	99	134	184	241	283	286	287	289
Fat cattle	106	108	136	141	152	157	160	164
Fat cows	108	113	145	153	152	148	161	166
Fat sheep	86	95	128	138	150	155	161	171
Fat ewes	93	97	153	165	165	165	165	173
Fat lambs	87	95	120	129	141	143	149	160
Bacon pigs	102	106	153	162	187	189	188	195
Pork pigs	104	108	141	143	154	155	155	159
Sows	108	118	174	169	169	169	169	169
Fowls	105	107	138	170	185	185	173	185
Ducks	101	104	137	171	211	208	167	201
Eggs	104	106	162	194	212	207	207	212
Milk	107	107	141	166	184	187	197	202
Butter	106	108	122	122	122	127	125	127
Cheese	102	101	156	161	195	185	191	..
Wool	75	91	116	135	153	152	152	152

1. Taking account of Exchequer payments but excluding subsidy on the 1938 crops of barley and oats under the Agriculture Act, 1937, and the Agricultural Development Act, 1939.
2. Excluding dairy cows and store stock.
3. Including acreage payments based on estimated quantities sold (1943 and subsequent crops).
4. Including acreage payments based on estimated total production (1941 and subsequent crops).
5. Tomatoes, cucumbers and grapes.

Source: Ministry of Agriculture and Fisheries

12.8 Stock and fertilizer price indices

England and Wales

	1938	1939	1940	1941	1942	1943	1944	1945
Stock[1]								
Dairy cows	106	108	131	172	188	185	181	180
Store cattle	106	109	128	148	159	163	169	167
Store sheep	88	93	108	129	147	155	168	181
Store pigs	107	119	115	141	158	184	214	170
Fertilizers[23]								
Total	102	102	133	138	137	138	138	138
Sodium nitrate	101	103	132	137	137	137	137	137
" Nitro-chalk "	101	101	125	130	130	130	130	130
Ammonium sulphate	102	102	128	133	133	133	133	133
Superphosphate	101	102	145	153	149	150	151	151
Basic slag	100	99	105	110	117	117	117	117
Ground rock phosphate	106	104	146	150	143	143	143	143

1. Base 1936-1938 =100.
2. Base 1937-1938 =100.
3. Taking into account Exchequer payments.

Source: Ministry of Agriculture and Fisheries

12.9 Wholesale prices (Annual averages)

Average 1938 =100

	Total	Food and tobacco	Industrial materials and manufactures				Building materials[2]
			Total (including fuel)	Basic materials[1]	Intermediate products[1]	Manufactured articles[1]	
1935	87.7	89.2	87.1	95.0	83.9	84.7	90.1
1936	93.0	94.2	92.4	106.5	89.3	87.6	92.9
1937	107.2	105.1	108.2	132.4	104.2	99.3	100.1
1938	100.0	100.0	100.0	100.0	100.0	100.0	100.0
1939	101.4	100.0	101.9	107.4	101.9	99.3	100.7
1940	134.6	136.4	133.7	158.6	138.7	119.3	117.0
1941	150.5	150.2	150.6	179.5	158.0	132.3	133.9
1942	157.1	161.1	154.6	181.8	161.9	135.8	139.2
1943	160.4	164.4	158.3	187.2	163.9	138.2	143.8
1944	163.7	162.4	164.5	198.3	167.5	141.5	147.3
1945	166.7	162.5	168.8	202.2	173.0	143.5	151.4

1. The greater rise in the basic materials index is essentially due to its containing various items such as paper-making materials, which rose very greatly in price and forwhich there were no corresponding quotations available under intermediate products or manufactured articles; similarly the index for intermediate products is raised above that for manufactured articles mainly because it includes timber.
2. Selected items included in the indices for industrial materials and manufactures.

Source: Board of Trade

BIBLIOGRAPHY

HSWW denotes that the title is part of the official History of the Second World War.

Place of publication is London unless otherwise stated.

Allen, R.G.D.1946. Mutual aid between the U.S. and the British Empire, 1941-45. *Journal of the Royal Statistical Society* 109: 243-71.

Allen, G.C. 1951. The concentration of production policy. In Chester 1951:168-76.

Behrens, C.B.A. 1955. *Merchant shipping and the demands of war*. HSWW.

Booth, A. 1989. *British economic policy 1931-49: was there a Keynesian revolution?* Hemel Hempstead.

Calder, A. 1969. *The people's war.*

Chester D.N. (ed.) 1951. *Lessons of the British war economy*. Cambridge.

Court, W.H.B. 1951. *Coal*. HSWW.

Department of Employment and Productivity. 1971. *British labour statistics: historical abstract, 1886-1968.*

Duncan Hall, H. 1955. *North American Supplies*. HSWW.

Duncan Hall, H. and Wrigley, C.C. 1956. *Studies in overseas supplies*. HSWW.

Feinstein, C.H. 1972. *National income, expenditure and output of the United Kingdom, 1855-1965*. Cambridge.

Ferguson, S. and Fitzgerald, H. 1954. *Studies in the social services*. HSWW.

Floud, R. and McCloskey, D. (eds.) 1994. *The economic history of Britain since 1700. Volume 3: 1939-1992.* 2nd edn. Cambridge.

Ford, P. 1951. The allocation of timber. In Chester 1951: 144-53.

Hammond, R.J. 1951. *Food. Volume I: the growth of policy*. HSWW.

Hancock, W.K. and Gowing, M.M. 1949. *The British war economy*. HSWW.

Hannah, L. 1979. *Electricity before nationalisation.*

Hargreaves, E.L. and Gowing, M.M. 1952. *Civil industry and trade*. HSWW.

Harris, J. 1992. War and social history: Britain and the Home Front during the Second World War. *Contemporary European History* 1: 17-35.

Harrison, M. 1988. Resource mobilization for World War II: the U.S.A., U.K., U.S.S.R., and Germany, 1938-1945. *Economic History Review* 41: 171-92.

Harrison, M. 1990. A volume index of the total munitions output of the United Kingdom, 1939-44. *Economic History Review* 43: 657-66.

Harrison, M. and Gatrell, P. 1993. The Russian and Soviet economies in two world wars: a comparative view. *Economic History Review* 46: 425-52.

Hornby, W. 1958. *Factories and plant*. HSWW.

House, F. H . 1965. *Timber at war.*

Howlett, P. 1993. New light through old windows: a new perspective on the British economy in the Second World War. *Journal of Contemporary History* 28: 361-79.

Howlett, P. 1994a. Resource allocation in wartime Britain: the case of steel, 1939-45. *Journal of Contemporary History* 29: 523-44.

Howlett, P. 1994b. The wartime economy, 1939-1945. In Floud and McCloskey 1994: 1-31.

Hurstfield, J. 1953. *The Control of Raw Materials*. HSWW.

Ince, G. 1946. The mobilization of manpower in Great Britain for the Second World War. *Manchester School of Economic and Social Studies* 14: 17-52.

Inman, P. 1957. *Labour in the munitions industries*. HSWW.

Johnson, P. 1994. The welfare state. In Floud and McCloskey 1994: 284-317.

Keynes, J.M. 1940. *How to pay for the war.*

Kohan, C.M. 1952. *Works and buildings*. HSWW.

Meade, J.E. and Stone, R. 1941. The construction of tables of national income, expenditure, savings and investment. *Economic Journal* 51: 216-33.

Meiggs, R. 1949. *Home timber production, 1939-1945* .

Milward, A.S. 1977. *War, economy and society.* Harmondsworth.

Milward, A.S. 1984. *The economic effects of the Two World Wars on Britain*. 2nd edn. Houndmills.

Murray, K.A.H. 1955. *Agriculture*. HSWW.

Overy, R.J. 1988. Mobilization for total war in Germany 1939-41. *English Historical Review* 103:613-39.

Paynton-Smith, D.J. 1971. *Oil: a study of war-time policy.* HSWW .

Pollard, S. 1983. *The development of the British economy*. 3rd edn.

Postan, M.M. 1952. *British war production*. HSWW.

Reddaway, W.B. 1951. Rationing. In Chester 1951: 182-99.

Robinson, E.A.G. 1951. The overall allocation of resources. In Chester 1951: 34-57.

Savage, C.I. 1957. *Inland transport*. HSWW.

Sayers, R.S. 1956. *Financial policy, 1939-1945*. HSWW.

Smithies, E. 1982. *Crime in wartime.*

Stevenson, J. 1984. *British society 1914-45.*

Stone, R. 1951. The use and development of national income and expenditure estimates. In Chester 1951: 83-101.

Supple, B. 1987. *The history of the British coal industry, Volume 4: 1913-1946: the political economy of decline.* Oxford.

Titmuss, R.M. 1950. *Problems of social policy.* HSWW.

Wiles, P. J.D. 1952. Pre-war and war-time controls. In Worswick and Ady 1952: 125-58.

Williams, H.T. 1954. Changes in the productivity of labour in British agriculture. *Journal of the Proceedings of the Agricultural Economics Society* 10: 332-47.

Worswick, G.D.N. and Ady, P. H. (eds.). 1952. *The British economy 1945-50*. Oxford.

DEFINITIONS AND NOTES

The purpose of this section is to supplement the footnotes given in each table and to make it possible to interpret the statistics more fully. The notes and definitions in this section are arranged in the same order as the tables. Certain definitions of general application throughout the Digest are also given in the Introductory Notes on page v.

1. POPULATION AND VITAL STATISTICS

POPULATION

1.3-1.5 For 1939 all figures for the population of the United Kingdom refer to the population actually in the country (resident population): they exclude members of the armed forces serving overseas and merchant seamen at sea. The number so excluded is estimated at about a quarter of a million at June 1939.

The figures for total population include from 1940 all members of the armed forces and merchant navy whether at home or overseas.

VITAL STATISTICS

1.6 Births

Figures for England and Wales relate to births occurring during the year; those for Scotland and Northern Ireland relate to the number of births registered in each year.

Birth rates have been calculated as follows:-

(a) For 1939 by relating birth registrations (occurrences in the case of England and Wales) to the resident population, that is excluding members of the armed forces overseas and merchant seamen at sea.

(b) From 1940 by relating birth registrations (occurrences in the case of England and Wales) to the total population, including members of the armed forces overseas and merchant seamen at sea.

1.7 Reproduction rates

Reproduction rates are an indication of the extent to which the female population of child-bearing age is being replaced by births. A rate of 1 represents exact replacement. In the "gross" rate no allowance is made for the losses due to death before completion of the child-bearing period. The "effective" and "net" rates both make provision for such losses but while the "effective" rate used for England and Wales assumes a continued improvement in mortality, the "net" rate used for Scotland is based on the mortality experienced in the year of calculation.

1.8 Infantile mortality

For England and Wales the rates of deaths of infants under one year of age are based on live births occurring in the several periods to which the deaths in the age groups comprising the first year of life relate. For Scotland and Northern Ireland the rates are based on live births registered in the year in which the deaths took place.

1.9 Deaths

The figures relate to the number of deaths registered during the year, the normal time lag between occurrence and registration being a matter of days only.

The figures for male deaths refer to civilians only for England and Wales and Scotland from 3rd September 1939 and for Northern Ireland from 1941.

The figures for female deaths refer to civilians only for England and Wales and Scotland from 1st June 1941 and for Northern Ireland from January 1941

2. SOCIAL CONDITIONS

PUBLIC HEALTH

2.3, 2.4 Deaths by cause and age

The figures are tabulated according to the Fifth Revision of the International List of Causes of Death from 1940 for England and Wales and Northern Ireland and from 1941 for Scotland. The figures for 1939 (and 1940 in the case of Scotland) are tabulated according to the Fourth Revision of the International List. The figures in brackets following each cause of death are the reference numbers to that particular cause in the Fifth Revision of the International List.

2.5 Notifications of infectious diseases

The figures for the years 1939 to 1943 for England and Wales incorporate such corrections as were reported on the weekly card returns and correspond with the numbers published in the quarterly and annual reports of the Registrar General. Those for 1944 and 1945 show the corrected number of notifications, incorporating revisions of diagnosis, either by the notifying medical practitioner or by the medical superintendent of the infections diseases hospital.

The term "formal notifications" as applied to cases of tuberculosis in England and Wales and Scotland covers new cases notified under the Public Health (Tuberculosis) Regulations, 1930. The figures exclude transfers between areas so far as they could be ascertained, duplicate notifications and a few cases brought to the notice of Medical Officers of Health otherwise than by formal notification under the regulations.

2.6 Venereal disease

The table shows the number of cases of venereal disease dealt with at civilian treatment centres in Great Britain and includes cases from the Services. The totals of all cases comprise cases under treatment or observation on 1st January of each year, cases removed from the register during any previous year which returned during the year in question for treatment of the same infection, new cases and cases dealt with for the first time during the year in question and known to have received treatment for the same infection or to have been under observation at other centres or Service hospitals.

In the number of new infections with syphilis are included cases of syphilis primary, secondary, latent in the first year of infection, all later stages and congenital. New infections with gonorrhoea include cases at first year of infection and at later stages.

NATIONAL INSURANCE

2.7, 2.9 National health insurance and pensions

The various enactments relating to national health insurance, widows', orphans' and old age contributory pensions and old age non-contributory pensions were consolidated in the National Health Insurance Act, 1936, the Widows', Orphans' and Old Age Pensions Act, 1936 and the Old Age Pensions Act, 1936 respectively. Similar legislation applies to Northern Ireland.

Persons insured for health and pensions comprised broadly the following classes:-

(a) Persons employed under contract of service by way of manual labour or (if non-manually employed) remunerated at a rate not exceeding £250 per annum up to 4th January 1942 and £420 thereafter. Seamen on foreign going British ships are included.

There are numerous exceptions in so far as national health insurance is concerned, the most numerous being civil servants, many employees of local authorities, railway companies and other statutory companies or undertakings, teachers covered by the Teachers Superannuation Acts, etc. Most of these excepted categories were, however, insured for pensions.

(b) Certain classes of persons not employed under contract of service, for example, outworkers, manual labour contractors, share fishermen and taxi drivers plying for hire with vehicles obtained under contract of bailment.

(c) Soldiers, sailors and airmen.

(d) Persons employed in certain classes of war occupation abroad.

(e) Voluntary contributors.

2.8 Unemployment insurance

Persons insured against unemployment under the Unemployment Insurance Acts were broadly the categories indicated at (a) and (d) on previous page for national health and pensions insurance with the following exclusions: (i) private domestic servants, (ii) female professional sick nurses and (iii) from 1942 persons engaged as a result of the war in employment for less than 30 hours a week.

JUSTICE AND CRIME

2.11- 2.18 It is necessary to preface these tables with the warning that differences exist in varying degree between the legal and judicial systems of England and Wales, Scotland and Northern Ireland which make it impossible to collate the statistics on a completely comparable basis. The differences between the systems of England and Wales and Scotland are the most pronounced.

Classification of offences

In all the relevant tables in this section offences are analysed under three broad headings. For England and Wales and Northern Ireland these are:

(a) indictable offences,

(b) non-indictable offences, and
(c) offences against Defence Regulations;
for Scotland they are:
(a) crimes,
(b) miscellaneous offences, and
(c) offences against war legislation.
Generally speaking these groups are broadly comparable.

The first two groups represent a division of criminal offences according to the nature of the proceedings in which the accused persons are tried. Thus, the procedure at Courts of Assize and Quarter Sessions is by a "bill of indictment" as opposed to a summons, warrant or charge at summary courts; therefore all offences which in the ordinary course are tried at Assize or Quarter Sessions are called "indictable" offences. All common law offences and all offences created by statute are indictable unless there is some statutory provision which expressly provides for some other mode of disposal. Originally, indictable offences could be tried at Assize or Quarter Sessions only, but there are now many offences committed by adults which may be dealt with summarily with the consent of the person accused. Offences which are ordinarily within the jurisdiction of summary courts only are designated "non-indictable" offences; such offences are created by statutes which contain express provision for summary treatment.

The last mentioned group (offences against Defence Regulations or war legislation) is of course a temporary one which came into existence during the war years and which arose out of the emergency powers taken by the Government to prevent acts which might be prejudicial either to the country's security or to the prosecution of its war effort. The difference in nomenclature of this group as between England and Wales and Northern Ireland on the one hand and Scotland on the other, is that the Scottish figures, in addition to covering offences under the various regulations made under the Emergency Powers (Defence) Acts, 1939 and 1940 (Defence Regulations), include offences under the National Registration Act, 1939, War Charities Act, 1940 and Goods and Services (Price Control) Act, 1941 which are included under non-indictable offences in the case of England and Wales and Northern Ireland.

2.11- 2.13 Finding of guilt and conviction

In the statistics for England and Wales the term "persons found guilty" covers not only persons convicted but also those found guilty without conviction (mainly persons dealt with under the Probation of Offenders Act, 1907 by dismissal, binding over or placing on probation). In the statistics for Scotland, however, persons so dealt with are not included in the term "persons convicted or found guilty" since there is in Scotland neither finding of guilt nor conviction in such cases.

Offences known to the police; persons proceeded against and found guilty

Offences known (or made known) to the police include offences reported to the police or otherwise coming to their knowledge within each year whether committed by the same or different persons and whether any apprehension took place within the same year or not.

A person proceeded against and charged at the same time with several offences appears as one person only. In selecting the offence for tabulation the principle is followed that a charge resulting in conviction has preference over any others, and where there are convictions on more than one charge the most serious offence (that is, the offence for which the heaviest sentence is awarded) is selected. Only cases disposed of within each year are included. Cases pending at the end of a year are included in the figures for the following year.

2.14- 2.16 Juvenile delinquency

For England and Wales and Scotland "juveniles" are defined as children or young persons under the age of 17; for Northern Ireland, however, the age limit is under 16 years.

2.17 Prison population

The prison statistics for Scotland are not altogether comparable with those for England and Wales and Northern Ireland. The main difference is in respect of the inclusion of criminal lunatics and mental defectives in the statistics for Scotland. In England and Wales and Northern Ireland the institutions in which criminal lunatics and mental defectives are detained do not come under the control of the Prison Commission, though the prison statistics may include such persons if received as ordinary prisoners before removal to the appropriate institution either by order of a court or by certification.

2.18 Divorce proceedings

During the years 1937 to 1939 new legislation relating to divorce was introduced which had a marked effect on the number of petitions filed. In England and Wales the Matrimonial Causes Act,

1937 came into effect on 1st January 1938 and gave additional grounds for divorce. The Divorce (Scotland) Act, 1938 gave additional grounds for divorce and also lowered the period of desertion necessary as a ground for divorce from four to three years.

The Matrimonial Causes Act (Northern Ireland), 1939 came into operation on 1st October 1939 and instituted a judicial for a legislative system of divorce. Before this Act the High Court of Justice in Northern Ireland had power to grant a decree of divorce a *mensa et thoro*, but such a decree did not dissolve the marriage and amounted only to what is known elsewhere as a judicial separation.

HOUSING AND BUILDING

2.20 Construction activity

This table shows the estimated value of work (both new work and repairs and maintenance) carried out by firms registered in the twelve main trades of the building and civil engineering industries; namely, general builders, building and civil engineering contractors, civil engineering contractors, plumbers, joiners and carpenters, painters, roofers, plasterers, glaziers, demolition contractors, scaffolding specialists and miscellaneous. Firms in these twelve trades consisting solely of working principals and therefore employing no operatives are excluded; a working principal is an owner, partner or director who also works as a craftsman or labourer.

The table also excludes building and civil engineering work carried out by the following:-
(a) Firms in the seven specialist trades, namely:- constructional engineers, reinforced concrete specialists, heating and ventilating engineers, electrical contractors, asphalt and tar spraying contractors, flooring contractors and plant hire firms.
(b) Building operatives employed directly by local authorities, Government departments, public utility and transport undertakings and by private firms outside the building and civil engineering industries.
(c) Prisoner-of-war labour.

The work done by the agencies excluded was, in 1946, about 40 per cent of the total output of building and civil engineering work. This percentage is not known for earlier years.

The figures for mining include the cost of raising opencast coal, since such work was undertaken by firms in the building and civil engineering industries. The item "all other work" includes all housing work other than new construction and war damage repairs and all work on shops, commercial premises, farm buildings, etc.

3. MANPOWER

3.3 Distribution of total manpower

The figures represent estimates of the total number of males aged 14-64 and females aged 14-59 gainfully employed, whether employers, employees or persons working on their own account, together with those who had not yet taken up employment since leaving HM Forces and insured persons registered as unemployed. Indoor private domestic servants are excluded. Women in part-time paid employment are included, two part-time workers being counted as equivalent to one full-time worker. The figures exclude prisoners-of-war but include such other foreign workers as had entered individually into civilian employment.

The heading "National Government Service" covers all employees of the Government except those employees in dockyards, royal ordnance factories, etc. who are included in their appropriate industry classifications. It also includes British employees of NAAFI.

ARMED FORCES

The figures in Tables 3.3-3.9 relate to men and women who served in the armed forces and auxiliary services of the United Kingdom, British subjects usually domiciled in Great Britain and Northern Ireland. Certain of the tables, annotated accordingly, include British subjects and other persons domiciled elsewhere who individually enlisted and served in the armed forces and auxiliary services of the United Kingdom.

All the tables exclude men and women who served in units and contingents of His Majesty's forces other than those of the United Kingdom or in Allied units and contingents under British or Allied command.

3.4 Strength

The term "strength" includes only those actually serving, that is, it excludes men whose service had been deferred, men or Reserve, men released to industry and, except where otherwise stated, men reported prisoners-of-war or missing. It excludes women whose service had been deferred and except in 1941, the ATS Unemployed List.

Men on T.124 agreements were merchant seamen serving with the Royal Navy under special agreements.

The nursing services include Queen Alexandra's Royal Naval Nursing Service, Queen Alexandra's Imperial Military Nursing Service, Territorial Army Nursing Service, Princess Mary's Royal Air Force Nursing Service and members of Voluntary Aid Detachments serving with the armed forces.

3.6, 3.8 Casualties

Casualties are given by date of notification and not be date of occurrence. The strength figures for the Army include a number of casualties which had not been reported at the dates to which the figures relate.

Casualties include the following categories:-

(a) Killed. Deaths from enemy action and injury are included, but not deaths from natural causes or (except in the case of the Royal Air Force) suicides. The figures for the Royal Navy, however, include deaths from diseases attributable to war service.
(b) Wounded. Non-battle injuries sustained on war service are included, but absence from duty due to sickness is excluded. The Army exclude all non-battle injuries and the Royal Air Force include injuries occurring during training.
(c) Missing.
(d) Prisoners-of-war and internees. The figures for prisoners in Europe were based on official notifications received from Germany and Italy. The figures for prisoners in Japanese hands were based partly on official notifications and partly on information received from the prisoners themselves.

In Table 3.6 the number of casualties represents those notified during the period less the missing who subsequently rejoined their units and repatriated prisoners. In Table 3.8 these two categories are included and the figures for prisoners-of-war also include internees. Men reported missing but subsequently reported killed, wounded or prisoners-of-war have been transferred from "missing" to the other category.

The figures relate to the gross number of casualties and not to the number of men who became casualties. A man who was reported missing, wounded or prisoner-of-war more than once has been counted as a casualty on each occasion so reported.

3.7 Releases

Men and women released for a temporary period are excluded, but those released locally abroad or repatriated from the United Kingdom are included.

The scheme of release from the forces after the end of hostilities of men and women called up under the National Service Acts provided for release in the following classes:-

(a) Class A in which release was based on age and length of service.
(b) Class B in which out-of-turn release was offered to men and women for employment in certain occupations essential to the reconstruction programme.
(c) Class C in which release was granted for an indefinite period on compassionate grounds.

Releases are counted from the date of dispersal and not from the date of completion of the period of paid leave.

CIVILIAN EMPLOYMENT

3.12 Agriculture

The table shows the number of workers (excluding occupiers and their wives, domestic servants and children still at school) employed on the day of the census on agricultural holdings of more than one acre in Great Britain.

Regular workers absent through sickness or holidays and working partners of the occupier are included.

Casual labour includes contract work, that is, labour supplied by County War Agricultural Executive Committees, contractors, etc., and all regular part-time agricultural workers, including those temporarily away through sickness or holidays.

The figures for the Women's Land Army relate to those in full-time employment in agriculture, horticulture and timber work.

3.13- 3.24 Manufacturing industries

The mid-year figures are based on the numbers of insured workers in each industry as estimated from the annual exchange of unemployment insurance books, less those registered as unemployed, together with one-half of the number of part-time female workers. The subsequent quarterly figures are obtained by application of the percentage changes in the numbers employed derived from the returns rendered by employers under various Orders made between 1940 and 1943, the last of the series being the Undertakings (Records and Information and Inspection of Premises) Order, 1943. The figures thus exclude employees over insurable age (65 for men and 60 for women), the relatively small number of non-manual workers whose earnings were above the salary limit for unemployment insurance, the employers themselves (proprietors, directors, partners, etc.) and persons working on their own account. Earlier figures have been adjusted to include an allowance for the extension of the salary limit for unemployment insurance from £250 to £420 per annum which came into force in September 1940 and to exclude women aged 60-64 who ceased to be insurable in July 1940.

The allocation between orders for Supply departments (Admiralty, Ministry of Supply and Ministry of Aircraft Production), home market and export has been made on the basis of figures supplied by employers in the employment returns referred to above. Employment on orders for Supply departments relates only to munitions and other equipment and stores for the use of the armed forces. Merchant shipbuilding and repairs is included in home market.

It should be noted that the figures shown for particular industries do not necessarily include the whole of the employment in the manufacture of the finished product; for example, part of the employment in the manufacture of aircraft parts and equipment is included in the general engineering, electrical engineering, scientific instruments, etc., industries.

3.25 Railway staff

The table shows all staff employed during the week of the census in March of each year by the railway companies of Great Britain (excluding the Manchester Ship Canal where staff fluctuated between 1,500 and 1,600 during the period), the London Passenger Transport Board and the Railway Clearing House. The figures represent the numbers receiving salaries or wages for the full week combined with the equivalent number of full-time workers where employees were paid for less than the complete week.

3.26, 3.27 Civil Service

The tables include both established and unestablished staff irrespective of their industrial classification. Staff in Northern Ireland, other than reserved and agency services, is excluded. Two part-time workers are counted as one whole-time worker. The figures are taken from returns made quarterly to the Treasury by all Government departments.

The table of non-industrial civil servants relates to clerical, executive and administrative staffs, their professional and technical counterparts and Post Office manipulative grades (postmen, telephonists, etc.).

In the case of industrial staff, in so far as they are employed in establishments which carry on work similar to that performed by employees of private firms (for example, engineering, building, etc.), they are also included in the tables for the particular industries concerned.

3.28 Government building programme

The table shows the labour employed on that part of the building programme subject to direct Government control. The figures cover male operatives aged 16 and over employed on the following types of work:-

(a) direct, authorised and assisted work of a Government department;
(b) licensed work;
(c) repair of houses made uninhabitable by war damage; salvage operations and war debris clearance; and first aid repairs carried out by the Special Repair Service.

"Direct" work is work on Government-owned property. "Assisted" work is work for which the Government granted financial assistance. "Authorised" work is work of construction or alteration for local authorities and public utility undertakings which required to be authorised by the appropriate government department. Repair and maintenance work for such authorities and undertakings and items of new work under £100 in value were exempted from authorisation.

Work for private firms, private institutions and individuals required to be licensed with the exception of items of work of a value below £100 and, until the end of 1941, all works of demolition, repair, decoration and maintenance.
The exemption limit of £100 for authorised and licensed work was reduced to £10 in the London Civil Defence Region in October 1944 and in certain other districts of the Home Counties in February 1945.

3.29 Government training centres and emergency training establishments

The table relates to the number of civilians trained or in training at Government training centres (excluding coal-mining training centres) and emergency training establishments. The latter utilised for training purposes all facilities available at technical colleges and industrial establishments not being used in operations essential to the war effort. The figures for completed training include all persons who completed the course in Government training centres together with terminations after passing the placing test in emergency training establishments. Trainees were required especially under schemes conducted by industrial establishments to undergo a placing test before completion of the course of training. These courses were of fixed duration, varying with the type of training required, but normally of eight weeks' duration.

4. AGRICULTURE AND FOOD

AGRICULTURE

4.3, 4.4 Area of crops and grass

The statistics of area are obtained from returns made by all occupiers of more than one acre of agricultural land in Great Britain. In Northern Ireland returns are required from all occupiers of one quarter of an acre or more of agricultural land. The areas shown exclude woodlands, buildings, roads, yards, ponds, etc.

The figures of specific crops relate to those which were actually in the ground on the date of the June census, or for which the land was being prepared at that date. Any catch crops grown for livestock feed or for ploughing-in in the period between the harvest and the sowing of the next season's main crop are not shown in the acreage returns. The case is similar for vegetable crops.

The number of acres under each crop was reported to the nearest quarter-acre. Any crops not specified in the return or grown in patches of less than one quarter of an acre are shown under the heading "Other crops".

The permanent grass acreage relates only to that grassland which was not under rotation.

4.5, 4.6 Crops and grass harvested

The estimates of the quantity harvested were for the most part obtained by combining the areas returned in June with estimates of yields made by technical officers employed by the Departments of Agriculture.

4.7, 4.8 Livestock

The tables show the number of cattle, sheep, pigs and poultry as returned by all occupiers of more than one acre of agricultural land in Great Britain and one quarter of an acre or more in Northern Ireland.

FOOD

4.11 Movement off farms

Wheat, barley and oats:

The series for wheat, barley and oats show as nearly as possible the sales of the home crops of these cereals as food. Thus no account is taken of farm sales specifically for animal feed, although small quantities were diverted for this purpose. The wheat figures show receipts by flour mills; the barley figures show receipts by brewers, maltsters, flakers, roasters, distillers, pot barley manufacturers, the Ministry of Food and (for a short period of 1943 and 1944 when flour was diluted) flour millers; the figures for oats are receipts by oatmeal millers (including a small quantity in 1943 for flour dilution), flakers and maltsters, and the Ministry of Food.

Potatoes:

The series shows the quantity of ware potatoes (excluding chat and seed) sold directly for food (including exports) and also for processing. The figures include the quantity of surplus ware potatoes fed direct to livestock under the Ministry of Food scheme or under special licences. Allowance has been made for human consumption on farms but production on allotments and gardens is excluded.

Sugar:

The production of refined and raw sugar (in terms of refined) from home-grown sugar beet. In 1939 the average relates to "the campaign year" - October, 1939 to January, 1940.

4.12 Animals purchased for slaughter

The figures relate to the number of animals purchased by the Ministry of Food from farms in Great Britain including fat animals imported from Eire and Northern Ireland for slaughter in Great Britain. Pigs fattened by pig clubs or other domestic producers and killed under licence are excluded.

4.13 Milk sales through the marketing scheme

The figures cover sales through the marketing scheme, for liquid consumption and for the manufacture of milk products including farm cheese. The quantity consumed by farm households and used on farms for butter production or calf rearing is excluded.

4.14 Processed food: Production

Wheat and oat milling

The series under the heading "Flour milling" show the quantity of home-produced and imported wheat milled and the resulting output of flour and offals. The latter two series include also the small quantity of oats and barley used for the dilution of flour in 1943 and 1944. The figures for oats show the quantity used by oatmeal millers, flakers and maltsters.

Seed crushing and vegetable oil consumption:
The five series show the quantity of oilseeds and nuts processed by crushing, expelling and extraction, the resulting production of crude oil and oilcake or meal and the consumption of the oil. The consumption figures include the crude oils used as such for soap and other industrial purposes, and the crude oil equivalent of the refined oils used for the manufacture of margarine and cooking fats and other food uses. Exports are included both in total disposals and in disposals for food. Castor meal, cocoa-cake and meal, which are unsuitable for animal feed, are excluded from the oilcake and meal figures.

Whale, herring and seal oil:
Consumption is calculated on the same basis as that of vegetable oils.

Meat:
Up to and including March 1940 the production of carcase meat and offal has been calculated from the estimated number of animals slaughtered. From April 1940 onwards the figures relate to sales by the wholesale meat supply associations and to meat and offal produced by pig clubs and other domestic producers. Meat from imported fat stock and fresh meat from Eire are included throughout.

Bacon and ham:
The figures relate to the output of curing factories from both home-killed and imported carcases. Bacon cured for pig clubs or other domestic producers is included.

Butter:
The figures relate to the output of home creameries. The production of butter on farms is excluded.

Cheese:
The series shows all graded cheese purchased by the Ministry of Food from creameries or farms. Processed cheese is excluded as being a remanufacture of graded cheese.

4.15 Food and animal feeding-stuffs: Consumption

The consumption figures relate to deliveries from stocks held or controlled by the Ministry of Food taking into account changes in stocks of wholesalers and manufacturing users. They should not be confused with retail purchases. In addition to deliveries to home food distributors, for civilians and for the Services, the figures include deliveries to manufacturers of products other than food and to exporters. Whenever these items are quantitatively important deliveries "for food" are shown separately. Where foods are used in the manufacture of other goods (for example, sugar in the manufacture of jam, biscuits, sweets) the quantities used for this purpose are included in the food column. The following points should be noted.

Rice:
The series gives total disposals which in addition to issues of whole rice, including issues of broken rice to manufacturers for brewing and for the production of ground rice, inedible starch, etc., and losses in recleaning as well as milling and drying losses.

Starch:
The series includes the quantity issued to industrial users as well as that issued to glucose and other food manufacturers.

Fresh, frozen and cured fish (landed weight):
Total disposals are the landed weight of fresh and frozen fish supplied to wholesalers, certain retailers and institutions, the Services, manufacturers of oil and fish meal and exporters, together with the quantity of cured fish issued to wholesalers, manufacturers and exporters. The condemned fish and offal which are included are taken by fishmeal manufacturers for the production of fertilizers and animal feed.

The figures for disposals for food in the United Kingdom give the landed weight of fresh and frozen fish and net weight of home-cured fish, but exclude quantities supplied to exporters and fish taken by fishmeal manufacturers.

Eggs in shell:
The figures show the consumption of imported and commercially-produced eggs plus an estimate of the number of eggs obtained by domestic poultry keepers.

Potatoes:
Total disposals exclude seed and chat potatoes, stock-feed outside Ministry schemes and waste on farms. Disposals for food in the United Kingdom further exclude stock-feed under Ministry schemes and exports, and relate to the distribution of

potatoes intended for human consumption. No allowance is made for waste in distribution or for feed to domestic animals.

Barley:
The figures for brewing and food show the quantity used by brewers, maltsters, flakers, roasters, distillers and pot barley manufacturers.

Maize:
Total disposals relate to the quantity used by manufacturers for production of edible starch, glucose and cereal breakfast foods, maize issued for pigeons and maize and maize meal used as feed.

Oilcake and meal:
This series covers sales of high, medium, and low protein oilcake by oilseed crushers to dealers together with the quantity processed by provender millers and compounders. Low protein oilcake, such as coconut cake and palm kernel cake, was issued as part of the "cereal" feeding-stuffs ration.

Milling offals:
The figures relate to sales by flour millers to dealers, together with the quantity processed by provender millers and compounders.

Conversion factors for items in the food tables

Flour:

Changes in the rate of extraction of flour from wheat:-

	Per cent
At 3rd September 1939	70
From 26th October 1939	73
From 28th April 1941	75
From 23rd March 1942	85
From 1st October 1944	82 1/2
From 31st December 1944 to 23rd February 1946	80

Oilseeds:

Crude oil equivalent:-

Cottonseed	17
Groundnuts decorticated	46
Groundnuts undecorticated	31
Copra	63
Palm kernels	47
Linseed	33
Rapeseed	38
Sunflower seed	26
Castor seed	44

4.16 Arrival of lend-lease foodstuffs

The figures given in this table cover arrivals of lend-lease food supplies originating in the United States of America only. Arrivals from other countries are shown in the small table at the foot of page 72.

5. FUEL AND POWER

COAL

5.3-5.5 Production, consumption and stocks

The series showing weekly averages for individual months are based on weekly or monthly returns. The weekly averages for each year are based on returns for the calendar year where available.

Saleable mined coal:
Production figures show the tonnage of coal raised and weighed at the pithead at coal mines in Great Britain, after deducting the weight lost in the elimination of stones and dirt by screening and washing. Miners' free and concessionary coal and all coal (of whatever quality) used for colliery purposes is included.

Opencast coal:
Coal obtained by opencast working of deposits near the surface.

5.4 Inland consumption

Public utility undertakings:
Gasworks include both statutory and non-statutory undertakings as well as gasworks of railway and transport undertakings.

Electricity undertakings comprise public supply and transport power stations.

Consumption of coal by railways is the amount used by the main line railways and the London Passenger Transport Board for locomotives, in workshops and stations and for marine purposes. It should be noted that coal consumed by the railways for the generation of electricity is included under "Electricity" and that for the production of gas under "Gasworks".

Coke ovens:
The series relates to coal carbonised by coke oven plants.

Industrial consumers:
The figures include only coal consumption of undertakings with an annual consumption of 100 tons or more of coal and coke.

Miners' coal:
Coal supplied by the collieries free of charge or at specially reduced prices to miners and their dependants, officials, clerks, etc., employed at the mines, miners' welfare bodies and other authorised persons and institutions.

Merchants' disposals:
The figures relate to the distribution of house coal, anthracite and boiler fuel by merchants to premises not separately programmed for their supplies and to other merchants for resale. In addition to private residences these premises include shops, offices, hotels, cinemas, institutions and the like and the smaller industrial consumers of solid fuel. House coal sold landsale by colliery undertakings acting as merchants is included.

Collieries:
The amount of coal, irrespective of quality, consumed at collieries for all purposes, including engine fuel.

Miscellaneous:
Water works, Service departments, shipments to Northern Ireland, industrial undertakings with an annual consumption of less than 100 tons, coastwise bunkers and non-industrial undertakings (that is, hospitals, schools, hotels, offices, shops, local authorities, Government buildings, etc., whose supplies are programmed and are not included in "merchants' disposals").

5.5 Distributed stocks
Distributed stocks relate to the amount of coal held by industrial consumers with an annual consumption of more than 100 tons of coal and coke, public utilities, railways, coke ovens, Government dumps (that is, coal held in Government stocking sites) and miscellaneous consumers and by merchants for domestic consumption. Stocks held in Northern Ireland are excluded.

5.6 Mined coal: Productivity
The figures before 1943 for the average number of shifts worked and possible and for the absenteeism percentage are based on returns collected by the Joint Accountants to the industry, in which the number of wage-earners differed from those obtained from the Ministry's own returns shown in the first column of the table. Average output per manshift before 1943 has not been calculated from these figures but from the annual statutory returns of the Ministry.

Wage-earners on colliery books:
This series includes all wage-earners, male and female, engaged in raising or handling coal or other minerals obtained with coal. Clerical and administrative staff are excluded.

Shifts worked:
The average number of shifts worked per wage-earner per week is the total number of manshifts worked in the period divided by the number of wage-earners on colliery books at the end of each week in the period.

Shifts possible:
Shifts possible are the sum of shifts worked and shifts lost through absenteeism of the workers. Shifts lost owing to recognised holidays, disputes, accidents, repairs, breakdown of machinery, etc., at the mines are not included.

Absenteeism percentage:
The absenteeism percentage is the total number of shifts lost through absenteeism multiplied by 100 and divided by the total number of shifts possible.

Output per manshift:
The average output in tons per manshift worked is the output of saleable coal divided by the total number of manshifts worked, at the coal face and overall.

COKE

5.7 produced at coke ovens consists of furnace coke and foundry coke. Production at gasworks includes coke used at these undertakings in the manufacture of water gas, in some cases that used for heating retorts and all other purposes.

Total inland consumption includes coke consumed at gasworks, blast furnaces and other industrial undertakings, by railways, non-industrial establishments and Service departments, disposals by merchants to domestic premises and shipments to Northern Ireland.

Total stocks relate to the amount held at producers' works, blast furnaces and other industrial undertakings, by railways, non-industrial establishments and Service departments and at merchants' yards. Stocks held in Northern Ireland are excluded.

GAS AND ELECTRICITY

5.9 Gas
Total gas available is the sum of gas produced at all authorised and non-statutory gas undertakings in Great Britain (excluding from the year 1943 that produced at works of railway and transport authorities) together with the amount bought from coke oven plants by gasworks for resale. Gas produced by coke ovens for the iron and steel industry and sold direct to other industries for consumption for other purposes is not included.

5.11 Electricity

The figures relate to authorised undertakings and railway and transport power stations only. Electricity generated by industrial establishments for their own use is not included.

PETROLEUM

The annual totals given in this series of tables and the weekly averages derived from them include certain revisions which have not been made to the monthly figures. The monthly figures in Tables 5.13 to 5.16 are for four or five week periods; in Tables 5.17 to 5.19 they are for calendar months.
The figures given for deliveries into consumption represent deliveries by the bulk petroleum distributors and not actual consumption.

5.13- 5.17 Petroleum products

Motor spirit:
Motor spirit includes distillation benzines used for industrial processes.

Lubricating oils
Lubricating oils include medicinal paraffin and mineral jelly.

Bitumen
Bitumen refers only to asphaltic bitumen refined by the distillation of asphaltic base crudes.

Process oils
Products intended for use as raw materials in refineries.

Approximate conversion factors

	Imperial gallons per long ton
Aviation spirit	310
Motor spirit	300
White spirit	284
Kerosine (paraffin)	276
Gas oil (including fuel for diesel-engined road vehicles)	264
Diesel oil	250
Fuel oils (imports)	235
Lubricating oils: White oils	255
Other	245
Crude and process oils	250

5.13 Arrivals of tanker-borne petroleum products and crude and process oils

The term "arrivals of tanker-borne petroleum products" covers liquid petroleum products carried in bulk in tankers; surplus bunkers removed from vessels of all descriptions; packed lubricants, whether carried as deck cargo or forehold cargo in tankers or in other vessels. It excludes paraffin wax, grease and natural bitumen. The figures for "refined petroleum products" refer to the quantities loaded at the port of shipment and are subject to a deduction of one-half per cent. for ocean leakage. Owing to differences in definition these figures which were provided by the Petroleum Board may differ, particularly in short-term periods, from the figures given in the Accounts relating to the Trade and Navigation of the United Kingdom.

5.15 Production from indigenous materials of petroleum products and substitutes

Indigenous production covers products obtained from refining shale oil and indigenous crude petroleum. It includes receipts by the bulk petroleum distributors from hydrogenation, low temperature carbonisation, tar distillation and benzole recovery plants. The figures under bitumen refer to the quantity of creosote used as a fluxing agent. The series quoted refer only to the output distributed by the Petroleum Board.

The figures for aviation and motor spirit include production of white spirit and kerosine.

Home production of fuel oil comprises mainly tar oils.

5.17 Deliveries into civilian consumption of motor spirit

This analysis of deliveries into consumption is based on coupon issues and does not take into account the use of coupons for purposes for which they were not intended. Consumption includes quantities delivered against coupons exchanged for Service department requisitions (private cars) and indents (public service and goods vehicles). Consumption by the armed Forces is excluded.

Private cars and motor cycles
Deliveries for cars taxed on horse-power and for motor cycles, including private hire cars and invalid carriages, but excluding cars and cycles operated by Government departments, local authorities and the police services.

Commercial vehicles
This heading includes deliveries for consumption by goods vehicles, buses, coaches, taxis, Government departments, local authorities, the police services, vehicles distributing petroleum products, etc.

Industrial uses
Deliveries for unlicensed vehicles, ambulances

(other than those owned by local authorities), vehicles operating on trade plates, plant, machinery and watercraft used for industrial purposes, lighting plants and motor spirit used for industrial processes.

Agricultural uses
Deliveries for farmers' vans, lorries and tractors not operating under carriers' licences or permits, agricultural engines (5s. class) and agricultural stationary engines.

5.18 Deliveries into consumption of fuel for diesel-engined road vehicles
This table is based on the total deliveries into consumption of gas oil on which duty is paid for use in diesel-engined road vehicles and on figures of coupon issues to consumer groups. The figures include quantities delivered against coupons exchanged for Service department indents.

5.19 Deliveries into consumption of gas, diesel and fuel oil
Bunkers
Including deliveries to certain coastal vessels which are linked with concerns operating ocean-going vessels.

Burning
Deliveries of oil for central-heating, steam raising and industrial furnaces.

Power
Deliveries of oil for stationary and mobile engines and for bunkers for fishing and coastal vessels excluding those linked with concerns operating ocean-going vessels.

Manufacture
Deliveries mainly for gas works and grease blending plants.

6. RAW MATERIALS

6.3 Iron ore and manganese ore
Iron ore
The ferrous content of home iron ore is about 30 per cent, compared with 55-60 per cent for imported iron ore.

Production figures for 1940-45 include small quantities of manganese ore.

Consumption figures relate to the consumption of raw and calcined ore as charged, except in the case of the figures for home iron ore in 1937 and 1938 which relate to raw ore and the raw equivalent of calcined ore. The 1937 and 1938 consumption figures for both home and imported ore include manganese ore, but exclude consumption in steel works. Consumption of imported ore in blast furnaces includes consumption in sinter plant.

Stocks of imported iron ore include ore in ships discharging and in transit to works.

Manganese ore
Stocks are the quantities held at works and in transit in the United Kingdom.

6.4 Pig iron
This comprises haematite, basic, foundry and forge pig iron, direct iron castings and blast furnace ferro-alloys.

Consumption includes refined and cylinder pig iron consumed in refined iron works.

Total stocks include stocks at wrought iron and refined iron works and in Ministry of Supply stock-yards.

Where cumulative adjustments have had to be made to annual figures for production and consumption, these may not correspond exactly with the monthly figures.

6.5 Iron and steel scrap and steel ingots and castings
Iron and steel scrap
Consumption figures relate to the quantity of steel and cast iron scrap (including scrap arising in own works) consumed in the production of steel ingots and castings, excluding the scrap consumed in blast furnaces.

Stocks are the quantities held at steel works and steel foundries.

Receipts of "bought" scrap are receipts of scrap bought in the home market. Figures before 1940 are estimated.

Steel ingots and castings
From July 1943 alloy steel figures relate to steel, other than high speed steel, containing a minimum of 0.4 per cent of chrome or nickel, 0.1 per cent of molybdenum, tungsten or vanadium, or 10.0 per cent of manganese. Before July 1943 the minimum proportions of these elements in alloy steel were 0.5 per cent, 0.25 per cent or 12.0 per cent. respectively.

Where cumulative adjustments have had to be made to annual figures for production and consumption, these may not correspond exactly with the monthly figures.

6.6 Semi-finished and finished iron and steel

Billets, blooms and slabs

Figures relate only to material for the production of heavy and light rolled products. From 1941 alloy steel is excluded.

Heavy rails and sleepers

Rails over 36 lb. per yard (perfects and defectives) and sleepers, fishplates and soleplates for use with them.

Heavy and medium plates

Boiler plate 3/16 inch thick and over; other plates 3/16 inch thick and over; medium plates and sheets under 3/16 inch thick, down to and including 3 mm. thick.

Other heavy steel products

Angles, tees and sections over 4 united inches; channels over 3-inch web; girders, joists and beams 3-inch web and over; rounds, squares and hexagons 3-inch and over, and flats over 5-inch wide; shell steel (ingots, billets and bars for shells, shot and bombs).

Light rolled products

Rails under 36 lb. per yard, and accessories; steel arches and accessories; angles, tees and sections 4 united inches and under; channels 3-inch web and under; joists and "H" bars under 3-inch web; wire rods; ferro-concrete bars and other bars, rounds, squares, hexagons, etc., under 3-inch and flats 5-inch wide and under; hot rolled hoop and strip.

Cold rolled strip

Under 18-inch wide.

Sheets

Under 3 mm. thick, coated and uncoated, but excluding tin, terne and blackplate.

Tin, terne and blackplate

Includes tinned sheets and uncoated tinplate base.

Steel castings

Net weight of fettled castings produced, machined as necessary to ensure soundness.

Steel forgings

Net forged weight of drop forgings and other type forgings.

Tyres, wheel and axles

Tyres, rolled rings, straight axles, solid wheels, disc wheel centres and assembled wheels and axles.

Stocks of steel

Ingots, semi-finished and finished steel held at producers' works, in British Iron and Steel Corporation stockyards and in transit in the United Kingdom. Consumers' stock are excluded.

6.7 Chrome ore and ferro-alloys

Chrome ore

Stocks are the quantities held by consumers, importers and the Ministry of Supply. Stocks in transit are excluded except in 1940.

Tungsten, molybdenum and vanadium

Production and consumption figures relate to the non-ferrous metal content of ferro-alloy and other finished products. Stock figures relate to the non-ferrous metal content of stocks of the ferro-alloys and of the ore (allowing for losses in refining) held by producers, consumers, merchants and the Ministry of Supply.

Ferro-chrome, silico-mangnese, ferro-mangnese, ferro-silicon, calcium silicide

Stocks are the quantities held at consumers' works, in British Iron and Steel Corporation stockyards and in transit in the United Kingdom. Figures for stocks and consumption of ferro-silicon exclude special grade used for aeronautical purposes.

6.8 Non-ferrous metals

Stocks

Except where otherwise stated, figures for stocks of copper, zinc, lead, nickel, tin, bauxite, cryolite, alumina and magnesite relate to quantities held by the Government and by consumers and include stocks in transit in the United Kingdom. Stocks of magnesium and magnesium alloys are Government stocks only and include stocks not taken on charge.

Refined copper

Production figures relate to production on toll contracts from imported blister, including scrap refined on private account from 1943.

Virgin copper

Unwrought copper (electrolytic, fire refined and blister).

Zinc concentrates

Consumption figures from 1942 include consumption other than for zinc production.

Virgin zinc

Unwrought zinc, excluding re-melted zinc. Some secondary material is included in the production figures for the years 1935 to 1939.

Refined nickel
Includes ferro-nickel.

Refined lead
English refined lead is included from 1942. Re-exports on toll transactions are included in total disposals and also in home consumption where fabrication had taken place before re-export.

Production figures for 1935 to 1942 relate to production from imported and domestic ores and concentrates; for 1943 to 1945 they relate to lead reclaimed from secondary and scrap material, and lead refined from domestic ores.

Virgin tin
Figures for production from 1942, and for total disposals throughout, include residues refined on toll and re-exported.

Bauxite
Expressed in terms of high grade bauxite.

Magnesium and magnesium alloys
Production includes scrap recovery. Consumption figures relate to despatches to consumers.

Magnesite (calcined and dead burnt)
Production figures refer to metal extracted from sea water.

6.9 Aluminium

Virgin aluminium
Consumption figures include the aluminium content of virgin alloys. Stocks are total stocks, including consumers' stocks and stocks in transit, and they include the virgin aluminium content of all alloys.

Secondary aluminium
Production includes production from crashed aircraft. Consumption figures relate to releases by the Light Metals Control. Stocks are total stocks, including consumers' stocks and stocks in transit.

6.10 Softwood and hardwood

Sleepers and crossings of all kinds are excluded, except in figures for production before 1942.

Softwood excludes pitwood, boxboards, pulpwood and poles. Hardwood excludes pitwood, logs for veneer production and staves.

Production of softwood and hardwood is the estimated output, based on deliveries from sawmills, of timber sawn from home-grown logs. In the figures for production after 1941 and in all figures for consumption of home-grown timber an allowance of 10 per cent. (softwood) and 5 per cent. (hardwood) has been made for conversion to square-edged material.

Consumption of home-grown softwood and hardwood is calculated from production and changes in stocks; that of imported, from the Timber Control's records of arrivals at ports to their account and changes in stocks.

Stocks of home-grown softwood and hardwood are the quantities held by the Home Timber Production Department, by merchants, by consumers (including railways) and in National stock. Ineffective stocks, estimated from July 1941 at 12,000 standards (softwood) and 1.25 million cubic feet (hardwood), are excluded.

Stocks of imported softwood and hardwood are National stocks (including stocks awaiting discharge), importers', merchants' and consumers' (including railways') stocks and stocks of recovered timber. Imported hardwood stocks exclude ineffective stocks of hardwood, which until August 1941 amounted to 4 million cubic feet and from September 1941 to 2 million cubic feet.

Stocks in the hands of firms whose normal stocks are less than 20 standards (softwood) or 1,000 cubic feet (hardwood) are excluded.

6.11 Pitwood and plywood

Pitwood
All mining timber specially prepared for use underground in mines for propping or shoring or as pit sleepers. It is shown in Gothenburg standards (equivalent to 180 piled cubic feet) calculated in the case of round pitwood in accordance with the Gothenburg scale, and in the case of other mining timber on an equivalent basis.

Round pitwood comprises pitprops, including sawn and quartered props, round bars and long pitwood. Sawn pitwood comprises other sawn mining timber.

The figures for production show the quantities despatched by the trade and by the Home Timber Production Department.

Consumption is calculated from deliveries to mines adjusted for changes in stocks at mines.
Stocks are National stocks (including stocks in transit and piling) and colliery stocks (including, from 1943, stocks held underground).

Constructional plywood
All rectangular boards, including block board, etc., of standard construction, excluding plywood of special shape or construction or of technical specification.

Production figures show the quantity of home-produced plywood taken into National stock.

Consumption is calculated from deliveries from National stock adjusted by changes in private stocks.

Stocks are National stocks, including stocks awaiting discharge. Merchants' and certain consumers' stocks are included up to June 1943.

Technical plywood
Plywood produced for special requirements of the Service departments.

6.12 Hides, skins and finished leather

Cattle hides
Production figures show deliveries to tanners of native raw hides. Stocks consist of native hides and imported wet, wet salted, dry and dry salted cattle and buffalo hides held by tanners and dressers. Stocks in transit in the United Kingdom are included.

Kips and calfskins
Production figures show deliveries to tanners of native raw kips and calfskins.
Stocks consist of native and imported kips and calfskins held by tanners and dressers.

Goatskins
Stock figures relate to imported goatskins held by tanners and dressers.

Sheepskins
Production figures show the quantity of native sheep and lamb pelts fellmongered, including deliveries of woolled skins to dressers for dressing with the wool on.

Stocks consist of native and imported sheep and lamb pelts and woolled skins for dressing with the wool on held by tanners and dressers and in Government reserve.

Rough tanned hides and kips
East Indian kips, calfskins and buffalo hides, including quantities in transit in the United Kingdom, held by tanners and dressers, factors and merchants.
Rough tanned goat and sheepskins
Imported rough tanned goat and sheepskins, including quantities in transit in the United Kingdom, held by tanners and dressers, factors and merchants.

Heavy leathers (leathers sold by weight)
Sole leather bends and offal, hide mechanical and textile leathers.

Consumption figures for heavy leathers represent deliveries by producers; for sole leather they also include imports and are adjusted for changes in certain stocks.

Stocks of heavy leathers comprise sole leather bends, offal and cut stock held by tanners, boot manufacturers, factors, merchants, sole cutters and heel builders and hide mechanical and textile leathers held by tanners, factors and merchants. Stocks in transit in the United Kingdom and any stocks in Government reserve are included.

Light leathers (leathers sold by area)
Upper and lining leather, gloving leather, chamois, upholstery, case, clothing, hat, bookbinding and other light leathers.

The consumption figures represent deliveries by producers; for upper and lining leather they also include imports and are adjusted for changes in certain stocks.
Stocks are the quantities held by producers, boot manufacturers, factors and merchants. Stocks in transit in the United Kingdom are included.

6.13 Rubber

Waste rubber
Crumb rubber is included in 1942.

Production is the collection of waste rubber from all sources including manufacturing scrap and domestic collections and the arrival of battlefield scrap at authorised dumps in the United Kingdom. From July 1944 the figures relate to collections at Ministry of Supply dumps only.

Consumption is the processing of waste into reclaimed rubber. From July 1944 the figures relate to issues from Ministry of Supply dumps only.

Stocks are the quantities held at Ministry of Supply dumps and, before July 1944, by cable strippers, licensed merchants, reclaimers, rubber manufacturers, and at Service dumps.

Reclaimed rubber
Natural, synthetic and, in the monthly figures for 1943, crumb rubber.

Production figures give production by reclaimers and, up to July 1944, by rubber manufacturers.

Consumption includes direct usage of waste rubber until July 1944. From that date figures are estimated and cover reclaimed rubber only.

Stocks are the quantities held by reclaimers, rubber manufacturers and the Ministry of Supply. Government lend-lease stocks are excluded in the figure for the end of 1941.

Natural rubber
Includes latex (except in the monthly figures for 1942) but excludes balata and gutta percha.

Consumption includes exports except in the monthly figures for 1942.

Stocks are the quantities held by H.M.Government, by manufacturers and, before January 1942, by importers and dealers in London and Liverpool. Stocks in transit are included from January 1942.

Synthetic rubber
G-R-S type, neoprene, butyl, N-type, and miscellaneous synthetic rubbers. "Thiokol" and "Novoplas" are excluded from July 1944. Consumption figures include exports.

Stocks are the quantities held by H.M. Government and by rubber manufacturers.

6.14 Chemicals

Industrial alcohol
Ethyl alcohol expressed as 68 O.P. spirit.

Consumption shows deliveries to consumers including methylators.

Stocks are quantities held on behalf of the Government and by producers.

Industrial methylated spirit
Consumption shows deliveries to consumers.

Methanol
Consumption shows deliveries to consumers.

Stocks are quantities held on behalf of the Government and by producers and consumers.

Urea
Consumption shows deliveries to consumers.

Nitric acid
Production in acid works, including Government acid plants.

Stocks are the quantities at acid works and Government plants.

Pyrites
Imported and home-produced pyrites for the manufacture of sulphuric acid.

Production figures relate to arrivals of home-produced material at acid works.

Stocks comprise the Government reserve and material at acid works, including Government acid plants. Stocks in transit in the United Kingdom are included from June 1943.

Sulphur (for acid)
Production figures relate to arrivals of home-produced material at acid works.

Stocks comprise the Government reserve and material at acid works, including Government acid plants. Stocks in transit in the United Kingdom are included from 1943.

Sulphur (regular)
Production figures relate to recovered sulphur. Stocks comprise the Government reserve and material at consumers' works and include manufactured forms. Stocks in transit in the United Kingdom are excluded.

Spent oxide and anhydrite
The figures relate only to material for use and consumed in the manufacture of sulphuric acid. Production figures show arrivals of home-produced material at acid works.

Stocks are the quantities at acid works.

Sulphuric acid
As 100 per cent acid. From 1941 acid made at Government factories is included.

Stocks are the quantities at acid works and Government plants.

Calcium carbide
Consumption figures relate to despatches from works.

6.15 Fertilizers, ammonia and molasses

Nitrogenous fertilizers (nitrogen content)
Production figures relate to ammonium sulphate, "Nitro-chalk" and concentrated compound fertilizers.

Consumption and stock figures relate to ammonium sulphate, "Nitro-chalk," concentrated compound fertilizers, Chile nitrates of soda and potash, Trail ammonium phosphate, ammonium nitrate, nitrate of lime and cyanamide.

Non-agricultural uses are excluded except in the series for total disposals which includes exports of ammonium sulphate for all purposes.

Superphosphate (P_2O_5 content)
Consumption figures relate to deliveries by manufacturers and from Government stores to merchants and farmers for direct application, and quantities used in ordinary compound fertilizers.

Stocks are the quantities held by manufacturers and by dry mixers. From February 1945 imported material is included.

Ground basic slag (P_2O_5 content)
Production figures relate to slag ground in the United Kingdom from home-produced raw slag.

Consumption relates to deliveries of home-ground material to merchants and farmers for direct application.

Stocks are the quantities held by manufacturers.

Ground phosphate (P_2O_5 content)
Production relates to phosphate ground in the United Kingdom from imported phosphate rock.

Consumption relates to phosphate ground in the United Kingdom delivered by grinders for direct application or for mixing in compound fertilizers.

Stocks are home-produced material held by manufacturers and compounders.

All other phosphatic fertilizers (P_2O_5 content)
Production figures relate to organic fertilizers, treated phosphate rock and concentrated compound fertilizers.

Consumption figures include in addition ammonium phosphate, triple superphosphate and, in 1943 and 1944 only, calcium metaphos. They relate to quantities delivered to merchants and farmers for direct application or used by compounders.

Stocks comprise treated phosphate rock, concentrated compound fertilizers and, in the figures for 1942 to 1945, triple superphosphate. The figures relate to home-produced and imported material held by superphosphate manufacturers and dry mixers.

Potash (K_2O content)
Agricultural potash only.
Consumption figures relate to quantities delivered in ordinary or concentrated compound fertilizers or for direct application.

Stocks are the quantities held by merchants and compounders.

Compound fertilizers (excluding concentrated compound fertilizers)
Total weight of product.

Consumption relates to deliveries by all compounders to merchants and farmers.

Stocks are the quantities held by compounders.

Phosphate rock
Consumption figures show the quantity used in the manufacture of fertilizers or for other industrial purposes.

Stocks are the quantities held for use in fertilizers by the Government, superphosphate makers and grinders, and quantities held by manufacturers for other industrial purposes

Ammonia
The figures exclude ammonia produced in by-product factories and converted directly into sulphate of ammonia.

Consumption figures show deliveries by producers to consumers and for export.

Stocks are the producers' stocks at works, including stocks in Government factories. Consumers' stocks are included in the figure for 1942.

Molasses
The figures are expressed in terms of blackstrap containing 52 per cent sugars.

Production is the production from sugar cane and sugar beet of molasses handled by the Government.

Consumption figures give deliveries for distilling; for cattle feed including silage, sweetened pulp and straw ration; and for tanning, solvents, yeast, core-making, citric and lactic acid, and Ministry of Food requirements.

Stocks are those held in depots and refineries and by consumers. The figure for 1945 includes the molasses equivalent of sugar awaiting conversion to high test molasses.

6.16 Plastics and materials for plastics

Home consumption covers consumption in producers' own factories and deliveries to consumers (including Government consumers).

6.17 Paper and papermaking materials

"Paper" means paper or board; "mills" means paper mills or board mills.

Papermaking materials other than woodpulp

Consumption figures relate to consumption by mills.

Stock figures of pulpwood, straw for papermaking, and esparto show the quantities held at mills. The stock figures for rags, waste ropes, etc., and waste paper are prepared from returns made by mills and merchants; they cover all mills and the principal merchants.

Paper equivalent

The paper equivalent figures show the approximate amount of paper which it is estimated can be produced from the papermaking materials other than woodpulp shown as consumed or in stock. The approximate paper equivalents are: pulpwood $37\frac{1}{2}$ per cent, straw 43 per cent, rags, etc., $66\frac{2}{3}$ per cent, waste paper 80 per cent, esparto 42 per cent.

Pulpwood

Imported pulpwood and home-grown timber, including wood waste and chippings.

Woodpulp for papermaking

This comprises chemical sulphite pulp (bleached, partly bleached, bleachable, easy bleaching, strong and bamboo), chemical sulphate pulp (bleached, partly bleached, bleachable, easy bleaching, knotter and screenings, and kraft); and mechanical pulp (wet and dry mechanical pulp) in terms of air dry weight used or held by papermakers and manufacturers of cellulose wadding.

Industrial woodpulp

The woodpulp held or used by manufacturers of rayon and transparent cellulose film.

Newsprint

Consumption figures for 1939 give the quantities of newsprint used by publishers of newspapers and periodicals; subsequent figures also include quantities licensed for other purposes, exports and re-exports.

Stock figures show the quantity of newsprint held at mills and by publishers of newspapers and periodicals.

Building boards and other paper and board

Building boards comprise insulation board, laminated wallboard and hardboard.

Consumption is derived by adding together the paper imported and the home-produced paper invoiced out by mills, and adjusting at the end of every four months for any reduction or increase in the stocks of paper held by manufacturers, merchants and large consumers.

Stocks are the quantities held by papermakers, paper merchants, bag makers, box makers, wallboard merchants, converters, manufacturing stationers and consumers. The returns made by bag makers, box makers, papermakers, and wallboard merchants are believed to cover all engaged in the trade. The principal converters who are omitted are periodical publishers and printers, although certain printers are included in the other categories where, for example, they operate also as merchants. The returns obtained from manufacturing stationers cover all those who are likely to hold considerable stocks, but the returns obtained from consumers relate only to a miscellaneous selection of large firms. National stocks of building boards are included in the figures for 1945.

6.18 Raw cotton, cotton waste and cotton linters

Raw cotton

The home consumption figures show the quantities used by (a) cotton spinning mills for cotton spinning, and (b) other consumers for spinning in mixture with cotton waste, wool, and asbestos and for the manufacture of surgical dressings, upholstery, rayon and, until March 1943, explosives.

Stocks are the quantities held by merchants until 1st April 1941 when such stocks were requisitioned by the Cotton Control. The estimated weight of raw cotton unloading at ports and in transit in the United Kingdom is included.

Cotton waste
Cleaning waste is included from January 1941.

Production figures relate to merchants' receipts of cotton waste from spinning, doubling, weaving and hosiery mills in the United Kingdom.

Home consumption figures show the amount of cotton waste used mainly in waste, woollen and cotton spinning and in the manufacture of surgical dressings, upholstery, cleaning waste and, until August 1943, explosives. Consumption in purification factories, for which the figures are Control deliveries to such factories up to the end of June 1941 and thereafter actual consumption, is included.

Stocks are the quantities held by the Cotton Control, merchants and commercial users (including stocks at purification factories).

Cotton linters
Home consumption figures show the use of imported first and second cut linters, United Kingdom and salvage linters, mainly in the manufacture of rayon, plastics, paper, bedding, surgical dressings, insulation material and explosives.
Stocks are those held by the Cotton Control, merchants, oilcake manufacturers and consumers.

6.19 Cotton yarn

Cotton yarn
Production figures give the total conditioned weight of single cotton yarn, whether sold or used in single or doubled form. They include yarn spun for sale, yarn used for further manufacturing processes in the same firm, and yarn spun on commission. They exclude yarn spun from waste, and spun rayon and mixture yarns.

Deliveries are the total weight of yarn delivered by cotton spinners or used by them for further processing against orders approved by the Cotton Control under the Cotton Allocation Scheme. Cotton waste yarn and cotton and spun rayon mixture yarn are included. Yarn for industrial uses is that used in certain manufactures (for example surgical dressings, hosiery, tyres and narrow fabrics), whether for home consumption or export, and for certain essential home services. Yarn for the export trade is yarn exported as yarn, thread, piece goods or made-up goods.

Consumption by weavers of cotton yarn is the amount of cotton and cotton waste yarns used in the manufacture of cotton fabrics and cotton and rayon mixture fabrics.

Cotton waste yarns
Production figures relate to yarns wholly of cotton waste.

Spindles running
Average of the number of single yarn spindles running during each week of the period on cotton only up to October 1941, and thereafter on cotton, spun rayon and mixture yarns. Figures are given as mule equivalents. Spindles running on waste yarns are excluded.

6.20 Rayon, rayon yarn and woven fabrics

Rayon
Production figures from 1941 give the quantity of rayon and other synthetic fibres produced in the United Kingdom on a delivered weight basis. Before 1941 the figures are excise figures less an estimated allowance for waste.

Spun rayon and mixture yarns
Production figures cover yarns of spun rayon, cotton and rayon mixtures, cotton and wool mixtures, and waste yarns other than those of cotton waste and raw cotton.

Woven cotton fabrics
Production is the output of grey and coloured-woven cotton cloth made for sale or on commission on looms of not less than 23-inch reed space. The figures cover jacquard cloths and cloth for made-up cotton goods, including towels, quilts, bed-coverings, surgical bandages and dressings and tyre cord and fabric. They exclude hosiery, lace net and machinery belting and other cotton smallwares. The figures represent the linear yardage of cloth in the grey state before undergoing finishing processes.

Woven rayon and mixture fabrics
Production is the output of fabrics made wholly from continuous filament or spun rayon, from nylon (after August 1944) and from mixtures of rayon, nylon and cotton yarn. Weaving is on looms of not less than 23-inch reed space. The fabrics included are those containing not less than 85 per cent by weight of cotton, rayon or nylon yarn. The

figures represent the linear yardage of cloth in the grey state before undergoing finishing processes.

Rayon yarn
Consumption figures give the consumption by weavers of yarns made of continuous filament, spun rayon (long or short staple) and other synthetic fibres (such as nylon) in the manufacture of rayon and mixture fabrics.

Looms running
Until December 1943 the average of the number of looms (of not less than 23-inch reed space) running on cotton, rayon, nylon and mixture fabrics during each week of the period. From January 1944 the figure given is the number of looms running on the last full working day of the month. The annual figures for 1944 and 1945 are monthly averages.

6.21 Wool and silk

Raw wool
Production figures show the intake of United Kingdom fleece and skin wool. From 1937 to 1940 the figures are estimated. From 1941 they give the actual weight of wool taken up by the Ministry of Supply, the Board of Trade or the Ministry of Agriculture and Fisheries.

Home consumption is the estimated clean weight consumed in combing, woollen spinning and felt making.

Stock figures show the estimated clean weight of raw wool in Government ownership or held by the UK/Dominion Wool Disposals, Ltd. (Joint Organisation), merchants, top-makers, spinners and manufacturers. Stocks held by farmers are excluded.

Worsted yarn
From 1942 the figures show the wool content of manufacturers' deliveries. The figure for 1937 relates to the production (total weight) of yarn wholly or mainly of wool, including admixtures amounting to about 5 inches wide.

Woven wool fabrics (excluding blankets)
Production figures relate to deliveries except in 1937. All lengths are expressed as the equivalent length of cloth 54 per cent.

Blankets
Production figures relate to deliveries computed on the basis of 1 blanket = 2½ linear yards and 4 cot blankets = 1 full size blanket.

Raw silk
Consumption figures from 1941 give the total amount of raw silk, undischarged weight, put into process. Figures for 1937 and 1938 show deliveries to mills.

Stocks are those held in the United Kingdom by consumers and by the Control, including stocks in transit but excluding material in process.

Silk noils
Production is by waste silk spinners. From March 1942 production from cartridge bag cuttings is also included.

Consumption shows quantity put into process.

Stocks are held by waste silk spinners, by noil spinners, and by the Government. From February 1942 garnetted material is included in Government stocks.

6.22 Jute, flax and hemps

Raw jute
The home consumption figures show the quantity of raw jute used in jute yarn spinning.

Stocks are those held by the Control, spinners and dealers.

Imported jute goods
The home consumption figures relate to deliveries by merchants against disposal licences issued by the Control; consumption by large consumers who buy direct from the Control; quantities sold by the Control to departments; and imported rove and other yarn sold by the Control to weavers, carpet manufacturers and other users. Home-produced goods from Control stocks are included from March 1942 to March 1945.

Stocks cover imported jute goods held by the Control, merchant distributors and consumers purchasing direct from the Control, and, from March 1942 to March 1945, home-produced goods taken into Control stock.

Flax
From April 1944, production includes imports from Eire.

Home consumption figures show the amount of flax spread for spinning by flax spinners and sales to the paper and other trades. Hemp and hemp tow used by flax spinners are included in the figures for 1940 and 1941.

Stocks are the quantities held by the Flax Control and by spinners. Hemp and hemp tow used by flax spinners are included in the figures for 1940 and 1941.

Soft hemps

True hemp comprises Italian, Central European (including Turkish) and Chilean hemp. The figures for consumption and stocks in 1940 and 1941 exclude some portion of true hemp taken over by the Flax Control and used by flax spinners.

Stocks of soft hemps are the quantities held by the Control and by spinners and papermakers, excluding stocks in transit in the United Kingdom.

Hard hemps

Sisal, manila, *phormium tenax* and other varieties.

Home consumption is the amount of hemp used by spinners, papermakers and bedding manufacturers.

Stocks are the quantities held by the Control and by spinners, papermakers and bedding manufacturers, excluding stocks in transit in the United Kingdom.

7. PRODUCTION

SHIPBUILDING

7.3-7.8 Figures of completions refer to vessels which have completed their trials and been handed over to their owners.

Standard displacement

The standard displacement of a *surface* vessel is the displacement of the vessel complete, fully manned, engined and equipped ready for sea, including all armament and ammunition, equipment, outfit, provisions and fresh water for crew, miscellaneous stores and implements of every description that are intended to be carried in war, but without fuel or reserve feed water on board.

The standard displacement of a *submarine* is the surface displacement of the vessel complete (exclusive of the water in non-watertight structure) fully manned, engined and equipped ready for sea, including all armament and ammunition, equipment, outfit, provisions for crew, miscellaneous stores and implements of every description that are intended to be carried in war, but without fuel, lubricating oil, fresh water or ballast water of any kind on board.

Deep displacement

Deep displacement of surface vessels is the same as standard displacement except that it includes fuel and reserve feed water.

Light displacement

Light displacement is the displacement of the ship complete with ammunition, but excluding oil, water, petrol, provisions, canteen stores, naval stores, officers' slops, navigation stores and paymasters' slops.

War load displacement

For landing craft, war load is the light displacement plus the full weight of armoured fighting vehicles, mechanical transport, troops, permissible ammunition, stores, fuel and crew.

Gross tonnage

Gross tonnage is the total volume of all the enclosed spaces of a vessel above the inner bottom. The unit of measurement is a ton of 100 cubic feet.

7.4 **Naval vessels: Ocean and coastal convoy etc.**

Minelayers

This series comprises fast minelayers, controlled minelayers, minelaying lighters and coastal minelayers.

Minesweepers, trawlers and boom defence vessels

These include fleet minesweepers; minesweeping, anti-submarine, and minesweeping anti-submarine trawlers; boom, gate and net vessels.

Mosquito craft

This series comprises steam gun boats, motor torpedo boats, motor anti-submarine boats, motor launches and motor minesweepers.

Landing craft

Types included are tank, flak, gun, mechanized, assault, support, personnel and infantry landing craft.

MUNITIONS

7.9-7.21 This section gives a summary of United Kingdom production of the more important munitions and warlike stores during the rearmament period immediately preceding the outbreak of war and during the war itself. The munitions section and the separate sections giving the production of military aircraft and naval vessels taken together cover the major groups of war production for the armed forces. There are important connections between this and the other two sections, for example, this section includes the production of guns for aircraft and naval vessels. A large part of the munitions tables relates to production administered by the Ministry of Supply, which was responsible not only for Army requirements but also for some production for the requirements of the Royal Navy and the Royal Air Force. The most important items of production of this type included in these tables are small arms ammunition, explosives and the filling of shells and bombs. Except for this production the other two Supply departments remained responsible for their major munitions requirements. Of the production shown in the munitions tables, the Admiralty was responsible for the production of all naval guns (Table 7.11), the Oerlikon gun (Table 7.12), naval propellant production (included in Table 7.17) and for most types of empty components for naval ammunition (Table 7.16); the Ministry of Aircraft Production was responsible for the production of aircraft guns including the Hispano-Suiza (Table 7.12) and to a varying extent for the supply of empty bomb components (Table 7.16).

The choice of items shown in the tables has necessarily been limited, although for certain groups the coverage of the figures is more complete than for others. For example, armoured fighting vehicles, artillery, light guns and small arms ammunition are comprehensively covered since these items lend themselves more readily to generic grouping than do certain others such as engineer stores, signal equipment and artillery instruments. The difficulty of dealing with groups of this latter type where only a limited selection of items has been included is overcome to some extent for Ministry of Supply production by prefacing the munitions tables with an index of munitions production (Table 7.9) from which the general trend of production in each main group can be readily seen. Some important groups are omitted entirely, both from these tables and from the index of production - for example, medical stores, clothing and general equipment and stores.

The statistics given in these tables come from two main sources. Those covering the period of the war and a small number of pre-war figures are extracted from the departmental records of the Admiralty and the Ministry of Supply (including the records of aircraft munitions production now in the possession of the Ministry of Supply). Most of the pre-war figures on the other hand come from Deficiency Progress Reports submitted to the Committee on Imperial Defence by Service departments during the rearmament period.

With one exception the tables cover new production only in the United Kingdom. The figures therefore exclude repairs, reconditioning, conversions and supplies from overseas. An exception is made for armoured fighting vehicles; overseas supplies of these vehicles were of exceptional importance and such supplies are shown alongside United Kingdom production in Table 7.18. Production of spare parts is excluded from all the tables.

The basis of enumeration in these tables is generally "deliveries passed inspection" and, for naval guns after January 1942 "acceptances after proof". For the few items where the basis is "deliveries ex factory" this is shown in the footnotes to the tables. The production figures relate to periods of three months (not necessarily ending on the last day of a calendar quarter) or to periods of 13 weeks ending near the end of the calendar quarter. The effect of these small variations in the time series is slight.

A double line drawn horizontally across a column indicates that the production of the particular item of equipment ceased in the preceding quarter.

The various abbreviations used in the column headings are listed and explained at the beginning of the Digest.

7.9 Index of Ministry of Supply munitions production

The index relates to Ministry of Supply production, that is, predominantly but not entirely to Army equipment. The major items in each of the groups shown in this table were included but the coverage varied with the different groups of stores. Owing to the very large number of spares produced and the lack of information regarding them, it was not found possible to make any allowance for spares in the index. From various estimates which were made, however, it is evident that the omission of spares from the index brings it appreciably lower towards the end of the war than it would otherwise have been.

The basis of the weighting system employed was fixed value. This was first calculated with prices ruling at October 1939, but a revision was made in mid-1942 as price changes had by that time appreciably affected the weighting. The revision was carried back to March 1941, the index being adjusted to produce a smooth join with the earlier figures.

As the index is based on fixed prices it relates to changes in deliveries and not to changes in expenditure. Any distortion due to differences in time between payments and deliveries is thus excluded.

The index is not adjusted for holidays.

7.10 Artillery equipment, instruments and tank and anti-tank guns

Deliveries of experimental or pilot models are not in general included in the figures.

The figures for light anti-aircraft equipment relate to the 40 mm. Bofors only. Up to the outbreak of war all supplies of this equipment were imported.

Only new production is included in this table and the figures therefore exclude the extensive programme of conversion which was in force immediately preceding and during the early stages of the war. The scale of this programme can be seen from the following figures:-

Equipment	*Number*		*Duration*
	Pre-war	*War*	*of programme*
Field 18 pdr. to 25 pdr.	611	829	1937 to Jun. 1941
A.A. 3-in. 20 cwt. (guns only)	431	30	1937 to Jan. 1940 1940
60 pdr. to 4.5-in.	1	64	1939 to Dec. 1940

7.11 Naval guns

The distinction between "short" and "long" range guns under anti-aircraft is broadly the same as that between "light" and "heavy" in Table 7.10. Short range guns comprise the 2 pdr. and 40 mm. Bofors. Long range covers all larger calibres.

7.12 Armoured fighting vehicles

This is the only table in the section to include supplies from sources other than the United Kingdom. The term "overseas" covers the United States of America, Canada, South Africa, Australia and New Zealand. Supplies of tanks were from the United States of America and Canada only. The term "supplies" includes deliveries not only to the United Kingdom, but also to United Kingdom, Dominion and Colonial forces in any theatre of war irrespective of whether the forces were under War Office control or not. The figures include 2,375 Canadian tanks retained in Canada and about 15,500 armoured carriers and cars retained in Canada and Australia for home defence.

The weight shown for tanks is the weight "in action", that is, including armament and allowance for ammunition, wireless and other equipment and crew.

7.13 Wheeled vehicles

The figures in this table cover production for the Service departments only. Total production of motor vehicles in the United Kingdom is given in Table 7.31.

The vehicles in this analysis, which are broadly designated as mechanical transport, include all mechanical wheeled vehicles except vehicles classified as fighting vehicles, that is, except armoured cars, scout cars and armoured command vehicles.

The classification used is based on broad general groupings. The various lorries and trucks are not all conventional load-carriers; a considerable number are vehicles with special bodies and fittings for special loads as well as for numerous technical purposes. It may, however, be useful to aggregate production in terms of load-carrying capacity and for this purpose heavy tractors should be regarded as equivalent to 6-ton lorries and light tractors and ambulances to 1-3-ton lorries; heavy cars are vehicles of 16 h.p. and upwards, while light cars and vans are below 16 h.p. It should be noted, however, that the load classification of Service vehicles in the main is not the same as for civil vehicles - for example, a Service 3-ton vehicle is the equivalent of a commercial 5-ton vehicle.

7.20 Signal equipment

This table gives a limited but representative selection of signal equipment. Radar equipment is excluded.

7.21 Engineer stores

Production of engineer stores covered a wide range of field, bridging and civil engineering equipment and amenity items, for example, refrigeration and air-conditioning equipment. The items included in this table are confined mainly to bridging equipment and are not a representative selection of engineer stores.

AIRCRAFT

7.23 Production of aircraft by structure weight

The structure weight of an aircraft is the empty weight of the fuselage, wings, undercarriage, engine nacelles and flying controls. Engines, propellers, turrets, guns, electrical equipment and radio sets are excluded.

7.24 Index of aircraft production
Neither structure weight nor unadjusted manhours taken separately were found to be a satisfactory basis for an index of aircraft production. Accordingly, this index is based on manhours standardised by reference to structure weight for the three main groups of aircraft produced, namely, heavy, medium and fighter bombers; other operational aircraft; and trainers.

7.25 Aircraft awaiting repair and repaired
The aircraft repair figures relate to repairs carried out by the Civilian Repair Organisation only and exclude repairs by squadrons.

7.26 Engines: Production, imports and repairs
The figures for imports relate to engines imported for the Royal Air Force and Royal Navy. They exclude engines returned to the United Kingdom for repair and re-export.

Repairs are those carried out by the Civilian Repair Organisation and exclude repairs by squadrons.

7.27, 7.28 Arrivals of aircraft from North America
The term "arrivals" covers aircraft despatched both by air and by sea and imported for the Royal Air Force and Royal Navy.

MANUFACTURED GOODS

7.29 Deliveries of machine tools, small tools, welding sets and electric motors

Machine tools
For definition see the Control of Machine Tools (No.12) Order 1942. The table excludes, except from the 1935 figures, metal-working and wood-working tools of value less than £50. The value figures exclude replacement parts.

Metal-working machine tools
The following types are included: automatics, borers, broaches, drills, gear-cutters, grinders, lappers and honers, capstans and turrets, lathes, millers, planers, presses, saws, shapers, shears, sheet metal working, slotters, screw, thread and miscellaneous metal-working machine tools.

Wood-working machine tools
The following types are included: saws of all types (except hand saws), drills, grinders and sharpeners, gluers, lathes, morticing and tenoning machines, dove-tailing machines, planes and moulds, routers, sanders, veneering machines and miscellaneous wood-working machine tools

Engineers' small tools
These include cutting tools, chucks, jigs and fixtures, press tools and gauges.

Welding sets
The value figures exclude replacement parts.

7.31 Locomotives and motor vehicles

Locomotives
The figures show the number of steam locomotives produced by railway workshops and by private makers and include production for the Services.

Main line types comprise passenger tender, passenger tank, freight tender (including mixed traffic), freight tank, Garratts and other steam types.

Industrial locomotives include shunters for docks.

7.32 Woven cloth, household textiles, hosiery and footwear
Supplies for home civilian use include retained imports where these are distinguished in the Trade and Navigation Accounts, supplies for N.A.A.F.I. and for local authorities, hospitals, etc., but exclude supplies for Government orders and for export. For 1935 the figures are based on the Census of Production, adjusted for retained imports and exports.

Woven wool cloth
Supplies are the deliveries by manufacturers of tissues containing 15 per cent and over of wool fibre, excluding hair fabric used for interlining and similar purposes. Cloth for uniforms for Civil Defence, transport purposes or hospitals, etc. is not included if specially issued by the Wool Control.

Woven non-wool cloth
Supplies are the deliveries by manufacturers and merchant converters registered under the Apparel and Textiles Order. Cloth for handkerchiefs and babies' napkins is included.

Wool hand-knitting yarn
All hand-knitting yarn, including yarn of Service shades and mending yarn, produced on wool machinery.

Blankets
The figures relate to supplies of full-size and cot blankets, and are based on manufacturers' deliveries.

Towels

"Other" towels include roller towels, tea towels, glass cloths, etc.

Hosiery

Garments made up from warp knitted fabric are excluded. The figures for children's garments cover all children under 14 and thus include infants' wear. The pre-war figures quoted are estimates for 1937.

Footwear

Total production for all uses is the output by manufacturers during the period. Production for home civilian use is the quantity of footwear transferred to warehouse stock by all manufacturers of leather footwear, excluding production for export or for which leather is procured under permit from the Director of Service Footwear; thus footwear for the Home Guard, Civil Defence and Women's Land Army is excluded. All rubber boots and shoes and canvas shoes with rubber soles are excluded, but other rubber-soled footwear is included under the appropriate heading. Children's footwear includes that for infants.

7.33 Pottery, hollow-ware and brushes

Production figures relate to manufacturers' sales. Supplies for home civilian use include retained imports where these are distinguished in the Trade and Navigation Accounts, supplies for N.A.A.F.I. and for local authorities, hospitals, etc., but exclude supplies for Government orders and for export.

Pottery

Small plates are those of 8-inch diameter or less, large plates are over 8-inch diameter.

Coffee-pots are included from March 1943 only.

Until February 1943 the figures for cooking-ware relate to pie and baking dishes only.

8. TRANSPORT

MERCHANT SHIPPING

Gross tonnage

The total volume of all the enclosed spaces of a vessel above the inner bottom. The unit of measurement is a ton of 100 cubic feet.

Deadweight tonnage

The number of tons (2,240lb.) of cargo, stores, bunkers, equipment, etc., that a vessel carries when floating at her summerload draught.

Net tonnage

Net tonnage is the gross tonnage less certain deductions on account of crew space, engine room, water ballast and other spaces not used for passengers or cargo.

8.3- Merchant shipping under British control
8.5 Foreign vessels

Bareboat charter transfers to the charterer, the responsibility for manning, upkeep and other functions normally assumed by the owner.

8.11 Shipping movement at United Kingdom ports: Entrances and clearances in the foreign trade

Foreign trade

Trading vessels engaged in voyages direct from any port abroad (including the Channel Islands and Eire) to a port in the United Kingdom (including the Isle of Man) or *vice versa*. Vessels calling at more than one United Kingdom port in the course of a single voyage are recorded as entered or cleared at one port only.

The figures exclude naval vessels or vessels with naval crews requisitioned or chartered for naval or military transport services, but vessels on Government service with mercantile crews are included. Other exclusions are pleasure yachts sailed privately, tugs engaged on the coasts of the United Kingdom, vessels entering ports for shelter through stress of weather and British fishing vessels.

Vessels with cargo

Vessels loading or unloading cargo, even though principally engaged in carrying passengers. Cargo consists of merchandise (other than Government stores, ships' stores or bunkers), bullion, specie or mail.

Vessels in ballast

Vessels other than those defined above under vessels "with cargo". The figures include vessels unloading or loading only Government stores, that is, goods consigned direct to Allied or Commonwealth forces in this country or reshipment of such goods; goods shipped by a United Kingdom Government department for the use of United Kingdom forces abroad or re-imports of such goods and imports of captured enemy military equipment.

8.12 Arrivals of shipping at United Kingdom ports

Vessels calling during the course of a single voyage at more than one port are recorded as arrived and departed at each port. The extent of the duplication, so far as inward movement is affected, can be seen by comparing the figures for foreign trade arrivals in this table with those for entrances in Table 8.11.

The terms "cargo" and "ballast" are defined as for Table 8.11.

RAIL TRANSPORT

8.16 Repair and availability of rolling stock

Locomotives
Steam, electric, petrol, oil and oil electric locomotives but excluding rail-motors. Figures do not necessarily show the number owned by the railway companies as account has been taken of loans made to and by the railway companies, the Service departments, the Ministry of Supply, etc.

Passenger-carrying vehicles
Rail motor vehicles and steam and electric coaches. Account has been taken of loans made to and by the railway companies, the Service departments, the Ministry of Supply, etc.

Trucks and wagons
Most of the privately-owned wagons in Great Britain were requisitioned in September 1939, with the exception of tank wagons, certain specially constructed wagons and wagons set aside for special traffic such as tarred road materials, cement, salt, etc.

8.17 Passenger and goods traffic

Passenger journeys
The figures of passenger journeys show the number of journeys originating on the railway system of Great Britain, including through booked passenger journeys commenced by road and completed by rail.

Children for whom tickets are issued are treated as adults, but infants in arms are excluded. Return tickets are counted as two journeys and the number of journeys by season ticket holders are on the basis of 600 journeys per annum. Government department traffic (for example, naval, military, etc.), tickets under bulk travel arrangements and other reduced fare traffic are included.

Estimated passenger miles
Figures relate to main line companies only and are estimated.

Goods, mineral and livestock traffic
The figures show the tonnage of revenue-earning traffic conveyed by trains on the railway system. Cross-channel traffic invoiced to interior stations is treated as originating at the port of entry.

Free-hauled traffic, which includes servicing materials for the railways conveyed without charge on revenue-earning trains, and traffic conveyed on ballast trains or departmental trains is excluded.

Estimated net ton-miles
The product of the load conveyed and the miles travelled including free-hauled traffic.

8.18 Operating statistics

Loaded train-miles
The distance run by all types of revenue-earning trains calculated on the actual distance worked to the nearest mile. Coaching trains are trains made up entirely of coaching vehicles for the conveyance of passengers and other traffic scheduled as passenger train traffic, such as parcels, mails, etc. Freight trains are those composed of wagons, trucks, etc., used for the conveyance of goods traffic at freight train charges. The mileage of trains consisting of both coaching and freight vehicles and scheduled as "mixed" has been divided equally between coaching and freight.

Loaded wagon-miles
The mileage of loaded wagons including those loaded with free-hauled traffic worked on revenue-earning trains. Each vehicle is counted irrespective of its capacity or its load. The distances correspond to those for train-miles but no mileage is included for the distances covered by wagons when being shunted.

9.19 Traffic receipts

From 1st September 1939, under the Railway Control Agreement, the receipts of the controlled undertakings (the four main line railway companies, London Passenger Transport Board, their joint lines and certain minor railways) were pooled and clearances between undertakings were not made. These figures represent, therefore, the originating receipts of the major portion of the Pool.

On 11th June 1939 railway passenger fares in the London area, including those on the London Passenger Transport Board, were increased by 5 per cent to the level of fares outside London; on 1st May 1940 railway passenger fares (except season tickets and workmen's fares) and freight rates were increased by 10 per cent; on 1st December 1940 this percentage was raised to $16^2/_3$. On the London Passenger Transport Board increases in railway passenger fares above 5d.

became effective from 1st May 1940 and increases in certain other railway and road transport fares became effective from 3rd July 1940 and 1st December.

Passenger receipts
Passenger receipts are the receipts from passenger fares of all kinds. Charges for platform tickets, seat reservations, left luggage, etc., which are classed as miscellaneous receipts are excluded.

Parcels, mails, etc.
Include receipts from the conveyance of small parcels and other merchandise by passenger train as well as mail and parcel post.

Merchandise
This class includes all freight train traffic except coal and coke and minerals and other commodities carried in bulk.

Minerals
This class covers traffic in Classes 1 to 6 of the general railway classification, that is, minerals and other heavy freight carried in bulk, for example, bricks, iron ore, lime, limestone, pig-iron, road stone and stone in the rough.

Coal and coke
Includes coal, coke, patent fuels, slack smudge, cannel and coal cinders for fuel.

ROAD TRANSPORT

8.20, 8.21 Vehicles with licences current and new registrations

These figures are compiled from information received by the Ministry of Transport from all licensing authorities in Great Britain which administer the relevant sections of the Roads Act, 1920. The statistics are thus a by-product of administration and the classes shown correspond in the main to taxation classes. The figures include all vehicles which pay tax and certain vehicles which are exempt from the payment of tax. Most of the latter carry a form of licence known as a "nil" licence.

Exempt vehicles are of three kinds: (a) vehicles which are designed and used for certain particular purposes; (b) those which make little or no use of public roads; and (c) vehicles owned by Government authorities.

Vehicles in the first class (such as ambulances, invalid vehicles, road construction vehicles and fire service vehicles) are registered when they are first brought into use and pay no tax but they do carry a "nil" licence. They therefore appear in the statistics of licences current. During the war, fire service vehicles were temporarily transferred to the National Fire Service and operated under O.H.M.S. certificates instead of "nil" licences, and during this period they disappeared from the statistics.

Of vehicles in the second class, those which are never used on the public roads (for example farm or works tractors used solely on the farm or site) are not required to bear a licence or to be registered, and are therefore outside the statistics altogether. Vehicles which make no use of roads repairable at the public expense, or make little use, that is, they travel not more than six miles per week while passing between different parts of the owners' lands, are registered but carry no licence. Therefore, they are not included in the statistics of licences current.

Vehicles belonging to the armed forces are not registered and carry O.H.M.S certificates. Hence they are not included in either table.

Agricultural tractors may fall into the 5s. or £12 class according to the uses to which they are put by the owner. The 5s. agricultural tractor class includes locomotive ploughing engines and other agricultural engines and covers those which are used on roads only for hauling their own equipment, farming implements and the like, or for hauling agricultural produce or requisites provided that the owner is engaged in agriculture and the vehicle is used primarily for work on the land. It also includes some trench diggers, excavators and mobile cranes which are used on roads only for proceeding to and from working sites. Mowing machines are also included. The £12 and over class includes tractors, agricultural tractors and engines (other than vehicles subject to a duty of 5s.) which are registered in the name of a person engaged in agriculture and which are used on the roads solely for the haulage of the produce of and requisites for his own agricultural land.

Agricultural vans and lorries are goods vehicles registered in the name of a person engaged in agriculture and used on roads solely for the conveyance of the produce of and requisites for his agricultural land.

9. EXTERNAL TRADE

9.3-9.10 The tables covering external trade have been compiled from information published in the Annual Statements of Trade of the United Kingdom and from the monthly Accounts relating to the Trade and Navigation of the United Kingdom.

Quantities and values

Both quantities and values are based on the declarations of importers and exporters, or their agents, which may be verified by Customs officials. The value of the imports represents the open market value as defined by Section 10 of the Finance Act, 1935. Briefly stated, this value is the price which the goods would fetch on sale in the open market at the time of import if the goods were delivered to the buyers at the port or place of importation, freight, insurance, commission and all other costs, charges and expenses incidental to the making of the contract of sale and the delivery of the goods at that port or place (except any duties of Customs and purchase tax) having been paid by the seller. The value of the exports represents the cost of the goods to the purchaser abroad, including packing, inland and coastal transport in the United Kingdom, dock dues, loading charges and all other costs, profits, charges and expenses (for example, insurance and commission) accruing up to the point where the goods are deposited on board the exporting vessel or aircraft or at the land boundary of Northern Ireland, and is known as the "free on board" value.

Imports and exports

Military stores

Stores owned by the Government of this country shipped for the use of United Kingdom forces abroad are excluded from the export figures. Similarly, military stores carried in Government vessels and captured enemy equipment imported by Government departments are excluded.

Stores and equipment imported direct by Commonwealth and allied forces and auxiliary bodies based in the United Kingdom are excluded. Imports by a United Kingdom Government department (unless carried in Government vessels) even though transferred subsequently to such forces within the United Kingdom are however included in the figures.

Stores for N.A.A.F.I., the Y.M.C.A. and other similar organisations are included.

Munitions

The figures for 1942 to 1945 exclude imports, exports and re-exports of "munitions", that is, aircraft and other vehicles and parts (except rubber tyres and tubes), arms, ammunition and military and naval stores. From 1938 to 1941 such goods are included under the appropriate headings of the Trade Accounts except that certain warlike stores imported for Government use are included under a comprehensive heading for Government stores (Class III, Group U (Miscellaneous articles wholly or mainly manufactured)).

Relief and rehabilitation, lend-lease and mutual aid

Exports of goods for relief and rehabilitation of liberated countries in Europe are included in the figures whether exported by U.N.R.R.A., by a United Kingdom Government department or on behalf of the country concerned.

Goods imported under lend-lease and mutual aid arrangements are included throughout under the appropriate headings; those imported by U.N.R.R.A. for its official use are excluded.

Parcels for prisoners of war and the armed forces

Parcels despatched to prisoners of war are excluded from the export figures.

Parcels despatched to United Kingdom or allied forces abroad are included as exports under the heading of "parcel post" except where they contain tobacco or other goods exported on drawback when they are included under the appropriate export heading.

Parcels from North America to United States and Canadian forces in this country are excluded. All other parcels are included as imports, those containing goods liable to import duty being recorded under the appropriate headings and not under parcel post.

Miscellaneous exclusions

Bullion and specie, ships' stores and bunkers and ballast of no commercial value are excluded from both exports and imports. In addition, exports exclude personal and household effects taken by passengers for private use and articles exported solely for temporary exhibition in galleries and museums abroad. Imports exclude fresh fish and shell fish of British taking landed from British ships, gifts for members of the forces and for approved war charities, etc.

10. PUBLIC FINANCE

10.4 Floating debt

Advances from the Bank of England

Ways and Means advances.

Advances from Government departments

Certain loans made to the Treasury by Public Departments, principally by the Paymaster-General and the National Debt Commissioners, out of accruing receipts.

Treasury bills

The total value of bills held by the market, by Public Departments and the Issue Department of the Bank of England.

Treasury deposits by banks

Loans to the Treasury by the banks for periods of six months.

10.5 Currency circulation and bank clearings

Currency circulation

The series showing the estimated circulation of notes and coin with the public relates to the total note issues of the Bank of England, the Scottish banks and the Northern Irish Banks, *plus* the estimated total of imperial silver, cupro-nickel, bronze and nickel-brass coin in circulation, *less* notes and coin held by the Bank of England (Banking Department), by the Scottish and Northern Irish Banks (as published in the London and Belfast Gazettes) and by the London Clearing Banks.

Bank clearings

The clearings reported by the London Bankers' Clearing House represent the total of bankers' effects (cheques, drafts, bills, interest warrants, etc.) passed through the clearing houses for collection from the banks.

Before the war the clearing house in London published its figures under three regions - Town, Metropolitan and Country - which covered broadly the City of London, the London suburbs and the rest of England and Wales (apart from the purely local provincial clearings) respectively. This classification ceased when the clearing banks' emerging operations came into force in September 1939.

During the war years the figures include the large volume of transactions settled between the head offices, and branches of the same banks but not cheques cashed over the counter. A partial return to pre-war methods, which excluded these transactions, began in October 1945.

Provincial clearings represent similar collections at the 12 clearing houses operating in the provinces.

10.6 External disinvestment

This summary table estimates, over the period from the outbreak of war in Europe to 30th June 1945, the effect of the war upon the United Kingdom in terms of capital loss in the overseas financial position. This loss took the form of the realisation of investments, the incurring of debts in the form of sterling liabilities, etc., and the running down of gold and dollar reserves. The sum of these represents the loss of overseas wealth which the United Kingdom suffered in order to meet overseas military expenditure and the cost of essential services and supplies from abroad.

10.7, 10.8 Lend-lease and reciprocal aid

The material contained in the two tables dealing with lend-lease and reciprocal aid has been extracted from a paper "Mutual Aid between the US and the British Empire, 1941-45" read before the Royal Statistical Society by Professor R.G.D Allen on 29th May 1946. A brief description of the nature of the material used and of its source is given below. Fuller information can, however, be obtained from Professor Allen's paper (Journal of the Royal Statistical Society, Vol. CIX, Part III, 1946, pp. 243-277).

United States lend-lease aid to the British Empire

The figures relate to goods transferred and services rendered under lend-lease as recorded by the Foreign Economic Administration (F.E.A.) and published in the Reports to Congress on lend-lease operations made quarterly by the President. Certain major revisions were made on the cumulative returns after June 1945. Aid to the British Empire shown in this table agrees with the revised F.E.A. figures cumulatively to 30th June 1945 and to 31st August 1945. The analysis by period to mid-1945 is obtained from differences in F.E.A. cumulative figures on the unrevised basis, except for adjustments in services and in industrial products (metals and machinery) arising from the revision. The analysis by periods must therefore be accepted with caution.

The classification adopted is as follows:

(a) Munitions: aircraft, ordnance, combat and motor vehicles and related equipment; small water-craft and naval equipment; signal engineer, quartermaster, medical, chemical warfare and other military stores.

(b) Ships (sail-away): naval and merchant vessels delivered under their own power.
(c) Other goods: agricultural products, raw materials, petroleum and manufactures.
(d) Services: ship repair, freights, ships' stores and other shipping services; ferrying of aircraft; training of personnel; storage and transportation; materials and charges for construction of bases; miscellaneous expenses.

Since Canada did not receive lend-lease aid, goods exported by the United States to Canada for the eventual use of the United Kingdom are included in the United Kingdom figures. Lend-lease aid has been shown as valued by the United States in dollars and reciprocal aid (in Table 10.10) as valued by the United Kingdom in £ sterling. Any direct comparison raises the difficult problem of the appropriate relation between the dollar and the £ sterling. The official rate of exchange has no relevance to the problem. What is required is either an evaluation of what lend-lease aid to the British Empire would have cost if the goods had been produced and the services rendered in British countries, or an evaluation of what reciprocal aid to the United States would have cost at the United States prices used in the accounting of United States lend-lease aid. For munitions and military stores (excluding food) an item by item comparison of unit costs in the United States and United Kingdom indicates that an appropriate average of conversion is around $7 to £1. For other goods and for services only a fragmentary comparison of the United States and United Kingdom prices used in mutual aid valuations is possible. The appropriate conversion rate, however, would seem to be not far from the official rate of exchange, that is about $4.03 to £1.

United Kingdom reciprocal aid

The figures have been derived from the White Papers on Mutual Aid (Cmd. 6483, 1943 and Cmd. 6570, 1944) and cumulative data subsequently compiled by the Treasury. Figures of petroleum provided in India are from United States Army records supplied to the F.E.A.

The classification follows closely that for United States lend-lease in the previous table. Military stores include all munitions and other stores for direct use by foreign forces with the exception of petroleum and food. Services are mainly transportation but also include building maintenance. The construction figure represents the cost to the Service departments of the construction of military installations and includes the whole cost of the Mulberry Harbour.

Aid to the United States in the United Kingdom comprises all transfers of goods and services to United States forces in the United Kingdom, but shipping services and petroleum tankers are on a world-wide basis. Aid in the United States includes both goods transferred in the United States as food and materials exported from the United Kingdom and the colonies to United States. Aid in overseas theatres includes transfers and construction in the colonies as well as in various theatres of war.

11. NATIONAL INCOME

Tables 11.3-11.9 have been prepared as far as possible on the same basis as those contained in "National Income and Expenditure of the United Kingdom 1946 to 1949" (Cmd. 7933, 1950). The correspondence, nevertheless, is not exact. While continuity has been preserved for the war years 1939-1945 there remains in certain points of detail an unavoidable break between the figures for this period and the figures for 1938 and for the post-war period. This applies chiefly to the accounts of public authorities.

It must be strongly emphasised, moreover, that the estimates given here are not based on exact knowledge, but are derived from information collected by government departments and private organisations for needs other than the estimation of national income. In some cases the information is very incomplete. No direct estimates of personal saving or of capital formation have been possible. Personal saving has been obtained by subtracting personal expenditure from personal income, and gross capital formation by subtracting all other components of national expenditure from the total of national income and depreciation.

For detailed definitions of terms reference should be made to Cmd. 7933. For items where the title is not self-explanatory, or to which special qualifications apply, brief notes are added below.

11.3 National income, depreciation and expenditure

The first part of this table presents estimates of the incomes received, in cash and in kind, by factors of production in producing the current output of goods and services of all kinds. The incomes are reckoned before tax, but after the amounts allowed for maintenance and depreciation in the calculation, for tax purposes, of net rent and profit. The total of these amounts together with the provision for maintenance by public authorities is given separately in this table.

Wages cover only the earnings of manual workers while *salaries* cover the earnings of administrative, professional, technical, clerical and office staff, including the earnings of shop assistants, commercial travellers, nurses and members of the police force and National Fire Service. In principle untaxed allowances of salary-earners and company directors' fees are also included in *salaries*.

Income from farming

This item represents the reward of the manual and managerial labour of farmers and their wives and the return on their capital. The estimates, still subject to revision, were originally calculated for crop years June to May. The figure given in the table for the calendar year 1938 includes five-twelfths of the income gained in the crop year 1937-38 and seven-twelfths of that for 1938-39; and similarly for other years. For example, the increase shown between 1938 and 1939 reflects in fact the higher profits reaped in the beginning of 1940.

Professional earnings

This item includes the earnings of doctors, dentists, lawyers, artists, journalists and other professional persons. It excludes the profits of brokers, auctioneers, estate agents and of other businesses where the profits made depend on the making of contracts on behalf of others or in the giving of commercial advice relating to contracts.

Profits of other sole traders and partnerships

This item includes the profits of all unincorporated enterprises other than those shown separately in income from farming and professional earnings.

Trading profits of companies

This item covers the trading profits of companies and mutual societies other than the profits included in "net income from abroad", together with the surpluses, before deduction of interest or dividends on sales, of co-operative societies and public boards.

Operating profits of public enterprises

The trading profits of local authorities before charging interest on, or amortisation of, debt *plus* the profit under the Railway Agreement *less* the loss incurred by the Exchequer in 1945 as a result of illicit trading operations abroad by members of the armed forces and other government employees. The definition of this item differs from that in Cmd. 7933 by the exclusion of the trading profits of the Board of Trade and Ministry of Supply and of the interest carried as a national charge in the commercial accounts of government trading branches.

Rent of land and buildings

This item represents the net rental value on a Schedule A basis of lands and personal and business property, together with excess rents assessed under Schedule D.

Net income from abroad

This item is made up of the profits remitted home by British companies operating abroad (other than oil, shipping and insurance companies, all of whose profits are included above) *plus* interest and dividends received from abroad *less* profits remitted abroad and interest and dividends paid (after deduction of tax) to non-residents.

National expenditure

The second part of Table 11.3 presents estimates of expenditure by residents of the United Kingdom on goods and services. The expenditure is recorded at market prices. From this expenditure is derived not only the incomes of the factors of production that produced the current output of goods and services, but also (i) the amounts to be provided for the maintenance, repair and replacement of the capital equipment used by the factors of production as part of the process of current output and (ii) the indirect taxes on outlay collected from producers by public authorities *less* subsidies paid to producers.

Gross national expenditure at market prices includes the amounts in both (i) and (ii). Gross national expenditure at factor cost excludes the amount in (ii) and is equal to national income plus depreciation.

Personal expenditure on consumers' goods and services

This item is described in the notes to Table 11.9.

Public authorities' current expenditure on goods and services

The term "public authorities" covers the central government, together with all extra-budgetary funds (in particular the Unemployment Fund and various national health insurance and pensions funds), and local authorities.

Only direct expenditure on goods and service is included, except that the provision made for maintenance is treated as a current cost and therefore as part of gross national expenditure. This provision is measured, in the case of the central government, by the amount actually spent on the maintenance of roads and buildings and, in the case of local authorities, by the amounts spent on maintenance of highways and bridges plus loan repayments and payments to sinking funds on rate-fund account, these being treated as the equivalent of depreciation allowances. Loan repayments or payments to sinking funds by the central government are excluded. Transfer payments (e.g., social security payments or subsidies) are also excluded, together with any transfers between one public authority and another. Expenditure refunded to the government or recovered by direct sales has also been excluded.

Capital expenditure by public authorities is included in the total of gross capital formation given separately below when it has been possible to distinguish it. But the separation is by no means complete. For example, it has not been possible to take full account of changes in government-owned stocks. All defence expenditure has been treated as current.

This item thus attempts to measure the value of the work currently performed on government account and the Exchequers' cash issues have been adjusted as far as possible for changes in department's cash balances and in the Government's liabilities to industry.

It is not, however, a consistent measure of the value of resources at the disposal of public authorities since lend-lease assistance has been excluded throughout with the one exception that the 1945 figure includes an amount of £161 million ($650 million) to cover the final settlement with the Government of the United States.

Gross domestic capital formation

This item is composed of gross expenditure, both public and private, on fixed capital and its upkeep (i.e., new additions, replacements and repairs) plus the increase in value of stocks and work in progress. It has been impossible to estimate this item directly for the war years and the figures given here have been obtained as a residual. They are therefore dependent on the accuracy of the estimates of each of the other items of national income and expenditure. Moreover, as explained above, part of capital formation may be included in public authorities' expenditure. The figures given here should therefore be treated with great reserve.

Net lending abroad and purchase of assets and financial claims from overseas

This item is an estimate of the net change in the external assets of the United Kingdom. It is equal to the surplus (or deficit) of the balance of payments on current account, i.e., to the difference between the country's current receipts from abroad and its current payments to foreigners. Lend-lease has entered into this item in only one year: the 1945 figure includes the liability of £161 million to the Government of the United States mentioned above.

11.4 Revenue account of persons

Personal income is made up of (i) incomes from employment for pay or gain (i.e., the first six items of Table 11.3); (ii) receipts by persons (treating charities, life insurance funds and other non-profit-making bodies, as persons) of net rent, dividends and interest paid by companies and public enterprises, debt interest paid by public authorities and income from abroad; and (iii) transfer incomes - social security benefits, war gratuities, etc. In all cases the income is reckoned before deduction of tax or insurance contributions.

Net saving is the amount left out of personal income after deducting current expenditure on consumers' goods and services, the tax liable on current income (whether paid currently or in the future) and taxes paid on capital (e.g., death duties).

11.5 Revenue account of public authorities

This table summarises the income and expenditure of public authorities after eliminating transfers between one public authority and another, such as Exchequer grants to local authorities and Exchequer contributions to insurance funds.

Miscellaneous income from property

This is made up of the profits of public enterprises and receipts of dividends, interest and rent (including national debt interest paid to the Unemployment Fund and national health insurance funds and debt interest paid by local authorities to the central government). Total national debt interest plus the total interest on local authorities' debt is treated as negative income from property.

11.6 Combined capital account

This table shows the sources from which gross capital formation was financed. Transfers from public authorities (the same as transfers to capital accounts shown in Table 11.5) consist of payments in respect of war damage claims and capital grants to local authorities.

11.7 Central government revenue

Tax revenue represents the net receipts by the Board of Inland Revenue and H.M. Customs and Excise as distinct from payments into the Exchequer.

11.8 The finance of the central government deficit on current account

Small savings

The increase in investments from the net deposits in the Post Office and Trustee Savings Banks together with receipts *less* repayments of National Saving Certificates and Defence Bonds.

Other public issues (net)

Receipts *less* redemptions, but excluding purchase of government securities by public departments.

Floating debt

Treasury bills, treasury deposit receipts and Ways and Means advances.

Lending and net capital formation

Includes loans to local authorities, Post Office loan expenditure, and Road Fund expenditure on improvement and new construction of roads.

11.9 Personal expenditure on consumers' goods and services

The totals shown in the table relate to expenditure out of personal income, i.e., the income of individuals and of charities and other non-profit-making bodies. The estimates for the different groups of expenditure include purchases by visitors to the United Kingdom and exclude purchases abroad by British troops and tourists. Rough adjustments for these factors are made at the end of the table.

Expenditure on consumers' goods and services by business firms and public authorities is as far as possible excluded except in certain cases where the object purchased is resold to persons as part of a composite product or service. Thus personal expenditure on meals in restaurants and hotels is spread over several categories. The cost to the establishment of the food used appears in the item "Food"; the rent of the building in the item "Rent, rates and water charges"; the chinaware and cooking utensils in the item "Durable household goods", and the allowance for the purely service and managerial element of expenditure in the item "Other services".

The figures represent the expenditure of consumers in the above sense on goods and services of all kinds whether these are provided out of new production or from stock. Second-hand goods are not included but an allowance is made for the costs, including profit, of handling and reconditioning them. For private motor vehicles this allowance is made in the item "Private motoring"; for other goods it is included in "Other services".

The figures in the second part of the table have been obtained by revaluing at the appropriate 1938 prices the quantities bought in any year of as many individual items as possible within each group of goods and services. The resulting products have then been added to arrive at a total for each group.

As it has been impossible either to allow for restrictions on consumers' choice due to rationing or to take full account of changes in quality, the resulting series must not be regarded as giving a reliable measure of changes in the standard of living.

Definitions of the miscellaneous categories of expenditure are given below.

Durable household goods

Furniture, soft furnishings, floor coverings, musical instruments, radio sets, pottery, glassware, electrical goods and all hardware.

Other household goods

Matches, soap, candles and miscellaneous cleaning materials.

Other services

Medical services not provided under national health insurance, domestic service, undertaking, laundry, hairdressing, hotel and restaurant services, repairs and other miscellaneous services not included elsewhere.

Other goods

Stationery, fancy goods, bicycles, sports and travel goods, chemists' wares and other miscellaneous goods not included elsewhere.

12. WAGES AND PRICES

12.3, 12.5 Average weekly earnings and hours worked in manufacturing and certain other industries

The figures relate to all wage earners other than office staff, shop assistants and outworkers; managers, commercial travellers, clerks, typists and salaried persons generally are excluded.

The industries covered are those for which separate figures are given together with mining and quarrying (excluding coal mining), treatment of non-metalliferous mine and quarry products, leather, fur, etc., woodworking, paper, printing, stationery, etc., miscellaneous manufacturing industries, Government industrial establishments, local authorities' non-trading services, gas, electricity and water supply services. The figures are based on returns from employers showing for a particular week in the month indicated, the number of wage earners actually at work, their aggregate earnings and the total number of manhours worked. The returns received at each enquiry covered five to six million workers, but in calculating the general averages and those for each of the groups of industries shown separately the averages for the individual industries have been "weighted" on the basis of the total number of wage-earners employed in each industry. In the case of women two part-time workers were, from July 1942 counted as one full-time worker.

The percentage increases in average earnings since October 1938 represent the combined effect of a number of factors, including (a) increases in rates of wages; (b) increases or decreases in the number of hours worked and in the proportion of hours paid for at overtime, week-end and night shift, etc., rates; (c) extensions of systems of payment by results in some industries, and increased output by the workers affected; (d) changes in the proportions of men, boys, women and girls employed in different occupations and (e) changes in the proportions of workers employed in different industries.

12.6 Wage rates and cost of living

Weekly wage rates

The figures are based on wage records in 69 industries, which include most of the principal industries and a proportion of the smaller industries. The principal industries or services which are not covered are the distributive trades, domestic service, the catering trades, National Government service and entertainment, sports, etc. The series shows the estimated percentage increase in all industries since the beginning of September 1939. Estimates are made monthly by the Ministry of Labour and National Service of the average percentage increase in rates of wages, for a full week's work, in industries, occupations and localities in which changes in the general levels of wage rates are regulated by collective agreements between organisations of employers and work people, arbitration awards or statutory orders. The percentages of increase since September 1939 vary considerably in different cases and in combining these percentages into a general average the Ministry of Labour has taken account of the approximate total pre-war wages bill in the various industries. The figures do not, however, take account of the effects on the general level of wages of the changes which have occurred since 1939 in the proportions of work people employed in different industries, nor of increases in wage rates granted by employers to individual workers. In the absence of comprehensive information as to the rates of wages actually paid by employers generally to their work people, the average percentages shown should not be regarded as more than rough approximations.

Working-class cost-of-living index

The figures are derived from the changes since 1st September 1939 shown by the Ministry of labour cost-of-living index. This index measured the average percentage increase in the cost of maintaining unchanged the standard of living prevailing in working-class families before August 1914. The percentage changes since July 1914 in the prices of the various commodities and services included in the index were combined by means of weights representing the estimated relative expenditure on these commodities and services by working-class families at that date. The 1914 weights for each of the main expenditure groups were: Food 7½, rent (including rates) 2, clothing 1½, fuel and light 1, other items included in the index ½.

12.7 Agricultural price indices

The prices used were the controlled prices or, where the product was uncontrolled, quotations made weekly by the Ministry's market reporters; Government payments such as acreage payments are taken into account. Thus so far as is possible the prices used are those relating to the point of first sale by the producer. In the case of fruit, vegetables and glasshouse produce, however, the prices are, for the most part, based not on prices realised by growers but on the prices realised by primary and secondary wholesalers at certain representative urban markets. Exceptional prices at the beginning and end of the season are excluded.

The index number for all products is the weighted arithmetic mean of the percentage price changes of 24 main items compared with prices in the base years.

The weight assigned to each commodity is proportional to the average value of the output of the five most recent crop years, re-valued at the prices of the base period 1927-29. Thus for the year 1945 the weights will be derived from the average quantities of output during the crop years 1939/40 to 1943/44 re-valued at the prices for 1927-29. As the system of moving weights involves a change in the weights used from year to year the following table allows a comparison to be made between weights in 1938 and 1945.

Moving weights used in the index of agricultural prices

	1938	1945
Total	**200**	**200**
Wheat	6	12
Barley	4	7
Oats	2	1
Potatoes	10	14
Hay	4	2
Fat cattle	18	16
Fat cows	7	6
Fat sheep	7	6
Fat ewes	3	3
Pork pigs	8	5
Bacon pigs	11	7
Fat sows	3	2
Milk	46	53
Butter	3	1
Cheese	1	-
Poultry (fowls and ducks, and, in annual index, geese)	5	4
Eggs	18	12
Sugar	7	8
Hops	2	2
Fat lambs	6	5
Wool	4	4
Fruit	10	12
Vegetables	12	14
Glasshouse produce	3	4

Both the wheat and potato indices include an allowance for acreage payments; for wheat the addition is based on the estimated quantity sold, for potatoes on the estimated total production. The indices for potatoes include only prices for January to June and September to December, and are based on the average of these months in the base years.

Index numbers calculated on the base 1927-29=100 have been multiplied by appropriate factors to convert them to the base 1936-38=100.

12.8 Stock and fertilizer prices indices

Prices for certain breeds quoted by the Ministry's market reporters are used in calculating the price indices for dairy cows, store cattle, store sheep and store pigs.

The index of fertilizer prices is calculated from quotations for basic slag, sulphate of ammonia, ground rock phosphate, nitrate of soda, nitro-chalk and superphosphate.

Weights used in the calculation for this index are as follows:-

Total	100
Ground rock phosphate	5
Nitrate of soda	6
Nitro-chalk	8
Sulphate of ammonia	33
Superphosphate	36
Basic slag	12

The method used is similar to that for agricultural prices but the weights applied to the different commodities are fixed and are proportional to the estimated average annual consumption of these materials in the calendar years 1937 and 1938.

12.9 Wholesale prices

The index is computed as a geometric average of 200 price changes. The number of varieties of each commodity chosen is as nearly as possible the same proportion of 200 as the value of the imports and production of the commodity (including any further stages of manufacture not separately represented in the index) is of the total for all articles in 1930. In a few cases (for example, other chemicals) in order to improve the representation, prices of several items are averaged to form a single series with a weight of one.

Thus while the index is computed as a simple average, a system of weighting is in reality achieved.

As far as possible, duplication between the various trades comprised within a group has been eliminated as has also the duplication between groups resulting from the inclusion in one group of a commodity which clearly forms a dominant material in another group. In this way the overweighting of certain commodities has been avoided. Thus coal, which is largely used in industry as a fuel or a raw material is to that extent already embodied in industrial output, and accordingly only receives representation in the index number in relation to its importance for other purposes including the production of gas and electricity for non-industrial uses.

The index is divided into two major groups, food and tobacco (68 items) and industrial materials and manufactures including fuel (132 items). Excluding fuel, the items in the latter are regrouped to form index numbers of basic materials (33 items), intermediate products (38 items) and manufactured articles (48 items). The latter relates to goods which are mainly manufactured rather than goods which are complete and ready for consumption for which it is difficult to get satisfactory price quotations. A further index number for building materials is also compiled; in this, the weight assigned to each commodity is based on its importance as a building material.

The price quotations used are for the most part weekly. For dutiable goods they include the appropriate amount of duty and for subsidised goods, the lower price (after deduction of the subsidy) is used. The weekly quotations are combined into monthly averages so that the index numbers relate to the average for the month. Annual indices are obtained by taking the geometric mean of the monthly indices.

Notes

Notes

Notes

INDEX

Figures indicate Table numbers

A

B

C

D

E

F

G

H

I

M

N

O

P

R

S

T

Y

Z

Printed in the United Kingdom for HMSO
Dd 300505 4/95 C40 559/1 59226